THE CONTEXTS
OF SCHOOL-BASED
LITERACY

Taffy E. Raphael

THE CONTEXTS OF SCHOOL-BASED LITERACY

Proceedings of the
Contexts of Literacy Conference
June, 1984
Directed by Taffy E. Raphael and Ralph E. Reynolds

RANDOM HOUSE   NEW YORK
This book was developed for Random House by Lane Akers, Inc.

First Edition

9 8 7 6 5 4 3 2 1

Published in the United States by Random House, Inc., and simultaneously in Canada by Random House of Canada Limited, Toronto.

Library of Congress Cataloging-in-Publication Data
Main entry under title:

The contexts of school-based literacy

"This volume . . . is the product of a conference cosponsored by Michigan State University and the University of Utah in June 1984."—Pref.
  Bibliography: p.
  Includes index.
  1. Reading—United States—Congresses. 2. Reading comprehension—Congresses. 3. Literacy—United States—Congresses. I. Raphael, Taffy. II. Michigan State University. III. University of Utah.
LB1049.95.C7 1986   372.4   85–14597
ISBN 0–394–35624–1

Manufactured in the United States of America

To my parents
Jean and Jack Raphael

Contents

Preface

There is no doubt that concerns about the development of a literate nation have been growing for the past decade. Reports from the National Assessment of Educational Progress (1982) suggest that there is much room for improvement. The importance of literacy has been underscored in articles from popular magazines (e.g., *Time*, 1984) to articles in major educational newspapers (e.g., *American Journal of Education*, 1984; *Journal of Reading*, 1984; *Reading Research Quarterly*, 1982). The need for literacy was quite simply stated in a recent issue of *Time* (1984, p. 48). While not a research-based publication, its point is one well recognized:

> Literacy is a defense against every form of extremism: social, political, even religious. It gives frustration and hostility another place to go instead of violence. It provides a perspective, a sense of past tradition and future possibilities, that can make ideas more viable than absolutes, and evolution more practical than revolution. . . . The whole idea of democracy is to resolve conflict through consensus, and literacy is essential to state both the conflict and its resolution.

That literacy is important is undeniable. That our educational system is not meeting the needs for the development of skills of literacy has been demonstrated. Goodlad (1984) studied classrooms from elementary, junior high, and high schools and found that reading occupies only 2 to 6 percent of the students' time. Further, only slightly more than 5 percent of the students' time was spent in organized discussions designed to promote students' speaking skills. Toch cites a review of 6,000 high school transcripts from 1964 to 1980 for the Commission on Excellence that "revealed a proliferation of courses not primarily designed to strengthen students' language skills . . . . (and a growth) of students in the less academically rigorous general track . . . . from 12 percent in the late 1960's to 42.5 percent in the late 1970's" (page L3, 1984).

Thus, our decision to focus on literacy derives from a very real need to examine what we, as researchers and educators, can do to improve the outlook of the development of literacy in schools today. This volume, *The Contexts of School-Based Literacy*, reflects a synthesis of four major strands of research: research on teaching, research on reading, research on writing, and research on social aspects of development. It is the product of a conference cosponsored by Michigan State University and the University of Utah in

June, 1984, directed by Taffy Raphael and Ralph Reynolds. At this conference researchers and educators from each of the four areas were brought together to examine potential ways in which each area might help the other to move closer toward our goal of developing a literate nation.

The identification of the four research strands is an extension of efforts begun in 1982 by Gerry Duffy, Laura Roehler, and Jana Mason in developing a joint seminar series between members of the Center for the Study of Reading at the University of Illinois and members of the Institute for Research on Teaching at Michigan State University. The resulting volume, *Comprehension Instruction: Perspectives and Suggestions* (1984), was the initial integration of two previously disparate bodies of literature—that on reading and that on teaching. Our thanks go to Jim Gavelek of Michigan State University for his initial suggestions about the need for expanding our efforts toward synthesis. As he suggested, a logical step forward was to examine the relationships between reading and writing, within the social context in which instruction occurs.

To examine these relationships, the volume raises and addresses four questions, each focusing on a critical question concerning the development of literacy in school settings:

1. What is the contextual view of the development of literacy?
2. How can contexts for learning to read and for developing strategic readers be characterized?
3. How can contexts for developing children's understanding and use of the writing process be characterized?
4. What influences the development of appropriate contexts for learning to read and write?

The volume's four sections consider each of these questions respectively.

THEORETICAL FOUNDATIONS

The first section provides the theoretical foundation for the volume. It presents a contextual view of learning in general and discusses this view in relationship to literacy. Fundamental to this section is the research on social aspects of development, for it emphasizes that learning is the result of a social interaction between the more experienced teacher (e.g., an adult, or a more experienced peer) and the learner. This contextual view is perhaps best exemplified by the theories proposed by Vygotsky, a Soviet psychologist of the 1930's, whose work has relatively recently been brought to the attention of American psychologists and educators (e.g., Vygotsky, 1978). Vygotsky underscores the relationships among language, thinking, and learning and emphasizes the social nature of the learning process. Gavelek describes the foundations of Vygotsky's theory as they relate directly to the development of literacy, examining concepts of "scaffolding" and "mediated learning" (i.e., types of instructional support) in terms of the acquisition of literacy in schools. Rogoff focuses on these aspects in terms of parents from different cultures guiding their children's learning, then proposes principles for guided participation of learning that can be applied to school settings. The social nature of learning and the variety of school contexts in which learning literacy skills occurs is the ongoing theme of the remaining sections.

SCHOOL CONTEXTS FOR READING INSTRUCTION

The second section focuses on the school contexts of reading instruction, primarily focusing on synthesis of research on reading and research on teaching. Pearson's chapter provides a historical context for the research described in each of the following articles. His chapter is followed by the work of Au and Kawakami who describe an application of Vygotskian principles to comprehension instruction. They discuss the social context of the reading group, and the types of teacher–learner interactions that should occur within such a setting to promote higher levels of comprehension and to promote the use of metacognitive skills. Paris elaborates on a program for enhancing comprehension through the use of analogies (e.g., taking a reading trip, becoming a reading detective). Mason, Stewart, and Dunning describe the influence of the social context of instruction on kindergarteners' perceptions of reading and their acquisition of reading skills. An important part of creating appropriate contexts for reading instruction is attributed to the teacher's verbal statements during instruction. The chapter by Roehler, Duffy, and Meloth directly integrates research on reading and research on teaching as they examine teachers' explanations during reading instruction. The guidelines for instruction they provide parallel Rogoff's suggested principles for guided participation of learning. The final two chapters in this section concern school-based contexts for developing reading skills outside the traditional reading period. Wixson and Lipson consider settings that reflect a contextual approach to the issue of the diagnosis and related remediation of unsuccessful readers. Fielding, Wilson, and Anderson describe current trends in out-of-school reading, then address the issue of how the teacher can create contexts to promote independent reading.

SCHOOL CONTEXTS FOR WRITING INSTRUCTION

The third section focuses on contexts of writing instruction, integrating research on the social aspects of development and on research on writing instruction. The chapters range from examining traditional classroom organizations to nontraditional contexts for writing, including the use of computers. DeFord characterizes contexts for children's school writing based on her observations in three classrooms over the course of a school year. Her observations reveal the direct impact the type of environment has on children's written products, again providing support for emphasizing the link between social contexts and the development and perceptions of literacy. Tierney, Leys, and Rogers continue this theme with their contrast between a traditional classroom and one that emphasizes interactions between writers and readers. Implementing contextual approaches to writing requires adjustments on the part of administrators and teachers as well as the students. The chapters by Hansen and by Rubin and Bruce describe the kinds of learning that must take place for each of these groups. Hansen discusses lessons learned by administrators, teachers, and students during the implementation of a process approach to writing in one school. Rubin and Bruce discuss lessons learned by students, teachers, and software developers as a computer-based writing environment was created in classrooms from Alaska to Massachusetts.

OTHER INFLUENCES ON
READING AND WRITING INSTRUCTION

The fourth section considers broader influences on the development of appropriate contexts for improving literacy, including an examination of student-teacher relationships, teachers, policy makers, and researchers and each one's unique influences on enhancing literacy. Weinstein considers how teachers may indirectly influence the development of reading skills by the implicit messages through which they convey their perceptions of their students' abilities. Schwartz discusses how teachers may directly influence the context for literacy by the strengths and limitations of their conceptual and procedural knowledge of the reading process. He describes the potential influence of such teachers' knowledge on children's reading development. Other sources that influence school contexts for literacy are the policy makers at the state and local levels and their information and application of research on reading, writing, and teaching. Winograd discusses the basis for tensions between policy makers, researchers, and teachers that may prevent smooth transition from research to practice. Clark considers such tensions from a different but important perspective. He discusses the need for increased communication and provides guidelines for communicating about ways to interpret and apply research to classroom and school settings.

The final chapter in this section, and the volume, provides a synthesis of what we have learned from the chapters and how this information fits the question, Where do we go from here? In this chapter Raphael addresses the four questions raised at the outset of the volume and considers possible responses in light of the information presented in the chapters and other available information. Future directions for researchers and practitioners are considered, particularly in the context of research that integrates instruction in reading and writing and focuses on the social context of the classrooms in which this instruction occurs.

Each section is preceded by a brief overview of the area of emphasis, an overview of chapters contained in the section, and a discussion of the relationships among the chapters.

This volume will appeal to a variety of audiences. For those conducting research in the areas of reading and writing within school settings, the volume presents an integration of research from different disciplines that focuses on the issues of school-based literacy. The cross-disciplinary nature of the content contributes to the value of the volume. For students interested in the study of school-based literacy development, this volume provides a review and synthesis of potential areas of continued research. Teachers interested in observing how research and theories may be translated directly into practice will find many valuable suggestions for classroom practice. Regardless of background, as a result of reading this volume the reader should be more sensitive to what we have accomplished in striving for the development of a literate society and more aware of the many areas still to be studied and understood.

Recognition and special mention are due the number of people who made this volume possible. First, the chapter contributors deserve thanks for the speed and conscientiousness with which each undertook his or her charge. High-quality chapters and an integration of ideas are visible throughout. Second, appreciation is due Henrietta Barnes, chairperson of the Department of Teacher Education, and Bill Schmidt, chairperson of the Department of Educational Psychology, both of Michigan State University, for their continued support of this project from the inception of the idea, through the conference, and through the preparation of the volume; and to Linda Magleby, conference administrator. Third, for helping to support the conference, recognition is due the University of Utah College of Education and the Division of Continuing Education. For assistance with editing and manuscript preparation, we thank Cindy Wolfe, Sally Quick, and Greg Gavelek. Lane Akers in particular deserves special recognition for guiding the publication of the volume.

REFERENCES

Goodlad, J. I. (1984). *A place called school: Prospects for the future.* New York: McGraw-Hill.

Time. July 9, 1984. p. 48.

Toch, T. (1984). America's quest for literacy. *Education Week* (September 5). Washington, D.C.: Editorial Projects in Education.

Vygotsky, L. S. (1978). *Mind in society: The development of higher psychological processes.* M. Cole et al. (Eds.) Cambridge, Mass.: Harvard University Press.

PART 1

THEORETICAL BASES OF INSTRUCTION IN LITERACY

The first question to be addressed in this volume is, *What is the contextual view of the development of literacy?* This first section outlines the underlying principles and assumptions of the volume, focusing primarily on the contextual view of learning. The theories of Vygotsky, the Soviet psychologist of the 1930s who promoted a contextual view of learning, are emphasized. This view is in contrast to the one that suggests children move through a universal set of stages with performance levels that can be generalized across a multitude of settings. Rather, the contextual view stresses the variability of learners' performances as a function of the task at hand, the setting in which the learning occurs, and the amount of support, or scaffolding, provided by the teacher. Particularly relevant to education is the importance Vygotsky places on the social context in which instruction occurs. This places a great responsibility on the teacher and the learner as cocontributors to the learning situation.

Both Gavelek and Rogoff introduce Vygotsky's concept of the *zone of proximal development* (ZPD), which is fundamental to the contextual approach. The concept suggests that instruction must occur in that zone where the child may not succeed independently, but where the child could succeed with proper adult support and guidance (i.e., mediation). This mediation is an important part of the context for learning in general, as well as for the development of specific abilities such as reading and writing. Gavelek focuses on the relationships among language, cognition, and the development of literacy, highlighting how Vygotsky's principles of learning may be applied to the development of literacy in school settings. Gavelek notes that Vygotsky emphasizes the need to transfer control of cognitive activity from the teacher to the learner, which is the basis for development of metacognitive skills. Readers interested in application of such a principle are directed to Paris' chapter in the next section for a discussion of a program designed to provide just such instruction.

Rogoff applies Vygotsky's general principles to the interpretation of parent-child interactions, using examples from her travels to Guatamala and her observations of children's learning, and parents' guidance of that learning, and from her observations of children and parents from this country in a variety of learning situations. From her observations of parents and children across these two cultures she outlines four characteristics of successful instruction. She terms effective instruction *guided participation*, in which the adult and the child together structure the context for learning. She then discusses how these principles of parent-child interactions can be applied toward enhancing instruction in school settings. For readers particularly interested in how these principles apply to instruction in classrooms, the chapter by Roehler, Duffy, and Meloth in the next section will be of interest. The guidelines they suggest for effective teacher explanation of cognitive strategies in reading parallel those proposed by Rogoff. A second extension to classroom settings is found in the Au and Kawakami chapter in the next section. They have applied the principles of guided particiation to small-group reading instruction and focus on how guided participation can enhance both cognitive and metacognitive development.

Thus, this section provides the theoretical foundation for many chapters throughout this volume, emphasizing the centrality of the interactions between teachers and learners and the contexts they jointly construct.

The Social Contexts of Literacy and Schooling: A Developmental Perspective

James R. Gavelek

OVERVIEW OF THE CHAPTER

To varying degrees children will have received some appreciation of literacy within the family prior to and concurrent with their attending school (Taylor, 1983). However, it is within the contexts of schooling that children of most societies acquire, refine, and learn how to make use of their skills of literacy. Indeed, so close is this association that it has been common to gauge a country's level of literacy by the average number of years of schooling its citizens have achieved. The emphasis upon literacy *and* schooling is important because it is often assumed that individuals' attainment of literacy is a measure of their level of intellectual functioning. So potent is the assumed relationship between literacy and thinking that some maintain that there is a "great divide" separating the cognitive ability of those who are literate from those who are not. Scribner and Cole (1981) however have presented compelling evidence suggesting that the contribution of literacy to individual cognitive functioning is neither so inevitable nor general as to be taken for granted. Based upon their study of the Vai, a people of West Africa some of whom become literate without the "contaminating" influence of schooling, Scribner and Cole concluded that there is little evidence for the notion that literacy bestows upon its users special intellectual capabilities unavailable to those who are nonliterate. The fact that literacy does not necessarily lead to cognitive enhancement should not, however, be taken as evidence that reading and writing make no difference.

It is not literacy per se, but the practice of literacy in certain contexts and in certain ways that *may* enhance an individual's cognitive development. In other words, it is not enough that an individual is able to read and write, one must determine both how and for what purposes these activities are put to use.

The purpose of this chapter is to consider whether or not literacy, when practiced in the contexts of the school, contributes, or might be made to contribute, to students' cognitive development. By cognitive development, I mean individuals' increasing ability to acquire and to make use of knowledge (i.e., cognition), as well as their ability to monitor and regulate these processes (i.e., metacognition).

A fundamental problem in relating literacy and schooling to cognitive development has been that the major theoretical framework in developmental psychology (i.e., Piagetian) has had relatively little to say about schooling, much less what the role of reading and writing should be in the schools. However, one cognitive developmental approach that has recently begun to grow in prominence is Vygotsky's sociohistorical theory (Vygotsky, 1962, 1978). More than any other developmental theorist, Vygotsky has called our attention to the function of instruction in fostering cognitive development and to the critical role played by the teacher as the mediator of both *what* and *how* knowledge is to be acquired and used. Further, Vygotsky saw language, both oral and written, as the primary vehicle by which adult-mediated instruction takes place.

This chapter will first discuss limitations of a Piagetian conception of cognitive development. It will present fundamental assumptions of Vygotsky's approach to cognitive development and instruction. It will discuss the consistency of current classroom practices with such an approach, specifically the classroom use of oral and written language and the extent to which this use promotes cognitive growth. It will suggest alternative classroom practices that follow from a Vygotskian perspective. Finally, it will consider the limits of school-based literacy in promoting cognitive growth.

LIMITATIONS OF A PIAGETIAN CONCEPTION OF COGNITIVE DEVELOPMENT

A fundamental obstacle in relating school-based literacy to the development of student thinking is the absence of a theoretical framework that incorporates the role of sociocultural factors (e.g., schooling and literacy) and their relationship to cognitive development.

Were one to ask a representative sample of educators to name the first person who comes to mind when they think of cognitive development, most would probable respond Jean Piaget. More than any other individual, he noted the fundamental change that children's thinking undergoes with development. Recently, however, his theory has been criticized by philosophers, psychologists, and educators alike.

Piaget emphasized the universal characteristics of humans as biological organisms while he deemphasized characteristics attributable to the unique historical, cultural, and social conditions under which humans have developed. According to Piagetian theory, development occurs as a result of the constructive activites that children carry out in interaction with their environment. However, the nature of these activities and their resulting cognitive structures are constrained by the individual's stage of development. These stages were assumed to change in an invariant sequence during the course of an individual's lifetime. To attain the highest stage of thinking, formal operations, a child first must pass through the sensory-motor, preoperational, and concrete-operational stages, and do so in that order. Thus, although interactional, Piaget's theory nevertheless attaches relatively more explanatory power to biological than social factors.

Nowhere is the absence of a focus on social influences so clear as is it with that most important cultural invention—schooling. Resnick (1981) suggests that the Piagetian view has encouraged a mistrust of instruction. She suggests that within a Piagetian framework "there is a sharp difference between natural environments and contrived or 'artificial' environments, and instruction falls clearly into the latter category" (p. 5).

To illustrate the nature of these criticisms, I would ask that the reader consider the implications for individual cognitive functioning of the following thought experiment:

A highly contagious but short-lived disease sweeps over the earth and in a period of weeks most of its population perishes. The only survivors are infants (six months and younger) who because of their temporary natural systems of immunization are unaffected by this disease. Fortunately, because of advances in robotics the biological needs of these infants (e.g., hunger, thirst, warmth, and so forth) have been provided, and the survival of most of them is insured. Moreover, the infants are reared in groups thus guaranteeing at least the opportunity for social interaction. Consider both the short- and long-term consequences of this adult-free world for the intellectual development of those individuals who do survive as well as for the generations to follow.

There is much that could be discussed concerning this thought experiment, but most relevant to the present concern is a consideration of how these children's development of oral and literate language would be affected and how this in turn would influence their general cognitive development. The infants in the experiment are no different biologically than infants as we presently know them. And yet, following such a cataclysmic event these children and their descendants for many generations thereafter would in all likelihood be condemned to nonliterate lives not unlike those of early prehistoric man. To be sure, they would live among a wealth of cultural implements associated with literacy, but with virtually no access to their functional use the implements would be mere fossilized artifacts of a time gone by. In short, such a thought experiment suggests in a most radical way the importance of instruction by language-using individuals (e.g., parents, teachers) in tethering children to historically evolved and culturally shaped instruments of thought.

Theories of cognitive development serve as lenses that enable one to analyze events more closely, but at the same time they may act as blinders that occlude one's vision to other important phenomena. For Piaget the blind spots were culture, the social interaction by which that culture is conveyed to the individual and the fundament cognitive change that is brought about as a result. Piaget's theory considers society to be a supportive context, not an active force in an individual's development (Meacham, 1977).

Clearly, there is a need for a theoretical framework that adequately addresses the relationship between important cultural practices such as those associated with language and instruction and their influence on a children's cognitive development. One approach that has become increasingly influential in this country over the last decade is the sociohistorical theory of Lev Semyonovich Vygotsky. More than any other developmentalist, Vygotsky recognized the relationship between historical and cultural practices and the development of the individual.

TOWARD A SOCIOHISTORICAL CONCEPTION OF COGNITIVE DEVELOPMENT

This year marks the fiftieth since Vygotsky's death. A brilliant scholar by all accounts, Vygotsky died young (38 years old), tubercular, and at the height of his career, which prompted the philosopher Stephen Toulmin to characterize him as the Mozart of psychology. During his short career, Vygotsky proposed a research agenda the implications of which are only now being appreciated in this country. After his death, during the Stalinist purge of the late 1930s, Vygotsky was declared a nonperson, and his work remained largely unknown outside of Russia. In 1962, the English translation of Vygotsky's classic book *Thought and Language* (Vygotsky, 1962) was published, but largely overshadowed by Piaget's theory of cognitive development, which also had been recently imported to this country. It was not until 1978 when an edited collection of Vygotsky's notes was published under the title *Mind in Society* (Vygotsky, 1978) that his theory began to receive any widespread recognition. Even today Vygotsky's theory of cognitive development is not widely known among educators; this despite the fact that it is a theory that explicitly speaks to, indeed has as its major focus, the interaction between the processes of learning and instruction and those of cognitive development. The small number of individuals in this country who have been influenced by and in turn have further extended Vygotsky's theory into education includes Jerome Bruner, Michael Cole, Sylvia Scribner, James Wertsch, Ann Brown, Courtenay Cazden, Katherine Au, and Barbara Rogoff. Collectively, the works of Vygotsky and of those whom he has influenced have been referred to as the Sociohistorical School of psychology. This school informs much of what follows in this chapter.

An Overview of the Theory

Vygotsky conceptualized development in somewhat broader terms that did Piaget. He believed that to adequately understand the nature of individual human cognitive development one must also understand the natural history and cultural variability of the development of collective human thinking. What is unique about humans is that they are able to acquire, practice, transform, and ultimately convey their culture to successive generations. The young of other species learn only by means of their own individual activity and the experiences that follow. Children also learn from their activity, but it is often joint problem-solving activity carried out in concert with other more knowledgable individuals. Throughout this process the use of language is extensive.

The important status accorded instruction in both informal and formal settings in Vygotsky's theory should be clear. Humans engage in what Erickson has called "taught cognitive learning;" that is, "instruction with aims for the content of learning that are deliberate and intentional" (Erickson, 1982, p. 149). Thus, essential aspects of this culturally designated curriculum are the content and tasks that its members consider important. Cultural tasks refer to the diversity of goals or purposes as well as the means practiced to attain these goals. For example, an important set of cultural tasks associated with school-based literacy is the learning of those activites (e.g., decoding, prediction, summarization, questioning) used in the comprehension of text-based knowledge. Human learning is thus largely a process of appropriating the social-historical experiences that members of one's culture consider important. It is by means of the language and tools that a culture has developed that human accomplishments are organized and that these processes of appropriation by successive generations are eventually brought about. It is the acquistion and internalization by the individual of knowledge concerning the use of culturally evolved tool and sign systems that most distinctively characterizes human learning.

Important to Vygotsky's conception of cognitive development was his distinction between elementary and higher psychological processes. Elementary processes are those common to all humankind and are exemplified by individuals' abilities to engage in activities such as abstract thinking, symbolization, and making inferences. However, human learning is not simply a collection of elementary processes built up through a process of accretion. Instead, these elementary processes are organized by one's culture into functional systems. The development of these functional systems results in a qualitative reorganization of mind and with it the necessity for new laws to account for the complexities brought about in human activity. For example, while members of all cultures engage in some form of symbolic representation, how and, indeed, whether these symbols are represented in written form depends upon the unique practices that are associated with that culture.

This relationship between the knowledge of individuals and that of their culture has been characterized as dialectical. Each form of knowldge interacts with the other and as a result new, emergent forms of knowledge are created. Vygotsky has called to our attention the importance of considering both the sociocultural and individual levels of development. Thus, in the next two sections each of these levels will be examined in detail, with specific attention given to the roles of literacy and instruction. First, the historical development and cultural variability of literacy and its relationship to instruction will be considered. Second, Vygotsky's account of individual development will be discussed, with particular attention given to the importance that he placed upon language and instruction.

HISTORICAL-CULTURAL INFLUENCES ON DEVELOPMENT

Two major questions are of interest in this section: (1) How has literacy, its purposes, and the various means by which these purposes may be achieved evolved historically? and (2) What role does cultural variability play in the establishment and organization of literacy-related higher psychological processes into functional systems?

The Historical Evolution of Literacy

Reference was made previously to the dialectical nature of the relationship between social-historical and individual development. Figure 1.1 visually depicts this relationship in the form of a double spiral. One strand of the spiral represents the social history of western literacy while the other strand represents the development of the individual at a given time. These parallel paths between historical and individual development should not be interpreted as suggesting that the mechanisms by which each occurs are the same, but, rather, are meant to convey the notion that the development of each is interdependent upon the other.

In what follows, several points along the social-historical path have been chosen to illustrate how the social context may channel individual cognitive development. However, it should be emphasized that while social contexts constrain development they themselves undergo a process of change. The examples presented below are meant to be representative but certainly not exhaustive (see also Cole & Griffin, 1983; Havelock, 1976; Mathews, 1966; Resnick & Resnick, 1977).

The first example relates to the changes brought about by the transition from syllabary to alphabetic systems of writing. The first evidence of individuals using signs to represent experiences in communication with others dates back some 300,000 to 400,000 years. Systematic writing systems did not appear until much later, between 4,000 and 3,000 B.C. It was around this time also that the concept of schooling evolved among the Greeks. Prior to this time instruction was primarily oral and usually occurred in less formal settings. The system of writing that the Greeks had to make use of was based upon the syllabary (i.e., the representation of words in terms of their directly communicable sound elements). Such a system

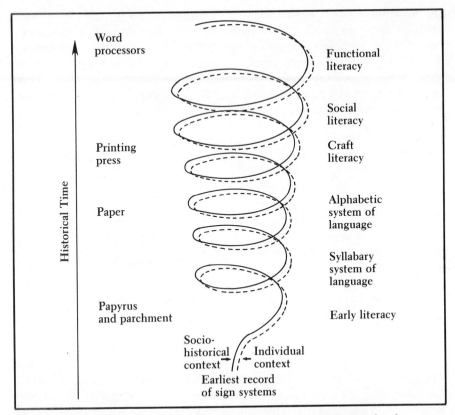

Figure 1.1 **Dialectical Nature of the Relationship Between Social–Historical and Individual Development**

was clumsy and imprecise and as a result made important transactions extremely difficult. It was not for another 2,000 years (approximately 1,000 B.C.) that an alphabetic system based upon a blending of the Greek and Semetic (Phoenician) languages evolved.

The transition from syllabary to alphabetic systems of writing (e.g., our own English) became what Cole and Griffin (1983) have described as the "bane of schoolchildren." While ultimately more powerful and economical, the second-order representation brought about by the alphabetic system nevertheless introduced another level of abstraction in children's ability to understand written language. No longer could language be represented by means of directly communicable sound elements. Children now had to learn about a system of signs that designated the sounds of spoken language that, in turn, referred to real-world experiences and relationships.

A second example of how the social history of Western literacy influenced individual development is based upon events occuring during the Dark and Middle Ages. In his book, *Origins of Western Literacy*, Havelock (1976) distinguishes between social and craft literacy. Social literacy refers to the condition where most people within a society can and do write. Craft literacy, on the other hand, represents the situation in which literacy is limited to the privileged class within a society. Havelock points out that during the Dark and Middle Ages social literacy disappeared. The general population of Europe ceased to read and write. Havelock (1976) suggests two reasons to account for the loss of social literacy during this historical period. First, calligraphic styles of writing during this time multiplied and became much less uniform:

> Calligraphic virtuosity of any kind fosters craft literacy and is fostered by it, but it is the enemy of social literacy. The unlikely careers of both the Greek and Roman versions of the alphabet during the Dark Ages and the Middle Ages sufficiently demonstrate this fact. (Havelock, 1976, p. 11)

A second somewhat more mundane but no less influential reason offered to explain the disappearance of social literacy is that papyrus and parchment, the primary sources for written material, became scarce.

A return to social literacy was ushered in by the invention of the printing press in the middle of the fifteenth century. One need not detail the many implications for the historical development of humankind of the social literacy made possible by such an invention.

A third example of the role of social-historical contexts in affecting individual development is more contemporary and more speculative. I refer to the discovery, or perhaps more accurately creation, of literacy-related learning disabilities that have occurred in the last half of this century. It seems a reasonable conjecture that 200 years ago such problems did not exist to the degree that they now do. It also seems extremely unlikely that humankind has changed biologically in any substantial ways over this period of time. The explanation of course is more apt to be found in the changing literacy-related demands that have been made of children over the last two centuries. Literacy, or at least reading, has become more important to effectively function in our society. Even today children are seldom referred for special help because they have specific learning disabilities in writing. Were one to project a step further into the future, a reasonable prediction would be that the learning disabilities of tomorrow will include various manifestations of computer illiteracy.

A final, related example also refers to more recent history. Members of the state board of education in Michigan in concert with practitioners and scholars of research on reading have worked toward a redefinition of reading. Extant definitions based upon older, bottom-up conceptions of reading no longer adequately capture either the richness of what we now know about the complex processes that comprise reading or the active role children play in their own learning how to read (Wixson & Peters, 1984).

Resnick and Resnick (1977) have documented the changing standards and teaching methods that have taken place with respect to Western literacy over the past four centuries. They note that historically the criteria defining literacy have become more demanding. Of importance is their finding that only as recently as the present century has the goal of elementary school reading instruction been to enable students to gain new information from texts. Finally, they conclude that if higher standards of literacy are to be achieved, then instruction will need to mirror changes in both the literacy criterion and the target population. One way of thinking about the nature of this pedagogy can be illustrated by Figure 1.1. As the area (i.e., quantity and quality of literacy-related knowledge) created by an upward-bound spiral describing the historical development of literacy increases, so does the necessity for more intensive social guidance in literacy instruction.

One important observation concerning this very brief historical account of literacy: the nature of this change has involved both the tool and sign systems of literacy. Thus, on the one hand we have witnessed the invention of paper, printing presses, and word processors; but equally important—the very nature of sign systems and what it means to be literate in the use of these sign systems have undergone substantial change.

Cross-Cultural Analysis: The Decoupling of Literacy from Schooling

The sociohistorical school uses cultural comparison as yet another approach in understanding human higher psychological functioning. Where historical comparisons may be used to study how literacy has developed over time, cultural analyses are concerned with the variability of the processes associated with literacy among different cultural or subcultural groups within the same period of time.

Of specific interest in this section is the relative role that schooling and literacy play in individual cognitive functioning. One difficulty in studying the relative contributions of schooling and literacy to students' cognitive development is that they so often occur together. In their book *The Psychology of Literacy* (1981) Scribner and Cole report the results of an elaborate study they conducted to decouple the influences of literacy and schooling as the two relate to individual cognitive functioning. Scribner and Cole suggest that three comparisons are necessary to address this problem.

One way to assess the effects of formal schooling is to compare schooled individuals with those who are not schooled. Indeed, there have been a number of studies in which such comparisons have been made. As a group, these studies have emphasized the differences between instruction that is based upon the oral (i.e., nonschool) and written (i.e., school) use of language. In general, these studies suggest that oral instruction tends to be much more tied to activity in the immediate context (i.e., is contextualized) while written instructions goes beyond the immediate context to permitting the individual to represent experiences and events that are spatially and temporally remote.

However, there is an inherent problem in studies that compare schooled and nonschooled populations in that it is not at all clear whether observed effects can be attributed to schooling, are the result of differences of literacy, or are some combination of the two. Logically, one may conceive of individuals developing and using the skills of literacy in the absence of any formal schooling. In reality, Scribner and Cole were able to find just such a group of individuals—the Vai of West Africa—a people among whom the skills of literacy had developed independent of any schooling. The existence of such a group of people enabled Scribner and Cole to carry out the second and third comparisons. The second concerned whether literacy per se, (i.e., literacy without schooling) makes a difference in individuals' performance on cognitive tasks (i.e., a comparison of Vai script literates to nonliterates). The third comparison concerned whether schooled and nonschooled literates were equivalent in their performance or whether schooling contributed to performance over and above literacy (i.e., a comparison of schooled and Vai script literates). Or in Scribner and Cole's words: "Is literacy a surrogate for schooling" (p. 20)?

Perhaps most important among Scribner and Cole's findings was a failure to obtain evidence for what they describe as "the great divide" (i.e., differences in cognitive functioning between literate and nonliterate people). They note that to the extent that such differences did exist they were between those who were schooled and those who were not. Schooled individuals were generally more able to provide verbal explanations than were nonschooled individuals. The authors attributed these effects to the verbal interaction (e.g., explanations) that takes place between teacher and students in the classroom, not to specialized skills attributable to knowing how to read and write. What is especially interesting about Scribner and Cole's findings with respect to the Vai's use of literacy is the fact that it was seldom, if ever, used for educational purposes. They describe it as "literacy without education" because it was not used for the acquistion of vicarious experience or new bodies of knowledge. For the most part, Vai script was used to engage individuals with familiar topics in new ways. In this sense, the Vai were no different from the Western literates prior to this century described by Resnick and Resnick (1977).

Scribner and Cole (1981) and other members of the Laboratory of Comparative Human Cognition (1983, 1984) suggest a "cultural practice" account of literacy and its relationship to cognitive functioning:

> Literacy is not simply knowing how to read and write a particular script but applying this knowledge for specific purposes in specific contexts of use. The nature of these practices, including, of course, their technological aspects, will determine the kind of skills ("consequences") associated with literacy. (p. 236)

It is culture through its social practices that determines the purposes of literacy, the means that are available for achieving these purposes, and the contexts within which this use takes place.

Thus, one should not misinterpret Scribner and Cole's findings and conclude that literacy cannot be used to enhance individual cognitive functioning. Literacy does not automatically bestow upon its users special capabilities. It is not literacy per se, but the way that literacy is defined and, ultimately, how it is practiced that is important. The Vai literacy studied by Scribner and Cole was literacy without education. One must look to the practice of Vai literacy if one is to understand why its uses were restricted.

Scribner and Cole conclude from their work that schooling enhanced students' capabilities to perform on cognitive tasks. Untested was the role of schooling without written literacy. While at one time knowledge conveyed in schools was based totally upon oralist traditions, it is difficult to imagine this today, given the sheer quantity and complexity of present-day knowledge. What, if anything, is important about the processes of reading and writing that makes schools uniquely well-suited for their practice? Or alternatively, what is there about practices in the contexts of schooling that are enhanced by written representation?

In summary, cognitive processes associated with literacy appeared relatively late in human history. The concept of schooling, while closely tied to this development of literacy, is not necessary for a system of literacy to evolve. As is the case with so many other psychological processes, literacy is a multifaceted concept and as such defies simple descriptive dichotomies such as literate or nonliterate. Instead, one must ask questions such as: What is the purpose for literacy? What are the culturally and historically established purposes for which the processes of reading and writing have been used? What means have been developed by the culture to achieve these purposes? These questions are especially important when examining the development of literacy by the individual and the role that schools serve in this development. More specifically, given the results of these historical and cross-cultural comparisons, a reasonable question to consider is how the tools and sign systems of a culture within a particular period of history are passed on to the individuals who comprise that culture. This is the question fundamental to individual cognitive development.

LANGUAGE, INSTRUCTION, AND INDIVIDUAL COGNITIVE DEVELOPMENT

The question considered in this section concerns how higher-order cognitive functions such as those associated with literacy (i.e., reading and writing) are acquired and used by the individual within the contexts of schooling. Central to Vygotsky's (1978) sociohistorical approach is his law of general cultural development that states:

> any higher mental function which has emerged in the process of human historical development appears on the scene twice. It first appears as a form of interaction and co-operation among people, as an interpsychological category. Then it appears as a form of individual adaptation, as a part of an individual's psychology, as an intra-psychological category. (p. 128)

What this means specifically with respect to childrens' learning and development is that what they initially can accomplish only with assistance, they are eventually able to do by themselves. Much of this internalization of thought takes place within the specific contexts of adult-mediated, goal-oriented, problem-solving activity. Children become able to problem solve independently "by incorporating into the structure of their own action and eventually internalizing the organizational principles inherent in the assistance which they receive from others" (Wozniak, 1980, p. 176).

Although modeling and physical guidance may characterize some of this activity, in academic tasks the primary medium of instruction is language. Vygotsky believed that inner speech is used by humans to plan and regulate their own behavior, and derives from participation in social speech activity during earlier development (Wertsch, 1980). Initially, language is tied to practical activity in the form of a dialogue between adult and child. Gradually children come to regulate their own problem-solving activities through the mediation of their own egocentric speech. This speech maintains its essential dialogic quality, but now it is an external dialogue carried on with the self. Eventually, regulation of one's own behavior "goes underground" in the form of inner speech that while still dialogic and self-directing is now no longer observable.

> Speech is first a communicative function. It serves the goals of social contact, social interaction, and the social co-ordination of behavior. Only afterwards, by applying the same mode of behavior to oneself, do humans develop inner speech. In this process, they, as it were, preserve the "function of social interaction" in their individual behavior. They apply the social mode of action to themselves." Under this condition, the individual function becomes in essence a unique form of internal collaboration with onself. (Vygotsky, 1962, pp. 450–451)

Vygotsky believed the distinction between oral and written forms of language to be especially important. The mastery of a system of reading and writing represents a major turning-point in the child's cultural development. Unlike spoken language that children acquire naturally, Vygotsky believed that the teaching of written language is based on artificial training. He stated that writing is given to the children from without, from the hands of the teacher, rather than founded on the needs and activities of children as they naturally develop (Vygotsky, 1978). This is so because a sign system represents a second-order symbolism that only gradually comes to be understood as a form of direct symbolism. In other words, written signs represent sounds before these sounds come to be understood directly as symbols representing experiences. How are the processes associated with reading and writing taught so that they are eventually owned and internalized by the individual?

An important concept in Vygotsky's sociohistorical approach to cognitive development is the zone of proximal development, that is:

> the distance between the actual developmental level as determined by independent problem solving and the level of potential development as determined through problem solving under adult guidance or in colaboration with more capable peers. (1978, p. 76) p 86?

For Vygotsky the most important instructional question was: How can education best assist children through the zone of proximal development?

Teachers as Mediators

Vygotsky believed that an important function of the teacher (formal or informal) is to mediate between children and those tasks that are beyond their independent levels of competence. The metaphor of the scaffold (Wood & Middleton, 1975) has been used to characterize this mediating function of the relationship between more knowledgable adult mediators and their students. The scaffold when applied to the activity of a mediator in an instructional setting is one who is able to offer *support* that is *adjustable* but *temporary*. The teachers' role as a mediator presents several challenges including those associated with the scaffolding of both the motivation and the thinking of their students.

In their role as mediators of motivation, teachers of reading or writing may be faced with the problem of presenting goals that students do not even understand, much less adopt as their own. Wertsch (1984) has further elaborated Vygotsky's concept of the zone of proximal development. He suggests that a critical dimension of the instruction that takes place within a learner's zone is the teacher and learner's definitions of the situation. By *situation definition* he means "the way in which a setting or context is represented by those who are operating in that setting" (p. 8). Wertsch suggests that even though both parties may be functioning in the same physical context, they have their own representation of the task at hand. Early in instruction these representations (i.e., definitions of a task) may be quite disparate. It is the role of the teacher to see to it that children eventually modify their definitions of a task to approximate that of the teacher. Wertsch maintains that this is accomplished by the establishment of intersubjectivity between a teacher and a student. This occurs when both share the same definition of a task and both are aware that they do so. Whereas this account may appear circular, it is not. Rather, it is meant to convey the idea that instruction is an ongoing process of negotiation and renegotiation between teacher and student. It is the teachers who initially must compromise their definition of a task, with the intent that students will eventually be brought back to "see" the task as the teachers do. Cole and his associates have described the master teacher as one who excells in "the artful subversion of children into the task of reading" (Laboratory of Comparative Human Cognition, 1982, p. 53). Similarly, Cazden (1981) suggests that in the acquistion of reading skills, performance often precedes competence. Thus, in the instruction of younger students and in the initial stages of teaching concepts to uninitiated, older students, instruction is more likely to proceed through a process of induction rather than abstraction. In other words, individuals may be induced into engaging in activities the instrumental function of which they only later come to understand. Throughout this process the use of language is critical.

In addition to the challenge of getting students to own the teachers' goals of instruction there are other problems related to the teachers second major role— that of mediator of student thinking. Fundamental among these is the problem of "privacy of cognitive activity." Privacy refers to the unavailability of observable cognitive processes that may serve as models for the students' own behavior. For most goal-oriented tasks associated with the acquisition and utilization of strategies of literacy in the classroom, the cognitive means or strategies used in the service of these goals by the already literate (e.g., teachers) are not likely to be observable to the newly initiated student. For example, as I read a passage of expository text, the processes that I use to enhance my understanding of that text occur largely beneath the surface. Moreover, even if the means I used were made observable, the fact that I engaged in an earlier cognitive strategy (e.g., self-questioning), which is instrumental to my eventually being able to understand what I have read, may not be self-evident to the novice reader. Thus, the teacher as an effective mediator must serve to make explicit the relationship between strategies and their eventual outcomes (Duffy, Roehler, & Mason, 1984).

A related function of teachers as mediators of their students' thinking is concerned with the assembly or integration of more complex cognitive processes from simpler ones. A major assumption of the sociohistorical approach is that before students can use cognitive strategies in the service of other higher-order goals these strategies must first be learned, indeed overlearned, as ends in and of themselves. For example, before students are able to effectively incorporate summarization as a strategy into their reading as a means of promoting comprehension, they must learn summarization as a goal itself. Indeed, requiring students to use comprehension-promoting strategies before they can do so efficiently may initially reduce rather than improve their comprehension of text. Note that the determination of *what* gets taught and *when* it is taught should be based upon functional and not formal considerations. In other words, it is the utility of the process associated with literacy that should determine whether it will be incorporated in the cognitive repertoire of the child. In effect, students must internalize culturally developed "functional systems," the components of which, when practiced by themselves, can be made meaningful to students while they become more and more skilled in their application.

A final important function of teachers in their roles as mediators of students' cognitive development is that of facilitating transfer of conceptual and strategic knowledge across settings or contexts. Students are often capable of using cognitive strategies that they nevertheless fail to spontaneously invoke in the service of new task demands. For example, while some children may be quite capable of uncovering contradictory statements in passages when prompted, they nevertheless fail to do so spontaneously.

A social-interactional conception of transfer may be contrasted with traditional views that tend to locate the ability to transfer either in the task or in the individual learners' head. Thus, from a behavioral perspective whether or not individuals are able to apply what they know to novel settings depends upon the similarity between the original learning and transfer tasks. In contrast, a Piagetian view of transfer assumes that the ability to transfer is a quality of the individuals and that their application of cognitive operations across tasks is related to their stage of development.

A sociohistorical analysis locates the ablity to transfer for any given culturally meaningful set of contexts on a continuum from social to individual control. In other words, we may think of classroom teachers in terms of the extent to which they do or do not promote practice in the application of concepts, principles, and strategies in contexts where they were not initally learned; and only gradually is the disposition to transfer internalized by students themselves (Laboratory for Comparative Human Cognition, 1984).

Teachers may promote the generalization of knowledge across contexts by the way that they:

1. Arrange for the occurrence or nonoccurrence of specific basic problem-solving environments.
2. Control the frequency of occurences of these environments; (repetition and redundancy minimize the problem of transfer).
3. Influence the patterning and cooccurence of events.
4. Regulate the level of difficulty of the tasks with which children are presented. (Laboratory of Comparative Human Cognition, 1983, 1984)

Cole and his colleagues suggest that the single most pervasive source of transfer is language itself (Laboratory of Comparative Human Cognition, 1983). The collective experiences of the world of a culture may be represented in its language and the way that this language is practiced. By representing the relevant relationships between different contexts, the culture precludes the necessity of transfer as an individual constructive activity. They further maintain that language in its written form (i.e., literacy) may be the single most important cultural tool for associating contexts since it represents a powerful means for storing and transferring information across both time and distance.

In summary, it is useful to think of students' zones of proximal development and the teachers' role in providing appropriate scaffolding within these zones in terms of a continuum of teacher and student engagement and responsibility. Thus, in the early stages of instruction, it is likely to be necessary that teachers will have to model and verbally direct students to goals that they as teachers will have specified. Later in instruction, however, it is to be expected that students will formulate their own goals and that when instructional assistance is necessary it will come at the determination of the students themselves (e.g., through student-generated questions). Intermediate between these two extremes one can imagine a graduated series of instructional interactions with increasingly more involvement and responsibility on the part of the students.

The Contexts of School-Based Literacy—
A Constructively Critical Analysis

Vygotsky's is an approach that conceives of instruction and cognitive development as interrelated processes.

Instruction is good only when it proceeds ahead of development and when it awakens and rouses to life those functions that are in the process of maturing or in the zone of proximal development. It is in this way that instruction plays an extremely important role in development. (1956, p. 278)

Sociohistorical theory provides a metric by which to evaluate the efficacy of current classroom practice as well as to suggest new practices that are likely to be effective. In short, the theory underscores the central role of teachers as interactive decision makers. The effectiveness of the decisions that they make is evaluated by how well their students are assisted through their respective zones of proximal development. To determine the goodness-of-fit between current teaching practices associated with reading and writing, and the type of instuctional principles and activities that follow from the Vygotskian framework described in the chapter, it is important to establish common assumptions concerning the tasks or curriculum of literacy. That is, how do the schools define literacy?

SCHOOL-BASED LITERACY: A CRITICAL ANALYSIS

A Vygotskian analysis of school-based literacy suggests three interrelated questions. First, what are the historically evolved and culturally shaped purposes and operations (i.e., the tasks) associated with literacy? Second, how are these tasks taught and practiced in the schools so as to promote their internalization and independent use by students who comprise the culture? And finally, how is it that teachers come to understand the tasks and practices associated with literacy instruction so that they are able to use these as knowledge-in-action? These questions will guide both the present analysis as well as suggestions for change.

The Tasks of School-Based Literacy

What *does* it mean to be able to read and write? We have seen that so apparently simple a question is in reality frought with significant conceptual as well as practical concerns. What are the culturally sanctioned purposes for which reading and writing are to be used? Reading is more than phonics and writing more than penmanship, but what more? At issue is the culturally prescribed curriculum (sign and tool systems) of school-based literacy in the broadest sense. The recent emphasis on the importance of functional literacy is consistent with the orientation of the present chapter. However, one must still ask: What are the functions to be learned?

In their review of "The Natural History of Literacy," Resnick and Resnick (1977) indicate that the expectation that the entire population be highly literate is of relatively recent origin. Moreover, we have seen that there is both historical and cross-cultural precedent for the occurence of literacy without education. Resnick and Resnick (1977) cited evidence suggesting that until the beginning of this century literacy was not used to promote the acquistion of new knowledge. Similarly, Scribner and Cole (1981) found that the present-day practice of literacy of the Vai of West Africa is not used as a way of communicating vicarious experience, new bodies of knowledge, or new ways of thinking about life problems. Thus, in neither case was literacy practiced so as to promote individual cognitive development. While it would be greatly exaggerated and unduly perjorative to characterize the current practice of classroom literacy in similar terms, it is nonetheless reasonable to inquire to what extent the tasks of school-based literacy serve to promote the growth of intellect and how our conceptualizations of these tasks might be improved.

In recent years, criticisms have been directed at the tasks of classroom literacy. Langer (1984) questioned the extent to which research findings from human learning and cognition have had an impact on literacy instruction in schools. She noted the abundance of seatwork and paperwork. Also, she noted relatively little thoughtful interaction between teachers and students, between students and students, or between students and the ideas about which they read or write. Findings from the National Assessment of Educational Progress (1981) suggest that while students seem to be acquiring the necessary basic skills associated with literacy there is little emphasis being placed upon the instruction of higher-level, critical-thinking skills. Summarizing a number of studies that have examined the use of language in instructional groups, Parker (1984) suggests that teachers spend little time in engaging students' higher psychological functions.

In her study of classroom reading instruction, Durkin found that less than 1 percent of the teachers' time was devoted to comprehension instruction. Instead, most of their time was spent giving assignments and asking questions. Other studies of questioning in the classroom suggest that of all questions asked 90 percent of these come from the teacher with most of students' questions focusing on procedural and not epistemic matters (Parker, 1984).

The state of the art in writing instruction has been even less encouraging. Graves (1983) found little emphasis on writing instruction in schools; indeed, he found that students are seldom even asked to write. When they do write, students essentially end up producing what Florio (1979) has referred to as "dead letters" (i.e., writing for which their is no real intended audience). Finally, there has been virtually no emphasis upon the integrated instruction of reading and writing (Jensen, 1983). Students can pass through school without recognizing that the activities of reading and writing are essentially related (Hansen, 1983).

It is too easy to lay such problems at the feet of teachers, for they are the ones ultimately and most visibly responsible for translating policy into practice. However, often overlooked are the formulators of policy themselves. It has been my experience that teachers frequently feel constrained in what they can introduce into their own instruction because of district policy that has failed to keep abreast of the current state of the art in instruction. This is often exacerbated by the skills emphasized in tests. Winograd (this volume) has provided a thought-provoking critique of policy making and literacy. Essentially, he concludes that policy makers and teachers are often working at cross purposes to each other. Until the goals of the two can be coordinated at a higher level, wide-scale constructive changes in literacy instruction are not likely to occur.

Thus, the tasks of literacy as currently practiced in schools tend to involve the low level practice of discrete skills. If we are to achieve a higher level of literacy we must alter our conception of what it means to be literate. At issue is not whether students should be functionally literate, but rather, what functions literacy best ought serve. Whereas it is no doubt important that individuals be able to balance checkbooks and follow written instructions, it is certainly no less important that they be empowered to use reading and writing for critical thinking and problem solving.

The Practice of School-Based Literacy

In their review of "The Natural History of Literacy," Resnick and Resnick (1977) note that the current expectation that the entire population be highly literate is of relatively recent origin. They suggest that if we are to achieve a higher literacy criterion, instruction will almost surely have to change to accommodate current conceptions of literacy. Given that literacy is culturally designated, how is it acquired by the individual? What do teachers do to promote this acquisition? How might this practice be improved?

There can be little argument but that the sort of instructional activities that follow from a such a Vygotskian perspective are highly labor intensive and, consequently, not likely to be used by a majority of teachers. Teachers are already concerned about the number and diversity of students that they must instruct. According to Vygotsky the most important instructional question is: How can education best assist children through the zone of proximal development? How can teachers as representatives of the prevalent culture arrange practice so as to promote its conception of being literate? An ultimate criterion of instructional success from a Vygotskian, or any other, perspective is that students eventually become able to effectively function independently. Indeed, the variety of social contexts that comprise literacy instruction may be thought of as falling along a continuum from more teacher responsibility to more student responsibility over the tasks (i.e., means and ends) of literacy.

The Social Contexts of the Practice of Classroom Literacy. It is useful to think of the social contexts of classroom literacy in terms of the amount of instructional support students are provided in setting and fulfilling various task demands. One may characterize the social contexts of classroom instruction both in terms of the size of the social unit and who it is that mediates or guides students learning within this unit. It may also be characterized in terms of the number of opportunities that teachers are able to create for individual and small-group instruction. Thus, on one level students may be engaged in one-to-one, teacher-student interaction, whereas on another level students may be expected to engage in whole-class instruction. There exists in addition a variety of different social contexts of instruction from reading groups to independent activities.

Dyadic or one-to-one instruction is usually considered the most optimal of teaching arrangements for a given student. Its major criticism, of course, is that it is not cost effective. Despite this limitation a suprising amount of individual instruction still takes place. Brophy (1983) suggests that:

> students in the early grades require a lot of one-to-one dyadic interaction with the teacher, who provides them opportunities for practice and feedback. Most of this dyadic interaction occurs within the small group setting, but it is dyadic interaction nevertheless.

Thus, there exists at least the potential for the sort of teacher-mediated literacy instruction that derives from a Vygotskian framework.

The most frequently occuring instructional setting in the early grades, however, involves students working alone. Estimates of the time that early elementary school age children spend in independent seatwork are as high as 70 percent. In a study of second graders' independent seatwork spent on reading and writing tasks, Anderson (1984) found that a substantial number of students defined as their major objective the completion of the assigned task. There was little evidence among these students of knowledge of the relationships between these tasks and improving cognitive processes such as reading comprehension. Thus, the problem with much of literacy instruction in these contexts is that it shares the goal of student independence without having adopted the means by which this is to be successfully achieved.

Graves (1983) describes writing workshops in which students are led initially by teachers to share their writing with their peers. First, teachers model for students how to "receive" each others writing, explaining what as readers they thought the piece was about and then asking the author questions about the paper. The questions range from asking where the idea came from to asking for specific information (e.g., how do whales sound when you are in the boat?). Initially, the teacher provides scaffolding through modeling, leading students to eventually meet with each other in peer writing conferences.

An example of a program of reading instruction that incorporates a transition from teacher-centered to student-centered control during the learning process is the work conducted by Palinesar (1984) using a reciprocal teaching procedure. Consistent with the maxim "to teach is to learn twice" Palinesar instructed groups of fifth grade low readers in the use of effective comprehension skills. Basically, this procedure involved instructing students to use four strategies known to promote effective comprehension: summarizing, predicting, questioning, and requesting clarity of text. Through a procedure that initially involved modeling and guidance accompanied by teacher scaffolding, students were eventually able to alternately assume the role of teachers themselves. The reciprocal teaching procedure involved extensive dialogue between teacher and student as well as between student and student. Analyses of the results of this procedure indicated that students reading scores were brought up to grade level and that they were able to make use of the earlier mentioned strategies in other instructional settings (i.e., transfer).

The general picture that emerges of current literacy instruction in the classroom often falls short of the sort of conditions Vygotsky suggests as important in promoting cognitive development. The size and composition of instructional groups are very real constraints in implementing Vygotskian informed instruction, but these are not constraints that are insurmountable. Through effective management of the classroom the teacher can create contexts that make possible mediated instruction (see Au, this volume). However, what becomes apparent from the combined consideration of the tasks and instruction of literacy and their relationship to student cognitive development is the necessity for highly knowledgable teachers. Through their instructional activities, or by means of the instructional conditions that they are able to create, they promote the internalization and independent use of the higher functions assumed to comprise literacy.

Teachers' Knowledge-In-Action

It is a truism to asert that students will benefit little from even the most optimal instructional settings (e.g., one-to-one instruction) unless teachers know how and when to guide and support their students' learning. It is important to characterize the knowledge that makes this teacher mediation possible (see Schwartz, this volume).

Hatano (1982) has made distinction between routine and adaptive experts that is useful when applied to understanding the knowledge of the teacher. Routine experts are able to carry out highly prescribed, more or less linear, activities that require little decision making. Adaptive experts, in contrast, are able to adjust their problem-solving activities as the task demands. Hatano suggests that what distinguishes adaptive from routine experts is the relative amount of conceptual knowledge that each possesses. Thus, in addition to having the know how or procedural knowledge that characterizes routine experts, adaptive experts have a much more elaborate network of conceptual knowledge.

The significance of the adaptive-routine distinction when applied to teachers should be clear. In order to effectively mediate students' academic problem solving in the way prescribed by Vygotsky, teachers must be adaptive experts. The problem, of course, is how to forge the requisite conceptual and procedural knowledge into action. Translated into the present context this means that teachers know not only that they need to provide mediated instruction but also when and how to go about doing so. Students in undergraduate education programs and practicing teachers recognize the importance of procedural knowledge, but so often minimize the importance of conceptual knowledge upon which practice is based, thus condeming themselves to the status of routine experts. Teacher educators, on the other hand, often extoll the virtues of conceptual knowledge, but then present this knowledge as inert abstractions far removed from the realm of practice.

In considering this fundamental problem of teacher preparation for literacy instruction, consider the following analogy. For the prospective teacher, like the students they will eventually instruct, learning is also a socially mediated process.

Like children-as-students, teachers-as-students must have their thinking guided by those who are themselves knowledgable in the domain for which they are mediating instruction. This is not a radical suggestion. What makes it unusual, however, is the amount and kind of guidance that may be necessary for the internalization of the cognitive skills associated with effective teaching. The various mediational roles of the teacher require an extraordinary amount of sophistication on the part of teacher educators. Thus, not only are the activities of teacher-as-mediators labor intensive but the preparation of teachers to be able to engage in this sort of instruction is itself labor intensive.

One need not search long for appropriate instructional models. Any professional who requires complex decision making requires complex and protracted socially mediated instruction (e.g., physicians, airline pilots, and so forth). Effective teaching is no less demanding.

THE ROLE AND LIMITS OF SCHOOL-BASED LITERACY

Whereas there are constraints on the uses of literacy in the classroom, many of these are potentially surmountable. A Vygotskian conception of instruction clearly places the role of teachers at the center, for it is they who have the potential to link their students to the various functions of literacy. They may do this by seeing to it that their students' motivation and thinking are mediated by those who are more experienced (i.e., themselves as teachers, or fellow classmates) in the tasks at hand. To accomplish this teachers must know when and how to create task structures that make possible opportunities for the mediation of student thinking. Teachers must also select and engineer the creation of contexts that promote the realization of the sort of goals that the larger culture deems useful. What emerges is a view of teachers as sophisticated decision makers. And what this chapter suggests is a model of teacher preparation far more involved than presently exists. In short, if teachers are to be effective at mediating their students' language processes, then they too must learn to do so by having their own thinking socially guided.

The more serious limits of literacy may relate to its inflated role in the general cognitive functioning of individuals. Scribner and Cole (1981) speak of the myth of the great divide, between the literate and nonliterate, and suggest that more important differences may be found between the schooled and nonschooled. More specifically, it is less the processes of literacy (i.e., reading and writing) and more an individual's ability to use and manipulate knowledge in a decontextualized fashion (i.e., in settings both spatially and/or temporally removed from the immediate context) that seems to divide individuals of varying cognitive sophistication (Scribner & Cole, 1981).

Finally, if there are fundamental limits in the use of literacy in classroom settings, they would seem to apply to the difficulty of representing tacit knowledge by means of language in either its oral or written form (Olson, 1977).

What seems clear is that if we wish children to use the higher-level cognitive functions associated with literacy (or, any other higher cognitive functions) for a diversity of purposes, we must instruct and provide practice in their use across a variety of contexts. As Rogoff (1982) suggests there are no context-free cognitive processes. What emerges, then, from Vygotsky's sociohistorical approach is a sort of relativity theory of literacy—indeed, of all higher cognitive processes—such that the utility or functionality of these (literate) processes can only be assessed in terms of their goodness-of-fit to the tasks deemed important by the predominant culture. What is literate today may not suffice in meeting the demands of tomorrow's literacy criteria.

REFERENCES

Anderson, L. (1984). The function of seatwork in a commercially developed curriculum. In G. G. Duffy, L. R. Roehler, & J. Mason (Eds.), Comprehension instruction. New York: Longman.

Applebee, A. N., & Langer, J. A. (1984). Instructional scaffolding: Reading and writing as natural language activities. In J. M. Jensen (Ed.), Composing and comprehending (pp. 183-190). Urbana, Ill.: The ERIC Clearinghouse on Reading and Communication Skills.

Au, K. H., & Kawakami, A. J. (1984). Vygotskian perspectives on discussion processes in small-group reading-lessons. In P. L. Peterson, L. C. Wilkinson, & M. Hallinan (Eds.), The social context of instruction (pp. 209-225). New York: Academic.

Brophy, J. E. (1983). Fostering student learning and motivation in the elementary school classroom. In S. G. Paris, G. M. Olsen, & H. W. Stevenson (Eds.), Learning and motivation in the classroom, (pp. 283-305). Hillsdale, N.J.: Erlbaum.

Brown, A. L., & Ferrara, R. A. (in press). Diagnosing zones of proximal development. In J. Wertsch (Ed.), Culture, communication, and cognition: Vygotskian perspectives. New York: Cambridge University Press.

Bruner, J. S. (1984). Vygotsky's zone of proximal development: The hidden agenda. In B. Rogoff & J. Wertsch (Eds.), Children's learning in the "zone of proximal development" (pp. 93-98). San Francisco: Josey-Bass.

Cazden, C. B. (1981). Performance before comptence: Assistance to child discourse in the zone of proximal development. The Quarterly Newsletter of the Laboratory of Comparative Human Cognition, 3(1), 5-8.

Cole, M., & Griffin, P. (1983). A socio-historical approach to re-mediation. The Quarterly Newsletter of the Laboratory of Comparative Human Cognition, 5(4), 69-73.

Day, J. D. (1983). The zone of proximal development. In M. Pressley & J. R. Levin (Eds.), Cognitive strategy research: Psychological foundations (pp. 155-176.). New York: Springer-Verlag.

Duffy, G. G., Rochler, L. R., & Mason, J. (1984). Comprehension instruction: Perspectives and suggestion. New York: Longman.

Erickson, F. (1982). Taught cogntive learning in its immediate environments: A neglected topic in the anthropology of eduction. Anthropology and Education Quarterly, 13(2), 149-180.

Florio, S. (1979). The problem of dead letters: social perspectives on the teaching of writing. The Elementary School Journal, 80(1), 1-7.

Graves, D. (1983). *Writing: Teachers and students at work*, Exeter, N.H.: Heinemann.

Hansen, J. (1983). The writer as meaning maker. In J. L. Collins (Ed.), *Teaching all children to write.* (pp. 10–18). New York: New York State English Council.

Hatano, G. (1982). Cognitive consequences of practice in culture specific procedural skills. *The Quarterly Newsletter of the Laboratory of Comparative Human Cognition,* 4(1), 15–18.

Havelock, E. A. (1976). *Origins of western literacy.* Toronto: Ontario Institute in Education.

Inagaki, K., & Hatano, G. (1983). Collective scientific discovery by young children. *The Quarterly Newsletter of the Laboratory of Comparative Human Cognition, 5*(1), 13–18.

Johnston, P. (1984). Instruction and student independence. *The Elementary School Journal,* 84(3), 338–344.

Laboratory of Comparative Human Cognition. (1982). A model system for the study of learning difficulties. *The Quarterly Newsletter of the Laboratory of Comparative Human Cognition,* 4(3), 39–66.

Laboratory of Comparative Human Cognition. (1983). Culture and cognitive development. In P. H. Musen & W. Kessen (Eds.), *Handbook of child psychology.* (Vol 1). New York: Wiley.

Laboratory of Comparative Human Cognition. (1984). Culture and intelligence. In R. Sternberg (Ed.), *Handbook of human intelligence.* New York: Cambridge University Press.

Luria, A. K. (1971). Towards the problem of the historical nature of psychological processes. *International Journal of Psychology,* 6(4), 259–272.

Luria, A. R. (1982). *Language and cognition.* J. V. Wertsch (Ed.). New York: Wiley.

Mathews, M. M. (1966). *Teaching to read: Historically considered.* Chicago: University of Chicago Press.

Meacham, J. A. (1977). Soviet investigations of memory. In R. V. Kail, Jr. & J. W. Hagen (Eds.), *Perspectives on the development of memory and cognition,* New York: Wiley.

Mehan, H. (1981). Social constructivism in psychology and sociology. *The Quarterly Newsletter of the Laboratory of Comparative Human Cognition.* 3(4), 71–77.

National Assessment of Educational Progress (1981). *Reading, thinking, and writing.* Denver, Colo: Education Commission of the States.

Olson, D. R. (1977). The language of instruction. In R. C. Anderson, R. J. Spiro, and W. E. Montague (Eds.), *Schooling and the acquisition of knowledge.* Hillsdale, N.J.: Erlbaum.

Palincsar, A. S., & Brown, A. L. (1984). Reciprocal teaching of comprehension-fostering and comprehension-monitoring activities. *Cognition and Instruction,* 1(2), 117–175.

Parker, R. P. (1984). Schooling and the growth of mind. In R. P. Parker & F. A. Davis (Eds.), *Developing literacy: Young children's use of language* (pp. 139–155). Newark, Del.: International Reading Association.

Resnick, L. B. (1981). Social assumptions as a context for science: Some reflections on psychology and education. *Educational Psychologist,* 16(1), 1–10.

Resnick, D. P., & Resnick, L. B. (1977). The nature of literacy: An historical exploration. *Harvard Educational Review,* 47(3), 370–384.

Rogoff, B. (1982) Intergrating context and cognitive development. In M. E. Lamb & A. L. Brown (Eds), *Advances in Developmental Psychology.* (Vol. 2). Hillsdale, N.J.: Erlbaum.

Rogoff, B., & Wertsch, J. (Eds.). (1984). *Children's learning in the "zone of proximal development."* San Francisco: Josey-Bass.

Scribner, S., & Cole, M. (1973). Cognitive consequences of formal and informal education. *Science, 182,* 553-559.

Scribner, S., & Cole, M., (Eds.). (1981). *The psychology of literacy.* Cambridge, Mass.: Harvard University Press.

Simon, Brian. (1971). *Intelligence, psychology, and education: A Marxist critique,* London: Lawrence & Wishart.

Taylor, D. (1983). *Family literacy.* Exeter, N. H.: Heinemann.

Vygotsky, L. S. (1956). *Collected psychological research.* Moscow: Academy of Pedagogical Sciences Press.

Vygotsky, L. S. (1962). *Thought and language.* E. Hanfmann & G. Vakar (Trans.). Cambridge, Mass.: The M. I. T. Press (Original work published 1934).

Vygotsky, L. S. (1978). *Mind in society.* M. Cole et al. (Eds.). Cambridge, Mass.: Harvard University Press.

Vygotsky, L. S. (1981). The genesis of higher mental functions. In J. V. Wertsch (Ed.), *The concept of activity in soviet psychology.* White Plains, N.Y.: Sharpe. 1981.

Wertsch, J. V. (1979). From social interaction to higher psychological processes: A clarification and application of Vygotsky's theory. *Human Development, 22,* 1-22.

Wertsch, J. V. (1980). The significance of dialogue in Vygotsky's account of social, ego-centric, and inner speech. *Contemporary Educational Psychology, 52,* 150-162.

Wertsch, J. V. (1984). The zone of proximal development: Some conceptual issues. In B. Rogoff & J. Wertsch (Eds.), *Children's learning in the zone of proximal development* (pp. 7-18). San Francisco: Josey-Bass.

Wertsch, J. V., et al. (1980). The adult-child dyad as a problem-solving system. *Child Development, 51,* 1215-1221.

Wixon, K. K. & Peters, C. W. (1984). Reading redefined: A Michigan Reading Association position paper. *Michigan Reading Journal, 17*(1), 4-7.

Wood, D., & Middleton, D. (1975). A study of assisted problem-solving. *British Journal of Psychology, 66,* 181-191.

Wozniak, R. H. (1980). Theory, practice, and the "zone of proximal development" in Soviet psychoeducational research. *Contempory Educational Psychology, 5*(2), 175-183.

2

Adult Assistance of
Children's Learning

Barbara Rogoff

Children's learning frequently occurs in social contexts that permit adults or more experienced peers to guide the young learner. This chapter examines several conceptions of the teaching-learning process and extends Vygotsky's concept of the zone of proximal development, in which cognitive skills such as reading are first practiced in social interaction with a more experienced person. This leads to internalization of the skill so that a child is able to carry it out independently. Adults or competent peers can support children's performance so that they can extend their activity beyond what could be accomplished independently (Vygotsky, 1978; Wertsch, 1979).

Research using the concept of the zone of proximal development has focused on what adults—parents or teachers—do to stretch children's learning. However, adults do not work alone. If children give no feedback or guidance as to their needs or understanding, adults can do little to structure the zone of proximal development. Children play an active role in their own learning. Not only do they assist the adult in setting the level of the lesson; through their motivation and self-directed attempts to learn, they require the adult to provide information or help. This chapter stresses that together the adult and the child manage teaching and learning in a process of *guided participation*.

Guided participation involves a finely tuned interaction between the assistance provided by adults and the children's skills in ensuring proximity to and involvement with more experienced people. Adults arrange the occurrence of children's activities and facilitate learning by regulating the difficulty of tasks and by modeling mature performance during joint participation in activities. On the many occasions that adults do not regard themselves as explicitly teaching children, they often nevertheless adjust their interaction and structure children's environments and activities in ways that provide support for learning.

To elaborate these concepts, I will describe a transformation in my thinking about the nature of teaching and learning. I began research in this area with the idea that instruction consisted of stimuli provided by the adult and information obtained by the child. I searched for modes of instruction used by adults to teach children. Such research focuses on the adult and child separately and emphasizes the means by which adults instruct. However, I gradually came to the view that separating the adult's contribution from the child's does not allow examination of the truly interactive nature of instruction. Thus my concept of instruction transformed to emphasize the joint problem solving involved in instructional communication.

MODES OF ADULT INSTRUCTION

Research on modes of instruction began with efforts to explain differences in cognitive test performance by children from different social classes or cultural backgrounds. One contrast in modes of instruction was formal versus informal teaching. Formal instruction is a caricature of school instruction, involving reliance on language used out of the context of practical activities. For example, in geography instruction, children often learn about places with which they have no contact, through oral or written lectures. Informal learning is characterized as involving activities that are embedded in the context in which the information and skills are to be used (Bruner, Olver, & Greenfield, 1966; Scribner & Cole, 1973). The adult demonstates the skill through practical activity, and the child observes and learns. An outgrowth of the formal versus informal dichotomy is interest in whether adults teach by verbal instruction or by demonstration.

In order to relate such differences in the mode of adult instruction to children's learning, I examined the relationship between verbal versus nonverbal instruction by mothers from two cultures and the memory test performance of their nine-year-old children (Rogoff, 1982). The mothers were to help their children construct tinkertoy objects according to models without actually putting the pieces together themselves. Mayan mothers in Guatemala made more use of nonverbal cues and less use of verbal cues than United States mothers, consistent with what would be expected from the literature contrasting formal and informal education. For the Mayan mothers and children, greater use of verbal instruction and less use of nonverbal instruction was associated with better performance on verbal memory tests. But the association was limited to verbal memory tests; there was no relation between mode of instruction and spatial memory test performance. This suggests a limited relationship between mode of instruction and memory test performance: children who receive greater exposure to verbal instruction from their mothers are skilled on verbal memory tests. Similar results were found by

Jordan (1977) for Hawaiian mothers and children. However, neither Jordan nor I found a relationship between mode of instruction and test performance using mainland United States mothers and children, perhaps because the United States mothers were all above some threshold in the use of verbal instruction.

Although this research contributes to our understanding of variation in the use of verbal and nonverbal instruction, I felt dissatisfied with the concept of instruction that it employed. One source of my dissatisfaction came from discussions I had with Guatemalan mothers about how they taught their daughters. In structured spot observations of the children's everyday activities, I had found very few occasions (6 out of 1,708 observations) in which the children were explicitly being taught anything. This puzzled me, because the children were obviously very skilled. Many of the girls were excellent weavers by early adolescence, and the tortillas made by young girls were much better formed than any I attempted. So how were they taught? I asked their mothers. The mothers insisted that they were not teaching these skills to their daughters; that the daughters just watched and learned. I began to wonder if my concept of teaching might be limiting my understanding of instruction in this context.

When I asked the mothers what they did to help their daughters learn, it was clear that the daughters indeed received guidance from their mothers. The mothers structured the learning process for the girls. For example, mothers organized learning to make tortillas as follows: At age five or so, a girl is given a little ball of corn meal dough to play with. After a little practice handling the dough, the girl is encouraged to try to make a tortilla. At age seven or eight the girl usually makes very imperfect tortillas, cracked and uneven. However, the mother puts these tortillas on the hot griddle for her, and they are the girl's dinner. During this process, the mother points out problems in workmanship and shows the girl how to hold and pat the dough appropriately. Not until age nine or so is the girl considered skilled enough to use her fingers to turn the tortillas on the hot griddle. Thus the mother allows the girl a greater role in the activity as her skills increase, and the mother provides instruction regarding how to improve the tortillas in the context of making them. The mother carried out a task analysis of what is involved in making tortillas as well as an assessment of the child's skills, providing guidance in the skill along the way. This all occurred in a relaxed fashion, rather than as an explicit lesson plan.

As I thought about this instruction, I felt that the main idea missing in my initial concept of teaching and learning was the notion of interaction. Instruction occurs *between* the mother and child, rather than involving a lesson provided by the mother that produces some general advance in development by the child.

In the next set of studies, I examined both the adult's and child's actions in an instructional situation, and related them to the child's learning of the specific information taught, rather than to skill on an unrelated cognitive test. This was a step in the direction of examining teaching and learning in a more interactive fashion. Instead of examining the adult's teaching and the child's learning on two separate occasions, they were examined together.

EVIDENCE FOR THE INTERACTIVE NATURE
OF INSTRUCTION

The next set of studies involved United States mothers and children classifying objects in two situations designed to simulate home and school tasks: sorting groceries onto shelves and sorting pictures into trays in a homework problem. Mothers were encouraged to teach as they would at home when organizing the kitchen after a shopping trip or when assisting their children on a homework problem.

In the first analyses (Rogoff, Ellis, & Gardner, 1984), both the adult's and child's participation were examined, but the adult's actions and the child's actions were considered separately. The instruction was coded in terms of the number of directives versus open-ended questions in the mother's discourse, her nonverbal instruction, and the child's contribution of verbal and nonverbal information. Following the instruction, the child was tested on learning and generalization of the category sructure by being asked to place some old and some new items in their proper locations.

The study examined two alternative predictions regarding the effects of the nature of the task and the child's age (six to seven versus eight to nine years) on mother's instruction and children's learning. Previous research indicates that older children receive more open-ended verbal instruction and fewer directives and nonverbal instructions than younger children. These developmental differences resemble the differences expected from the literature contrasting formal and informal instruction. Hence, the effect of the interaction of child's age and instructional context might be expected to be additive, with the greatest use of directives and nonverbal instruction in the home task with the younger children and the most open-ended verbal instruction in the school task with the older children.

An alternative hypothesis that considers the difference in the children's expertise with the two tasks leads to a different prediction: that mothers would adjust their instruction according to their perception of the child's need for assistance in the task. The younger children are new to formal schooling and thus might be expected to need more assistance with the school task than the older children who have had more school experience. Both age groups are relatively familiar with chores at home, so there may be little difference in the assistance they receive from their mothers, and it would be less than the assistance the younger children receive in the school task.

The results supported the hypothesis that instruction would be adjusted to the perceived needs of the children. There was more instruction of all kinds for the younger children in the school task. The mothers and children seemed to expect the school task to be more difficult, though it was arranged to be similar in difficulty to the home task. Mothers and children adopted a more formal stance and spent more time in instruction in the school task. It appeared that mother-child dyads adjusted instruction to provide more support for the younger children in the school task, in which they would be expected to be less expert. Interestingly, this adjustment was accompanied by slightly better performance on the learning test by the younger children in the school task. The findings were replicated with a sample of unrelated women teaching seven year olds in the two tasks (Ellis, unpublished manuscript).

These results focus attention on the interactive nature of teaching and learning. Younger children are usually expected to perform less successfully than older children on such learning tests. But with the dyads adjusting for the "harder" task with the younger children, slightly better performance was achieved by the less expert group of children. These findings fit nicely with Vygotsky's (1978) argument that instruction is tailored to the learner's needs in the zone of proximal development, allowing the child to stretch skill and understanding with adult assistance.

With this demonstration that instruction is indeed an interaction between teacher and learner, I was led to consider more carefully the nature of the interaction. It appeared that instead of separating the adult's and the child's actions so that they could be analyzed independently, it might be fruitful to regard the teacher-learner dyad as an integrated unit. In considering the mother's and child's actions in isolation from each other, their behaviors lose the meaning available in the flow of the interaction. The actions of each individual are less interpretable when examined independently of both the history of immediately preceding actions and the purpose linking them with the joint direction pursued by the dyad. The meaning inherent in the jointly developed framework of instruction is obscured by dividing the cooperative actions of mother and child into behaviors for which only one is given credit.

Studying the interaction itself involves a shift in perspective from one in which the individual is regarded as the basic unit of analysis to one in which the unit is social (Vygotsky, 1978; Wertsch, 1979). Rather than regarding what happens between people as secondary to the primay phenomemon of two coexisting individuals, such an approach takes the interaction as primary. The emphasis of analysis thus shifts from attempting to remove the interactive context in order to attribute actions to one person or the other, to examining both people's contributions to the interactive event. This shift in perspective led to my characterizing the instructional interaction between adults and children as guided participation in skilled activities.

INSTRUCTION AS GUIDED PARTICIPATION IN SKILLED ACTIVITIES

In the instructional process of guided participation, the adult leads the child through the process of solving the problem, and the child participates at a comfortable but slightly challenging level. The child is actively involved in the joint solution of the problem. The adult does not simply solve the problem and report the answer, nor does the child passively observe the adult's work and absorb the information spontaneously. The adult and child are both involved in working on the problem. The adult assesses the child's current understanding of the material and adjusts the necessary support of the child's contribution, while the child simultaneously adjusts the pace of instruction and guides or even manages the adult's construction of a supporting "scaffold" [to borrow Wood, Bruner, & Ross' (1976) term]. The child thus carries out simple aspects of the task under the adult's guidance, participating in the problem's solution and internalizing some aspects of the joint problem-solving process.

The notion of guided participation in problem solving integrates the child's activity with the adult's. Both verbal explanation and demonstration, if offered without the involvement of the child in the activity, yield one-sided instruction.

Guided participation may be important for both formal and informal instructional situations. The distinction between formal and informal instruction is overdrawn, limiting the conception of formal instruction to verbal explanation out of context and the conception of informal instruction to demonstration without explanation. Instead, guided participation may be important to effective instruction in both school and everyday practical situations. There is some literature to support this reconciliation of the concepts of formal and informal instruction. Mehan and Reil (in press) challenge the view that verbal explanation out of context is the primary means of exchanging information in school, with their observation that most messages in the classroom rely upon both verbal and nonverbal communication as the teacher guides students through tasks. Ethnographic observations (Fortes, 1938; Mead, 1964; Ruddle & Chesterfield, 1978) suggest that informal instruction may be better characterized as careful guidance and graduated participation in tasks—as with the Mayan mothers teaching their daughters to make tortillas—rather than as nonverbal demonstration.

Five general statements regarding instruction as a process of guided participation arise from such ethnographic observations of formal and informal instruction, as well as from ethnographic observations of the mothers assisting children in the home and school tasks (Rogoff & Gardner, 1984). Guided participation:

1. Provides a bridge between familiar skills or information and those needed to solve a new problem.
2. Provides structure for problem solving.
3. Involves the transfer of responsibility for management of problem solving.
4. Involves active participation by the child as well as the adult.
5. May be tacit as well as explicit in the everyday arrangements and interactions between adults and children.

Guided Participation Provides a Bridge between Familiar and Novel

Adults help children find the connections between what they already know and what is necessary to solve a new problem. In order to communicate successfully, the adult and child must find a common ground of knowledge and skill. Otherwise the two people would be unable to share a common reference point, and understanding would not occur. This effort toward understanding in communication draws the child into a model of the problem that is more mature yet understandable through links with what the child already knows. In the process of communicating, the adult translates the new task into terms that are familiar or comfortable to the child, drawing connections between what the child already knows and the new situation.

For example, many of the mothers in the classification task in the kitchen drew parallels between the laboratory kitchen and their kitchen at home, to guide the child's transfer of relevant information about classification to the laboratory task. One mother explained, "We're going to organize things by categories. You know, just like we don't put the spoons in the pan drawer and all that stuff. So we're going to organize the groceries by categories, okay?" Thus the mother helps the child figure out how to do this experimental task by tying it to a task with which they are more familiar. This mother went on to point out explicitly that making the link between the home situation and the laboratory would be useful, "See, that's the same way we do it at home, isn't it?" Most of the mothers provided some such link between the laboratory task and a more familiar context, assisting the children in stretching their understanding to encompass the new situation.

Guided Participation Provides Structure to Organize Problem Solving

The adult structures the task by determining the problem to be solved, the goal, and how the goal can be segmented into more manageable subgoals. The adult's structuring of the problem may be tailored to the child's level of skill. With a novice, the adult may take responsibility for managing the subgoals as well as making sure the overall goal is met. With a more experienced child, the child make take responsibility for the subgoals, and eventually for the whole task. For example, during early phases of learning to plan a birthday party, the child may participate in decisions at the most detailed level. They may decide whom to invite or what kind of drink to provide. But the adult structures the planning by managing the focus of decisions. When one subgoal is accomplished, the adult may steer decision making to another subgoal by saying something like: "Okay, that sounds like a fun party with all those kids—What would you like to have for them to eat?" In this way, the adult manages the overall goal and subgoals, with the child participating at a comfortable level. As the child's skill in planning parties advances, the child participates not only in the detailed levels of the subgoals but also in managing the subgoal or even in integrating the subgoals to reach the goal.

People vary in the effectiveness with which they structure a task for a learner. While most of the adult teachers structured the home and school classification tasks by providing the rationale for grouping particular items together, nine year olds who worked with six year olds seldom managed to provide such structure for learning the organization of items. Almost all of the children left out the subgoal of providing the rationale for putting things into particular categories. Instead of structuring the task to ensure that the category rationale was learned, the nine year olds focused on the more immediate task of placing items in their locations (Ellis & Rogoff, in press). Of the nine year olds, 88 percent provided *no* category structure to organize the items, while only 7 percent of the adults neglected to provide this structure. In the school task, the nine year olds also seemed to operate on an assumption that doing too much for the learner would be inappropriate. They frequently required the learner to guess the placement of each item without any clues. Even when an error was made, the child's teacher would supply minimal assistance ("Nope . . . Nope . . . Pretty close . . . GOOD! I bet you'll go to second grade next year!"). Their less effective teaching may have resulted from their revealing idea of what teachers are "supposed to" do, as well as the complexity for nine year olds of managing instruction and classification simultaneously. The results illustrate that the effectiveness of people's structuring of learning situations for others varies.

With effective guidance in learning, the adult not only takes initial responsibility for structuring the aspects of the task that are beyond the child but also ensures that as the child gains expertise the child takes over responsibility for relevant aspects of the task. The latter feature of guided participation is elaborated in the next section.

Guided Participation Transfers Responsibility for Managing Problem Solving

In guided participation, the child takes on an increasing role in managing problem solving during the course of a lesson and during the course of years. Effective transfer of responsibility for problem solving from the adult to the child requires sensitivity to the child's competence in the particular task so that responsibility is given when the child is able to handle it. It involves a task analysis of what is required to solve the problem and a tacit theory of the course of development of skill in that domain.

In the home and school classification tasks, the transfer of responsibility was evident in changes in who placed the items—the mother placed the items at the beginning, while the child was more likely to place them at the end of the session. In the placement of the first few items, the mother generally identified the appropriate location and provided a category rationale for the decision. As the session proceeded, the child would take increasing responsibility for portions of the routine. By the end, the child often independently determined the item's location and the rationale for its association with others in the same location. In such cases, the mother's supportive scaffolding was removed as it became unnecessary, and the child participated at a continually changing optimal level.

An example of adjustment of support by a mother to encourage participation by a child involves one dyad's development of mnemonic strategies in preparation for the child's posttest. They constructed a story associating the category labels with their locations. The mother devised the story for the first three category boxes, explaining, "We'll remember those things go there . . . we'll make a little story," as she invented mnemonics involving a daily routine. The child contributed slightly to the story for the fourth category, and invented part of the story for the last two (fifth and sixth) category boxes. Thus, by the end, the child took over the responsibility for developing the story line, an activity that likely had mnemonic benefits. But the idea was the mother's, and during the course of instruction, she transferred it to the child. It was clear that the mother was attempting to involve the child in developing the story, because she would pause and look at the child, pointing to the next box without filling in that part of the story, encouraging the child to fill in the blanks in the story. Finally the mother asked the child to tell the story independently as a review. The mother managed the story construction so that by the end the child was a major participant in the preparation for the test.

Such transfer of responsibility has also been noted in classroom reading instruction (Brown & Campione, 1984). In initial sessions the teacher primarily modeled strategies for comprehension, but gradually the teacher's demands for student involvement increased as the student began to perform parts of the task, until finally the students independently produced strategic behavior that resembled that modeled by the teacher.

Attempts to assess the child's readiness for greater responsibility are often subtle and embedded in the ongoing interaction, appearing as negotiations of the division of labor. At the beginning of the classification sessions, mothers often provided redundant information to ensure correct performance. For example, they might simultaneously point at the correct shelf, repeat the category level for the shelf, and look toward the shelf. The mothers decreased such redundancy as the session preceeded, but increased it again if the child appeared not to understand. The child's errors or hesitance were used to diagnose problems in the child's understanding and to adjust the mother's support for the child's performance.

In the ongoing interaction, the mothers frequently evidenced subtle diagnosis of the child's readiness and corresponding adjustment of maternal support. The mothers and children used hesitation, glances, and postural changes, as well as errors by the children, to adjust their relative responsibilities for problem solving. For example, one mother encouraged her child to determine where the next item went. When the child hesitated, the mother turned slightly toward the correct location. When the child still hesitated, the mother glanced at the correct location and moved the item slightly toward its intended location. Finally, she superficially rearranged other items in the correct group, and with this hint, the child finally made the correct placement. Thus the mother encouraged greater responsibility by the child, and masked her assistance as random activity rather than correction of error, adjusting her support to the child's level of understanding.

Guided Participation is Managed by the Child as Well as the Adult

It is difficult to focus on the activity of two people at once. This may account for the fact that much research on instruction examines only the activity of the adult. Although it is certainly true that adults carry great responsibility in instruction—they are more knowledgeable and have authority—children are also very active in gaining skill through the social interaction. The previous section notes that children participate through indicating their readiness for greater responsibility. In addition, children may at times manage the transfer of information.

In the home and school classification tasks, a few of the children took over the management of the instruction, despite their mothers' assigned responsibility to prepare them for the upcoming test and the fact that only the mothers had access to a cue sheet indicating the correct placement of items. One nine year old took control of the instruction when his mother indicated that she was totally confused about how to proceed and the items were in disarray. The child told her, politely but insistently, to look at the cue sheet. She followed the suggestion but was still confused, so the child led her through the process of checking the correctness of placement of items, picking up one item at a time and asking, "Is this one right? Look at the sheet." The child clearly managed the situation to solicit the information he needed from the mother.

In situations in which the adult is not formally labeled as the teacher, the child is probably likely to take a large role in learning on a routine basis. Parents go about their own activities, rather than focusing on instructing the child. And children may be more free to ask for help or join in with the adult in everyday situations, without worrying about overstepping bounds of the teacher. In the example above, the boy certainly felt he was stepping out of his appropriate role; he continually tried to mask the fact that he was telling her what to do. In explicit teaching situations an important part of the learner's role is helping to preserve the greater status of the teacher by avoiding being "uppity." In everyday situations, children may be more free to manage their own learning.

Their attempts to learn from adult activities may go unnoticed by parents, who are likely to view children's attempts to help or be involved in adult activities as just an inevitable aspect of childhood. Whereas the adult may be more concerned with getting the dishes clean or the gift wrapped, the young helper may be gaining an understanding of the principles of soap and water or the geometry of fitting paper around a gift. The fact that young children often insist on being involved is evidence that they are managing their own learning. My daughter, at age four, asked, "Can I help you with the can opener by holding onto your hand while you do it? . . . That's how I learn." And at age five she often suggested to her younger sister and brother that they hold onto her hand while she did something so they could learn how to do it. Such incidents illustrate the eagerness with which children approach the possibility of learning things from others, as well as their active role in managing their own learning (See also Nelson-Le Gall, in press, on children's help-seeking behavior in learning.) Children arrange for participation in activities, and adults tacitly (sometimes even unwillingly) provide information.

Guided Participation May be Tacit as Well as Explicit in Everyday Arrangements and Interactions between Adults and Children

Arrangements for learning often involve tacit and opportunistic communication of information, rather than explicit lessons on how to solve problems. As an adult and a child work together, the adult may point out crucial features of the task, indicate choice points, and provide assistance in handling difficulties. But this is often embedded in the context of practical activity rather than set off as explicit instruction. This tacit process is illustrated in the inconspicuous supporting role adults play in the development of children's narrative skills (McNamee, 1980). When a young child tells a story or recounts an event, a listening adult does not provide explicit lessons on how to narrate. Rather, the adult assists the child at stopping points by providing prompts, such as, "Who else was there? . . . What happened next?" These questions not only draw the child out, but demonstrate the structure of topics to be used in narration. McNamee argues that through experience with such social support, children internalize the adults' questions to structure more developed independent narratives. The listening adult is unlikely to conceive the prompts as instructional; more likely the adult is just conversing with the child or investigating what happened at school that day. But this tacit guidance is likely to be influential in helping the child develop skill in the culturally appropriate form of narrative.

Tacit guidance of children's cognitive development is also evident in aspects of adult-child relationships that do not involve direct interaction. Parents and teachers devote a great deal of energy to making arrangements for children. They select activities and materials they consider appropriate for the child. For example, parents choose toys and books, and teachers select textbooks; they assign some tasks and prohibit other activities; they arrange the social environment to promote or discourage particular friendships. Though adults may expect such choices to influence the child, they probably do not regard this as instructional activity. However, by making such choices and adjusting tasks and materials to the child's competence and needs, adults tacitly guide the child's development. This guidance is similar to the way in which the Mayan mothers assist their daughters in learning to make tortillas by providing relevant materials and encouraging participation in different aspects of the process according to the child's skill.

Thus adults arrange for children to be involved in specific cognitive tasks and adjust the difficulty of the task in accord with the child's skill. For example, children are guided in learning to use books by being introduced as infants to relatively indestructible books made of cloth or cardboard, with easily understood pictures and few printed words. Toddlers are given books of paper, with pictures portraying more complex concepts and words tying the pictures into stories. In books for preschoolers, the words begin to assume a more central role, but the meaning is still clarified by redundancy carried in the accompanying pictures. Gradually during the grade school years, books wean children away from reliance on pictorial representation and substitute skills in deriving meaning from the printed word. This progression illustrates how parents and teachers, and authors and publishers unknown to the child, provide guidance through the arrangement of materials.

SUMMARY

Thus adults provide guidance in cognitive development through the arrangement of appropriate materials and tasks for children, as well as through tacit and explicit instruction occurring as adults and children participate together in activities. Adults' greater knowledge and skill allow them to assist children in translating familiar information to apply to a new problem and to structure the problem so that the child can work on manageable subgoals. The effectiveness of adults in structuring situations for children's learning is matched by children's eagerness and involvement in managing their own learning experiences. Children put themselves in a position to observe what is going on; they involve themselves in the ongoing activity; they influence the activities in which they participate; and they demand some involvement with the adults who serve as their guides for socialization into the culture that they are learning. Together, children and adults choose learning situations and calibrate the child's level of participation so that the child is comfortably challenged.

Reflections on Guided Participation

How do the principles of guided participation elaborated here apply to a classroom situation, where one adult is involved with dozens of children rather than one to one? I will conclude by offering some speculations on how guided participation in the classroom may resemble or differ from the dyadic communication described above. It is certainly the teacher's goal to help students translate familiar information and skills to handle new problems. Gallimore and Tharp (1983) argue that teachers' questions bring children's past experience to bear on understanding text in comprehension-based reading lessons. It is also part of the teacher's job to structure the learning situation so that the students can deal with manageable subgoals while the teacher makes sure that the overall goal is reached. In addition, classroom learning would not occur without the teacher arranging for students to take on increasing responsibility for the material as their understanding grows. Brown and Palincsar (in press) emphasize the importance of gradual transfer of control to students learning to read strategically.

However, with a few dozen students it is likely to be more difficult for an adult to monitor readiness of individuals and adjust levels of responsibility for the material accordingly. So in a classroom situation, the limitations on an individual adult's stamina and attention, as well as requirements for efficiency in dealing with many chidren at once, may produce a looser relationship between the child's readiness and the level of responsibility given to the child. In addition, there may often be less room for the children to take initiative in managing their own learning, as they must be responsive to the needs of the group. Finally, the teacher's instructional role may more often involve explicit lessons with the intent to impart information than is the case with parents in everyday situations. As professionals, teachers would more frequently be aware of the instructional function of even their casual remarks. However, the exigencies of communication with a group of children would likely mean that the teacher would less frequently interact directly with individual children and would rely instead on more distal forms of communication and arrangements of tasks, such as workbooks or learning centers that can be monitored in a time-sharing fashion rather than requiring constant interaction with an individual.

Despite the complications arising from dealing with a number of students at once, evidence indicates that teachers use principles of guided participation in managing reading lessons and in supporting students' learning of classroom discourse (Au & Kawakami, in press; Cazden, 1979; Raphael, 1984). A teacher managing reading and language instruction with groups of five or six Hawaiian children (Tharp et al., 1984) determines the points at which assistance is needed by being responsive to the rapid flow of evidence provided by the children regarding their learning. She alters her teaching "in flight," decreasing the complexity of the conversation when the children give cues of not understanding. She extends and recodes the children's utterances to stretch their understanding and encourages the children's active participation in conversation and in interpretation of texts.

Although there is undoubtedly variation among teachers and across different classroom contexts in the use of guided participation as an instructional process, I consider it to be a frequent practice as well as a goal of classroom instruction. In learning to read, as in learning to make tortillas, children may benefit from the assistance of adults in stretching their skills to solve new problems, as children participate with adults in learning situations.

REFERENCES

Au, K. H., & Kawakami, A. J. (in press). Vygotskian perspectives on discussion processes in small group reading lessons. In L. C. Wilkinson, P. L. Peterson, & M. Hallinan (Eds.), *Student diversity and the organization, processes, and use of instructional groups in the classroom.* New York: Academic.

Brown, A. L., & Campione, J. C. (1984). Three faces of transfer: Implications for early competence, individual differences, and instruction. In M. E. Lamb, A. L. Brown, & B. Rogoff (Eds.), *Advances in developmental psychology* (Vol. 3, pp. 143–192). Hillsdale, N.J.: Erlbaum.

Brown, A. L., & Palincsar, A. S. (in press). Reciprocal teaching of comprehension strategies: A natural history of one program for enhancing learning. In J. Borkowski & J. D. Day (Eds.), *Intelligence and cognition in special children: Comparative studies of giftedness, mental retardation, and learning disabilities.* New York: Ablex.

Bruner, J. S., Olver, R. R., & Greenfield, P. M. (Eds.), (1966). *Studies in cognitive growth*. New York: Wiley.

Cazden, C. (1979). Peekaboo as an instructional model: Discourse development at home and at school. *Papers and reports on child language development*, No. 17. Department of Linguistics, Stanford University.

Ellis, S., & Rogoff, B. (in press). Problem solving in children's management of instruction. In E. Mueller & C. Cooper (Eds.), *Process and outcome in peer relationships*. N.Y.: Academic.

Fortes, M. (1938). *Social and psychological aspects of education in Taleland*. Oxford: Oxford University Press.

Gallimore, R., & Tharp, R. G. (1983). *The regulatory functions of teacher questions: A microanalytic analysis of reading comprehension lessons*. Tech. Rep. No. 109. Honolulu: Kamehameha Eductional Research Institute, The Kamehameha Schools.

Jordan, C. (1977). Maternal teaching, peer teaching, and school adaptation in an urban Hawaiian population. Paper presented at the meetings of the Society for Cross-Cultural Research, Michigan.

McNamee, G. D. (1980). *The social origins of narrative skills*. Ph.D. Diss., Northwestern University.

Mead, M. (1984). *Continuities in cultural evolution*. New Haven, Conn.: Yale University Press.

Mehan, H., & Reil, M. M. (in press). Teachers' and students' instructional strategies. In L. L. Adler (Eds.), *Issues in cross-cultural research*. N.Y.: Academic.

Nelson-Le Gall, S. (in press). Help-seeking behavior in learning. In E. Gordon (Ed.), *Review of research in education* (Vol. 12).

Raphael, T. E. (1984). Teaching learners about sources of information for answering comprehension questions. *Journal of Reading*, 27 (4), 303–311.

Rogoff, B. (1982). Mode of instruction and memory test performance. *International Journal of Behavioral Development*, 5, 33–48.

Rogoff, B., Ellis, S., & Gardner, W. (1984). The adjustment of adult-child instruction according to child's age and task. *Developmental Psychology*, 20, 193–199.

Rogoff, B., & Gardner, W. P. (1984). Adult guidance of cognitive development. In B. Rogoff & J. Lave (Eds.), *Everyday cognition: Its development in social context*. Cambridge, Mass.: Harvard University Press.

Ruddle, K, & Chesterfield, R. (1978). Traditional skill training and labor in rural societies. *The Journal of Developing Areas*, 12, 389–398.

Scribner, S. & Cole, M. (1973). Cognitive consequences of formal and informal education. *Science*, 182, 553–559.

Tharp, R. G. et al. (1984). Product and process in applied developmental research: Education and the children of a minority. In M. E. Lamb, A. L. Brown, & B. Rogoff (Eds.), *Advances in developmental psychology* (Vol. 3, pp. 91–141). Hillsdale, N.J.: Erlbaum.

Vygotsky, L. S. (1978). *Mind in society: The development of higher psychological processes*. M. Cole et al. (Eds.). Cambridge, Mass.: Harvard University Press.

Wertsch, J. V. (1979). From social interaction to higher psychological processes: A clarification and application of Vygotsky's theory. *Human Development*, 22, 1–22.

Wood, D., Bruner, J. S. & Ross, G. (1976). The role of tutoring in problem solving. *Journal of Child Psychology and Psychiatry*, 17, 89–100.

PART 2

THE CONTEXTS OF
READING INSTRUCTION

The second section of the volume concerns the contexts of reading
instruction, addressing the question, *How can contexts for learning to
read and for developing strategic readers be characterized?* A historical
context is set in the chapter by Pearson as he traces the development of
current lines of research. In addition to the description of the major
research strands, he provides an analysis of the effectiveness of this
research towards effecting change in today's schools. He also provides a
context or perspective for understanding the differences in focus of a
contextual approach to reading instruction, in contrast to the more
decontextualized views traditionally held. He highlights the work of Au
and Kawakami and of Paris as exemplars of large-scale programs that
have promoted improved comprehension abilities of elementary school
children from a variety of backgrounds. The reader should note that in
Pearson's descriptions of exemplary current practices, he continues with
the theme suggested in the first two chapters: the importance of social
interaction to encourage active learning. The theme of the importance of
social contexts is further expanded by Mason, Stewart, and Dunning's
discussion of the different perspectives to the social context of their kindergarten instruction.

If effective instruction involves active guided participation of
learners, a critical component is what teachers can and should do to
promote such active learning. The chapter by Roehler, Duffy, and
Meloth considers such an issue, paralleling the principles proposed by
Rogoff and applying them directly to classroom reading instruction.
Examples of programs that have adopted or adapted such principles are
described in the chapters by Au and Kawakami and by Paris. The former
describes a program that focuses on comprehension instruction, with a
particular emphasis on the guidance provided by the teacher during

group reading instruction. The latter describes a program that focuses on developing children's metacomprehension ability through teacher modeling and the use of analogies in large-group settings.

Instruction takes place, or should occur, in settings outside the context of the reading group. Two chapters focus on other contexts of instruction. Wixson and Lipson consider the context of the reading clinic, applying principles of guided participation and active learning to issues of assessment and remediation. Their discussions of diagnostic teaching and dynamic assessment are sound examples of guided participation in clinical settings. Fielding, Wilson, and Anderson examine the use of free-reading activities to encourage independent reading, addressing both the motivational aspects of free reading and the relationship between such activities and success during formal reading instruction. Their focus is not only on the lack of children reading outside school settings but on what teachers can do to encourage students' independent reading.

Thus, the focus of this section is on guided participation within a variety of reading contexts, from reading groups to clinical settings, from whole-class activities to independent reading designed to promote the development of both comprehension and metacomprehension in young learners.

3

Twenty Years of Research in Reading Comprehension

P. David Pearson

The purpose of this chapter is to characterize the patterns of development in three related domains: theory and research about basic processes in reading comprehension, research about reading comprehension instruction, and practices in teaching reading comprehension (as reflected by what practitioners think and do and by suggestions in basal reader manuals about how to develop children's reading comprehension ability). I begin by trying to characterize our knowledge and beliefs in the period from 1965–1970. Then I try to answer the question, What have we learned since 1970? Finally, I speculate what the future holds for us in terms of possible advances in our knowledge of both process and practice.

THE SCENE IN 1970

What We Knew about Process in 1970

In 1970 our knowledge of reading comprehension was fairly well defined by four research strands: readability, the cloze procedure, factor analytic studies, and, the child-bride of the field, psycholinguistics.

Readability research (studying what made texts easy or difficult to understand) by that time had a history of 35 to 40 years stemming back to Gray and Leary (1935) and Lorge (1939) in the 1930s, carried on by Flesch (1948) into the 1940s and George Klare (1963) into the 1950s and 1960s. Basically what the

The research reported herein was supported in part by the National Institute of Education under Contract No. NIE 400-81-0030.

research told us was that long words and long complex sentences were hard to understand. But we were not sure why. We did not know whether long words and sentences caused, or were merely symptoms of, content that was hard to read for other reasons, such as concept density.

The cloze technique (a procedure in which one deletes every fifth or tenth or nth word in a text and requires students to guess what fits in the resulting blanks) had been with us for a decade and a half. Taylor (1954), Rankin (1965), and Bormuth (1967, 1969) had used it to great advantage in refining research in comprehension and readability. If nothing else, we knew that we had a good dependent variable for measuring comprehension: It was objective (it did not depend on a test writer's judgment about what questions were important to ask), easy to score, and highly reliable.

It is probably fair to say that Davis (1944) made factor analysis studies [factor analytic studies try to determine whether different tests measure the same or different underlying trait(s)] of reading comprehension respectable. Between 1944 and 1969 several important factor analytic studies of reading comprehension all shared the common purpose of trying to isolate independent components of reading comprehension. All found only a few factors, such as word difficulty and reasoning, to be independent components of reading comprehension.

If readability, cloze, and factor analytic studies represented the conventional wisdom concerning reading comprehension, then psycholinguistics (the interface between psychology and linguistics) was the hope of the future. Simons' (1971) review of reading comprehension reflected this hope. After reviewing and discussing the conventional perspectives on reading comprehension, Simons raised the banner of transformational grammar as the guiding light of the future.

Psycholinguistics had tremendous, immediate, and unprecedented appeal. Part of its appeal stemmed from the impact that Chomsky's (1957) views had on the psychology of language in the decade of the 1960s. Based upon studies like those of Miller and Isard (1963), Mehler (1963), Gough (1965), and Slobin (1966), there was genuine feeling that behavioristic views of language development and processing would have to be replaced by views that were both nativistic (people are born with a genetic capability to learn language) and cognitive (admitting that there is more than a blank black box in the brain) in orientation. Furthermore, these research studies seemed to suggest that the transformational generative grammar created by Chomsky might actually serve as a model of human language processing. Thus, there was a ready-made theory waiting to be applied to reading comprehension. And psycholinguistics commanded academic respectability. There was something invigorating about standing on the shoulders of the new psychology, working within a paradigm for which there was a model that made fairly precise predictions and, thus, had testable hypotheses.

Beginning in the late 1960s and extending into the mid-1970s, considerable empirical and theoretical work was completed within the psycholinguistic tradition. The influence of psycholinguistics on reading is nowhere better demonstrated than in the work of Kenneth Goodman (1965) and Frank Smith (1971). For both Goodman and Smith, looking at reading from a psycholinguistic perspective meant looking at reading in its natural state, as an application of a person's general cognitive and linguistic competence. It seems odd even to mention their names in discussing the influence of psycholinguistics on comprehension research because neither Goodman nor Smith distinguishes between reading and reading comprehension. Their failure to make the dinstinction is deliberate, for they would argue that reading *is* comprehending (or that reading without comprehending is *not* reading). Similarly, a distinction between word identification and comprehension would seem arbitrary to them.

For others, the influence of the psycholinguinstic tradition (particularly the use of transformational-generative grammar as a psychological model) on views of reading comprehension was quite direct. The work of Bormuth (1966, 1969), Bormuth et al. (1971), Fagan (1971), and Pearson (1974–1975) reveals a rather direct use of psycholinguistic notions in studying reading comprehension.

Such was the scene in the early 1970s. The conventional modes of research, while still strong, were being challenged by a new interloper from the world of linguistic research—psycholinguistics.

What We Knew about Practice in 1970

Unlike the late 1970s and early 1980s, there were few complex and thorough analyses of how comprehension was taught in classrooms or in basal series prior to the early 1970s. The following attitudes and practices regarding the teaching of reading comprehension skills seem evident:

1. Many scholars wondered whether comprehension skills could be taught at all.
2. Some thought it was a matter for the later grades, to be dealt with once decoding skills were mastered.
3. Most thought that comprehension skill resulted from practicing separable skills within a balanced scope and sequence extending across the elementary years.
4. The most common criterion for sequencing comprehension skills was from literal to inferential to creative.
5. Children's ability to answer questions was considered to be the most basic piece of evidence that they could comprehend and was thought by many to be the best path to nurturing comprehension.

Can Comprehension be Taught?   Perhaps the clearest argument for the resistance of comprehenstion to direct teaching came from the philosophy underlying the so-called *linguistic readers* that were fairly popular from 1963 through the early 1970s. These readers forbade asking comprehension questions in the early books, and they used content that was not at all predictable from a student's oral language base. The rationale for avoiding comprehension questions at all in the early grades was that once children could decode written symbols into a speech code, they could comprehend by *listening* to themselves say the words. Therefore, questions were superfluous. The rationale for unpredictable language was that guessing could get in the way of the real task confronting the child: learning the code for translating print to speech. These attitudes toward comprehension were not limited to those who sided with a lingistic approach to beginning reading. Further evidence for the view that comprehension cannot be taught is found in the emphasis upon questioning [what Durkin (1978–1979), later came to call assessment] and the practice of guaranteeing that students completed worksheets on a wide range of comprehension skills; after all, if comprehension cannot be taught, then simply allowing students to practice doing it may be the sensible avenue to improvement.

Decoding First–Comprehension Later. Not all reading series adopted the decoding first–comprehension later philosophy absolutely; in fact, this philosophy can only be found in early versions of linguistic series. However, the *relative* emphasis given to decoding versus comprehension activities in the early versus later grades in all basal series indicates a bias toward this decoding first–comprehension later viewpoint (see Chall, 1967).

Balanced Diet of Separable Skills. Regarding a balanced diet of separable skills, even a cursory examination of any of the popular basals of that period (or today, for that matter) reveals a solid reliance on making sure that many different skills are practiced at all grade levels (see Pearson & Johnson, 1978).

Sequencing Skills. The progression from literal to inferential to creative comprehension comes packaged in many different ways: from getting the facts straight to using the facts, reading the lines to reading between the lines to reading beyond the lines. But the underlying phlosophy is the same: Students cannot do anything with the facts until they have them straight; hence, literal comprehension has to be emphasized first. The evidence for this progression comes from Guszak's (1967) study. He found that the proportion of higher-level questions in basal story discussion increased from Grades 2 to 4 to 6; however, even at Grade 6, the overall emphasis was on literal comprehension questions.

The Dominance of Questions. The dominant reliance on questions for assessing and "instructing" comprehension emerges clearly in Guszak's study, as well as in an examination of basal manuals in that era. There is reason to believe that patterns have changed little since that period.

There is little evidence from this period that the research and theoretical work about the *process*(es) of comprehension were influencing *practice* in comprehension instruction. Note, for example, the widespread use of long lists of comprehension skills in the face of factor analytic studies demonstrating few distinguishable skills. This tension between research and practice seems to transcend historical periods; it will resurface when we evaluate the impact of more recent research and theory on current practices.

WHAT WE HAVE LEARNED SINCE 1970

About the Process

The force behind the shift from behavioristic to cognitive views of lanuage was a linguist, Noam Chomsky. He exposed the prevailing views on the psychology of language for their gross inadequacies and provided an alternative model (transformational grammar) of language processing. Fittingly, the motive force behind the exodus from a narrow psycholinguistic view based upon transformational grammars was another linguist, Charles Fillmore. In 1968 he published a paper in which he argued for the resurrection of a centuries-old case grammar approach to linguistic explanation. Case grammars are based upon the different relationships between the verb in the sentence and the case (nominative, accusative, recipient, and so forth) that the nouns take in relationship to the verb.

Fillmore's case grammar was appealing to psychologists and educators who were experiencing great difficulty with models of comprehension based upon a transformational generative grammar. Those very models that had seemed to be sensible and alluring only five years earlier had not withstoood tests of empirical verification. With their emphasis on transformations to realize a variety of surface structures from a single deep structure, transformational models had to stress an analytic view of comprehension. Yet researchers (e.g., Bransford & Franks, 1971) were collecting data that indicated that comprehension consisted of synthesis (integrating ideas) rather than analysis (decomposing ideas). Other researchers (e.g., Sachs, 1967) found that comprehension and recognition memory seemed to be more sensitive to semantic rather than syntactic factors, contrary to the emphasis in a transformational model. Still others, like Pearson (1974-1975), found that the predictions from a derivational theory of complexity (i.e., the theory that comprehension difficulty varies as a function of the number of transformations necessary to travel from the surface structure of a sentence to its deep structure) were exactly the opposite of results obtained in several comprehension studies.

In such a milieu, something like Fillmore's case grammar was quite appealing; it emphasized synthesis rather than analysis and semantic rather than syntactic relations. In addition, case grammar allowed one to begin to examine relations that held between linguistic ideas that crossed sentence boundaries.

The psycholinguistic tradition, based as it was on Chomsky's transformational grammar, had concentrated upon the sentence as the basic unit of analysis. Somewhere in the early to mid-1970s the proposition (basically, a verb plus the nouns, adjectives, and adverbs that go along with it) replaced the sentence as the basic unit of analysis. Researchers in artificial intelligence began using it in the early 1970s (Minsky, 1975; Schank, 1973). Lindsay and Norman (1975), Frederiksen (1975), Thorndyke (1977), and Stein and Glenn (1977) were all using propositions to parse texts and analyze recall protocols by the mid- to late 1970s.

The proposition fit nicely with an emphasis on case grammar. Just as the verb is the center of a proposition [another way of defining a proposition is as a predicate (active or stative verb) and its arguments (nouns, adjectives, adverbs)], so the verb is the central node in a case grammar parsing (parsing is a sort of fancy diagramming) of a sentence. All other form classes revolve around the verb. Also, many of the case relations in a case grammar are really relations among propositions (e.g., cause, condition, time, manner).

As we moved into the late 1970s, no new revolutions occured; fine tuning better characterizes what took place. The perspective that spawned case grammars and propositions persisted, but the problems researchers addressed changed substantially. In the early 1970s text researchers were still preoccupied with relations within and between sentences, and their research reflected this emphasis on what we have come to call *microstructure*. Text researchers in the late 1970s were more concerned about relations that obtain between whole episodes in stories or whole paragraphs or sections in informative test; we have come to call this more wholistic emphasis *macrostructure*. Accompanying this shift in the study of text was a shift in the study of how human memory is organized, in particular how humans are able to store and retrieve large bodies of information. This latter movement came to be called *schema theory*.

Researchers in this period tended to fall into two categories: those who tried to characterize relations among ideas in texts and those who tried to characterize relations among ideas stored in human memory. Neither group denied the importance or necessity of the other's work; each group simply chose to emphasize one area over the other. Hence, researchers like Rumelhart (1975), Stein and Glenn (1977), and Thorndyke (1977) gave us plausible macrostructures for narative material in the form of story grammars. Researchers like Meyer (1975) or Halliday and Hasan (1976) tried to provide more general structural accounts that would apply equally well to expositions. Alternatively, the work of Schank (1973), Minsky (1975), Anderson (1977), and Rumelhart (1980; Rumelhart & Ortony, 1977) was more concerned with the structure of knowledge within the human processors (i.e., readers). Still others, such as Kintsch (1974) or Frederiksen (1975), seemed to be trying to provide a balanced emphasis on text and knowledge structure. These differences are more a matter of degree than kind. All of the researchers were concerned with human infomation processing; they simply tended to emphasize different aspects of the processing. Therefore, researchers focusing on the structure of the text were likely to emphasize something like the number of high-level propositions within the story that were recalled. Conversely, those emphasizing the structure of the reader's knowledge were more likely to dwell upon something like nontextual inferences made during recall or how a reader's prior knowledge determines aspects of the text that will be remembered. Put differently, the former group were likely to highlight text structures while the latter group were likely to highlight knowledge structures.

Sometime during the late 1970s, a new interloper burst onto the research stage, bearing the cumbersome but intellectually appealing label *metacognition*. It seemed a logical extension of the rapidly developing work on both schema theory and text analysis. These latter two traditions emphasized *declarative* knowledge, knowing *that* X or Y or Z is true, but were scant on specifying *proce-*

dural knowledge, knowing *how* to engage a strategy for comprehension or memory (see Gavelek, this volume; Paris, this volume; or Schwartz, this volume). This is precisely the kind of knowledge that metacognitive research has emphasized. The key words associated with metacognition reveal its emphasis: awareness, monitoring, control, and evaluation.

Two parallel strands of research dominated the early work in metacognition. The first, metamemory research, is most typically associated with John Flavell and his associates at Stanford. They have discovered that along with the capacity to remember more information, human beings develop tacit and explicit strategies for remembering. The second line of research, metacomprehension, is more typically associated with Ann Brown and Joe Campione and their colleagues at Illinois, and more recently with Ellen Markman at Stanford and with Scott Paris at Michigan. It emphasizes the strategies that readers use while they are reading as they monitor, evaluate, and repair their comprehension of written text. This line of research has grown so rapidly that it has been reviewed several times within the last few years (Wagoner, 1983; Paris, Lipson, & Wixson, 1983; Baker & Brown, 1984).

Given the tremendous outpouring of research on basic processes in comprehension since the mid-1970s, it is fair to ask what we have learned from it all. The answer, I think, is that we have learned a considerable amount. We view comprehension very differently from the way we did in 1970. Our knowledge is both more extensive and more refined. Here is a sampling of some insights that we have gained.

Prior knowledge (in the form of schemata) influences our comprehension to a much greater degree than earlier research would have suggested. Anderson (1984) has summarized the influences that schemata play in our comprehension in these generalizations (these are close paraphrases of Anderson's assertions):

1. Schemata provide ideational scaffolding for assimilating text information. Schemata have slots that readers expect to be filled with information in a text. Information that fills those slots is easily learned and remembered.
2. Schemata facilitate the selective allocation of attention. Put simply, schemata guide our search for what is important in a text, allowing us to separate the wheat from the chaff.
3. Schemata enable inferential elaboration. No text is ever fully explicit. Schemata allow us to make educated guesses about how certain slots must have been filled.
4. Schemata allow for orderly searches of memory. For example, suppose a person is asked to remember what he did at a recent cocktail party. He can use his cocktail party schema, a specification of what usually happens at cocktail parties, to recall what he ate, what he drank, who he talked to, and so on.
5. Schemata facilitate editing and summarizing. By definition, any schema possesses its own criteria of what is important. These can be used to create summaries of text that focus on important information.

6. Schemata permit inferential reconstruction. If readers have a gap in their memory, they can use a schema, in conjunction with the information recalled, to generate hypotheses about missing information. If they can recall, for example, that the entree was beef, they can infer that the beverage was likely to have been red wine.

So powerful is the influence of prior knowledge on comprehension that Johnston and Pearson (1982; see also, Johnston, 1984) have found that prior knowledge of topic is a better predictor of comprehension than is either an intelligence test score or a reading achievement test score.

Reading is a dynamic, interactive process. To use the language of Collins, Brown, and Larkin (1979), as we read, we are constantly revising our model of what the text means. To view an individual's comprehension of a text as an inadequate reproduction of the original text misses the whole point about the reader's enormous contribution to the comprehension process.

Reading involves the use of many different kinds of knowledge. We have already discussed two of these, declarative and procedural knowledge. Recall that declarative knowledge, knowing *that*, includes our knowledge of the world at large and our knowledge of the world of text (prototypical structures and authorial devices); recall that procedural knowledge, knowing *how*, includes the strategies we use to become aware of, monitor, evaluate, and repair our comprehension. To these, Paris (Paris, this volume; Paris, Lipson & Wixson, 1983) argues convincingly that we should add conditional knowledge, knowing *when* and *why* to call up a particular strategy to aid our comprehension. The point is that we cannot characterize comprehension processes without including all of these kinds of knowledge.

Reading and writing are a lot more similar in process than we had ever thought. Traditionally, in comparing the language arts, we have tended to think of reading and writing as mirror images of one another—that when we read, we more or less *undo* what writers do when they write. Even the attributes we assign to them—productive versus receptive language—reflect this oppositional view. While the research base arguing for the similarity rather than the difference between reading and writing is weak (see Hansen, in press; Tierney, Leys, & Rogers, this volume), many theorists have begun to emphasize essential similarities (e.g., Murray, 1982; Tierney & Pearson, 1983; Pearson & Tierney, 1984). Even though strict comparative research is just beginning, one can make the argument for similarity by examining the conclusions permitted from research on the role that schemata play in comprehension (cf. pp. 49–50). Notice that terms like constructive and reconstructive processes are used to describe what we know about comprehension; these are the very terms writing researchers use to describe the writing process.

About Practice

It is fair to conclude that more research about reading comprehension practices has been conducted since 1975 than in the 100 years prior to 1975. One reason for this sudden barrage is that we understand the basic processes involved in comprehension better than we used to. However, another reason is that practitioners are more concerned about teaching comprehension skills now than they ever have been. Perhaps the gradual decline of SAT scores and the consistent drop in inferential reasoning scores on National Assessment tests have contributed to awareness and concern.

Research on reading comprehension instruction tends to fall into one of three categories (see Pearson & Gallagher, 1983). Some studies attempt to *describe* what is going on in the name of reading comprehension, either in our schools or our textbooks. Other studies attempt to try out different ways of teaching or allowing students to practice reading comprehension strategies or activities. They represent what we might call *pedagogical experiments* and try to evaluate competing practices over relatively short but intensive treatment periods (1 to 10 weeks). A few studies with more of a *program evaluation* flavor examine a practice or set of practices embedded into a larger curriculum.

Descriptions.   From descriptions, we have learned much about what is *not* being done in schools and what is *not* suggested for teachers to do in manuals. Durkin, in two studies (1978–1979, 1981), has demonstrated that little direct instruction of comprehension skills occurs in intermediate grade classrooms (1978–1979) or is suggested in teacher manuals (1981). Instead of offering students advice about how to employ reading skills, teachers and manuals tend to *assess* comprehension by asking or suggesting many questions about the selections students read and by providing enormous quantities of practice materials in the form of worksheets and workbooks. Sometimes, teachers or manuals "mention," or say just enough about the skill so that students understand the formal requirements of the task. Rarely do teachers or manuals require application of the skill to reading real texts. Even more rarely do they discuss the kind of conditional knowledge suggested by Paris et al. (1983). Most recently, Durkin (1984) has found that teachers *rarely use* that section of the teachers' manual suggesting backgound knowledge activities but *rarely skip* story questions or skillsheet activities.

Beck and her colleagues at Pittsburgh (1979) have found several features of commercial reading programs that may adversely affect comprehension. Among them are the use of indirect language (using high-frequency words such as *this* or *him* instead of lower-frequency but more image-evoking words like *garbage can* or *Mr. Gonzalez*), elaborate but misleading pictures, inappropriate story divisions, misleading prior knowledge and vocabulary instruction, and questions that focus on unimportant aspects of the stories students read.

Other descriptive studies have concentrated more on pupil texts than on teacher manuals or classroom instruction. For example, Davison and Kantor (1982) studied the kinds of adaptations publishers make when they rewrite an adult article for students in order to meet readability guidelines. They found a number of examples of practices that may actually make passages harder rather than easier to understand:

1. Reducing sentence length by destroying interclausally explicit connectives.
2. Selecting simpler but less descriptive vocabulary.
3. Altering the flow of topic and comment relations in paragraphs.
4. Eliminating qualifying statements that specify the conditions under which generalizations are thought to hold.

Anderson and Armbruster (Anderson, Armbruster, & Kantor, 1980; Armbruster & Anderson, 1981, 1982, 1984) have examined a number of dimensions of student text material in social studies and science that may cause unintentional difficulty. Among their observations are that content area texts often:

1. Fail to structure the information within a predictable and recurrent frame (like a schema for text).
2. Use subheadings that do not reveal the macrostructure of the topic.
3. Avoid using visual displays of information, particulary to summarize information presented textually.
4. Use obscure pronoun references.
5. Fail to use obvious connectives, such as *because, since, before,* and *after,* even when these connectives clearly fit.

To make the picture even drearier, Bruce (1984) has compared basal stories to those found in trade books and concluded that basal stories avoid features commonly found in stories, such as inside view, internal conflict, and embedded narratorship. In a similar vein, Gallagher and Pearson (1982) found a wide discrepancy between the kinds of text structures found in informational selections in basals and in content area textbooks.

Any summary of the descriptive research cited thus far is doomed to be dismal. Many texts are hokey and misleading; teacher manual suggestions tend to be scant, misleading, or unhelpful, and teachers do not seem to teach very much in the way of comprehension skills and strategies. Perhaps pedagogical experiments will yield a more optimistic view of comprehension instruction.

Pedagogical Experiments. Since 1975 a renaissance has taken place in instructional research, and most of the work has been directed toward the development of reading comprehension strategies. While it is beyond the scope of this overview to review that research in depth (see Pearson & Gallagher, 1983, or Tierney & Cunningham, 1984, for complete summaries), the following is a summary of the conclusions that I believe are permitted from this research.

1. Students understand stories better if they are asked questions that focus on integrating story parts than if they are asked questions that do not have a focus (e.g., Beck, Omanson, & McKeown, 1982; Gordon & Pearson, 1983; Singer & Donlan, 1982; Tharp, 1982).

2. Students understand informational texts better if discussions are guided by

an attempt to help them see how all the pieces of information in a text fit together than if discussions are guided by a close but piecemeal interrogation of the main points and facts (Gallagher & Pearson, 1983).

3. Vocabulary instruction that focuses on building rich semantic networks of related concepts facilitates transferable growth in both vocabulary and comprehension. It is even better than either a definitional or a context approach (Beck, Perfetti, & McKeown, 1982; Johnson, Toms-Bronowski, & Pittleman, in press; Schachter, 1978).

4. Vocabulary growth is also facilitated by simply reading; however, it is likely that such growth is better characterized as the development of what Isabel Beck (1984) calls an "acquaintanceship" with words rather than "ownership" of concepts (Nagy, Herman, & Anderson, 1985).

5. Building background knowledge prior to reading facilitates comprehension of the upcoming story or article, *and* it helps to develop a set within students for learning and evaluating new material in terms of what they already know (Hansen, 1981; Hansen & Pearson, 1983).

6. Teaching the so-called comprehension skills in a model that begins with a fairly heavy reliance on the teacher and builds toward students independence and ownership *and* that includes demonstrations of how to perform the skill is superior to a model that emphasizes practice, assessment, and more practice (Baumann, in press; Gordon & Pearson, 1983; Palincsar & Brown, 1984; Raphael & Pearson, 1985; Raphael & Wonnacutt, 1985).

7. Approaches that emphasize students' awareness of their own strategies suggest alternative strategies and help students learn techniques for self-monitoring result in sizable gains in comprehension performance (Palincsar & Brown, 1984; Paris, this volume).

8. Approaches that emphasize inferential thinking result in greater growth in inferential thinking (at no loss to and sometimes a gain in literal comprehension) than do approaches that emphasize literal comprehension (Gordon & Pearson, 1982; Hansen, 1981; Hansen & Pearson, 1983).

Of these conclusions, numbers 6 and 7, both of which speak to the promise of explicit instruction in comprehension strategies, deserve special emphasis. In a sense, the studies that support these conclusions justify Durkin's (1978–1979) concern about the lack of comprehension instruction in intermediate grade classrooms, for they suggest that student performance improves when teachers take the time and effort to help students learn *how* and *why* and *when* they should perform some of the complex comprehension and problem-solving tasks that we require of them in schools.

Program Evaluations. There have been two projects in which after new ideas about reading comprehension have been incorporated into a curriculum, the more or less long-term effects of that curriculum have been evaluated against competing curricula. The first project is located in Honolulu, and the effects of a comprehension-focused curriculum have been studied over a five-year period (see

Au & Kawakami, this volume; Tharp, 1982). The second, located in Michigan evaluated a metacognitive training program over a single school year, with a follow-up eight months after the project ended (see Paris, this volume).

What is remarkable about these two program evaluation studies is the similarity between their conclusions and those derived from the previous section on pedagogical experiments. While the tasks in the two sets of studies are sometimes different, the principles leading to effective performance are remarkable similar. Explicit instruction associated with guided practice, lots of opportunity to practice and apply strategies independently, as well as attention to monitoring the application of such strategies seems to help students perform better on a variety of comprehension measures.

The State of Practice in 1984

Given all the criticsms of current practice derivable from the descriptive research presented earlier, given the new insights implied by the basic research conducted since 1970, and given the promise of new and exciting techniques for teaching reading comprehension strategies emanating from recent pedagogical experiments and program evaluations, it is fair to ask whether or not reading programs used in today's schools are any different from those used in 1978 (the period that spawned the texts so heavily criticized). To answer this question, I conducted a very cursory examination of three popular basal series in their 1984 editions, looking for changes from earlier editions of the same series. Both positive and negative findings resulted.

On the Positive Side. Story questions are focused more on helping students develop the central thread of the stories they read. The proportion of inferential questions has risen dramatically, from about 20 percent to almost 50 percent, at least in the three series I have examined. Provisions for building background and setting purposes are stronger than ever, but then Durkin's recent article (1984) suggests that building background is the least used section of basal manuals.

Publishers seem to be trying to take Durkin's comments (1978–1979, 1981) on the paucity of direct comprehension instruction in classrooms and manuals seriously; unfortunately, the efforts have not worked too well. The problem here, I think, is that good comprehension instruction is too interactive and dynamic to be captured easily in an abstract set of directions written for some hypothetical teacher working with a hypothetical set of students. Nonetheless, the old adage that comprehension cannot be taught seems to have died a graceful death. There is evidence that we are at least trying to do it.

The decoding first–comprehension later philosophy seems also to have found its grave. All aspects of comprehension, including inferential questions and skills, are included early and often. Interestingly, this has not resulted in a loss in emphasis placed on decoding skills; if anything, early decoding programs are stronger than ever. I think that now there is simply more to teach in the early programs. In this regard, it is important to note that the linguistic series that exemplified this philosophy most clearly are now little more than items of historical curiosity.

On the Negative Side. The long lists of comprehension skills in a scope and sequence chart persist. All the work emphasizing the similarity of most comprehension tasks (remember those early factor analytic studies) seems not to have found its way into reading series yet.

The emphasis on assessment (story questions) and practice (lots of worksheets) that Durkin found in the late 1970s remains, and, if anything, is even stronger. This is apparent not only in the mainline workbook and worksheet components, but also in the supplementary components that are available for students who, by virtue of low mastery test scores, earn the opportunity for more "practice."

A new development, since the 1970 editions of basal series, is the systematic inclusion of mastery tests for all the levels (and often all the units within a level) in a series. The tests are provided to assess mastery of skills that are taught at that level (or in that unit). The net effect of these mastery test components has been to heighten the emphasis on practice as the primary means of skill improvement and remediation (since more worksheets is the usual remedy for a noted deficiency).

A Note about Impacting Materials

The potential for impact by changing the materials of instruction is great. We know that students read basals and that teachers use manuals. I am encouraged by the receptivity of publishers to new ideas from research. At the Center for the Study of Reading, we have been involved in two conferences (and are planning a third) in which researchers and publishers have met together to address both general and specific issues about improving materials. But if we really want new and different approaches in basals, then consumers, those who buy basals for schools, will have to carry the bulk of the responsibility in persuading publishers to change. Book companies are, in fact, profit-making organizations; they are therefore unlikely to produce something that they do not think their customers want.

What I have said about basals also applies, of course, to tests, and here the need for reform is even more crucial. Assessment in American education truly does drive instruction, even that in basals. We are unlikely to convince people that they should be teaching metacognitive monitoring skills, for example, if what teachers think they are accountable for is literal comprehension and sequence of events. Conversely, if we can infuse these new strategies into widely used tests, then these strategies are more likely to be taught (or at least practiced).

SOME FUTURE HISTORY

Basic Process Research

The schema theory tradition has provided us with an alternative world view about comprehension processes. But it has emphasized the effect of existing knowledge on comprehension. In the future, researchers will turn their attention to the more difficult questions of schema acquisition, or, if you will, the effect of comprehension on knowledge. We will look more carefully at what Bransford, Nitsch, and

Franks (1977) identified as the issue of "changing states of schema." And when we do, we will, of course, be returning to a recurrent theme in psychology usually labelled "learning." A vital component of this work on schema acquisition will focus on the issue of vocabulary (it has, in fact, begun—see Nagy & Anderson , in press; and Nagy et al. 1984), for we will finally recognize that words are but the surface representations of our knowledge.

The text analysis tradition will change its focus also. Now that we can do a decent job of parsing texts to characterize underlying relations among ideas, we will turn to an age-old issue, What makes a text readable? And our search will be guided by principles very different from long sentences and hard words. In their place, we will substitute principles that come under the label of considerateness (see Armbruster & Anderson, 1981; 1982; 1984); these principles will emphasize whether authors provide frameworks for interrelating ideas, analogies that permit cross-topical comparisons, and examples that solidify concept acquisition.

Schema-theoretic and text-analysis traditions will merge so as to become indistinguishable from one another. This even will result from our discovery that the goal of every author is the same as the goal of every reader—to represent knowledge in as coherent a framework as possible.

We will learn much more about basic relationships between reading and writing, more specifically between comprehension and composing strategies. The promise of an exciting integrated view of language processes, expressed so eloquently by many in recent years, will finally reach fruition.

Finally, we will develop the grace and good judgment necessary to overcome our tendency to debate whether reading is a word-based or a meaning-based process so that we can come to understand the intrinsic relationship between growth in comprehension strategies and growth in word identification abilities, particularly in beginning reading.

Instructional Practice Research

We will discover the precise ways in which writing activites benefit reading comprehension and vice versa. We will also develop and evaluate programs in which children are taught to read texts for different purposes and from different perspectives (see Wixson & Lipson, this volume). For example, we will learn that even young children can be taught to read texts from the perspective of an editor or a critic, and that such instruction benefits both their own writing and their critical reading skills.

We will discover that the benefit of explicit instruction found in many of the existing pedagogical experiments and program evaluation studies of the early 1980s derives not so much from the explicitness of the instruction as it does from the considerateness of that instruction and from the collaboration that is required when teachers and students learn that it is all right to share cognitive secrets publicly.

We will make even greater strides in learning how to help students develop those mysterious evaluation, monitoring, and repair strategies that come under the rubric of metacognition. Our greatest progress will come in the area of repair strategies.

We will learn that we can get by without an entire compendium of comprehension skills in our scope and sequence charts. We will finally admit what we have known for 30 years: that they all reduce to a few basic cognitive processes like summarizing, detecting relationships in an explicit message, filling in gaps in incomplete messages, fixing things up when they go wrong, and detecting tricks authors use to try to con us.

The State of Practice in 1990

What, then, will be going on in our schools in the year 1990 in the name of reading comprehension? Will any current or future research find its way into practice? The answer to these questions is quite complex for it requires that we consider not only issues of reading comprehension processes and instruction but also issues of dissemination and change. While I think the gap between research and practice will always exist, I am optimistic about narrowing it. My optimism stems from two observations. First, the research of the last decade is more deserving of implementation than that of earlier decades. It is more central to what reading is all about, and it is more focussed on issues that impact what teachers are responsible for in their classrooms. Second, practitioners are more receptive to research findings than they have been at least during the 20 years that I have been in the field.

Let me close by outlining what I believe to be the requirements of an effective collaborative program for promoting educational change in our schools. There are several essential ingredients that have to be present in such efforts in order for them to work effectively.

1. Teachers have to *want* to try something new. There has to be some disequilibrium in their own minds as a motive for trying something new. It takes a fair amount of courage to admit (even to ourselves) that what we are doing presently is not what we want to be doing.

2. Teachers have to have at least some administrative support. The more the better. They need someone up there saying that this is a good idea.

3. The people who are doing the changing—the teachers—have to have a voice in planning for change. Others can try to legislate it, but it proceeds much more smoothly when teachers feel a sense of ownership of the project. Parity between teachers and change agents is essential.

4. Services must be delivered at the level of the people doing the changing. It's not really enough to give a couple of lectures to a group of administrators and supervisors. Change occurs more rapidly when the change agents work directly with teachers in their classrooms and schools.

5. Change agents have to establish a forum in which teachers can interact with one another on things that matter and in which teachers are rewarded for behaving professionally. In two efforts I have been involved with this last year, I

have come to the conclusion that my most important role as a change agent is to establish such a forum. Teaching can be very lonely profession, even when you are in the constant company of your peers. A friend of mine says that the best index of the professional climate of a school is the topic of conversation in the teachers' lounge. She is probably right. Indeed, the teachers in our two projects have corroborated just such a phenomenon in their schools: they have found themselves discussing different issues than they used to, and they find themselves using one another as resources.

6. Change efforts need time!

Now, how does what I have said about comprehension research fit with what I have just outlined as a set of requirements for effective change? I do not want to conclude that disseminating knowledge about research is any better or any worse than working with teachers directly on change efforts. Whereas direct collaboration is probably more powerful, without the production and dissemination of new knowledge we might not have any ideas worth implementing. Materials and tests will continue to have an impact on practice whether we like it or not—to avoid getting our hands dirty in this arena is to seal our fate as powerless bystanders. But neither the new knowledge nor the new material will do us any good unless we learn to work together on matters we care about. I see that cooperative potential all over the country: in Hickory Hills, Illinois, and at Metcalf School in Bloomington, Illinois; in Orange County, Florida, and in Kalispell, Montana; in New York City and in Zion, Illinois, and in Fairfax County, Virginia; in Montgomery County, Maryland, and in Honolulu; in Wading River, New York, and Media, Pennnsylvania. But there is hope in our discontent. Many teachers are tired of curricula and testing programs that drive teachers into corners and children away from books. There is also hope, and high expectation, amidst the dillusionment espoused by the critics of education and the fear engendered by those who want to coerce us into change through legislation requiring new and tougher standards for skills we know are not at the heart of literacy. Working together is our only option; for if we do not, we will lose the day to the more hostile forces of coercion. I'd rather we changed our school curricula because we realized that we had found more effective choices than because some quasi-official body told us we had to.

REFERENCES

Anderson, R. C. (1977). The notion of schemata and the educational enterprise. In R. C. Anderson, R. J. Spiro, & W. E. Montague (Eds.), *Schooling and the acquisition of knowledge*. Hillsdale, N.J.: Erlbaum.

Anderson, R. C. (1984). Role of the reader's schema in comprehension, learning, and memory. In R. C. Anderson, J. Osborn, & R. J. Tierney (Eds.), *Learning to read in American schools*. Hillsdale, N.J.: Erlbaum.

Anderson, T. H., Armbruster, B. B., & Kantor, R. N. (1980). *How clearly written are children's textbooks? Or, of bladderworts and alfa*. Reading Education Rep. No. 16. Urbana: University of Illinois, Center for the Study of Reading. ERIC Document Reproduction Service No. ED 192 275.

Armbruster, B. B., & Anderson, T. H. (1981). *Content area textbooks*. Reading Education Rep. No. 23. Urbana: University of Illinois, Center for the Study of Reading. ERIC Document Reproduction Service No. ED 203 298.

Armbruster. B. B., & Anderson, T. H. (1982). *Structures for explanations in history textbooks, or so what if Governor Stanford missed the spike and hit the rail?* Tech. Rep. No. 252. Urbana: University of Illinois, Center for the Study of Reading.

Armbruster, B. B., & Anderson, T. H. (1984). *Producing considerate expository text: Or easy reading is damned hard writing*. Reading Education Rep. No. 46. Urbana: University of Illinois, Center for the Study of Reading.

Baker, L., & Brown, A. L. (1984). Metacognitive skills of reading. In P. D. Pearson (Ed.), *Handbook of reading research*. New York: New York: Longman.

Baumann J. F. (in press). The effectiveness of a direct instructional paradigm for teaching main idea comprehension. *Reading Research Quarterly*.

Beck, I. L. (1984). Developing comprehension: The impact of the directed reading lesson. In R. C. Anderson, J. Osborn, & R. J. Tierney (Eds.), *Learning to read in American schools*. Hillsdale, N.J.: Erlbaum.

Beck, I. L. et al. (1979). *Instructional dimensions that may affect reading comprehension: Examples from two commercial reading programs*. Pittsburgh: University of Pittsburgh, Learning Research and Develoment Center.

Beck, I. L., Omanson, R. C., & McKeown, M. G. (1982). An instructional redesign of reading lessons: Effects on reading comprehension. *Reading Research Quarterly, 17*, 462–481.

Beck, I. L., Perfetti, C. A., & McKeown, M. G. (1982). The effects of long-term vocabulary instruction on lexical access and reading comprehension. *Journal of Educational Psychology, 74*, 506–521.

Bormuth, J. R. (1966). Readability: A new approach. *Reading Research Quarterly, 1*, 79–132.

Bormuth, J. R. (1967). *Implications and use of cloze precedure in the evaluation of instructional program*. Occasional Rep. No. 3. Los Angeles: University of California, Center for the study of Evaluation Instructional Programs.

Bormuth, J. R. (1969). An operational definition of comprehension instruction. In K. S. Goodman & J. F. Fleming (Eds.), *Psycholinguistics and the teaching of reading*. Newark, Del.: International Reading Association.

Bormuth, J. R. et al. (1971). Children's comprehension of between- and within-sentence syntactic structures. *Journal of Educational Psychology, 61*, 349–357.

Bransford, J. D., & Franks, J. J. (1971). The abstraction of linguistic ideas. *Cognitive Psychology, 2*, 331–350.

Bransford, J. D., Nitsch, K. E., & Franks, J. F. (1977). Schooling and the facilitation of knowledge. In R. C. Anderson, R. J. Spiro, & W. E. Montague (Eds.), *Schooling and the acquisition of knowledge*. Hillsdale, N.J.: Erlbaum.

Bruce, B. (1984). A new point of view on children's stories. In R. C. Anderson, J. Osborn, & R. J. Tierney (Eds.), *Learning to read in American schools*. Hillsdale, N.J.: Erlbaum.

Chall, J. (1967). *Learning to read: The great debate*. New York: McGraw-Hill.

Chomsky, N. (1957). *Syntactic structures*. The Hague: Moulton.

Collins, A., Brown, J. S., & Larkin, K. M. (1979). Inference in text understanding. In R. J. Spiro, B. C. Bruce, & W. F. Brewer (Eds.), *Theoretical issues in reading comprehension*. Hillsdale, N.J.: Erlbaum.

Davis, F. B. (1944). Fundamental factors of comprehension in reading. *Psychcometrika, 9*, 185–197.

Davison, A., & Kantor, R. N. (1982). On the failure of readability formulas to define readable texts: A case study from adaptations. *Reading Research Quarterly, 17,* 187–209.

Durkin, D. (1978–1979). What classroom observations reveal about reading comprehension instruction. *Reading Research Quarterly, 14,* 481–533.

Durkin, D. (February 1981). *Do basal reader manuals provide for reading comprehension instruction?* Paper presented at the Center for the Study of Reading Publishers' Conference, Tarrytown, N.Y.

Durkin, D. (1984). Is there a match between what elementary teachers do and what basal reader manuals recommend? *The Reading Teacher, 37,* 734–745.

Fagan, W. T. (1971). Transformations and comprehension. *The Reading Teacher, 25,* 169–172.

Fillmore, C. (1968). The case for case. In E. Bach & R. G. Harms (Eds.), *Universals in linguistic theory.* New York: Holt, Rinehart & Winston.

Flesch, R. F. (1984). A new readability yardstick. *Journal of Applied Psychology, 32,* 221–233.

Frederiksen, C. H. (1975). Representing logical and semantic structure of knowledge acquired from discourse. *Cognitive Psychology, 7,* 371–458.

Gallagher, M. C., & Pearson, P. D. (1982). *An examination of expository texts in elementary instructional materials.* National Reading Conference, Clearwater, Fla.

Gallagher, M. C., & Pearson, P. D. (1983). *Fourth grade students' acquisition of new information from text.* National Reading Conference, Austin, Tex.

Goodman, K. S. (1965). A linguistic study of cues and miscues in reading. *Elementary English. 42,* 639–643.

Gordon, C., & Pearson, P. D. (June 1983). *The effects of instruction in metacomprehension and inferencing on children's comprehension abilities.* Tech. Rep. No. 277. Urbana: University of Illinios, Center for the study of Reading.

Gough, P. B. (1965). Grammatical transformations and speed of understanding. *Journal of Verbal Learning and Verbal Behavior, 4,* 107–111.

Gray, W. S., & Leary, B. E. (1935). *What makes a book readable: An initial study.* Chicago: University of Chicago Press.

Guszak, F. J. (1967). Teacher questioning and reading. *The Reading Teacher, 21,* 227–234.

Halliday, M. A. K., & Hasan, R. (1967). *Cohesion in English.* London: Longman.

Hansen, J. (1981). The effects of inference training and practice on young children's reading comprehension. *Reading Research Quarterly, 16,* 391–417.

Hansen, J., & Pearson, P. D. (1983). An instructional study: Improving the inferential comprehension of fourth grade good and poor readers. *Journal of Educational Psychology, 75,* 821–829.

Johnson, D. D., Toms-Bronowski, S., & Pittleman, S. (in press). An investigation of the effectiveness of semantic mapping and semantic feature anlysis on vocabulary acquisition and retention. *Reading Research Quarterly.*

Johnston, P. (1984). Prior knowledge and reading comprehension test bias. *Reading Research Quarterly, 19,* 219–239.

Johnston, P., & Pearson, P. D. (June 1982). *Prior knowledge, connectivity, and the assessment of reading comprehension,* Tech. Rep. No. 245. Urbana: University of Illinois, Center for the Study of Reading.

Kintsch, W. (1974). *The representation of meaning in memory.* Hillsdale, N.J.: Erlbaum.

Klare, G. (1963). *The measurement of readability.* Ames: Iowa State University Press.

Lindsay, P., & Norman, D. (1972). *Human information processing.* New York: Academic.

Lorge, I. (1939). Predicting reading difficulty of selections for children. *Elementary English Review, 16,* 229-233.

Mehler, J. (1963). Some effects of grammatical transformations on the recall of English sentences. *Journal of Verbal Learning and Verbal Behavior, 2,* 346-351.

Meyer, B. J. F. (1975). *The organization of prose and it effects on memory.* Amsterdam: North-Holland.

Miller, G. A., & Isard, S. (1963). Some perceptual consequences of linguistic rules. *Journal of Verbal Learning and Verbal Behavior, 2,* 217-228.

Minsky, M. A. (1975). A framework for representing knowledge. In P. Winston (Ed.), *The psychology of computer vision.* New York: McGraw-Hill

Murray, D. M. (1982). Teaching the other self: The writer's first reader. *College Composition and Communication, 33,* 140-147.

Nagy, W. E., & Anderson, R. C. (1984). How many words are there in printed school English? *Reading Research Quarterly, 19,* 304-330.

Nagy, W. E., Herman, P., & Anderson, R. C. (1985). Learning words from context. *Reading Research Quarterly, 20,* 233-253.

Palincsar, A. M., & Brown, A. L. (1984). Reciprocal teaching of comprehension-fostering and comprehension-monitoring activities. *Cognition and Instruction, 1,* 117-175.

Paris, S., Lipson, M., & Wixson, K. (1983). Becoming a strategic reader. *Contemporary Educational Psychology, 8,* 293-316.

Pearson, P. D. (1974-1975). The effects of grammatical complexity; on children's comprehension, recall, and conception of certain semantic relations. *Reading Research Quarterly, 10,* 155-192.

Pearson, P. D., & Gallagher, M. C. (1983). The instruction of reading comprehension. *Contemporary Educational Psychology, 8,* 317-344.

Pearson, P. D., & Johnson, D. D. (1978). *Teaching reading comprehension.* New York: Holt, Rinehart & Winston.

Pearson, P. D., & Tierney, R. J. (1984). On becoming a thoughtful reader: Learning to read like a writer. In A. Purves & O. Niles (Eds.), *Becoming readers in a complex society.* Chicago: National Society for the Study of Education, 144-173.

Rankin, E. (1965). Cloze procedure—a survey of research. *Yearbook of the South West Reading Conference, 14,* 133-148.

Raphael, T. E., & Pearson, P. D. (1985). Increasing students' awareness of sources of information for answering questions. *American Educational Research Journal, 22(2),* 217-236.

Raphael, T. E., & Wonnacutt, C. A. (1985). Metacognitive training in question-answering strategies: Implementation in a fourth grade developmental reading program. *Reading Research Quarterly, 20(2),* 282-296.

Rumelhart, D. E. (1975). Notes on a schema for stories. In D. G. Bobrow & A. M. Collins (Eds.), *Representation and understanding: Studies in congitive science.* New York: Academic.

Rumelhart, D. E. (1980). Schemata: The building blocks of cognition. In R. J. Spiro, B. C.

Bruce, & W. F. Brewer (Eds.), *Theoretical issues in reading comprehension*. Hillsdale, N.J.: Erlbaum.

Rumelhart, D. E., & Ortony, A. (1977). The representation of knowledge and memory. In R. C. Anderson, R. J. Spiro, & W. E. Montague (Eds.), *Schooling and the acquisition of knowledge*. Hillsdale, N.J.: Erlbaum.

Sachs, J. S. (1967). Recognition memory for syntactic and sematic aspects of connected discourse. *Perception and Psychophysics, 2*, 437–442.

Schachter, S. (1978). *An investigation of the effects of vocabulary and schemata orientation upon reading comprehension*. Ph.D. Diss. University of Minnesota.

Schank, R. C. (1973). Indentification of conceptualizations underlying natural language. In R. C. Schank & K. M. Colby (Eds.), *Computer models of thoughts and language*. San Francisco: Freeman.

Simons, H. D. (1971). Reading comprehension: The need for a new perspective. *Reading Research Quarterly, 5*, 338–363.

Singer, H., & Donlan, D. (1982). Active comprehension: Problem solving schema with question generation for comprehension of complex short stories. *Reading Research Quarterly, 17*, 166–186.

Slobin, D. T. (1966). Grammatical transformations and sentence comprehension in childhood and adulthood. *Journal of Verbal Learning and Verbal Behavior, 5*, 219–227.

Smith, F. (1971). *Understanding reading: A psycholinguistic anyalysis of reading and learning to read*. New York: Holt, Rinehart & Winston.

Stein, N. L., & Glenn, C. G. (March 1977). *A developmental study of children's construction of stories*. Paper presented at the Society for Research in Child Development conference, New Orleans.

Taylor, W. (1954). *Application of "cloze" and entropy measures to the study of contextual constraint in samples of continuous prose*. Ph.D. Diss. University of Illinois at Urbana-Champaign.

Tharp, R. G. (1982). The effective instruction of comprehension: Results and description of the Kamehameha Early Education Program. *Reading Research Quarterly, 17*, 503–527.

Thorndyke, P. W. (1977). Cognitive structures in comprehension and memory of narrative discourse. *Cognitive Psychology, 9*, 77– 110.

Tierney, R. J., & Cunningham, J. (1984). Research on teaching reading comprehension. In P. D. Pearson (Ed.), *Handbook of reading research*. New York: Longman.

Tierney, R. J., & Pearson, P. D. (1983). Toward a composing model of reading. *Language Arts, 60*, 568–580.

Wagoner, S. (1983). Comprehension monitoring: What it is and what we know about it. *Reading Research Quarterly, 18*,(3), 328–341.

4

Influence of the Social Organization of Instruction on Children's Text Comprehension Ability: A Vygotskian Perspective

Kathryn Hu-pei Au • Alice J. Kawakami

In this chapter we look closely at the social dynamics of a particular context of literacy: classroom reading lessons. Our research on these lessons is an effort to consider some of the classroom implications of the constructivist view of the reading process (e.g., Spiro, Bruce, & Brewer, 1980). In the constructivist view, reading is defined as the process of constructing or composing meaning from text (Pearson & Tierney, 1984). One of the practical implications of this view is that reading comprehension, rather than word identification, becomes the focus of most lessons. Thus, our research is directed at learning how the social organization of lessons can support the development of children's reading comprehension ability.

Specifically, we discuss three studies of relationships between the cognitive and social dimensions of classroom lessons targeting reading comprehension. These studies were all of lessons where the teacher worked with a small group of children on constructing the meaning of a particular text.

The ideas of Vygotsky provide the framework for our research. He suggested that the child's development proceeds on the basis of experiences in the social world (for more detailed discussion, see chapters by Rogoff and by Gavelek, this volume). This position assumes that:

> any function in the child's cultural development appears twice, or in two planes. First it appears in the social plane, and then on the psychological plane. First it appears between people, as an inter-psychological category, and then within the child as an intrapsychological category. (Vygotsky, 1981, p. 163)

In our studies we are examining the roots of reading comprehension development on the social plane, trying to understand how classroom reading lessons can help develop children's proficiency in reading comprehension.

PREVIOUS RESEARCH

Little research has been conducted on naturally occurring classroom reading comprehension lessons. One obvious reason, reflected in the results of Durkin's (1978–1979) large-scale observational study, is that such lessons may be difficult to find; classroom reading lessons typically do not focus on comprehension. Furthermore, even when comprehension is targeted, instruction may be poorly organized and carried out (Durkin, 1978–1979; Mason, 1983).

Comprehension instruction is, however, at the heart of the reading program developed by the Kamehameha Elementary Education Program (KEEP) in Honolulu, Hawaii, where our research was conducted. This program was designed to boost the reading achievement of disadvantaged students of Polynesian–Hawaiian ancestry. Daily lessons in reading comprehension, 20 to 25 minutes long, are given to groups of about five children, all at a similar instructional level. Improvement in student achievement is reflected in standardized test scores (Tharp, 1982), even though items in these tests are not necessarily the best measures of the kind of comprehension development we are trying to promote (Crowell, Au, & Blake, 1983).

By analyzing videotapes of reading comprehension lessons given by teachers in the KEEP program, we are beginning to identify the characteristics of effective comprehension instruction. Although, following Vygotsky, we think that the "cognitive" and "social" aspects of instruction are in a sense inseparable, being experienced by students as one, we find it useful for analytic purposes to distinguish between the two.

The cognitive dimension of instruction in the KEEP reading lessons is operationally defined in our studies by the *experience-text-relationship* or ETR approach to teaching comprehension (Au, 1979). This is the approach the teachers typically use to organize their lessons, although they have been observed to use about seven different methods for teaching comprehension (Au, Oshiro, & Blake, in preparation), including the *directed reading–thinking activity* or DRTA (Stauffer, 1969) and *question-answer relationship* or QAR training (Raphael, 1982).

The ETR method, while very general, gives teachers a structure for organizing comprehension lessons, which in our program are generally based on selections from basal readers. Experience-text-relationship lessons incorporate three broad phases of instruction: (1) the experience (E) phase focuses on schema activation, or the accessing by the students of background knowledge relevant to the topic of the text; (2) the text (T) phase centers on the close literal reading, as well as interpretation, of text information; and (3) the relationship (R) phase attends to the integration of information read with prior knowledge and experience.

The idea behind use of the ETR method is that repeated experience in these lessons will enable students to internalize a general approach to text comprehension. This is consistent with Vygotsky's idea that learning begins at the interpsychological and then moves to the intrapsychological plane. In the small-group setting, teachers involve students in silent reading and guided discussion of the text. They do this in a way that minimizes the isolation of either bottom-up or top-down processes while encouraging the interaction of both. (For a brief description of bottom-up versus top-down theories of reading, see Ringler & Weber, 1984, pp. 35–45.) The approach is one of a gradual approximation to mature reading by assisting the child's performance of the whole act of reading for meaning (cf. Holdaway, 1979; alternative approaches are generally based on a task or subskills analysis).

Within the cognitive framework provided by the ETR method, our first work on the social dimension of instruction had to do with the importance of cultural compatibility in the patterning of teacher-pupil interaction (Au & Jordan, 1981; Au, 1980a). Patterns of interaction in lessons taught by effective teachers showed similarities to those in talk story (as described by Watson, 1975), an important nonschool speech event for Hawaiian students.

In the KEEP reading lessons, the most common form of teacher-pupil interaction is the *talk story pattern*. The teacher begins by asking a question, but does not then ask for volunteers to answer or call on individual children. Rather, the teacher leans forward and looks at the five or so children, often smiling and nodding at them. The children begin to answer the teacher's question without raising their hands and waiting to be called on. They usually build upon one another's answers, or in some cases argue with one another, working as a group to frame a complete answer to the teacher's question. This manner of speaking, termed *joint performance,* is characteristic of talk story as a speech event outside of the classroom (Watson, 1975).

The talk story pattern can be constrasted with the *conventional classroom recitation pattern* for organizing discussion in lessons (Au & Mason, 1981). The characteristics of this recitation pattern are thoroughly described in the work of Sinclair and Coulthard (1975) and of Mehan (1979). Basically, teacher-led discussion is structured according to a three-part sequence. First, the teacher asks a question or poses a problem. The students generally bid for a turn to answer, and the teacher selects one of them. Second, that student, and that student alone, frames an answer to the teacher's question. Finally, the teacher may evaluate the student's response. If the student answers incorrectly, the teacher may provide the correct response or call on someone else to answer.

In the reading comprehension lessons we study, which are generally those given by experienced and effective teachers, the conventional classroom recitation pattern occupies perhaps a third of the time in any given lesson. It can, however, take up 70 percent of the time in lessons given by a teacher inexperienced in working with Hawaiian children (Au & Mason, 1983).

Having identified these two major patterns of teacher-pupil interaction in reading lessons, we then looked at their probable effects on Hawaiian children's learning to read (Au & Mason, 1981). In a microanalysis of sample lessons, we found lessons incorporating the talk story pattern to be associated with higher rates of academically productive classroom recitation pattern than lessons excluding the talk story pattern.

The primary purpose of the next study in this line of research, exploring relationships between the cognitive and social dimensions of reading lessons, was to test the relevance to ETR lessons of Vygotsky's concept of the zone of proximal development (Au & Kawakami, 1984a). The zone is defined in the following way:

> *It is the distance between the actual developmental level as determined by individ-ual problem solving and the level of potential development as determined through problem solving under adult guidance or in collaboration with more capable peers.* The zone of proximal development defines those functions that have not yet matured but are in the process of maturation, functions that will mature tomorrow but are currently in an embryonic state. (Vygotsky, 1978, p. 86, italics in the original)

From this perspective, we suppose that reading comprehension lessons can be effective only if the teacher, as the more capable other, engages the children in text-understanding activity within the zone of proximal development.

What might it mean, in terms of teacher and student behavior, for instruc-tion to be conducted within the zone of proximal development? First, many of the questions posed by the teacher at the start of an interchange drew incorrect responses from the students. When this happened the teacher almost always tried to elicit answers from the students rather than telling them the information. She either waited for a correct answer to be given or asked a follow-up question, making sure that the students did as much of the cognitive work as they were able. Second, the students would occasionally introduce a text topic for discussion on their own. The teacher then encouraged the group to build upon these student-initiated topics in the same way that she encouraged them to respond to her own questions.

Both of these patterns of behavior appeared consistent with Vygotsky's ideas about the zone of proximal development and how learning takes place. Within lessons students work with slightly as well as highly developed text comprehension abilities. The students received the teacher's help in working out the answers to difficult questions, having the opportunity to carry out rather advanced compre-hension skills if only with considerable asistance. On the other hand, in initiating topics students took a large share of responsibility for the text interpretation pro-cess. Thus, initiations might be taken as a sign of the maturing of certain text comprehension abilities.

The three studies to be discussed here are further explorations of the relationships between the cognitive and social dimensions of instruction in the context of small-group reading comprehension lessons. In the first study we look at the match between patterns of interaction and particular instructional goals. In the second study we look at how instuction can be said to lead development in classroom reading lessons. Finally, in the third study we look at the transfer of control over text comprehension processes from teacher to student, as it can be seen in comparisons of reading lessons given to first and third graders. The common thread in all cases is how the social organization of instruction, or the social dimension of lessons, can serve to support students' learning to read, or the cognitive outcome of lessons.

MATCHING PATTERNS OF INTERACTION WITH DIFFERENT PHASES OF COMPREHENSION INSTRUCTION

In this study (Au, 1980b) we looked at differences in the structuring of interaction in the three phases of an ETR lesson. Our hypothesis was that effective teachers structured interaction in the phases differently in order to accomplish the different instructional purposes associated with each. Following Vygotsky, such a match should strengthen opportunities for development to proceed on the interpsychological plane.

The lesson analyzed in this investigation was taught to a group of four disadvantaged Hawaiian second graders. As in each of the studies to be described, we prepared a transcript from the videotaped lesson. We then identified the E, T, and R phases in the lesson, each phase being marked by a key question and related, supporting questions. A key question asked during an E phase was:

What would you do with a frog?

A key question during the T phases was:

How does Freddy feel about using the frog for bait?

In the R phases a key question was:

Why do you think the frog might have done that (jumped out of Freddy's hand into the grass)?

This 22-minute lesson opened with a string of five E phases. Then there was a period of silent reading, followed by six T phases and three R phases.

The next step was to look at the way interaction was managed in each of the three phases. This highly skilled teacher varied greatly the patterns of interaction in the lessons. Sometimes she spoke herself, forbidding the children to speak. Sometimes she had the children answer in a chorus. Sometimes she used the conventional classroom recitation pattern and allowed only one child to speak at

Table 4.1 **Time in Each Pattern of Interaction During E, T, and R Phases**

Phase	Pattern of Interaction				Total Seconds
	Teacher Only	Chorus	One Child	More Than One Child	
E	5[a] (1.87)[b]	15 (5.62)	47 (17.60)	200 (74.91)	267
T	36 (8.14)	52 (11.76)	204 (46.15)	150 (33.94)	442
R	0	13 (5.53)	106 (45.11)	116 (49.36)	235
Total	41 (4.34)	80 (8.47)	357 (37.82)	466 (49.36)	944

[a]Seconds
[b]Percentage of total time

a time. Finally, she sometimes encouraged more than one child to speak, thus permitting the talk story pattern to occur (for details of this analysis, see Au, 1980b).

The bottom row of Table 4.1 shows the time in seconds that these four different patterns prevailed. There was hardly any time at all (less than 5 percent) when the teacher spoke without permitting the children to speak, too. Not much time (less than 9 percent) was spent having the children reply in a chorus. However, a considerable amount of time was taken up in the other two patterns, conventional classroom recitation with only one child speaker (about 38 percent) and talk story (about 49 percent). Therefore, we were primarily interested in how time in these last two conditions was distributed across the E, T, and R phases.

As seen in Table 4.1, nearly three-quarters of the time in E phases was spent in the talk story pattern, with less than 18 percent in the conventional classroom recitation pattern. We see marked differences between the management of interaction in T as opposed to E phases. In T phases much more time (about 46 percent) is spent in the recitation pattern and less (about 34 percent) in the talk story pattern. Also during T phases, more time is spent in patterns when only the teacher speaks, or when the teacher requires the children to answer in a chorus, than during any other type of phase (about 8 percent and 12 percent of the time, respectively). Time in R phases is divided quite evenly between the talk story and recitation patterns (about 49 percent and 45 percent).

These results show how teacher-pupil interaction probably should be managed to meet the purposes of E, T, and R phases. In E phases the teacher needs to build children's interest in the text. Thus, it makes sense to allow the children to respond whenever they want to, as long as their remarks are on the right topic. The openness of the interactions reflects the rather wide range of acceptable responses, and the free-responding procedure makes it easy for several children to participate at once.

In contrast, during T phases the teacher should try to restrict response opportunities, perhaps slowing the pace of the lessons somewhat to encourage close attention to the information in the text. In T phases the appropriate responses will generally be fewer, and perhaps more difficult to elicit from the children. Thus, the teacher should assume more control over the course of the discussion and generally should call on one child at a time to respond.

As the lesson moves into R phases, the teacher will probably want to vary the nature of the interaction, sometimes allowing the children to call out answers and sometimes having them wait to be chosen before answering. In R phases there will be moments when speculation is invited, and the children should be permitted to speak freely. But there will also be times when information from the text should be reviewed and summarized, and students' responses should be more carefully monitored by the teacher.

The results of this study suggest one form of influence that the social organization of lessons can have on learning to read. It may be that a careful match between patterns of interaction and instructional goals, as described above, will boost learning on the interpsychological plane. This matching may be especially important in the case of culturally different students, whom teachers might otherwise find difficult to draw into active processing and discussion of the text.

KEEPING INSTRUCTION IN THE ZONE OF PROXIMAL DEVELOPMENT

In this study (Au & Kawakami, 1984b) one of our major goals was to see if earlier findings (Au & Kawakami, 1984a) concerning the zone of proximal development would hold up across a series of lessons on the same text (in the KEEP program, more than one lesson is usually required to complete the reading of a single basal reader selection). For this purpose we analyzed a series of four reading lessons given by a talented teacher to a group of six gifted second-grade students, all of Hawaiian ancestry.

Our principal unit of analysis was the *interchange*. An interchange is a segment of discussion that centers on the working out of a particular text or text-related idea and concludes when the teacher and children have reached agreement on, or a shared understanding of, that idea. In analyzing interchanges we attend explicitly to the group process aimed at the cooperative or collaborative construction of the meaning of the text.

With this method we look at the overall pattern of results in two ways, first, treating interchanges as equivalent units and second, according to the time in seconds within each interchange. Both measures revealed the same patterns, so we report below only the results for interchanges as units.

In 18 of the 84 interchanges (21 percent) that opened with a teacher question, the initial set of student responses was either incorrect or incomplete. The teacher asked quite a few questions that the students were not able to answer correctly on their own. Following the thinking of Vygotsky, we take this as a sign that the children were being challenged to perform at a higher level than they were able to achieve independently.

The teacher's reaction to these incorrect responses was entirely consistent across the set of lessons. She always asked follow-up questions, working to elicit the correct answer from the children. She never just gave away the answer. Instead, the point at issue was discussed until the children worked it out.

Again following Vygotsky, we see this as a positive sign. The teacher should be supporting the students' text comprehension processes so that they will succeed in answering her orginal question and eventually, in a much condensed internal process, be able to understand text on their own. For learning to take place, she needs to prompt them to take as much responsibility as they can for the reading-as-problem-solving task.

The text for these lessons was entitled "Annie and the Old One" (Miles, 1971). Annie is a young Navaho girl and the Old One is her grandmother. At the beginning of the story the Old One tells her family that when the rug Annie's mother is weaving is taken from the loom she (the Old One) will return to Mother Earth. Annie takes her grandmother's words literally and tries several schemes to keep the rug from being completed. Finally, the Old One takes Annie out into the desert and helps her understand the natural cycle of life, death, and rebirth.

The excerpt below, from the transcript of the fourth and final lesson in the series, gives the flavor of our comprehension lessons at their best. It encompasses two interchanges, the start of the second being marked with an asterisk. Material in brackets is speech we were not able to transcribe with certainty. Overlapping speech is marked with slashes.

TEACHER: Now grandmother, in a very simple way, tries to explain to her about time. How did she do that? How did she explain to Annie about the dying and about time? What did she compare it to?

RACHEL: The sun.

TEACHER: Okay, tell me about the sun, Rachel.

RACHEL: (*Reads from text*) "The sun comes up from the edge of earth in the morning. It returns to the edge of earth in the evening. Earth, from which good things come for the living creatures on it. Earth, to which all creatures finally go."

TEACHER: That's very nice. So what is like the sun?

KENT: Life.

TEACHER: Can you tell me now, what—when they say life, when they say the sun rises, how does that relate to life?

KENT: Um, you get born.

JOEY: Someone get born.

KENT: It's like years passing when the sun finally goes down and you die.

JOEY: Sets—sets. And then it comes up again when somebody else is born and [inaudible] it again.

TEACHER: That's very nice. I like the way you said that.* But she also compared it/when she said—/

JOEY: /The cactus./

TEACHER: Okay, tell me about the cactus, Joey.

JOEY: Oh, I know about the cactus.

TEACHER: [What did you] find about the cactus?

JOEY: (*Reads from text*) "The cactus did not bloom forever. Petals dried and fell to earth."

TEACHER: Okay, what is she trying to tell Annie by using that analogy of the cactus?

ROSS: That people die of old age. That people just don't die when they say so.
TEACHER: Well, yeah, okay, that's—that's true. But what did they mean when they said, "The cactus did not bloom forever"?
ROSS: That people, they got to die.
KENT: That means that when it starts blooming a life will start, but when it falls the life will end.

Although nonverbal behavior is not noted here, we can see on the videotape that the children were not raising their hands and bidding for turns to answer. Rather, they gained turns simply by beginning to speak in response to the teacher's questions, following the talk story pattern. The teacher's follow-up questions came in response to the children's initial answers. As shown in the transcript excerpt above, these questions required the children to give fuller or more complete formulations of their interpretations of the text. The sequence of events just described was typical of these lessons. In about 85 percent of the interchanges more that one student spoke on the same topic, and the teacher asked one or more follow-up questions, either to have them clarify or refine their responses.

At the start of the second interchange Joey began to answer the teacher's question before she had finished speaking it. This is not considered an initiation, however, because his idea might have been cued by the teacher's first few words. At this point, though, he clearly had a very good understanding of where the discussion was heading. Understanding of this kind seemed to be supported by the social organization of the lessons, which encouraged the students to follow a sophisticated story line and to express complex thoughts.

When we looked at who initiated the topic of discussion, the teacher or one of the students, we saw a preponderance of teacher-initiated discussion, 84 of the 103 interchanges (about 82 percent). In 19 interchanges (about 18 percent), however, the topic of discussion was initiated by a student.

In looking at how the teacher reacted to the students' initiations, we were interested in knowing whether she built upon the idea and helped the group develop it, or ignored it and caused it to be dropped. In 15 instances she picked up on student ideas by asking follow-up questions, and in only four did she merely comment on or acknowledge what the student had said. Thus, she recognized their ideas to be as important to the text interpretation process as those she introduced herself.

In most instances, as we saw in Joey's case, what seemed to be happening was that the children anticipated the direction in which the teacher was moving the discussion. Consistent with Vygotsky's ideas, we think this is evidence that the transfer from other- to self-regulation is beginning to take place.

The results of this study suggest a second kind of influence of the social dimensions of instruction upon the cognitive. This has to do with whether the teacher involves students in text comprehension activities in the zone of proximal development. First, this teacher created a conversational environment where the students felt able to take risks. They were willing to suggest answers to the rather difficult questions she posed to open the interchanges. The children always tried to respond, even though, as mentioned earlier, they were unable to answer correctly on one out of every five occasions. The social organization of these lessons also permitted the students to show initiative by suggesting topics for discussion. The teacher encouraged these initiations by building the discussion around them, thus communicating a respect for the children's own ideas.

In both cases, whether accepting the challenge of responding to a difficult teacher-posed question or of themselves introducing an idea for discussion, the children were "stretching their minds." This behavior seems consistent with Vygotsky's (1978) idea that instruction is effective only if it leads development. That is, lessons should cause the child to use abilities still in the process of developing.

TRANSFERRING CONTROL OVER COMPREHENSION PROCESSES TO THE STUDENTS

Viewing reading lessons from the framework provided by Vygotsky, we looked in our third study (Kawakami & Au, 1983) for ways in which control over text comprehension processes might gradually be transferred from teacher to students. We assume that comprehension performance has two aspects, metacognitive and cognitive (Brown, 1980). The metacognitive has to do with awareness and control of the cognitive skills that should be applied. In the KEEP reading lessons, of course, the cognitive skills are those defined by the ETR method. Thus, an increase in child as opposed to teacher control over the execution of E, T, or R phases of discussion might be taken as a sign of metacognitive development.

We hypothesized that E, T, and R comprehension abilities could go through three stages of mastery. In Stage 1 the teacher controls both cognitive and metacognitive aspects of performance. The teacher exercises metacognitive control by initiating the discussion topic for each interchange. In so doing, the teacher chooses the appropriate phase within the ETR approach and cues the students as to which it is. The teacher then guides students' cognitive performance by providing feedback and assistance. For example, as we saw, this may be by asking questions leading to a clarification of text ideas.

In Stage 2 as students become better able to read with understanding, they are provided with opportunities to control certain aspects of the lesson. At this stage it seems they may have control over *either* cognitive or metacognitive aspects of comprehension performance. As yet, though, they are unable simultaneously to carry both out on their own. Thus, Stage 2 performance may take two forms. In one form, students initiate a topic but require specific questioning from the teacher before being able to carry on the discussion. In this case they appear to have control over the metacognitive aspect of performance. In the other form, the teacher sets the topic, but students are able to discuss it with very little guidance. In this case, then, they appear to have control over the cognitive aspect of performance.

In Stage 3 students control both aspects of comprehension performance. At this stage of mastery, they are capable of independently identifying and carrying out the appropriate E, T, or R phase in the comprehension process. The teacher serves merely as a facilitator, rather than a director, of the comprehension discussion. In proposing these three stages, then, we tried to lay out more specifically the process of transfer, or movement from other- to self-regulation, suggested by Vygotsky.

We analyzed videotapes of two first- and two third-grade lessons. The first-grade students had not had much experience with ETR lessons, while the third graders had had this type of instruction for almost three years. The basic unit of analysis, again, was the interchange.

As expected, there was much more teacher-controlled comprehension discussion in the first- than third-grade lessons. About 85 percent of the discussion time in the first-grade lessons showed Stage 1 performance by the students, being teacher initiated and guided. In contrast, about 60 percent of the time in the third-grade lessons was in Stage 1. Put another way, about 40 percent of the time in the third-grade lessons was spent in Stage 2 performance, while in the first-grade lessons only about 15 percent of discussion time fell into this category.

Stage 2 interchanges were further examined for qualitative differences in the performance of first and third graders. On the basis of the limited data available, their performance did seem very different. Most of the Stage 2 time in the first-grade lessons was spent in student-initiated interchanges (75.3 percent in one lesson and 100 percent in the other). These younger children were able to initiate appropriate topics for discussion. Then, however, they required the teacher's assistance in working through their ideas. This pattern was reversed in the third-grade lessons (about one-third of Stage 2 time was in student-initiated and about two-thirds in teacher-initiated discussion). Thus, older students were more often able to execute the steps on their own once the teacher had set the discussion topic.

This finding must be viewed with caution because it is based on such a limited amount of data. It suggests, however, that metacognitive awareness of some skills may develop *before* the ability to perform them independently. This is an idea to be explored in future studies, where we will work with a four- rather than three-stage model. In Stage 1 in this new model, teacher support is required for both metacognitive and cognitive aspects of performance. In Stage 2, students can carry out the metacognitive aspects but need teacher guidance with the cognitive. In Stage 3 teacher support is needed for the metacognitive aspects but the students can carry out the cognitive. Finally, in Stage 4 students can carry both out on their own.

We also found Stage 1 time to be unevenly distributed among the E, T, and R phases of instruction. This effect was partly due to text variables, for example, whether events were presented in chronological order (for details, see Kawakami & Au, 1983). In short, however, allowing for differences among the texts, it seems children first master the cognitive skills required for E-phase performance. They then appear able to carry out R-phase discussion with relatively little teacher help. Independence in T-phase performance seems to come last.

The results of this study bring out a third kind of influence that the social dimensions of instruction may have upon the cognitive: The social organization of lessons can support the orderly transfer of control over text comprehension processes from teacher to student. To maximize this kind of impact, future research is needed to understand how instruction should change over time. Two aspects of change have to be understood: first, the cognitive goals or types of text comprehension ability that should be targeted, and second, the patterns and characteristics of teacher-pupil interaction which may further students' independent use of certain comprehension abilities.

CONCLUSION

In this chapter we discussed three studies, each exploring relationships between the social and cognitive dimensions of small-group lessons on reading comprehension. The results of these studies suggest three ways that the social organization of lessons might have an influence on cognitive outcomes in learning to read.

In the first study we considered the positive impact of achieving a match between patterns of teacher-pupil interaction and phases of instruction targeting different aspects of comprehension performance. This study built on previous research on the importance of cultural compatibility in the structuring of talk during ETR lessons given to Hawaiian children. E phases of instruction, in which the cognitive goal is the accessing of existing schemata or prior knowledge, appear logically to be best supported by the talk story pattern of interaction. T phases of instruction, where the goal is close analysis and interpretation of the text itself, seem more effective when most of the time is spent in highly teacher-directed patterns of interaction, including the conventional classroom recitation one. Finally, R phases, when the goal is a fitting together of text information with prior knowledge and experiences, seem best supported by a balance between talk story and conventional classroom recitation patterns.

Our specific findings apply to reading lessons given to Hawaiian children, but the basic idea is probably generalizable to students from other groups. If the goal of instruction is to improve students' ability to construct meaning from text, lessons centered on discussion of text ideas are likely to be an important part of the classroom reading program. In this event the teacher needs to encourage students' active involvement with text and the discussion of text ideas. The goals of instruction, as set out in the ETR approach, may not change from group to group, but the patterns of interaction may need to be adjusted, depending on the rules governing speaking, listening, and turn taking [or participation structures (see Shultz, Erickson, & Florio, 1982)] in the students' homes and community. The idea is to find a match between lesson *content* (or instructional goals and material) and *context* (or patterns of interaction). This study suggests that such matching should take place *within* as well as between lessons, if different types of intellectual processes are being targeted at various times.

In the second study we considered the importance of keeping instruction within the zone of proximal development, or the region of greatest sensitivity to instruction. Two types of results were highlighted. First, we examined the difficulty level of teacher questions, which led to students' answering incorrectly at the start of about one out of five teacher-initiated interchanges. Second, we saw that students, and not the teacher, introduced the topic of discussion for about one out of every five interchanges.

These findings suggest the importance of students' willingness to take risks during discussion of text. Risk taking was shown in the students' proposing of answers to difficult questions and in their suggesting of topics for discussion. The teacher created an interactional climate where the students took such risks regularly, without the fear of being punished. When their responses were incorrect or incomplete, she helped them to work out a correct or more complete response. She always pushed and prodded them to do more. When a student suggested a topic for discussion, the teacher generally accepted this idea and encouraged the other students to elaborate upon it. Risk taking by the students seemed to be part of an unspoken pact with the teacher: "We'll keep answering if you'll help us get it right!" Through this pact, a substantial amount of the discussion appeared to be kept near the upper limits of the students' text comprehension abilities.

In the third study we focused on the orderly movement from other- to self-regulation in the development of students' reading comprehension. We saw how third graders differed from first graders in their overall independence in applying text comprehension abilities during reading lessons. Also, this independence was not uniform, but seemed to be highest in the application of E-phase ability, somewhat lower in R-phase ability, and lowest in T-phase ability. These results suggest a third kind of influence of the social dimensions of instruction upon cognitive outcomes: in contributing to a systematic transfer of control over text comprehension processes from teacher to students.

Given the results of these three studies, it seems that the development of students' ability to comprehend text will proceed well in lessons where there is:

1. A match between patterns of teacher-pupil interaction and the type of comprehension skill being targeted.
2. Risk taking by the students, so a substantial proportion of the group's text processing discussion can be kept within the zone of proximal development.
3. Student control over the text comprehension and discussion process in areas where they are more proficient, but teacher control over areas where their proficiency is lower.

Possible practical implications of these results for teachers may be the following. Teachers who give unscripted text discussion lessons will need to know something about the interactional patterns comfortable for their students. They will want to think about structuring interaction somewhat differently at different times in lessons, depending upon whether a divergent, wide-ranging or convergent, narrowly focused type of discussion is wanted.

Teachers will want to ask challenging questions and create a lesson climate in which students are willing to take the risk of answering incorrectly. Incorrect answers often reveal the nature of a student's reasoning. In this sense, it may give the teacher a better idea of what the student is thinking, and therefore be more valuable to instruction than a correct one. Teachers need to communicate to students, too, that they are after well-reasoned, to-the-point responses, and not carelessly formulated ones. Students should be required to give reasons for their responses, referring back to the text for evidence, if necessary.

Finally, teachers should look for signs that students are able to take over responsibility for certain aspects of the text comprehension and discussion process. One sign is when students introduce appropriate topics for discusssion, particularly topics that serve to keep discussion on the central theme of the text. On these occasions teachers should incorporate these topics into the discussion and, where possible, assume the role of discussion facilitator rather than director. Taking these steps gives students the incentive to become increasingly independent in comprehending text.

REFERENCES

Au, K. H. (1979). Using the experience-text-relationship method with minority children. *Reading Teacher, 32*(6), 677–679.

Au, K. H. (1980a). Participation structures in a reading lesson with Hawaiian children: Analysis of a culturally appropriate instructional event. *Anthropology and Education Quarterly, 11*(2), 91–115.

Au, K. H. (1980b). Effective use of the ETR method: Matching patterns of teacher-pupil interaction with instruction goals. Honolulu, Hawaii: Kamehameha Early Education Program.

Au, K. H., & Jordan, C. (1981). Teaching reading to Hawaiian children: Finding a culturally appropriate solution. In H. T. Trueba, G. P. Guthrie & K. H. Au (Eds.), *Culture in the bilingual classroom: Studies in classroom ethnography.* Rowley, Mass.: Newbury House.

Au, K. H., & Kawakami, A. J. (1984a). Vygotskian perspectives on discussion processes in small group reading lessons. In P. L. Peterson, L. C. Wilkinson & M. Hallinan (Eds.), *The social context of instruction: Group organization and group processes.* New York: Academic.

Au, K. H., & Kawakami, A. J. (April 1984b). Understanding interactional dynamics in the effective teaching of comprehension. Paper presented at the annual meeting of the American Educational Research Association, New Orleans.

Au, K. H., & Mason, J. M. (1981). Social organizational factors in learning to read: The balance of rights hypothesis. *Reading Research Quarterly, 17*(1), 115–167.

Au, K. H., & Mason, J. M. (1983). Cultural congruence in classroom participation structures: Achieving a balance of rights. *Discourse Processes, 6*(2), 145–167.

Au, K. H., Oshiro, M., & Blake, K. (manuscript in preparation). Variation in implementation of the KEEP reading program, 1983–1984. Honolulu, Hawaii: Kamehameha Elementary Education Program.

Brown, A. L. (1980). Metacognitive development and reading. In R. J. Spiro, B. C. Bruce, & W. F. Brewer (Eds.), *Theoretical issues in reading comprehension.* Hillsdale, N.J.: Erlbaum.

Crowell, D. C., Au, K. H., & Blake, K. (1983). Reading comprehension questions: Differences among standardized tests. *Journal of Reading, 4*, 314–319.

Durkin, D. (1978–1979). What classroom observations reveal about reading comprehension instruction. *Reading Research Quarterly, 14*(4), 481–533.

Holdaway, D. (1979). *The foundations of literacy.* Sydney: Ashton Scholastic.

Kawakami, A. J., & Au, K. H. (April 1983). Metacognitive development and text variables in the teaching of reading comprehension. Paper presented at the annual meeting of the American Educational Research Association, Montreal.

Mason, J. M. (1983). An examination of reading instruction in third and fourth grades. *Reading Teacher, 36*(9), 906–913.

Mehan, H. (1979). *Learning lessons.* Cambridge, Mass.: Harvard University Press.

Miles, M. (1971). Annie and the Old One. In W. K. Durr, J. M. LePere, & R. H. Brown (Eds.), *Passports.* Houghton Mifflin Reading Program, 1976. Boston: Houghton Mifflin.

Pearson, P. D., & Tierney, R. J. (1984). On becoming a thoughtful reader: Learning to read like a writer. In A. C. Purves & O. Niles (Eds.), *Becoming readers in a complex society.* Part I. Eighty-third yearbook of the National Society for the Study of Education. Chicago: University of Chicago Press.

Raphael, T. E. (1982). Question-answering strategies for children. *Reading Teacher, 36*(2), 186–190.

Ringler, L. H., & Weber, C. K. (1984). *A language-thinking approach to reading.* San Diego: Harcourt Brace Jovanovich.

Shultz, J., Erickson, F., & Florio, S. (1982). Where's the floor? Aspects of the cultural organization of social relationships at home and at school. In P. Gilmore & A. Glatthorn (Eds.), *Ethnography and education: Children in and out of school.* Washington, D.C.: Center for Applied Linguistics.

Sinclair, J. M., & Coulthard, R. M. (1975). *Toward an analysis of discourse: The English used by teachers and pupils.* London: Oxford University Press.

Spiro, R. J., Bruce, B. C., & Brewer, W. F. (Eds.). (1980). *Theoretical issues in reading comprehension.* Hillsdale, N.J.: Erlbaum.

Stauffer, R. (1969). *Reading as a Thinking Process.* New York: Harper & Row.

Tharp, R. G. (1982). The effective instruction of comprehension: Results and description of the Kamehameha Early Education Program. *Reading Research Quarterly, 17*(4), 503–527.

Vygotsky, L. S. (1978). *Mind in society: The development of higher psychological processes.* M. Cole et al. (Eds.). Cambridge, Mass.: Harvard University Press.

Vygotsky, L. S. (1981). The genesis of higher mental functions. In J. V. Wertsch (Ed.), *The concept of activity in Soviet psychology.* Armonk, N.Y.: Sharpe.

Watson, K. A. (1975). Transferable communicative routines: Strategies and group identity in two speech events. *Language in Society, 4*, 53–72.

5

What to Be Direct about in Direct Instruction in Reading: Content-Only versus Process-into-Content

Laura R. Roehler

Gerald G. Duffy

Michael S. Meloth

The classroom is a major context of literacy. It is in the classroom that the teacher provides instruction and, as research on teaching has repeatedly demonstrated in recent years, what the teacher does to directly instruct makes a difference in student reading achievement (Duffy, 1981; Good, 1983; Rosenshine, 1983; Brophy & Good, in press). However, there are differences regarding what to be direct about in direct instruction, especially when teaching low-aptitude students. Some reading educators emphasize the content of the selecton being read; others emphasize the process used to make sense of the content. This chapter examines the *content-only* versus *process-into-content* approaches to direct reading instruction. It uses

Work on this chapter was sponsored in part by the Institute for Research on Teaching, College of Education, Michigan State University. The Institute for Research on Teaching is funded primarily by the Program for Teaching and Instruction of the National Institute of Education, United States Department of Education. The opinions expressed in this publication do not necessarily reflect the position, policy, or endorsement of the National Institute of Education. (Contract No. 400-81-0014) descriptive data from three years of research of classroom reading instruction to characterize direct instruction of process-into-content and argues for greater attention to this emphasis when creating an instructional context for low-aptitude students.

BACKGROUND

In the broadest sense, reading educators do not disagree about the outcomes of reading instruction. We all want children to be good comprehenders; to construct the messages authors send in text. Similarly, in a broad sense, reading educators accept the research findings that teachers make a difference by being direct in providing reading instruction. Consequently, the recent literature of instructional research in reading focuses almost exclusively on direct techniques for developing comprehension (see, among others, Duffy, Roehler, & Mason, 1984; Anderson, Osborn, & Tierney, 1984; Purvis & Niles, 1984).

However, there are two positions regarding what to be direct about in developing comprehension outcomes. One view argues for developing comprehension primarily through direct instruction of the *content* of the message in the text; another argues for developing comprehension primarily through direct instruction of the *process* by which the content of text is understood. In the former, the assumption is that all children posses an intuitive understanding of how to make sense out of text and that if they are directed explicitly to the content they will unconsciously make use of this intuitive understanding of the language system (the content-only approach); the latter, in contrast, assumes that children, especially low-aptitude students, must be made conscious of the language system one uses to make sense out of text and must be shown how to consciously use this understanding when constructing messages from text (the process-into-content approach).

The Content-Only Emphasis

The content-only emphasis is reflected in traditional instructional techniques such as sustained silent reading and guided reading. Allington (1977) is a major proponent of *uninterrupted sustained silent reading* (USSR). He argues that one reason poor readers remain poor readers is the fact that they read less connected text than good readers. Although Allington's (1977) now classic question, "If they don't read much, how are they ever gonna get good?" is intuitively appealing, and his plea that teachers should give poor readers more time to read connected text is no doubt sound, his position nevertheless minimizes the reader's conscious use of strategies useful to the reading process. The implication seems to be that by engaging in sustained silent reading low-aptitude students will spontaneously come to understand the cognitive processes involved in figuring out how to get meaning from text and, hence, will become better readers.

The numerous variations on guided reading are based on a similar assumption. For instance, the *directed reading lesson* (DRL) used as a standard pattern in most basal reading textbooks focuses only on content as the teacher introduces the story; introduces the vocabulary words; sets a purpose for the reading; assigns silent or oral reading of either the entire selecton or of designated parts; and then asks questions of the students about the story. Guided reading techniques such as the *directed reading and thinking activity* (DRTA), reviewing techniques, semantic mapping, structured overviews, study guides, and study techniques such as Survey, Question, Read, Recite, and Review (SQ3R) also focus only on content. Nowhere does the teacher explicitly say anything about how reading works or how to get meaning from text. Because the task is to understand the selection and to answer questions about the selection, the focus is limited to content only. The apparent expectation is that, in the process of understanding the content, students will *infer* the existence of a language system and subconsciously use it to comprehend.

The content-only emphasis is also reflected in the reading educator's traditional preoccupation with questioning techniques (Raphael & Gavelek, 1984). For instance, Guzak (1967) recommends that teachers ask questions which call for higher-level thinking; Pearson (1983) calls for questions based on story grammars, Beck, Omanson, and McKeown (1982) call for asking questions based on a story map analysis; and Tharp (1982) calls for questioning based on the relationship between the text and the reader's experience. In all cases, the assumption seems to be that if the *teacher* explicitly understands the reading process and asks questions about the content of text based on this understanding *students* will naturally come to understand the system upon which the teacher based the questions.

The Process-Into-Content Emphasis

The proponents of a process-into-content emphasis, in contrast, argue for teaching students how the language system works and how to apply this knowledge when making sense out of text. For instance, Collins and Smith (1980) state:

> We do not argue that reading curricula should not stress interpretation. We argue only that a reading curricula should also try to teach how to construct intepretations. . . . If we do not teach these skills, then the better students will develop them on their own, and the worse readers will find reading very frustrating. (p. 28)

Roehler and Duffy (1984) take a similar position:

> our concept of direct explanation focuses on the skills that represent the processes used to comprehend. In contrast to researchers such as Beck (Beck, Omanson, & McKeown, 1982) and projects such as the Kamehameha Early Education Program (Tharp, 1982) in which the focus of instruction is on the interpretation of the story content, our emphasis is on the mental processing involved in comprehension skills and how competent readers do such processing in interpreting stories. (p. 266)

Note that neither advocates teaching process as isolated skills independent of comprehension. Rather, process is taught as a way to acquire understanding of text when engaged in sustained silent reading, guided reading, or any other reading activity. The instructional emphasis is on mental awareness of how to make sense of text and on the connection between this mental processing and the content of the text. Hence, neither is content nor are techniques such as USSR and DRLs abandoned; rather, content is the context in which process knowledge is applied.

This view of process is based on our growing understanding about the strategic behavior employed by good readers (Paris, Oka, & DeBritto, 1983; Paris, this volume). Research on metacognition (Brown, 1978; 1980; 1982; Brown & Campione, 1981; Brown, Campione & Day, 1981) has shown convincingly that as learners mature they acquire a wide variety of strategies for learning and remembering. When used extensively over time, these stategies take on the appearance of automatic unconscious processes (Brown, 1980) although at a subconscious level there remains an awareness of when and how to apply a particular strategy or set of strategies. Significant positive correlations have been found between the degree of metacognitive awareness and performance of complex problem-solving tasks (Brown, 1980; Brown & Smiley, 1978). Good readers proceed on "auto pilot" until a triggering event alerts them that their expectations of text are disrupted. They then consciously identify what is wrong and the steps that are required to eliminate the disruption. This is apparently similar to what happens in mathematics and problem solving where it has been found that children who display consistent patterns of incorrect calculations often do so because of an inaccurate conceptual understanding of the process governing mathematics (Resnick, 1981; Resnick & Ford, 1981). Such studies emphasize that strategic knowledge plays a role in mathematical problem solving as well as in reading, and that process knowledge needs to be activated in the form of the strategies (Greeno, 1978; Greeno, Magone, & Chaiklin, 1979).

Hence, the process-into-content emphasis is neither a call for back to basics in the tradition of skills monitoring systems nor the brand of direct instruction that emphasizes the automatized application of isolated decoding skills. Rather, it urges sharing with students (1) the knowledge of how the reading system works and (2) how they can consciously apply this knowledge in the stategic manner that distinguishes good readers from poor readers.

This emphasis is reflected in Raphael's (1984) research on *question and answer relationship* (QAR) in which conscious awareness of the kind of question being posed is used to predict how to answer questions about the content of specific text; in Hoffman's (1984) study of instruction in story structures as a means for teaching students to summarize first-grade stories; in Paris's (1984) use of metaphoric descriptions of reading process to improve the comprehension of content; and in our research of direct explanation of reading strategies to improve comprehension of content (Duffy et al., 1984). The goal is for students to monitor their comprehension, stop and analyze the situation when a blockage to meaning-getting occurs, activate their schema for how the language system works as a means for trouble-shooting the situation, apply an appropriatae strategy to remove the blockage, and then continue on with the act of constructing meaning from the text. The strategies themselves are not skills, algorithms, rules, or procedures to be memorized and applied automatically and inflexibly. Rather, strategies are flexible and adaptive plans for dealing with situations; they are consciously applied within a larger understanding of the sense-making function of reading.

Proponents of a process-into-content emphasis also take a different view of the role questions play in instruction. Rather than believing that good questions trigger in students an implicit understanding of process (even when there has been no explanation of the process), questioning is seen as part of the teacher's ongoing assessment effort that includes data collection about process as well as content. When teaching a new strategy, for instance, teachers ask content questions, but always follow-up with questions designed to assess how students got their answers, such as, "How did you figure that out?" or "How did you know that?" Such questions are important to ask, whether the student's answer to the content question is correct or not. If the answer is incorrect, the process question provides data about what the sudent needs to use the language process correctly; if the answer is correct, the process question provides data about whether the students used what Resnick (1981) has called *buggy algorithms* to figure out the answer. In short, getting the right answer is not all there is to comprehension; it also involves a schema for comprehension that the reader consciously applies as needed.

Current Views and Practices

Reluctance to include how the reading process works as part of the instruction of reading is pervasive among reading educators. There are two reasons for this. First, as Pearson (1984) states, some educators doubt whether process can be separated from content:

> Process factors . . . refer to how data are processed instead of what data are processed. To discuss them in a paragraph separate from content factors may seem to imply that I think they are separate from and independent of content factors. To the contrary, I know of no data base that would allow us to determine the independence of content (data) and process (control) factors. (p. 223)

Second, a process-into-content emphasis requires an analysis of how reading works and a sequential presentation of this analysis to students. It is this piece-by-piece sequence that many reading educators currently object to, primarily because they associate it with traditional skill instruction. Goodman (1984), for instance, says, "Learning to read involves getting the process together. That's harder if instuction takes it apart" (p. 112). Similarly, Tierney and Cunningham (1984) say:

> we are uneasy with the linear and mechanical approach to presenting reading to students. However the brain functions, the experience of reading has all the components of art and experience. To date our comprehension instruction has tended to emphasize the systematic, sequential, and piecemeal at the expense of the aesthetic, experiential, vicarious, and the wonder of reading. (p. 634)

Views such as these cause many reading educators to take what seems to be a contradictory position. On the one hand they argue persuasively for the existence of a language system that governs the meaning-getting process, but on the other they argue against directly sharing with students knowledge about how this system works. For instance, Harste and Mickulecky (1984) discuss the *sign complexes* which readers must use, Goodman (1984) specifies the various *cue systems* that must be learned, and Beach and Appleman (1984) describe the *text types* with which readers must be familiar. However, despite the apparent importance of such aspects of the language system, these same authors make no mention of sharing these sign complexes, cue systems, and text types with students. Instead, it is assumed that students will learn about them while reading. For instance, Harste and Mickulecky (1984) state that "any instance of reading allows language users the opportunity of learning reading" (p. 57) while Beach and Appleman (1984) suggest that students acquire knowledge of text types "from their reading and viewing experiences" and from "extensive reading of certain texts" (p. 140).

Understandably, the reading educator's emphasis on content-only is also reflected in practice. It is a content-only emphasis that Durkin (1984) finds in her studies of comprehension instruction, and it is a processes-into-content emphasis that Duffy and McIntyre (1982) failed to find in a study of primary-grade teachers. Teachers, following the lead of reading educators, move students through reading materials offering little direct assistance on how reading works or how to get meaning from text.

MacGinitie's work (1984) is particularly revealing in this regard. He points out that when students do not understand a text teachers talk about what the text is about (content-only), not about how to figure out what the text is about (process-into-content). He observes that "the more obvious or painful the student's lack of comprehension, the more likely that the teacher will explain the content rather than the text" (p. 145).

The Relevance to Low-Aptitude Students

The issue of content-only versus process-into-content is particularly relevant for the low-aptitude students who do not learn to read by reading. The fact that some students *do* learn to read by reading has been established, as has the fact that most of these students are high-aptitude students. Low-aptitude students, in contrast, have more difficulty learning to read.

Allington (1983) has attributed the difficulties of low-aptitude readers to differential instruction, arguing that high-aptitude readers become better readers because they get more opportunity to read connected text fluently than low-aptitude readers. However, from the standpoint of a content-only versus process-into-content perspective, low groups and high groups receive identical types of instruction. Whether teaching the low group or the high group, the teacher focuses on content-only, having students read the selection and asking for answers to questions about the selection and about various kinds of exercises that accompany the selection. Neither the high group nor the low group gets instruction on how to use knowledge of the language process to make sense of text. What Allington may be observing, then, is not differential instruction, but, rather, differential student and teacher responses to a situation. That is, some students (usually in the high group) catch on spontaneously to the teacher's questions and probes about content while other students (usually in the low group) do not. The teachers in the latter case then provide more structure so that the students will get the right answers.

Concern about whether low-aptitude students respond to content-only instruction is shared by several reading educators. For instance, Calfee (1981) says:

> Instruction that emphasizes examples and leaves it up to the student to discover the significant generalizations will work only for that small proportion of students who, by inclination or previous education, seem always to search for, and often come up with, deeper understanding. (p. 42)

Similarly, Farr (1984) makes the following analogy:

> A child learning to propel himself on a playground swing is likely to first be placed on the swing and pushed by a parent or friend. Even though the child is "engaged in" swinging, he has not learned to swing. Although he may be able to tell about swinging or describe feelings of swinging, he has not learned to swing. By observing how others pump themselves by pulling on the ropes and swinging their legs, he may learn to swing. But because some children may learn from observation and experience does not mean that all will. Others seem to need more direct teaching in the form of explanations, demonstration, and guided practice. Independent practice and testing may follow teaching, but they are not equivalent to teaching. So to argue that some children learn to comprehend by imitation and practice is to ignore the fact that many do not, or that they may learn to read faster or better with direct instruction. (p. 40)

Hence, the disagreement is strongest in a particular context—that of teaching low-aptitude children. Content-only proponents argue for wholistic instuction—teaching children how to read by emphasizing only the content of the textual message in the expecation that the process of how one figures out the message will develop naturally as the student reads. In contrast, process-into-content proponents argue that low-aptitude students need (1) to be made aware of how readers use knowledge of the language system to make sense out text and (2) guidance in consciously and intentionally applying this knowledge to the content in the text. Direct instruction, therefore, is not only direct about the content of the selection but also direct about how the language system can be used to interpret that content.

DESCRIPTIVE CHARACTERISTICS OF PROCESS-INTO-CONTENT INSTRUCTION

What does direct instruction in reading look like when the teacher is being direct about process? To answer this question we provide here excerpts from lesson transcripts collected as part of an experimental study of teacher explanation during reading instruction (Duffy et al., 1983; Duffy et al., 1984). The study was guided by two concepts. The first was the content-only and process-into-content distinction articulated above. The second was a view of instruction that focuses on the role of social mediation in the acquisition of knowledge (Vygotsky, 1978; Feuerstein, 1980; Wertsch, 1978; Laboratory for Comparative Human Cognition, 1982; Gavelek, this volume; Rogoff, this volume). Such research argues that the internalization of all higher psychological processes are socially mediated; internalization begins with a mediator (parent, teacher, tutor) who provides guidance in situations new to the learner; and this guidance is gradually withdrawn as learners assume more control over their problem solving. This organization of instruction from other- to self-regulated learning occurs within an individual's zone of proximal development (ZPD), that instructional level where the learner cannot do the mental function independently but can profit from the assistance of a mediator. Feuerstien (1980) and Campione, Brown, and Ferrara (1982) note that inadequate mediated learning is a possible explanation for poor academic performance of low-aptitude learners, suggesting that the teacher's mediational role may be crucial. Consequently, we study the teachers mediational role when explaining process-into-content. The following seven characteristics describe this role: outcome emphasis, process as a means to a goal, transferring process to content, emphasizing the mental process, making visible the invisible mental process, allowing students to verbalize the mental process, and maintaining a process focus.

Outcome Emphasis

The intent of all reading instruction is that students make sense out of text. However, when the focus is content it is the *only* outcome; when the focus is process-into-content an intermediate outcome is whether students are aware of how to use process knowledge to make sense of text. In our study, student interviews following instruction about strategies are used to determine whether this intermediate outcome is being achieved. The following fifth-grade student is typical of those who possess such awareness:

I: What were you learning in that lesson I just watched?
S: Well, we had to divide different words up into syllables to figure out the meaning.
I: Why do you think that is important to learn?
S: Well, if we are ever reading a book, like right now when I am reading a book and I find a big word, I usually skip it. She doesn't want us to do that, she wants us to figure it out.
I: Okay, so why does your teacher think it is important?
S: So you get the meaning; it is an important word.
I: Maybe the word that you skip might be important so you need to know what it is?
S: Yes.
I: Okay, Well, now, tell me, how is it that you go about figuring out the word.
S: Well, first we divide it up into syllables, either the VCCV rules—vowel, consonant, consonant, vowel—or we figure them out by the—okay, like if there is a vowel, a

consonant, and then a vowel, if you put the line between the first vowel and the consonant, then the first vowel would be long. If you put it after the consonant and before the second consonant, then the first vowel is short. So you figure it out that way.

The following fifth grader demonstrated less awareness following a lesson on prefixes and suffixes.

I: Why do you think your teacher taught you about prefixes and suffixes?
S: Because when we get in junior high and other grades we have to know all this stuff to pass.
I: Why do you have to know it?
S: In order to pass, you have to know your division, your times, your prefixes, your suffixes, your base words, your pluses and take aways.
I: All that stuff, huh? Well, when would you use your prefixes and suffixes and base words?
S: You would use the base word on a word. She teaches compounds too.
I: Compounds, too?
S: Yes, they are two words put together to make one word.
I: Now, let me see here. Now, if you were reading, how would you get a chance to use what you learned today? If you were in a book, for example. When would you get a chance to use prefixes, suffixes, and base words in a book.
S: In a book?
I: Yes.
S: Well, you wouldn't use them in a book. But you would when she says to you, "Write a word and write the prefix and a suffix and a base word." And you would make an arrow, like right here is a compound word.
I: Right.
S: Then you make an arrow, that's the prefix, that's the suffix, and that's the base, Well, like in *mailbox*. In the middle you put the base word. And out here on the side of the word you put the suffix and then like that you put the prefix.

The conscious awareness illustrated in the first student's interview response is characteristic of process-into-content instruction. Students taught by a content-only orientation are less aware of how the reading system works and often respond to process questions in a manner similar to the second student.

Process as a Means to a Goal

When teachers emphasize process-into-content, their teacher talk includes statements about where the strategy will be used in text; they emphasize that the strategy is the means and that gaining additional content knowledge is the goal. Note how the following teacher achieved this when teaching fifth graders what to do if their meaning getting was blocked by unknown words in text that they could not decode. First, the teacher specified four ways to figure out unknown words in text and that it was important to be able to use these strategies when needed. She then said:

All right, I'm going to ask you to pretend that you have just picked up a book in the library and sometimes you will find some words in there that will not make any sense at all. There are some ways that you can figure out new words without having the teacher around, and I'd like to share with you some of those ways that I have used over the years.

She returned to the use of the strategies again later in the lesson:

T: Would it just be used for reading in class?
S: No (in unison).
T: Where?
S: English.
T: Anything. It would help you in reading newspapers, magazines, comic books, anything that you have.

The teacher completed the lesson by having the students state where they would use what they learned:

T: Why did I do this today? Why did I show you how to use these four strategies?
S: When you're by yourself, you can figure it out.
T: What could you be doing when you need these four strategies?
S: When you're alone—in the library or something. When you read a book and you get a word you don't know.

Content-only teachers rarely discuss strategies, and when they do they tend to treat them as skills to be learned as ends in themselves.

Transferring Process to Content

Process-into-content teachers have students consciously use process knowledge when reading selections such as those typically found in a directed reading lesson or sustained silent reading. In the following excerpt, the teacher taught a lesson on how to use context clues to remove word-meaning blockages encountered while reading. She followed the lesson immediately with a social studies assignment where the students were directed to read a selection from their text while using their newly learned strategy. After setting the content purposes for the reading and developing background knowledge needed to understand the author's intent, she directed them to the words in dark print (those words whose meanings the authors had decided were unknown):

T: Open your books to page 75. Alicia, find the word *tornado* on the bottom of the page. It is in dark print. Authors of this book do that when they think you may not know the meaning of the word. Read the sentence aloud for me.
S: (*Reads sentence*)
T: We can use the context strategy we just learned to help us understand the meaning of this word. Who can tell us what *tornado* means and how you arrived at the answer?
S: (*Gives definition and explains how he got the answer*)

The teacher then had the students read the selection, discussing with them the content about tornadoes and weather in the midwest and providing opportunities for students to consciously use the context strategy as they encountered other word-meaning problems that caused blockages in their meaning getting.

Emphasizing the Mental Process

Process-into-content instruction is characterized by an emphasis on the thinking one must do in order to make sense out of text. Consider the following excerpts. In the first, a teacher is teaching how to use context clues to determine the meaning of an unknown word. Note the focus on the mental process involved in using the strategy:

> I don't know what *upbraided* means. I have to figure it out. What do I do first? I look for clues. Are there any clues that might tell me what that means? I look at the words around it and then. . . .

After carefully directing students through this example, the teacher continued to emphasize the mental process when interacting with students:

T: You are reading and you come to that sentence. How are you going to figure out that word? Matt, what would you do first?
S: I would look through the context. I see *rage* (inaudible).
T: Yes. *Did not come* is a clue. When Jerry didn't come, whatever it was he caused, it was caused because he didn't come. Now you are thinking about what you know when people don't come and people getting in rages. What do you suppose that means he was?
S: He was angry or mad at the person.
T: So, do you have a one-word synonym that you could put there?
S: *Mad.*
T: How do you check to see if that makes sense?
S: When he didn't come, Jerry was so mad that he left in a rage.
T: Does that sound reasonable? Yes. Let's try the next one.

In contrast, the mental processing is ignored and answer accuracy is emphasized in the following lesson on main idea taught by a content-only teacher:

T: All right, now here are some possibilities [for a short title]: "A Trip Downtown," "The New Shirt," "The Shirt That Didn't Fit." Let me read them again: "A Trip Downtown," "The New Shirt," "The Shirt That Didn't Fit." Now, of those three possibilities, which one would go best? Annie?
S: "A Trip Downtown."
S: "A Trip Downtown."
T: Okay, Tim, what do you think?
S: "The New Shirt."
T: Don, what was your choice?
S: "The New Shirt."

T: I think the girls decided on "The Trip Downtown," and the boys liked "The New Shirt." Mainly, what was the story about?
S: A trip downtown.
S: Getting a new shirt.
T: Getting a new shirt, wasn't it?

Making Visible the Invisible Mental Process

Process-into-content teachers talk out loud to help students visualize the invisible mental process. For instance, note how this teacher made visible the invisible mental processing she employs when using the pronunciation key of a glossary:

Let me show you how that's done. For instance, I'm reading a story and a sentence says, "The man sent the student to the unemployment *agency*." I see this word *agency* and I cannot pronounce it. So I'm going to take my glossary and I'm going to turn to page 368 where I see that word. First, I see the word written, then I see it rewritten in parenthesis. I see *a* then I have *j* with an upside-down *e* and *n* and then *see*. I put the sounds together like this: *a-jen-see*. I have *agency*.

In contrast, the following teacher does little to make visible for students the mental processing involved in determining whether two words are synonyms or antonyms:

T: The first two were done for you. Let's see if we can go over these today and figure out what the word means. All right. Let's do the first two, just for practice. All right, the first one there is *buffalo* and *ox*, and those two words mean what? The same or almost the same, so they are synonyms. All right, the next one there?
S: Antonyms.
T: *Patiently* and *impatiently*, and, of course, you can look at those words and automatically tell that they are . . .
S: Antonyms.
T: Antonyms because they mean?
S: Opposite.

Allowing Students to Verbalize the Mental Process

Another characteristic of process-into-content teachers is that they encourage students to verbalize how they make sense of text. For instance, while teaching a lesson on context clues the following teacher encouraged a student to verbalize the mental process when, in response to his answer, she said the following:

T: Are you saying that *divulge* means *mention*? Oh, you jumped ahead to the end. You went through all the clues in your head and you are saying that this means *mention*. How did you know that? How did you figure out that it is *mention*?

Content-only teachers, in contrast, do not have students verbalize the mental process used to make sense of text. For instance, the following teacher focused on content, not on the process used to get meaning:

T: Number 5, Annie.

S: (*Student reads sentence*)

T: Very good. Tell me what you know about the sentence, Annie.

S: (Inaudible)

T: Tell me. Look at the sentence and tell me what they are talking about in the sentence. They are talking about something . . .

S: The club.

T: What kind of a club is it?

S: Secret.

T: A secret club. And they also have something else that is secret. What is that?

S: Password.

T: A password. So if you *divulge* the name of the secret club, you might as well tell the name of our secret password as well. So they are talking about something secret, and if it is secret, what don't you do?

S: Tell.

T: You don't tell. So would *divulge* mean (A) *ask*, (B) *tell*, or (C) *forget?*

S: B.

Maintaining a Process Focus

Process-into-content teachers are characterized by an ability to relate a particular aspect of process to a particular content, focus on that particular process, and then apply the process element to the content specified at the outset. However, this is sometimes difficult to do. Note, for instance, the difficulty this fifth-grade teacher has maintaining a focus on how to determine the main idea while using a text about bears hibernating:

T: Let's talk about animals that hibernate. Okay, you know what *hibernate* means, right? What does *hibernate* mean?

S: (Inaudible)

T: Okay, animals that sleep through the winter, right? Now, what are some animals that might hibernate?

S: A bear.

T: Okay, bear.

S: Rabbit.

T: Rabbit.

S: Fox.

T: I'm not sure about all the animals. Squirrels, okay, But don't you see squirrels in the winter?

S: Yeah.

S: Yeah.

T: Then are they hibernating?

S: No.

S: Yeah.

T: Maybe they do. I don't know. Maybe that is something that I should check out, too.

At this point ther teacher realizes that she is not teaching students how to figure out the main idea; she is focusing on the story content about animals that hibernate. She tries to shift the focus back to the main-idea strategy by generating the following nonexample:

T: Okay, let's say we were talking about those animals that hibernate and I said, "Oh, many, many animals sleep through the winter. Some of the animals are bears. Bears hibernate in cages." And I talk about bears, but then all of a sudden I say, "Fish swim in the sea."
S: How do fish hibernate in the cold water?
T: I didn't say they hibernate. I said, "Fish swim in the sea," "Birds fly south." Is that about animals that hibernate?
S: No.
S: Yeah.
T: No. So, would this be included in my paragraph?
S: No.
T: No. So, what is a main idea? A main idea is a group of sentences that do what?
S: Hibernate.

The moral of this story is, of course, that students learn what teachers emphasize. If teachers emphasize process and how to use it to make sense out of textual content, that is what students learn; if they emphasize the story content, that is what students learn. To be sucessful as a process-into-content teacher, the focus on process must be maintained from the introduction of the content to which it will be applied through the transfer to this content when the strategy is actually used.

Summary

Content-only instruction is characterized by a focus on the story content. Typically, teachers asks questions about the content, students answer those questions, and teachers provide corrective feedback regarding the accuracy of the answer. In process-into-content instruction, in contrast, the focus is on helping students consciously employ knowledge of the language system to make sense out of the content in texts. As illustrated above, it emphasizes student metacognitive awareness of their schema for how reading works and the application of this knowledge to the task of making sense out of text.

CONCLUSION

The classroom and the instruction provided in classroom are crucial contexts of literacy, especially for the low-aptitude group. The question posed here is whether low-aptitude students learn to read efficiently when the instructional emphasis is limited to content.

Tierney and Cunningham (1984) oppose the process-into-content emphasis we espouse:

Teaching children our theories about how they think in order to get them to think better seems to us to be fraught with danger. It is true that we should be concerned with process, but to the extent that comprehension is like gardening, we must be more interested in the vegetables produced than the tools in the shed. (p. 634)

They and other reading educators argue for giving students real gardens and real books where they can grow real vegetables and get content knowledge without consciously understanding how to use the accumulate knowledge of how agriculture works. However, we suspect that low-aptitude students must be taught how to use the tools of reading because waiting for them to be learned naturally often means that there is no harvest of textual content. We argue for sharing with students what we know about the tools of reading in the belief that low-aptitude students require more explicit explanations of how to use language tools (the process) to achieve the aesthetic and functional rewards of reading (the content). Further, we argue that the important question about direct instruction is whether we should be direct about the content of the selections only or about the connection between the processes of reading and how these are used to make sense of textual content. Finally, we argue that if the reading performance of low-aptitude students is to be improved, teacher educators must arm prospective teachers with the professional knowledge needed to make pedagogical decisions about how to apply process knowledge to content rather than leading prospective teachers to believe that universal literacy is acquired by a content-only emphasis.

REFERENCES

Allington, R. (1977). If they don't read much, how they ever gonna get good? *Journal of Reading, 21,* 57– 61.

Allington, R. (1983). The reading instruction provided readers of differing ability. *Elementary School Journal, 88,* 255-265.

Anderson, R., Osborn, J., & Tierney, R. (Eds.). (1984). *Learning to read in American schools: Basal readers and content texts.* Hillsdale, N.J.: Erlbaum.

Beach, R. & Appleman, D. (1984). Reading strategies for expository and literary text types. In A. Purves & O. Niles (Eds.), *Becoming readers in a complex society.* Eighty-third yearbook of the National Society for the Study of Education (Part I, p. 115-143). Chicago: University of Chicago Press.

Beck, I., Omanson, R., & McKeown, M. (1982). An instructional redesign of reading lessons: Effects on comprehension. *Reading Research Quarterly, 17*(4), 462-481.

Brophy, J., & Good, T. (in press). Teacher behavior and student achievement. *Third Handbook of Research in Teaching.* New York: Rand McNally.

Brown, A. L. (1978). Knowing when, where and how to remember: A problem of metacognition. In R. Glaser (Ed.), *Advances in instructional psychology* (Vol. 1, pp. 77–165). Hillsdale, N.J.: Erlbaum.

Brown, A. L. (1980). Metacognitive development in reading. In R. Spiro, B. Bruce & W. Brener (Eds.), *Theoretical issues in reading comprehension* (pp. 453-481). Hillsdale, N.J.: Erlbaum.

Brown, A. L. (1982). Learning and development: The problems of compatibility, access, and induction. *Human Development, 25,* 89– 115.

Brown, A. L., & Campione, J. C. (1981). Inducing flexible thinking: A problem of access. In M. Friedman, J. P. Das, & N. O'Connor (Eds.), *Intelligence and learning* (pp. 515-529). N.Y.: Plenum.

Brown, A. L., Campione, J. C., & Day, J. (1981). Learning to learn: On training students to learn from texts. *Educational Research, 10*(2), 14-211.

Brown, A. L., & Smiley, S. S. (1978). The development of strategies for studying texts. *Child Development, 49*, 1076-1088.

Calfee, R. B. (1981). Cognitive psychology and conceptual practice. In D. C. Berliner (Ed.), *Review of research on causation* (Vol. 9 pp. 3-13). Washington, D. C.: American Educational Research Association.

Campione, S. C., Brown, A. L., & Ferrara, R. A. (1982). Mental retardation and intelligence. Research on exceptional children: Implications for theories of intelligence. In R. J. Sternberg (Eds.), *Handbook of human intelligence* (pp. 392-490). Boston: Cambridge University Press.

Collins, A., & Smith, E. (1980). *Teaching the process of reading comprehension.* Tech. Report No. 182. Urbana, Ill.: Center for the Study of Reading, University of Illinois.

Duffy, G. (1981). Theory to practice: How it works in real classrooms. Research Series No. 98. East Lansing: Institute for Research on Teaching, Michigan State University.

Duffy, G., & McIntyre, L. (1982). A naturalistic study of instructional assistance in primary grade reading. *Elementary School Journal, 83*(1), 15-23.

Duffy, G. G. et al. (1983). *Instructional characteristics which promote strategic awareness in reading.* Paper presented at the annual meeting of the National Reading Conference, Austin, Tex.

Duffy, G., Roehler, L., & Mason, J. (Eds.). (1984). *Comprehension instruction: Perspectives and suggestions.* New York: Longman.

Duffy, G. et al. (1984). *A study of the relationship between direct teacher explanation of reading strategies and student awareness and achievement outcomes.* Paper presented at the annual meeting of the American Educational Research Association, New Orleans.

Durkin, D. (1984). Is there a match between what elementary teachers do and what basal manuals recommend? *The Reading Teacher, 37*(3), 734-745.

Farr, R. (1984). Reaction to "Do basal manuals teach reading comprehension?" In R. Anderson, J. Osborn, & R. Tierney (Eds.), *Learning to read in American schools* (pp. 39-44). Hillsdale, N.J.: Erlbaum.

Feuerstein, R. (1980). *Instrumental enrichment: An intervention program for cognitive modifiability.* Baltimore, Md.: University Park Press.

Good, T. (1983). Research on classroom teaching. In L. Shulman, & G. Sykes (Eds.), *Handbook of teaching and policy* (pp. 42-80). N.Y.: Longman.

Goodman, K. (1984). Unity in reading. In A. Purves, & O. Niles, (Eds.), *Becoming readers in a complex society* (Part I, pp. 79- 114). Eighty-third yearbook of the National Society for the Study of Education. Chicago: University of Chicago Press.

Greeno, J. G. (1978). Understanding procedural knowledge in mathematics instruction. *Educational Psychologist, 12*, 262-283.

Greeno, J. G., Magone, M. E. & Chaiklin, S. (1979). Theory of construction and set in problem solving. *Memory and cognition, 7*, (6), 445-461.

Guzak, F. J. (1967). Teacher questioning and reading. *The Reading Teacher, 21*, 222-234.

Harste, J., & Mickulecky, L. (1984). The content of literacy in our society. In A. Purves, & O. Niles, (Eds.), *Becoming readers in a complex society.* (Part I, pp. 47-78). Eighty-third yearbook of the National Society for the Study of Education. Chicago: University of Chicago Press.

Hoffman, J. (1984). *Personal communication*. University of Texas, Austin, Tex.

Laboratory for Compartive Human Cognition. (1982). Culture and intelligence. In R. S. Sternberg (Ed.), *Handbook of human intelligence*. Cambridge, Mass.: Harvard University Press.

MacGinitie, W. (1984). Readability as a solution adds to the problem. In R. Anderson, J. Osborn, & Tierney, R. (Eds.), *Learning to read in American schools* (pp., 141-152). Hillsdale, N.J.: Erlbaum.

Paris, S. (1984). *Improving children's metacogition and reading comprehension with classroom instruction*. Paper presented at the annual conference of the American Educational Research Association, New Orleans.

Paris, S., Oka, E., & DeBritto, A. (1983). Beyond decoding: Synthesis of research in reading comprehension. *Educational Leadership, 41,* 78-83.

Pearson, P. D. (1983). *Asking questions about stories*. Ginn Curriculum Series. Boston: Ginn.

Pearson, P. D. (1983). Direct explicit teaching of reading comprehension. In G. Duffy, L. Roehler & J. Mason (Eds.), *Comprehension instruction: Perspectives and suggestions* (pp. 222- 233). N.Y.: Longman.

Purvis, A., & Niles, O. (Eds.). (1984). *Becoming readers in a complex society* (Part I) Eighty-third yearbook of the National Society for the Study of Education. Chicago: University of Chicago Press.

Raphael, T. (1984). Teaching learners about sources of information for answering comprehension questions. *Journal of Reading, 27*(4), 303-311.

Raphael, T., & Gavelek, J. (1984). Question-related activities and their relationship to reading comprehension: Some instructional implication. In G. Duffy, L. Roehler, & J. Mason (Eds.), *Comprehension instruction: Perspective and suggestions* (pp. 234-250). N.Y.: Longman.

Resnick, L. (1981). Instructional psychology. In M. R. Rosenzweig & L. W. Porter (Eds.), *Annual review of psychology*. Palo Alto, Calif.: Annual Review.

Resnick, L. B., & Ford, W. W. (1981). The psychology of mathematics instruction. Hillsdale, N.J.: Erlbaum.

Roehler, L., & Duffy, G. (1984). Direct explanation of comprehension process. In G. Duffy, L. Roehler & J. Mason (Eds.), *Comprehension instuction: Perspectives and suggestions* (pp. 265- 280). N.Y.: Longman.

Rosenshine, B. (1983). Teaching functions in instructional programs. *Elementary School Journal, 83*(4), 335-352.

Tharp, R. (1982). The effective instruction of comprehension: Results and description of the Kamahameha early education program. *Reading Research Quarterly, 17*(4), 462-481.

Tierney, R., & Cunningham, J. (1984). Research on teaching reading comprehension. In P. D. Pearson (Ed.), *Handbook of reading research* (pp. 609-656). N.Y.: Longman.

Vygotsky, L. S. (1978). *Mind in society: The development of higher psychological processes*. M. Cole et al. (Ed. and Trans.). Cambridge, Mass.: Harvard University Press.

Wertsch, J. W. (1978). Adult-child interaction and the roots of metacognition. *Quarterly Newsletter of the Institute for Comparative Human Development, 1,* 15-18.

6

What Kindergarten Children Know about Reading

Jana Mason

Janice Stewart

David Dunning

INTRODUCTION

In the last six years we have seen a new focus on early literacy and kindergarten reading instruction. At this point the research is primarily descriptive. There are case studies of individual children (Bissex, 1980; Taylor, 1983; Dyson, 1984; Soderbergh, 1977; Sulzby, 1983). There are studies on what preschool children know about how to read and what their strategies are for trying to read (Clay, 1979; Ehri, 1979; Ferreiro & Teberosky, 1982; Hiebert, 1981; Mason, 1977, 1980; Mason, McCormick, & Bhavnagri, in press; McCormick & Mason, 1984; Teale & Sulzby, in press; Yaden & Templeton, in press). With observations that show how children begin learning to read at home we are ready to measure their knowledge about reading at school and to study their perceptions about how they are learning to read.

This chapter is organized around two aspects of kindergarten reading: children's ability to read and spell three- and four-letter words and their approaches to identifying words and comprehending stories. The set of tasks and interview questions provide a window into kindergarten children's understanding of reading.

In 1974 we directed a preschool program for 40 children and, with the help of the preschool teachers, developed an experimental early-reading program. Reading materials were constructed for the classroom, the children were observed in the playrooms, their parents filled out a questionnaire at the beginning and end of the school year, and we tried using alternative techniques for measuring their progress (Mason, 1977; 1980). Those experiencs helped us realize that young children begin learning about how to read at a much earlier age than was described in the literature. One reason for the apparent inconsistency is that traditional reading readiness tasks did not adequately capture what young children knew about print.

EARLY READING TEST APPROACH

In our attempt to use readiness tasks that would reveal what children know about print, a number of tasks were developed and tried out with average-ability kindergarten children (Mason & McCormick, 1979; McCormick & Mason, 1981). Our testing approach has the following features: individual administration of test items; probes of children's knowledge about letters, words, and story reading; examination of changes in children's word and story recognition strategies; and analyses of children's awareness of the reading process.

Individual Administration

Individually administered production tasks are used because children understand them better than activities that involve selecting from alternative choices and also because production tasks elicit more interpretable responses. We ask children to name letters or words, write and spell, read a book, and talk about their reading. Individually adminstered tasks enable the researcher, teacher, or observer to record both verbal and nonverbal responses, adding clues about the child's thinking and attitude towards tasks.

Probing Children's Knowledge of Reading

We select items that vary in difficulty and probe children's knowledge with the variety of items. We arrange items so that the easier ones are presented first, thus the harder ones can be omitted if there is a high error rate. For example, we ask children to name upper-case letters before lower-case letters. We check them on consonant-vowel-consonant (CVC) words before trying words with harder patterns (CVCe, CVCC, CVVC).

We test children's ability to identify words that their parents say they are learning to read and words that their teachers have taught them to read. For test development purposes we used words that we had taught during a testing session and words that we had taught them to read in a story. From scoring their answers and studying their errors, we have gained the following insights into how to test young children's word knowledge:

1. A test of early word reading needs to include the kinds of words that preschool children try to read. High-frequency (book) words (e.g., words from the Dolch list or from a basal reader primer) and common words that appear on signs and labels (traffic signs, food and beverage labels) are appropriate. Both are important because children typically identify words from signs and labels during their fouth and fifth years. As the kindergarten year progresses, many begin to read one-syllable, common (book) words.

2. Words can be taught and measured before children know how to read. We obtained the following effects: (1) children learned more words when they matched them with their pictures than when they matched the words to their initial letter; (2) words we had teachers teach in September by associating them with their meaning were better recognized one and five months later than were words teachers taught by spelling and sounding out; and (3) a letter-sound rule could be used to try to read new words if children had first learned words in a story that fit the rule (Suber & Mason, 1977).

3. Early-reading tasks can measure the extent to which preschool children are constructing appropriate letter-sound rules for recognizing words. We found that they typically figure out consonant sounds before vowels, and short-vowel patterns before other vowel patterns. We also obtained high intercorrelations among spelling, reading pseudowords, and reading achievement (Mason & McCormick, 1979). Asking children to read pseudowords that contain varying patterns (CVC, CVCe, CVVC) and asking children to spell similarly patterned words test acquisition of general letter-sound principles.

4. When we gave words in a story or sentence, we were not sure whether children were guessing by using picture-context cues or were actually reading. So, our first version of the Early Reading Test (ERT) was limited to letter naming, spelling, and reading lists of words, measuring, principally, children's knowledge of the form of print. We have since developed simple-to-read caption books as testing materials. Some of the results in this chapter describe our first attempts to expand the ERT in this way.

5. It is assumed that an important aspect of reading comprehension is the development of metacognitive strategies for recognizing and interpreting text information. This is described here with interview questions to children about their awareness of inconsistencies we placed in a story, their ability to describe how they are learning to read, and their explanation of how they figure out printed information.

Probing Changes in Children's Strategies

Test items are selected with the intention that errors would occur and could then be analyzed. Examination of systematic errors divulges the strategies that children use for recognizing and remembering words and for figuring out words in stories. These patterns help to determine what children understand about how written language is structured. For example, we ask them to spell and read similar words to learn whether they use the same strategies with both tasks. We give sign words, real words, and pseudowords in order to see whether they are willing or able to apply their strategies to words they have never seen before. We ask them to read in and out of context and with misleading context to see what strategies they try to employ.

Children's approaches to identifying words, for example, can be analyzed through the kinds of word recognition and spelling errors they make. Following analyses by Read (1971) of spelling errors and Mason (1976) of word-reading errors, we collect both spelling and word-reading errors to uncover a developmental progression in word recognition that is relatively unaffected by instruction. Children use similar strategies to read and to spell isolated words, but over time changes in their approaches to the two tasks indicate their progress.

Awareness of the Reading Process

We ask children questions about how they are learing to read, how they figure out particular words, and what part of the text they were using to read. For example, after trying to read a printed label, whether or not they are correct, they are asked how they knew what it said or how they figured it out. We ask them how they might teach a younger child to read and have them draw pictures that describe what younger children need to do to learn to read. In these ways the children explain what and who they think helped them learn to read and how they approach and remember printed information.

USING THE ERT TO STUDY
TWO KINDERGARTEN PROGRAMS

Although there are predictable developmental changes in children's knowledge about how to recognize words (Ferreiro & Teberosky, 1982), spell (Ehri, 1984; Hiebert, 1984), and write (Sulzby, 1983), we are just beginning to interpret this development in conjunction with home experiences in reading (Taylor, 1983; Heath, 1983; Bissex, 1980) and preschool reading experiences (Mason, 1980; Mason, McCormick, & Bhavnagri, in press). The following investigation concerns learning to read in kindergarten.

Method

Tracing children's knowledge about the form of print and their comprehension strategies has been initiated with a study of children who attended kindergarten in the 1983–1984 school year in either a rural or a city school. We worked with a total of 140 students from four classrooms, two in each school. Some of our tests were given to all the children in the two schools, whereas other tests were administered to smaller groups. For the interview tasks, 9 to 11 children were selected from each classroom. For observation of home behavior during the summer following kindergarten, four children were studied.

Pine School, in a rural area, used a commercial letter-identification program followed by a basal program with teacher-directed, whole-group instruction of letters and letter-sounds. During the last two months, instruction was given to small ability-level groups, where ability was determined by performance in the letter program. The children were usually expected to work silently at their table after receiving instruction or directions for independent work.

Water School, in an urban setting, used an individualized reading approach. The teachers worked with children one at a time listening to them read simple books usually chosen by the teacher. They were encouraged to read to themselves and to each other. Because it was a whole-language approach to reading, letter and phonics instruction was occasionally provided, but was secondary to book and language experience story reading.

Pine School's commercial alphabet program was Alpha Time, followed by Macmillian basal readers. All children were also given Houghton Mifflin's reading readiness book. All the children completed Alpha Time and the readiness book. However, only the higher two groups read stories from the basal. The middle groups completed both preprimers and the high groups completed preprimers and the primer. The lowest groups were given more letter and phonics work in place of the preprimers.

In this school there were few breaks for free play, story reading, art, or music, and there were no field trips. The classes were half-day, with identical programs for morning and afternoon groups. Reading was taught principally within the confines of the first hour and a half of instruction. Teachers shifted activities frequently so that most of the children usually appeared to be on task. Children began learning through whole-class sessions with oral drill and practice, written multiple choice, and copying exercises, followed by reading group participation and worksheets at their tables. Stories were made available for children to hear about three times a week. These were usually read-along books or books brought in by the children.

Children attending Water School read from books published by Modern Curriculum Press (each book contained one story of 6 to 12 pages in length), prereading skills books from Economy, and Houghton Mifflin's reading readiness books. All of the children used the Economy and Houghton Mifflin materials. In addition to the language experience stories, about one-third of the children read 10 to 15 of the Curriculum Press books, one-third read 20, and one-third read 40 or more books. The teachers also read stories to them nearly every day.

Water School had a flexible schedule that encompassed reading, math, and a free play, which took the first two to three hours of the day. Many school days were frequently interrupted by field trips, assemblies, and other special events.

Instruction was often conducted by asking children to read to the teacher individually. In the meantime the other children read to themselves or to another child, did other work, or played. As the reading instruction began each day, children were observed playing, reading alone or with a friend, or talking to friends. However, after about 10 minutes all the children were usually involved in math activities or were reading in books that the teacher or child had selected. Lan-

Table 6.1 **Percentage Correct Scores on ERT Subtests**

	Pine School			Water School		
	Fall	Spring	Gain	Fall	Spring	Gain
Labels in context	71	82	11	70	86	16
Labels out of context	20	45	25	26	53	27
Spelling	6	54	48	42	69	27
Pseudowords	3	43	40	38	77	39
Common words	1	28	27	17	48	31

Table 6.2 **Case Study Children's Responses on the Spelling Task in September and May**

	Word to Spell					
	PAT	TIP	TAPE	KITE	SACK	SICK
	September					
Joseph	a	a	a	a	a	a
Donna	ET	AP	b	b	b	b
Sani	CSTP	TEPC	TPCA	ITC	KAES	SKC
Erica	PIC	EKE	TIPCSE	TACKE	TCE	KESIA
	May					
Joseph	PAT	TEP	TAP	KIT	SAK	SEK
Donna	PAT	TIP	TAP	KIT	SAK	SEK
Sani	PATEK	TPE	TAP	KTI	SKA	CKE
Erica	PAT	TIP	TAPE	KITE	SAC	SIC

[a]Rearranged letters
[b]No attempt

Table 6.3 **Case Study Children's May Responses on the Sign and Label Task, Showing Percentage Correct and Examples of Errors**

	Percentage Correct	Words	Child's Response
Joseph	50	crayons	call
		coca cola	door
		baby powder	chocolate milk
Donna	90	crayons	coke
Sani	30	EXIT	mix
Erica	80	baby powder	baby porridge
		Nestle's Quick	quick

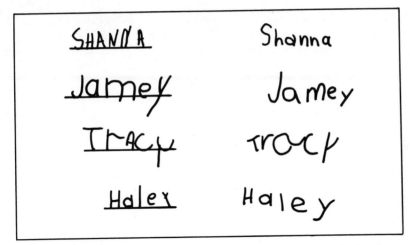

Figure 6.1 **Examples of Children's First Name at the Beginning (September) and the End (May) of Kindergarten**

guage experience charts were used almost daily with children sitting in one group on the rug. After an activity such as planting seeds the children and teacher would compose a story and then read it together several times. As new stories were written the children learned to read them, yet could continue reading the old stories that hung on the classroom walls. While reading the children were also asked to pick out words or talk about sounds, letters, and meanings. Questions were encouraged and the children were expected not only to listen but to participate. Show and tell, with the teacher extending the children's knowledge through demonstrations and questions, was an integral part of the daily program.

Results

This study compares the kindergarten children in the two schools (the means for form of print tasks are in Table 6.1) and describes four of the children in more detail. Two of the children (Joseph and Donna) attended Pine School and the other two (Sani and Erica) attended Water School. We discuss the following tasks and interviews: letter naming and printing; spelling CVC, CVCe, and CVCC words; reading sign and label words; reading CVC pseudowords; reading common three-letter words; reading predictable and unpredictable labels; story reading; telling stories; and awareness of how to read.

Upper-Case Letter Naming and Printing Most of the children entered kindergarten knowing how to name upper-case letters and to print part of their names, although most used only capital letters, and only a few used upper- and lower-case letters appropriately. Figure 6.1 provides examples of children printing their first names at the beginning and the end of kindergarten. Note that at year's end fewer uppercase letters are formed and reversed letters are omitted.

Spelling A large number of entering kindergarten children could not use letters to spell words (84 percent in Pine, and 28 percent in Water School scored zero in the fall). At the end of the year, only 4 percent to 6 percent of the children received a score of zero. Children in both schools had made large gains in spelling. Table 6.2 indicates the spelling changes of the four children in our case studies. Notice the letterlike quality of September responses and that Erica shows a partial understanding of the task; she correctly chose two initial letters. At the end of the year the children are appropriately using most of the consonants in the words.

Reading Sign and Label Words Children in both schools were similarly able to name the sign and label pictures, particularly *STOP* and *EXIT*, and they knew about a third of the words without the picture context. Table 6.3 indicates the May results made by the four children.

Reading Pseudowords In the fall most children could not read any pseudowords (96 percent of the Pine School and 33 percent of Water School students knew no pseudowords as the year began). At the end of the year the number of zero scores dropped to 35 percent at Pine School and 4 percent at Water School. There were large overall gains in both schools. Examining our case study children, Table 6.4 indicates that ony Erica, who was using initial letters to spell, attempted to read pseudowords in the fall. Donna did not improve much over time, but the others made reasonable gains.

Common Book Words Children knew few words in the fall, with 97 percent of the Pine School students and 41 percent of Water School students performing at the zero level. At the end of the school year, the percentage of zero scores dropped to 15 and 9 for the two schools respectively; 6 percent of Pine and 22 percent of Water children read 10, 11, or all 12 words. The four case study students' spring responses are described in Table 6.5. Notice that Joseph used initial-letter information and tried to figure out the words, but he, as well as Sani, confuses *b* with *d*. Donna would not try words she did not know.

Reading Pictured Labels To obtain the clearest possible measures of children's approaches to word recognition, we gave 66 of the children labled pictures that were either predictable (under a picture of a toy train was the word *train*) or unpredictable (under a picture of a car was the word *wheels*). We asked, "Show me where there is something to read. . . . What does it say? . . . How do you know?" This task, given at the end of the kindergarten year by Peterman (Peterman & Mason, 1984), followed closely one devised by Ferreiro and Teberosky (1982).

Only one child ignored the print, pointing to the picture and naming it when we asked, "Show me. . . ." The rest of the children knew that information was in the print. But did they use the print to identify the words? Twenty-three percent talked about the picture rather than graphics when they were asked to explain how they knew what the word said. They misread all the unpredictable

Table 6.4 **Case Study Children's Responses on Pseudoword Task in September and May**

Words:	fam pag lac tak caf jao ras gat maz naj san kap	
	September	*May*
Joseph	No attempt	11/12 correct (*as* for ras)
Donna	No attempt	No attempt
Sani	No attempt	3/12 fat (fam) paguh (pag) ars (rag) emay (maz) grum (gat) kake (kap)
Erica	fat (fam) cat (caf) teep (tak)	12/12 correct

labels, telling us, for example, that the word *wheel* under the picture of a car was *car*. Twenty-eight percent said they knew the words because of the letters or hesitated when they came to the unpredictable label, but still gave us the name of the picture for the unpredictable label. Thirty-six percent tried to decode and to integrate one with the other (e.g., by calling the car labeled *wheel*, *wagon*, and by thinking of two semantically appropriate words for the two-word labels *wood blocks* such as *building blocks*). These children figured out some of the unpredictable labels. Only one child was able to read all the labels correctly and without hesitation.

Assuming that these kindergarten children are fairly representative of most kindergarteners who are given readiness or reading instruction, we can say that whereas they are aware that print carries a message they are more likely to look to the picture information for the message than to the print. However, a majority knew that they *should* look at the print. Their error in relying on picture information in kindergarten is understandable because the printed information that they usually read is in predictable, pictured contexts. Still, we found that children's ability to read unpredictable text was related to other reading and listening abilities. The more able early readers were likely to read or try to read using letter information.

Reading Simple Stories A task given at the beginning of kindergarten and repeated at the end of the school year allowed us to study children's approaches to reading a book with pictures and captions (McCormick & Mason, 1984). To measure children's attempts to read, we handed them a book, told them what it is about, and asked them to read it. If they objected, saying that they could not read, we said to "pretend" to read it. In this way all the children participated. They labeled the pictures, constructed a story about the pictures, or tried to read the words. Since at the beginning of the kindergarten year few children are actually reading, we coded their remarks by the extent to which they used or elaborated on the picture information. Later, we counted how many words they read and asked them how they figured out some words.

In our testing at the beginning of kindergarten, we noticed that most of the children simply labeled pictures, ignoring the story possibilities; some told an

Table 6.5 **Case Study Children's Responses on the Common Book Word Task, Showing Percentage Correct and Type of Error in May**

	Percentage Correct	Words	Child's Response
Joseph	33	ran	red
		but	dut
		had	hat
		may	mister
		ate	at
Donna	50	ran	run
Sani	8	ran	rode
		at	cat
		did	pate
		ten	teen
		had	hat
		say	soup
		may	mom
Erica	83	use	us
		ate	at

elaborate story from the pictures; and a few were able to read. For example, for a text that read "Stop car; stop truck; stop bus; stop, step,* stop; stop for the cat," one child simply labeled each page, saying, "Cat; car; truck; bus; car and no monkey car and bike; and truck, cat, car, bus." Another child elaborated, saying:

> The car is going down the road and the sign said stop and he stopped. Then a truck was going down the road and the sign said stop so he stopped. A school bus was going down the road. Another sign said stop so the school bus stopped. And the semi and the bike and the car and the kitten were going down the road, and the sign said stop so they stopped. And then the bus, the car, and the kitten were going down the road, and the sign said stop and they stopped.

At the end of the year when we again asked them to read the same stories, a few children simply labeled the pictures or made up stories, but most of them read part or all of the stories. After they read or tried to read we asked several questions. One was, "Where does it say *stop?*" Some pointed to the pictured sign, not acknowledging any other source of print, and some told us the imformation was in the print below the picture. With respect to the last page of the story, whether or not they read it correctly, we asked, "How did you know that it said that?" and then, "What does it say here (pointing to the words *the cat*)?" These children gave us varying reasons for knowing how they could read the print ("I just knew the words"; "I saw the word before"; "It matches with the sign"; "I sounded it out"; "I saw the word before"; "It matches with the sign"; "I know how to read").

---

* This error was deliberately placed in the text to determine whether children would read it correctly or not or comment on it.

From among the children who had ignored the print, a few changed their method of attending to the story as we questioned them. They looked more carefully at the words that they had just ignored and, to our surprise, read the words correctly. They even continued reading the print with the next story. We hope to learn later why the more primitive strategy is sometimes chosen over a more effective one.

It appears that children who were elaborators at the beginning of kindergarten are more likely to become readers than those who were picture labelers. Possibly, children who began kindergarten as story elaborators have parents who provide a good grounding for story comprehension by reading to their children and talking to them about stories. Perhaps kindergarten children learn to make better use of context when they read if they are in a story-reading rather than a letter-identification program. We hope that later analyses will permit us to separate some of these instructional effects from children's personal styles and home support.

Telling and Retelling Stories　At the beginning of the school year, children constructed stories from four-picture sequences. In March they retold a story that their teacher had just read to them. The second task tapped the extent to which they could organize information around a narrative framework. Both tasks measured whether they could describe the intentions of the main character. We looked for specific vocabulary terms (e.g., *want, think, need, try*) and phrases that explained why an action was performed.

This extends work by Hall, Nagy, and Nottenburg (1981) and Torrance and Olson (1982) who found the construct of intentionality to be related to reading achievement. We found a wide variation in these children's use of intentionality. In the four-picture sequence task many children simply labeled pictures and gave no indication that they saw a set of connected events; some tried to tie the picture information together with *and* or *and then;* others put *intention* relationships into their responses. These three kinds of responses describe, we suspect, three levels of story understanding.

For example, one of the picture sets showed (1) a little girl waving at an ice cream truck, (2) being given an ice cream cone, (3) eating it, and (4) throwing something in the trash box. One child told the story, "Getting ice cream, eating it, throwing the cone away." Another using the *and* relationship said, "She's giving her ice cream and she's eating it. And she's going to throw it away." And a child who relied on *intention* said, "One time a little girl was trying to get a ice cream cone and some lady gave it to her. Then she walked and when she was done she throwed it in the garbage can."

We used recall of a story children had just been read as another way to measure intentionality. Some never mentioned the main character's intention or the problem involved in accomplishing that intention. Others gave the problem but not the intention. Only a few were able without probing to tell us why the little girl in the story wanted to visit someone and why there would be a problem if she did. Interestingly, not mentioning this information was not due to lack of attention to the information, because when probed about half of the children could tell us both the intention and problem.

These tasks show promise of being applicable for testing children's way of organizing story information, an important aspect of reading comprehension. We expect it will be a predictor of later reading ability.

Awareness of How to Read   To assess children's awareness of how to read, we constructed three interview questions. One question is, "How are you learning to read [at home]?" and another is, "How is your teacher helping you learn to read?" We scored their use of metacognitive terms (e.g., *think, remember, learn*), their use of metalinguistic terms (e.g., *write, read, spell, sound out*), and the number of different ideas that were related to learning to read. They used more than twice as many metalinguistic terms as metacognitive terms ($M = 1.7$ vs. .6). They reported ideas such as, "People are helping me"; "I try to read books at home"; "We start by the sounds of stuff"; or "She don't teach me to read. We just say the word and fill in the lines."

Another quesition was, "How would you help this stuffed animal or doll to read?" Most chidren pretended the animal was a child and showed us how they would "teach" it. In the process they either modeled a teacher or a parent, providing indirect evidence of how they perceived reading and reading instruction. For example, one child picked up a book, read to the animal, then placed a book in front of the animal and said, "This says *a, b,* . . . you say it now," modeling the teacher. This child's responses for learning at home was, "My mommy reads it again and again and then she tells me to read it."

We also asked children to write down or draw three ideas for next year's kindergarten children to help them learn to read, then to explain what they drew or wrote. Most of the children (90 percent) were able to describe at least one way for kindergarten children to learn. Typical advice was, "Listen to your teacher"; "Sound out words"; and "Have your mom read to you." Children varied in their use of metacognitive and metalinguistic terms, again using more metalinguistic than metacognitive terms. *Read* and *listen* were common terms. The results from this task indicate that most children, whether they are learning by using books or using letters, believe that learning the alphabet, reading books, and having mothers help them are the important ways to learn to read.

Case Studies

Four children, two each from the contrasting instructional settings, were studied in depth through the summer to ascertain their out-of-school literacy experiences and the support provided by their parents. There is no doubt that the children had made reading progress in school. How they interpreted their school instruction within their home environment becomes clearer from these vignettes.

Joseph   Joseph, a very popular child at Pine School is beginning to use letter-sound strategies for consonants but not for vowels. He seldom relies on context clues so his comprehension may be limited. His awareness of how to read appears not be centered around word identification. For example, he told us the teacher helps him learn "by spelling the words for us, helping us to learn letters." His response to learning at home, however, reflects a different approach, "My cousin, he's in first grade, helps me read. He listens to me try to read and tells me words."

Family Perspective   The father works for the town repairing streets and the mother is a homemaker. Neither parent studied beyond high school. There are two children, Joseph and a younger brother. Joseph likes to play outside with his friends. His mother says she can trust him, he is very responsible, a pleasure, easy to manage, and a leader. She commented that Joseph does not like to take time out from playing outside to do any reading, but he does have a favorite read-along record that he has memorized and reads this to his younger brother in the evening. He spends little time watching Sesame Street or Saturday morning cartoons during the summer months.

Teacher Perspective   He listens and is a good learner. He volunteers during lessons and is well liked by classmates. He was ranked fourteenth in a class of 20.

Self-perspective   He told us, "Reading is easy for me because I have to sound out the letters. It's easy. I'm a good reader."

Observer Perspective   He is not a fluent reader, but is very self-assured. He shows leadership qualities in giving orders and getting children to follow.

Donna   Donna is also attending Pine School. Her responses to some of the readiness tasks are similar to those made by Joseph. However, she is less willing to try to read words that she was not taught. Her responses to the awareness task indicated reliance on school materials for reading at home with, "My green book (the school primer) helps me to read (at home). It has children in it." About learning in school she said, "We learn letters so we can spell. We read names of children in a reader. My book helps me."

Parent Perspective   Her father works as a laborer and her mother is a homemaker who gives piano lessons occasionally. Both parents attended junior college. There are two cousins that come to visit often. All the children in this extended family are younger than Donna. She is very motherly with them and helpful. There are many books in the living room. Her mother encourages her to teach the younger brother.

Teacher Perspective   She is a good student and was placed in the highest reading group. She expects her to do well in first grade. She was ranked sixth in a class of 20.

Self-perspective   "Reading is easy because it's fun. I am a good reader."

Observer Perspective   Donna can be quiet and clinging (to her mother) but can also be forceful and persistent. She is an independent and calm child and functions well in familiar surroundings. At school she sometimes has to be coaxed to respond. When she is reading she will labor, read without meaning, word by word, unless she is familiar with the story. Sometimes she ignores the picture information in her concentration on the words.

Erica   Erica attends Water school. She was ahead of the other children in developing letter-sound recognition strategies, and continues to progress successfully. She is developing a good balance between comprehension and decoding. The awareness task revealed her unusual ability to express how she is learning to read at home and school. She said:

> At home, I read books and play school with my sister; she's 2. I be the teacher. I read. I'm a good writer by sounding out words.
> At school, she lets us read in class the books. She lets us read sentences. We put the writing and we read them to ourselves. She lets us sound out words. She tells us to sound it out. She tells us to look at the picture and that tells us what they are doing and then you can read it.

Family Perspective   Her mother works for a preschool program during the school year and there is no father at home. Erica is one of five children and has a three-year-old niece living with her as well. Her mother went to junior college, but her father did not finish high school. Her mother watches the children carefully and keeps them working and learning. For example, she noticed that Erica was reversing letters last year so she sent her to an early childhood program in addition to Headstart. She constantly buys workbooks, puzzles, records, and little books for the children. She looks for programs at the library and free movies and lessons at the city park. Erica goes everywhere with her mother during the summer.

Teacher Perspective   The teacher believes Erica will be very successful in school, expecially since she knows how to get what she needs to help her learn. For example, she would observe the teacher and wait for a free minute to have the teacher listen to her read. She is also very competitive and makes sure that her friends do not get ahead of her in learning new things. She is ranked ninth in a class of 23.

Self-perspective   She said, "Reading is easy because I'm learning how to read. I am a good reader."

Observer Perspective   Erica is very sure of herself and independent, yet also clings to her mother. She can do almost anything and seems to know that she is smart. If something is too hard, she simply asks for help. She takes the initiative to learn and has high ambitions. For example, after joining the library club, she read one book while there and had read five more within the week. When she reads she tries to understand it. She seems to read in phrases and looks at the picture information for cues. She wants people to see her reading.

Sani Sani also attends Water School. Sani is later than most in his class developing letter-sound recognition strategies; often he ignores context because of his attempts to identify words. His awareness responses reflect the language experience approach used in his classroom. He told us:

> At school she reads to us and we be thinking and we write sentences and after we write our sentences we write our picture and she reads and then she helps us learn. Sometimes I ask her words. She tells me some of them.

At home Sani said he learned by "practice reading to Mom and Dad. They tell me words I don't know. Somebody reads a book to me the first day and the next day I can read it myself."

Parent Perspective Sani's father works as a laborer in a factory, but also writes for a newspaper; his mother babysits. Sani is the youngest of six children. The family stresses academic success. An older child is on the honor role, and the family has sit-down programs for academic work each week. Sani's mother is worried about him because he still does not seem to be very interested in reading. When she tried to teach him earlier this year, he would put his hands over his ears, preferring to play. He responds better to instruction from his father than the mother. They insisted that he sign out books at the library this summer instead of toys. Both parents are reading to Sani, and he is beginning to read little books. He is a very willing helper at home, but is strong willed: "You can't tell him anything, you've got to prove it to him."

Teacher Perspective She believes that Sani is a bright child but needs encouragement to learn. She's not worried about him, however, because she expects the family to work with him. She ranked him eighteenth in a class of 23.

Self-perspective He said, "Sometimes reading is hard, because I haven't read a lot. Yes, I'm going to be a good reader."

Observer Persepctive He is self-confident and independent. He likes to be a leader. For example, if a game is not going as he thinks it should, he walks away. He is a full participant with 10-year-old children in kickball and soccer. He seems relaxed in school, unconcerned about doing well. When doing experience charts, he will try if called on but does not volunteer.

Discussion

Two contrasting kindergarten reading programs were chosen for this study to examine how early instruction affects children's progress in learning to read as well as their awareness about how to read. This first report suggests that both programs have an equivalent influence on development of the form of print. The average gain made by students on the ERT subtests was about the same for each school, 30 percent for Pine School and 28 percent for Water School; however, ceiling effects in Water School may have curtailed greater gains (see Table 6.1).

Average gains, however, are only part of the story. First, there were large within-school score differences. Few of the subtests showed normally distributed score patterns (U-shaped and negative skews in the spring for Pine School; negative skews in the spring for Water School). This suggests that a larger proporation of low-achieving children in Water School than in Pine School are profiting from the instruction. In a follow-up study these same children will be tested during first grade to examine potential patterns.

Another school difference is the pattern of gain score correlations (Table 6.6). There are moderate correlations in both schools between the word-reading tasks: reading label words out of context and reading common (book) words were correlated .40 in Pine and .57 in Water. There are similar correlations between the phoneme identification tasks: spelling and pseudoword reading were correlated .48 in Pine and .52 in Water. However, only Pine School shows moderate correlations between gain scores for combined measures of word reading and phoneme identification (Water School with a correlation of .11 and Pine School with a correlation of .60). We hope to explain these differences after the first-grade tests are given.

A third school difference is apparent in the analysis of the four children. The two from Pine School are thought by their parents, the teacher, and themselves to be progressing normally. Yet neither child is very involved in literacy activities during the summer. The boy plays with his friends and the girl follows her mother, helping to care for younger children. The Water School children, coming from a more book-oriented school environment and encouraged by their parents, are reading much more during the summer. The boy would rather be outside playing, like Joseph. The girl, however, appears to be self-motivated to read but with significant support from her mother.

IMPLICATIONS

The ERT has been successfully extended beyond the measurement of the form of print to aspects of reading and listening comprehension. Having children try or pretend to read a caption text or labeled pictures and then tell us where certain words are and how they figure out particular words or phrases appear to be effective tasks. Having children recall a story they heard divulges large differences in remembering and structuring important information. Interviewing children reveals their perception of how they are learning to read at school and at home. These are understandable tasks to young children, they are not threatening, and they tap a wide range of responses. As a result, we expect to find changes over the summer and during first grade in word recognition and comprehension that will help explain later reading progress.

Table 6.6 Intercorrelations for Gain Scores on Form of Print Tasks (values above the diagonal are from Pine School, and values below the diagonal are from Water School)

	Labels in Context	Labels out of Context	Spelling	Pseudo-words	Common Words
Labels in context		.16	−.03	−.07	−.09
Labels out of context	.43		.30	.38	.40
Spelling	.15	.06		.48	.37
Pseudowords	.05	.01	.52		.65
Common Words	.22	.57	.10	.25	

At this point we are unable to determine whether kindergarten reading program differences will be long lasting. The data indicate that most children begin reading in kindergarten whether they receive book instruction or letter-and-word instruction. Still to be determined is whether there will be differing patterns of learning and reading strategy or interest in reading that stem from the instruction.

REFERENCES

Bissex, G. (1980). *GNYS at WRK: A child learns to write and read.* Cambridge, Mass.: Harvard University Press.

Clay, M. (1979). *Reading: The patterning of complex behavior.* Exeter, N.H.: Heinemann.

Dyson, A. (1984). *Emerging literacy in school contexts: Toward defining the gap between school and curriculum and child mind.* Paper presented at the American Education Research Association, New Orleans.

Ehri, L. (1979). Linguistic insight: Threshold of reading acquisition. In T. Waller & G. MacKinnon (Eds.), *Reading research: Advances in theory and practice.* New York: Academic.

Ehri, L. (1984). *Do beginners learn to read visual or phonetic word spelling more easily?* Paper present at the American Education Research Association, New Orleans.

Ferreiro, E., & Teberosky, A. (1982). *Literacy before schooling.* London: Heinemann.

Hall, W., Nagy, N., & Nottenburg, G. (1981). *Situational variation in the use of internal state words.* Tech, Rep. No. 212. Urbana: University of Illiniois, Center for the Study of Reading.

Heath, S. B. (1983). *Way with words—Language, life and work in communities and class-rooms.* Cambridge, Mass.: Harvard University Press.

Hiebert, E. (1981). Developmental patterns and interrelationships of preschool children's print awareness. *Reading Research Quarterly, 2,* 236–260.

Hiebert, E. (1984). *Perspectives on young children's acquisition of reading.* Paper presented at the American Education Research Association, New Orleans.

Mason, J. (1976). Overgeneralization in learning to read. *Journal of Reading Behavior, 8,* 173–182.

Mason, J. (1977). Refining phonics for teaching beginning reading. *Reading Teacher, 31,* 184–197.

Mason, J. (1980). When do children begin to read: An exploration of four-year-old children's letter and word reading competencies. *Reading Research Quarterly, 15*, 203–227.

Mason, J., & McComich, C. (1979). *Testing the development of reading and linguistic awareness.* Tech. Rep. No. 126. Urbana: University of Illinois, Center for the Study of Reading. ERIC Document Reproduction Service No. ED 170 725.

Mason, J., McCormick, C., & Bhavagri, N. (in press). How are you going to help me learn? Lesson negotiations between a teacher and preschool children. In D. Yaden & S. Templeton (Eds.), *Metalinguistic awareness and beginning literacy.* Exeter, N.H.: Heinemann.

McCormick, C., & Mason, J. (1981). What happens to kindergarten children's knowledge about reading after a summer vacation? *Reading Teacher, 35,* 164–172.

McCormick, C., & Mason, J. (1984). Intervention procedures for increasing preschool children's interest in knowledge about reading. In W. Teale & E. Sulzby (Eds.), *Emergent literacy: Writing and reading.* New York: Ablex.

Peterman, C. & Mason, J. (1984). *Kindergarten children's perceptions of the form of print in labeled pictures and stories.* Paper presented at the National Reading Conference, St. Petersburg, Florida.

Read, C. (1971). Preschool children's knowledge of English phonology. *Harvard Educational Review, 41,* 1–34.

Soderbergh, R. (1977). *Reading in early childhood: A linguistic study of a preschool child's gradual acquisition of reading ability.* Washington, D.C.: Georgetown University Press.

Sulzby, E. (1983). *First-graders' reading from three text types: Self-authored texts, commercial story books and basal readers.* Paper presented at the National Reading Conference, Austin, Texas.

Surber, J., & Mason, J. (1977). Effects of rule consistent examples in learning letter-sound correspondences. *Journal of Reading Behavior, 9,(31),* 1–11.

Taylor, D. (1983). *Family literacy: Young children learning to read and write.* Exeter, N.H.: Heinemann.

Teale, W., & Sulzby, E. (Eds.). (in press). *Emergent literacy: Writing and reading.* New York: Ablex.

Torrance, N., & Olson, D., (1982). *Oral language competence and the acquisition of literacy.* Paper presented at the American Education Research Association, Montreal.

Yaden, D., & Templeton, S. (in press). *Metalinguistic awareness and beginning literacy.* Exeter, N.H.: Heinemann.

7

Teaching Children to Guide Their Reading and Learning

Scott G. Paris

American education has been criticized recently because school children have inadequate reading comprehension. The most recent National Assessment of Educational Progress (1981) found that students in intermediate and secondary grades especially had difficulty understanding, inferring, and recalling meaning from texts. In a cross-national study of educational achievement, Lee, Stigler, and Stevenson (1985) found that students in second and sixth grades in Taiwan and Japan consistently scored higher than American students on both reading and mathematics tests. Growing alarm about poor reading skills has sparked reexamination of American educational practices and has led to many of the suggestions in this book. In this chapter several contributing factors to students' poor reading comprehension will be indentified and then conceptual and practical alternatives discussed.

Reading instruction in most classrooms is virtually determined by three factors: teachers' knowledge about reading, the choice of instructional methods, and the availability of reading materials. Of course, the success of instruction depends on additional factors such as classroom dynamics and student characteristics, but for the moment the focus is on teachers, methods, and materials. A central problem of instruction is the limited information that many teachers have about reading. The growth of knowledge from research during the past 15 years has been

This research was supported by a grant from the National Institute of Education and could not have been conducted without the collaboration of Marjorie Lipson, David Cross, Evelyn Oka, Janis Jacobs, Ann Marie DeBritto, and the excellent cooperation of teachers and administrators in Farmington and Waterford School districts.

explosive, and many teachers have had only limited exposure to these new ideas. Because of age, training, or habit, many teachers today teach reading in the same way that they were instructed as children. Recent information about the importance of cognitive strategies, schemata, attributions, and metacognition (Brown, Armbruster, & Baker, 1984) are just beginning to supplement traditional emphases on phonics, decoding, and vocabulary.

Traditional views of reading also influence instructional methods. Reading groups based on ability are omnipresent in elementary grades and round-robin oral reading interspersed with periodic questions from the teacher about the passage are standard. Indeed, sometimes these are the only instructional methods that students experience. Comprehension skills are assumed to emerge from these activities. However, Durkin (1978–1979) found that teachers in intermediate grades rarely provided explicit instruction on comprehension strategies. She also found that basal readers and teachers' manuals did not encourage comprehension instruction (Durkin, 1981). The manuals direct teachers to engage in question-and-answer sessions about the content of students' reading but they offer little instruction about strategies to improve comprehension.

Certainly some of the homogeneity in reading instruction is due to the similarity among materials usually found in classrooms. Most teachers use basal readers and the accompanying workbooks. These materials are designed according to commercial interests and marketability and have severe limitations (Osborn, Jones, & Stein, 1984). The lengthy cycles for development and production of basal series means that advances in reading education may take 5 to 10 years, at best, to trickle down to classroom materials. Perhaps that is why many basal series still use drill and skill exercises such as questions about passage content, repetitive phonetic discriminations, and language skills removed from relevant content reading to "teach" comprehension. How to use context, titles, and prior knowledge or how to skim, reread, infer, or monitor comprehension are seldom explained and practiced. If these types of comprehension strategies are worthy instructional objectives, and much research suggests that they are, then it may be necessary to promote new knowledge, methods, and materials for teachers so that they can convey the skills directly to students.

The intent of this discussion is not to attribute blame for students' poor reading on either teachers or publishers. Neither the causes of poor reading nor the solutions are simple. Yet with the renewed interest in reading education and a great deal of new research, this is an ideal time to reevaluate our educational practices. Recent advances in developmental, cognitive, and instructional psychology have direct implications for how students learn to read. In our projects we have tried to incorporate those findings into a practical approach to improve students' reading comprehension skills. We have tried to provide information directly to teachers and students about various strategies that can facilitate comprehension. We have also created instructional alternatives or supplementary activities to traditional reading groups that can be used flexibly by teachers. Thus, the project described in this chapter was motivated by theoretical concerns about comprehension strategies as well as pragmatic concerns for effective instruction.

During the past five years, our research team at the University of Michigan has been developing and testing an instructional program that we call Informed Strategies for Learning, or ISL, (Paris, Cross, & Lipson, in press; Paris et al., 1984). Informed Strategies for Learning is a research project designed to test the relation between children's awareness about reading strategies and their reading skills, but it is also a practical approach to classroom instruction. There are three basic objectives in ISL. The first is to increase young children's understanding of reading tasks, goals, and strategies by describing what, how, and why various strategies influence reading. The second objective is to provide an experimental test of the relation between metacognition and performance. Can children's reading skills and comprehension levels be promoted by teaching them information about reading strategies? The third objective is to develop an instructional method for informing children about reading that is interesting, easy to use, and suitable for young readers. Informed Strategies for Learning involves instruction given to the entire class that includes extensive discussion and teacher-student interaction so that students can increase their understanding about reading as well as their skills and motivation.

PRINCIPLES OF ISL

The central tenet of our approach is that reading strategies can be explained directly to children. If they perceive the strategies as sensible and useful courses of action, we would expect children to use them appropriately and spontaneously in their subsequent reading. Our emphasis is thus on how children's awareness about reading, or metacognition, can facilitate intentional use of particular strategies. The nature of reading strategies will be considered prior to a discussion of how they can be instructed.

A strategy is more than a successful action. After all, you could hit a winning shot in tennis by accident or because someone told you what to do. Likewise, students could correctly answer questions about texts they have read for reasons other than the deployment of good strategies. Strategic readers combine knowledge about the task with motivation to act accordingly. Their plans are self-generated and their actions are self-directed. Unlike strategic reading, some students are only following directions and, thus, when unsupervised, may not be aware of when to transfer their actions to other tasks and settings. Consider the kinds of strategies that teachers would like to observe in 10 to 12 year olds when reading. Skilled readers might evaluate the task and its purpose, examine the topic, and estimate the difficulty before reading. They might pause as they read to check on their understanding. They will also probably make inferences, reread parts, and summarize the main points when they finish. These actions are unlikely if students are uninformed of the procedures and their utility, or if they are not motivated to use the strategies (Brown, 1980).

Brown, Palincsar, and Armbruster (1984) reviewed many reading curricula and identified six fundamental comprehension strategies: understanding the purpose of reading, activating relevant background knowledge, allocating attention to main ideas, critical evaluation, monitoring comprehension, and drawing inferences. These comprehension activities are important because strategic reading leads to self-directed learning. Awareness of cognitive strategies, their existence, application, and benefits, can promote the development of self-directed learning. Despite consensus about the importance of these strategies, however, there are few instructional methods designed to teach students how to use them.

We created ISL methods and materials to teach students about strategies, and we based our approach on three fundamental principles of effective teaching: (1) students need to understand the skills they are expected to learn; (2) students need the opportunity to share their thoughts and feelings about what they are learning; and (3) students need to be guided and coached to successively better and more independent levels of performance. These key instruction activities—informing, discussing, and coaching—will be discussed briefly.

Removing the Mystery of Reading

Beginning readers often have vague and mistaken notions about reading (Reid, 1966). They may not know word boundaries, print conventions, or even that pictures do not "tell the story." Older students may remain just as naive about the goals, strategies, and text complexities of reading comprehension (Myers & Paris, 1978). They frequently do not understand different purposes. Even when task goals are well-defined and understood, children may fail to invoke deliberate plans. They may not be aware of potential actions that will achieve the goal or they may not judge differences in the utility of various actions and thus behave haphazardly. A pervasive problem is the insensitivity of young children to the need to recruit any special actions (Paris & Lindauer, 1982).

Cognitive and developmental psychologists have examined the kinds of knowledge that are acquired as learners change from novices to experts. These accounts have emphasized two major types: declarative and procedural knowledge, or knowing *that* and knowing *how* (Resnick, 1983). These kinds of knowledge are crucial for becoming strategic. Declarative knowledge includes propositions about task structure and task goals. For example, I know that most stories introduce the setting and characters in the opening paragraph, and I know that my comprehension goals differ when reading newspapers and textbooks. Declarative knowledge can also include beliefs about the task and one's abilities (e.g., "reading is boring" or "I'm a slow reader"). In sum declarative knowledge includes propositional beliefs about the existence of task characteristics and personal abilities. It includes the kind of information that can help in setting goals and adjusting actions to changing task conditions.

Procedural knowledge includes information about the execution of various actions; knowing how to skim, how to scan, how to summarize, and so forth for reading. There are many reading procedures that children learn quickly, such as the directionality of reading. Other procedures such as determining pronoun references and an author's point of view remain difficult even for older children. Procedures are the large range of actions involved in any task such as reading.

They are the repertoire of behavior available to the agent who selects among them to attain different goals. Therefore, procedures are fundamental to strategic action. Procedural knowledge can be acquired from direct instruction or induced from repeated experience. Thus, children who receive instruction on how to skim passages may develop a greater appreciation of the skill, and they may be able to describe their idiosyncratic procedures for skimming in detail. This kind of understanding can facilitate the development of strategies for reading.

However, declarative and procedural knowledge alone are not sufficent to ensure that children read strategically. They only emphasize the knowledge and skills required for performance and do not address the conditions under which one might wish to select or execute actions (Paris, Lipson, & Wixson, 1983). Because strategic behavior involves intentionality and self-control, any analysis that ignores learners' motivations is incomplete. Conditional knowledge includes knowing *when* and *why* to apply various actions. For example, skimming is a procedure that is only appropriate for some tasks and situations. The procedure needs to be applied selectively to particular goals in order to be a strategy. Reading only some of the words and sentences in text is not a strategy by itself; such skimming could be the result of skipping difficult words, poor visual tracking, or laziness. The systematic employment of skimming to accomplish goals of speeded reading or previewing, however, would be strategic reading. Conditional knowledge describes the circumstances of application of procedures. An expert with full procedural knowledge could not adjust behavior to changing task demands without conditional knowledge.

Declarative, procedural, and conditional knowledge are necessary ingredients for strategic behavior. Students can learn about these features of reading by direct instruction as well as by practice. Part of a teacher's job is to explicate strategies for reading so that students will perceive them as useful and sensible. This is where persuasion needs to be added to information and brings us to the second principle of ISL.

Making Thinking Public

Awareness or metacognition does not have to be private; knowledge about strategies can be shared among students and teachers. How can teachers convey information to students about the benefits of strategies and the necessity to use them on their own? Most researchers agree that interactive learning facilitates persuasion. Students need to talk with each other about the tasks and options in order to see how various plans might be implemented. In reciprocal teaching (Palincsar & Brown, 1984) or peer tutoring situations, children can act as teachers as well as students. In this fashion they can adopt the role of an external monitor for someone else just as they need to act as an internal monitor for their own reading. Of course, such monitoring depends on children's knowledge about the strategies, but this kind of interactive learning helps to shift the responsibility for recruiting and applying cognitive strategies from teachers to students (Pearson & Gallagher, 1983; Vygotsky,1978).

We think that classroom dialogues are fundamental to this transfer because they give students opportunities to express their ideas. By listening to students' ideas, teachers can appreciate students' concepts and attitudes about reading, as well as diagnose their misconceptions (Wixson & Lipson, this volume). Conversations in classrooms also help to "make thinking public" so that students can learn from one another. As they assert, defend, and question their ideas about their own reading and studying skills, they are being persuaded about the value of effective strategies. There are many ways in which teachers can stimulate Socratic discussions about thinking skills. We have found that these dialogues can be facilitated by using metaphors to describe the strategies. For example, we have encouraged children as young as seven or eight years old to talk about what they need to do in order to "be a reading detective" or "plan your reading trip." These metaphors stimulate children to relate reading to other problem-solving tasks so they can generate similar plans and strategies for cognitive objectives such as reading, skimming, and studying. The metaphors offer easy vehicles for communicating about abstract skills. They make the strategies seem sensible and tangible because students can relate specific actions to each one. They can also perceive the need to use them by analogy.

Cognitive Coaching

Knowing about strategies will not ensure that students use them while they read. Teaching is more than telling; the information must be supplemented with a rationale for using strategies. This is where motivation blends with knowledge and where teaching and learning interact. The reponsibility to use reading strategies must be shifted from teachers to students so that learning is self-regulated and not done merely for compliance or external rewards. Students need to internalize guidance that is provided initially by someone else so that they can provide their own criticism and encouragement. The steps involved in shifting responsibility can include the following forms of instruction: informing, modeling, guiding, observing, correcting, and encouraging. Repeated cycles of such learning and teaching resemble coaching more than didactic information giving. Indeed, this type of guided learning is how parents usually teach children routine skills such as cooking, fishing, and game playing (Rogoff & Gardner, in press). Coaching students about cognitive skills includes guided practice, feedback, faded support, and generalization to related tasks so that students can recruit strategies apropriately and independently (Pearson & Gallagher, 1983).

Guided learning through social interactions also provides pragmatic benefits to children. Instruction that accompanies aided practice offers information and assistance in task completion. Most instruction for young children occurs sporadically and informally as various situations arise. Paris, Newman, and Jacobs (1985) point out that a great deal of socially guided learning is accomplished tacitly as parents show, tell, model, coax, and correct their children to do simple things such as play with toys or help to prepare food. Regardless of the formality of instruction, most situations include the same principles of interaction. Whether we refer to interactive learning as guided participation, proleptic instruction (Wertsch & Stone, 1978), or informed instruction (Palincsar & Brown, 1984), many researchers are emphasizing a set of common principles that reflect good coaching. We want to call attention to three general characteristics. First, coaching implies a set of shared objectives between tutors and pupils. Expertise of pupils is the standard of success, and both teacher and pupil strive to achieve it. Because learning is a joint responsibility, coaches and parents have a large stake in students' progress. After all, poor learning can reflect poor coaching. This arrangement permits (perhaps elicits) a strong interpersonal commitment to succeed for the other person's sake and enhances motivation by providing a goal of social solidarity and mutual achievement (Maehr, 1983).

A second principle of coaching is an emphasis on accurate evaluation of a pupil's starting point. Coaches need to assess what pupils know and how they perform before they can form reasonable expectations and appropriate plans for training. Parents have some distinct advantages in assessment as they teach cognitive skills to children. They usually know what is familiar and novel to children so that they can connect new information or responses to old ablities. Thus, parents can avoid imposing task redundancy that breeds boredom or overly challenging tasks that may produce failure. Assessing a pupil's starting point and adjusting standards for performance can be considered progressive evaluations and advances in the zone of proximal development, a term used to denote incipient learning (Vygotsky, 1978). Parents can also assess children's *willingness* to be coached. They can structure tasks or arrange the environment in subtle ways so that children encounter progressive demands on their skills yet still receive incentives and rewards. The coaching metaphor is appropriate because it includes sensitivity to the pupils' physical, social, cognitive, and motivational progress.

A third characteristic of coaching is mutual regulation. Shared goals, accurate assessments of pupils' readiness and willingness, and good plans may be unsuccessful if coach and pupil do not modify their behavior as they interact. Feedback and dialogues are needed so that mutal criticism is constructive, not destructive or threatening. Parents model this role of critic, and children should internalize the criticisms as suggestions for progress rather than as pejorative evaluations of their self-worth. The essence of mutual regulation in coaching is the shifting of responsibility for positive direction and correction from coach to pupil. The shift is gradual in time and graduated according to skill development. As young children become more skilled readers, teachers and parents should provide fewer supports and raise their expectations for children's unaided comprehension.

In summary, teachers do not directly instruct students about reading strategies very often. This is paradoxical given the importance of strategies and the readiness of students to learn about them. Guided instruction appears to be an effective way to inform students about the existence of reading strategies. It also provides modeling, feedback, and persuasions so that students can internalize teachers' regulation of comprehension skills. Group discussions and direct instruction can provide information about declarative, procedural, and conditional aspects of strategies. Classroom dialogues also provide stimulation and motivation to use the strategies. In the following section the methods and materials of ISL are described as one example of how these instructional principles can be implemented.

INSTRUCTIONAL TECHNIQUES OF ISL

Our methods of teaching children about reading strategies may be characterized as "direct instruction" or "informed training" (Brown, Armbruster, & Baker, 1984) because we taught children about strategies explicitly. We based our methods on several tenets of research on teacher effectiveness that emphasize the importance of (1) directing students' attention to the material to be learned, (2) providing an academic focus to learning activities, (3) ensuring high levels of student participation and involvement, and (4) using frequent practice with immediate feedback. We tried to promote these features of effective teaching by designing half-hour group lessons that stimulated students to think and to talk about (as well as to use) different reading strategies. The following five techniques were part of the lessons:

1. Informed teaching
2. Metaphors for strategies and bulletin boards
3. Group dialogues
4. Guided practice
5. Bridging to content-area reading

Informed Teaching

Informed teaching simply means that teachers told students *what* a particular strategy is, *how* it operates, and *when* and *why* to use it. Thus, teachers were told about the declarative, procedural, and conditional aspects of reading strategies so that they could pass on the knowledge to their students. For example, skimming seems like such a simple strategy to adults, but when you ask 8 to 10 year olds how to skim, many may respond by saying, "You read the little words," or "Just read the first and last sentences." They often do not know why skimming can be a good preview or review technique or they think about the value of the strategy weighted against the extra effort. Teachers often forget how naive students are about such strategies. But researchers and academics also often overlook teachers' naivete. Some teachers do not teach students about the declarative, procedural, and conditional knowledge of reading strategies, because they do not understand those characteristics well, and there are no descriptions of these strategies in teachers' manuals. That is why ISL provides *teachers* with information on what, how, when, and why strategies operate so that they in turn can convey it directly to students.

Metaphors for Strategies

In this project we created metaphors for reading strategies, because we wanted the strategies to be concrete, meaningful actions, and the metaphors seemed to make cognitive strategies sensible to young readers. We drew analogies between pre-reading activities and planning in general by using the metaphor "plan your reading trip." To make summarizing more concrete, we used the metaphor "round up your ideas." Evaluating text difficulty and reading purposes was depicted by analogy in "be a reading detective." These metaphors made the strategies sensible by analogy and they provided concrete, vivid cues for image, recall, and discussion. Consider, for example, the quintessential comprehension strategy of every scope and sequence chart—identifying the main idea. Informed Strategies for Learning tries to teach this strategy by drawing the analogy of a sleuth using clues to "track down the main idea." The clues include pictures, titles, prior knowlege, setting, and so forth. Students are taught how to use these clues to deduce or abstract the theme of the text or main idea. Thus, the metaphor affords a vehicle for communicating information about the declarative, procedural, and conditional features of the strategy.

We also capitalized on the visual impact of our selected metaphors by creating colorful bulletin board displays of each one. The bulletin boards were incorporated into the lessons so that children attended to them. Focal questions that students should ask themselves about each strategy were included on the bulletin boards. These served as daily reminders to think about and to use the strategies. The themes of the metaphors, such as detectives or planning a trip, were also incorporated into worksheets so that strategies became tangible, sensible, and functional.

Group Discussions

There is evidence that teachers and students do not have adequate opportunities to talk about the strategies and skills that they are learning. Students need the opportunity to express confusion, distress, or pride publicly. They need to know that they are not alone, that other students have similar thoughts and feelings. There are personal and idiosyncratic aspects to reading strategies just as there are personalized aspects of comprehension and appreciation that can be shared non-competitively because there is not always a "best" strategy. We found that group discussions provided for readers of all abilities an outlet that was satisfying and informative. Talking also seemed to promote cooperative learning and to encourage the breakdown of boundaries created by reading groups.

Teachers learned a great deal from these discussions and often seemed suprised at one extreme by the unexpected naivete, or at the other by the depth of understanding demonstrated by some students. These dialogues afford teachers with informal assessments of their own instruction. It takes some teachers time to get used to so much discussion and democracy in the classroom, but we have found that dialogues inject spirited enthusiasm into what may often be dull drill-skill practice. We hasten to add that the quality of teacher talk during these dialogues is critical. Duffy et al. (1984) found that effective teachers emphasize:

1. Assistance during reading rather than procedure or assessment.
2. Knowing how you know.

3. Conscious connections to previous and future learning.
4. The context to which new skills will be applied.
5. Making invisible cognitive skills tangible.
6. Responding to student confusion with advice about how to think strategically.

Obviously the quality and content of the group dialogues must match the information in the informed instruction and students' levels of understanding.

Guided Practice

As part of each ISL lesson students read a selection and applied the strategy that they were learning. Immediately after reading, the group discussed the strategy—how it worked, the effort required, and students' evaluations of its usefulness. Worksheets built around each metaphor were also provided so that students could read and use the strategies individually. We found that teachers frequently used the metaphors to refer to students' performance, for example, "You didn't follow your reading map," or "You forgot to use the clues." Here we can see how the metaphors for strategies promote communication about cognitive processes, and how teaching resembles cognitive coaching.

Bridging to Content-Area Reading

Our final technique was to fade explicit support in the instruction and worksheets so that students had increasing demands to recruit and apply the strategies independently. We taught generalization of the strategies to content-area reading by including a bridging lesson periodically. In this lesson teachers used reading selections from science, social studies, and so forth to reinforce the instructed strategy. In this manner students could learn directly that the strategies should be applied beyond reading instruction.

MATERIALS AND METHODS FOR ISL

The ISL program of reading instruction currently includes 20 modules designed for Grades 3, 4, and 5. Each module is designed to be used by teachers independently, but we have worked closely with more than 60 teachers who have used ISL. Each module emphasizes one comprehension strategy and includes three separate half-hour lessons, the last one being a bridging lesson. The standard format is as follows:

Topic   *Metaphor*

Strategy description
Rationale

Goals
Bulletin board
Lesson A
Lesson B
Lesson C
Stories/passages
Worksheets

There are approximately 20 typed pages of material for each module with stories and worksheets ready for thermofax or photocopying. The lessons provide detailed information about strategies, metaphors, and how to foster group discussions of them.

The set of 20 modules is arranged into four groups as follows:

1-5   Planning for reading
6-10   Identifying meaning
11-15 Reasoning while reading
16-20 Monitoring comprehension

The entire list of modules, with metaphors and strategies listed separately, is shown in Figure 7.1.

While the methodology for instruction remained roughly the same each week, the content varied, with each week building on previously learned information. We focused our training program on building metacognitive awareness in the belief that such awareness, in itself, might promote better comprehension in young readers. Our goals were to make children aware of the requirements of skilled reading, to teach some strategies to effect good comprehension, and to promote the belief that these strategies are useful and worth employing.

In order to examine more closely the content of one of our lessons, one module will be discussed in detail. This module, entitled "Road Signs for Reading" was designed to help children focus on planning for efficient reading. As always, the goals for the lessons built on previously learned material. Goals for this week included persuading children to: (1) use their clues to plan the reading trip; (2) reach the goal (i.e., meaning); and (3) use their "bag of tricks" to get there. These objectives clearly specify that the children will use the information and strategies that they learned in earlier lessons. The purpose of this particular lesson was to instruct children to activate previously learned information—to plan to use it during their reading activities.

The bulletin board of this module (used in a 1983 *Weekly Reader* poster) included a winding road with various signs along the way. The title focused on children's attention to the analogy and prompted lively discussions of how reading and taking a trip are similar. The focal questions (e.g., (1) Do I know what clues to attend to, what to do to get ready for a reading trip? (2) Did I use the

Figure 7.1 **Comprehension Skill Training Modules**

I. Awareness of Reading Goals, Plans, and Strategies

    1. Goals and purposes of reading
        "hunting for reading treasure"
    2. Evaluating the reading task
        "be a reading detective"
    3. Comprehension strategies
        "a bag full of tricks for reading"
    4. Forming plans
        "planning to build meaning"
    5. Review

II. Components of Meaning in Text

    6. Kinds of meaning and text content
        "turn on the meaning"
    7. Ambiguity and multiple meanings
        "hidden meaning"
    8. Temporal and causal sequences
        "links in the chain of events"
    9. Clues to meaning
        "tracking down the main idea"
  10. Review

III. Constructive Comprehension Skills

  11. Making inferences
        "weaving ideas"
  12. Preview and review of goals and task
        "surveying the land of reading"
  13. Integrating ideas and using context
        "bridges to meaning"
  14. Critical reading
        "judge your reading"
  15. Review

IV. Strategies for Monitoring and Improving Comprehension

  16. Comprehension monitoring
        "signs for reading"
  17. Detecting comprehension failures
        "road to reading disaster"
  18. Self-correction
        "road repair"
  19. Text schemas and summaries
        "round up your ideas"
  20. Review
        "plan your reading trip"

tricks to guide my reading?) emphasized the goals of the lesson and provided children with an easy reference throughout the week. The children were instructed to ask themselves these questions each time they read—a cue to use the strategies being taught that week.

In order to highlight the salient features of comprehension monitoring, the bulletin board contained additional aids. Under each of the "road signs," we gave children specific directions to follow during their reading. For example, before children began on their reading trip, they were instructed to find a "quiet zone." This directed them to find a quiet place, to decide what kinds of reading they had to do—to get ready to read. The "stop sign" directed them to "stop and think" about their reading and the "dead end" sign told them they had hit a dead end—they needed to go back and reread because they had missed the meaning.

While discussing the bulletin board and focal questions, children identified ways in which reading was like taking a trip. They were encouraged to remember where they would be going (to the meaning), to adjust their speed, to watch their progress, and to retrace their route (i.e., reread) if they became lost. As soon as these ideas had been fully discussed, children were provided with an opportunity to take their own reading trip by completing a worksheet that included road signs that encouraged children to yield to unknown words, to get needed help, to stop and think periodically to see if they were understanding, and to slow down when the material was difficult.

By the second session of the week, we expected children to work with fewer explicit prompts. Worksheets for the second day included no explicit directions (road signs). In their place were boxes in which children were expected to write down the information called for by the passsage itself. That is, if they found it difficult, they could draw a "go slow sign"; if they had not understood, they would draw a "dead end sign" to demonstrate that they had gone back to reread.

The content of this lesson is clearly focused on the planning and regulation aspects of reading. It is metacognitive in the sense that we are concerned with demonstrating to children that these aspects of reading are required if they are going to "make a successful reading trip." As noted earlier, this increased awareness was one goal of the intervention. The other involved persuading children to use these skills. Therefore, each week we attempted to instill the importance of using each strategy. We provided a rationale for its use. In the case of the lessons just discussed, we talked about how much easier it was to read if you followed the signs, thought about what you were reading, and checked to see if you were getting nearer to the goal (meaning). In addition we followed several weeks later with an entire weekly module entitled "The Road to Reading Disaster," which focused on the consequences of not using the road signs for reading.

The use of concrete metaphors, promoting awareness of task characteristics, group discussion, immediate practice, and immediate feedback combined essential elements of direct instruction into a flexible, stimulating, effective program of group-reading instruction. Informed Strategies for Learning is not linked to any one set of curricular materials or any one method of reading instruction. Unlike DISTAR, for example, which dictates both content and method, the metacognitive intervention described here is adaptable to any reading series and, indeed, to all content areas. Many of the skills we addressed could best be taught during social studies or science, for example. Nothing was more satisfying than when teachers in the project indicated that they had tried one of our strategies to teach a chapter from a social studies unit or had encouraged children to use the skills while reading a basal selection. Indeed, we would hope that given the conceptual framework provided here teachers would find many more and better ways of incorporating the lessons into their daily classroom routine. The magic is in the strategies and awareness; their ordered presentation to children; and teachers' communication that these strategies are important and beneficial.

CONSEQUENCES OF ISL

In our research during the past five years with more than 2,000 students we have documented the advantages of teaching children about comprehension strategies. Informed Strategies for Learning has significantly increased students' awareness about comprehension strategies, and we have shown that students who are most cognizant of strategies score highest on several tests of reading comprehension (Paris & Jacobs, in press). We have also shown that direct classroom instruction is relatively easy to implement and that brief group lessons can significantly increase children's use of cloze and error detection strategies (Paris, Cross, & Lipson, in press). Informal evidence also suggests that increased strategy awareness may enhance students' confidence and motivation for reading.

We believe that ISL combines cognitive skill and motivational will in students because the program emphasizes the functional value of strategic reading. Students who understand what they are learning and who appreciate the value of the extra effort required to use cognitive strategies may be more motivated for three reasons. First, the strategies have become personally significant as sensible, valuable actions that are applied intentionally and selectively at the reader's discretion. They are therefore personalized means to chosen goals. Second, there is a rationale provided for the strategies because they have utility and economy—using them results in better comprehension and savings of time in rereading or relearning. Third, the strategies are self-controlled and can be managed by students as personal resources. Failures can be attributed to strategy choice or inefficiency rather than inability, and success in reading can be promoted by effective use of strategies. These functional features of students' learning seem a natural reflection of pragmatic instruction. We believe that reading comprehension can be facilitated by emphasizing the principles and techniques embodied in ISL. The challenge is to inform students about cognitive strategies so that they perceive them as useful aids to reading. There are many methods and materials that can be developed for this purpose and the initial success of ISL should encourage others.

REFERENCES

Brown, A. L. (1980). Metacognitive development and reading. In R. Spiro, B. Bruce, & W. Brewer (Eds.), *Theoretical issues in reading comprehension.* Hillsdale, N.J.: Erlbaum.

Brown, A. L., Armbruster, B. B., & Baker, L. (1984). The role of metacognition in reading and studying. In J. Orasanu (Ed.), *A decade of reading research: Implications for practice.* Hillsdale, N.J.: Erlbaum

Brown, A. L., Palincsar, A. S., & Armbruster, B. B. (1984). Instructing comprehension fostering activities in interactive learning situations. In H. Mandle, N. Stein, & T. Trabasso (Eds.), *Learning from texts.* Hillsdale, N.J.: Erlbaum.

Duffy, G. G. et al. (1984). Instructional characteristics which promote strategic awareness in reading. Paper presented at the American Educational Research Association, New Orleans.

Durkin, D. (1978-1979). What classroom observations reveal about reading comprehension instruction. *Reading Research Quarterly, 14,* 418-533.

Durkin, D. (1981). Reading comprehension instruction in five basal reading series. *Reading Research Quarterly, 16,* 515-544.

Lee, S., Stigler, J., & Stevenson, H. (1985). Beginning reading in Chinese and English. In B. Foorman & A. Siegel (Eds.), *Learning to read: Cognitive universals and cultural constraints.* Hillsdale, N.J.: Erlbaum.

Maehr, M. (1983). On doing well in science: Why Johnny no longer excels: Why Sarah never did. In S. Paris, G. Olson, & H. Stevenson (Eds.), *Learning and motivation in the classroom.* Hillsdale, N.J.: Erlbaum.

Myers, M., & Paris, S. G. (1978). Children's metacognitive knowledge about reading. *Journal of Educational Psychology, 70,* 680-690.

National Assessment of Educational Progress (1981). Three national assessments of reading: Changes in performance, 1970- 1980. Report 11-R-01. Denver: Education Commission of the States.

Osborn, J., Jones, B. F., & Stein, M. (1984). The case for improving textbook programs: An issue of quality. A preconference report prepared for the National Forum on Educational Reform, "Excellence in our schools: Making it happen," San Francisco.

Palincsar, A. S., & Brown, A. L. (1984). Reciprocal teaching of comprehension fostering and monitoring activities. *Cognition and Instruction, 1,* 117-175.

Paris, S. G. et al. (1984). *Improving children's metacognition and reading comprehension with classroom instruction.* Paper presented at American Educational Research Association, New Orleans.

Paris, S. G., Cross, D. R., & Lipson, M. Y. (in press). Informed strategies for learning: A program to improve children's reading awareness and comprehension. *Journal of Educational Psychology.*

Paris, S. G., & Jacobs, J. E. (in press). The benefits of informed instruction for children's reading awareness and comprehension skills. *Child Developement.*

Paris, S. G., & Lindauer, B. K. (1982). The development of cognitive skills during childhood. In B. Wolman (Ed.), *Handbook of developmental psychology.* Englewood Cliffs, N.J.: Prentice-Hall.

Paris, S. G., Lipson M. Y., & Wixson, K. K. (1983). Becoming a strategic reader. *Contemporary Educational Psychology, 8,* 293– 316.

Paris, S. G., Newman, R. S., & Jacobs, J. E. (1985). Social contexts and functions of children's remembering. In C. J. Brainard & M. Pressley (Eds.), *The cognitive side of memory development.* New York: Springer-Verlag.

Pearson, P. D., & Gallagher, M. C. (1983). The instruction of reading comprehension. *Contemporary Educational Psychology, 8,* 317–344.

Reid, J. (1966). Learning to think about reading. *Educational Research, 9,* 56–62.

Resnick, L. B. (1983). Toward a cognitive theory of instruction. In S. Paris, G. Olson, & H. Stevenson (Eds.), *Learning and motivation in the classroom.* Hillsdale, N.J.: Erlbaum.

Rogoff, B., & Gardner, W. P. (1984). Adult guidance of cognitive development. In B. Rogoff & J. Lave (Eds.), *Everyday cognition: Its development in social context.* Cambridge, Mass.: Harvard University Press.

Wertsch, J., & Stone, C. (1978). Microgenesis as a tool for developmental analysis. *Quartarly Newsletter of the Laboratory of Comparative Human Cognition, 1,* 8–10.

Vygotsky, L. S. (1978). *Mind in society.* Cambridge, Mass.: Harvard University Press.

8

Reading (Dis)Ability:
An Interactionist Perspective

Karen K. Wixson • Marjorie Youmans Lipson

Clem is in the fourth grade and was recently classified as learning disabled. His teacher reports "he is working below grade level in all areas but math. His academic problems all seem to stem from his poor reading skills." The results of an informal reading inventory indicated that Clem's instructional level was at the second grade. However, when asked to read selections of 300 to 400 words from three different fourth-grade-level library books on sports topics, Clem read each selection with over 95 percent accuracy in word recognition and with 90 percent comprehension.

Linda is in the third grade and receives special help in phonics from the learning center in her school and from a tutor after school. Her parents report a history of ear infections. An informal reading inventory placed Linda's word recognition skills at the preprimer-primer level. Informal teaching sessions indicated that a whole-word approach was an effective means of teaching her to identify words. After 20 sessions of instruction, Linda's word recognition scores were 90 percent and 98 percent respectively on the Grade-2 word list and passage of the informal reading inventory.

Are these children reading disabled or not? What is reading disability? Who is disabled? Those who do not perform, those who are not learning, those who cannot learn? Or, is it better to ask how children learn and perform in different situations, and what this means for instruction?

The answer to these questions depends on the conceptual framework that is used to define reading and reading disability. In practice we actually use different models to guide our decision making for able and disabled readers. When an able reader fails to successfully complete a particular reading task, we typically view this failure as the result of some aspect of the task and alter the task accordingly. However, when a disabled readers fails, we presume that the failure reflects some internal disorder and initiate what Sarason and Doris (1979) call "the search for pathology." Although we are quick to accept the fact that variability in performance is a normal part of the process for able readers, we rarely allow for this possibility in evaluating the performance of less able readers.

In this chapter we argue that reading disability, like ability, is interactive. In other words, the *conceptual context* is the same for both reading ability and disability. The first section of the chapter presents an interactionist view of reading ability and disability. The second section considers the implication of this view for assessment and presents several examples of interactive assessment procedures.

AN INTERACTIONIST VIEW OF READING ABILITY AND DISABILITY

Recent theory and research in the area of reading indicate that reading is the process of constructing meaning through the interaction among the reader, the text, and the context of the reading situation. An essential finding of reading research is that the degree of interaction varies as a function of factors such as the reader's prior knowledge (Anderson et al., 1977); motivation and interest (Asher, 1980; Butkowsky & Willows, 1980); sociocultural background (McDermott, 1977); the type of text (Meyer, 1975; Stein & Glenn, 1979); the task demands (Williams, Taylor, & Ganger, 1981); and contextual factors (Mosenthal & Na, 1980).

Reading ability is most commonly evaluated in terms of performance on measures of word recognition and comprehension. Because the reading process is highly variable, it can be expected that performance on different measures of reading ability will vary according to the conditions of assessment. The following examples taken from the current literature support the view that children's performance on various measures of word recognition and comprehension can be expected to vary as a function of the conditions under which they are being evaluated.

Word Recognition

The ability to recognize words is frequently measured by asking students to read lists of isolated words or to read orally a series of short paragraphs. Students' errors are then counted and analyzed to determine their word recognition ability. Although recognition skill has traditionally been viewed as a stable and invariable ability, research suggests that children's performance on measures of word recognition is influenced by factors such as the reader's background and the nature of the words and passages to be read. For example, tests of word recognition are obviously composed of a subset of all possible words a child might know. Since basal reading programs do not all teach the same words, children may perform differently on various measures of word recognition depending on the words that they have been taught in a particular series. This possibility was explored by Jenkins and Pany (1978) who found discrepancies in the grade-equivalent scores that would be expected on commonly used standarized tests given the words that are taught in several different basal reading programs. In discussing their results, the authors emphasize that the child's actual reading skills would not have changed, only that the achievement test results would have been different.

We also know that the ability of young children of all skill levels (good, average, and poor) to recognize words varies depending on characteristics of the words themselves. When words contain regular phonic patterns, children are better able to recognize them. Further, children are more successful when reading high-frequency words than words that occur with low frequency in our language (Juel, 1980). The results of studies like these indicate that a child's poor performance on measures of word recognition in isolation may not be evidence of failure to learn, but may be a result of the particular words used on a given test.

Other measures of word regnition evaluate a reader's ability to recognize words in context. This skill is frequently measured by analyzing patterns of oral reading errors or *miscues* (Goodman, 1969; Goodman & Burke, 1972). A small sample of readers' miscues is often used to characterize their performance in all reading contexts. However, the research on miscue analysis indicates that children's miscue patterns are highly variable and are influenced by many factors (Wixson, 1979). These factors include: the instructional method (Barr, 1974–1975; DeLawter, 1975); the type of materials (Brazee, 1976); the syntactic difficulty of the text (Christie, 1977); the presence or absence of a stated purpose for reading (Thornton, 1973); the length of the passage (Menosky, 1971); the reader's prior knowledge of the material being read (Rousch, 1972); and, finally, the difficulty of the passage being read (Hutson & Niles, 1981; Kibby, 1979). Thus, it appears that miscue patterns reflect the strategies a reader employs in interaction with a particular reading activity. As such, they may or may not be representative of the strategies used in other reading situations.

Comprehension

The second area that is most commonly evaluated in assessments of reading ability is reading comprehension. Reading comprehension is frequently measured in terms of a student's ability to answer open-ended, multiple choice, or true-false questions following reading, and/or their ability to "recall" the content of a passage they have read. As in the case of word recognition, research suggests that children's performance on measures of comprehension is influenced by a number of factors including background knowledge, motivation and interest, text organization, the nature and content of the task, and the setting in which reading occurs.

One of the most powerful factors in determining children's performance on tests of comprehension is their prior knowledge of the passage topic or, as it is sometimes referred to, the familiarity of the passage. This factor has been studied in a variety of ways, but always with the same result. Higher levels of prior knowledge result in improved performance on measures of reading comprehension. For example, Pearson, Hansen, and Gordon (1979) demonstrated that children with more background knowledge prior to reading are better able to answer inferential questions about the passage than children with less background knowledge. Similarly, Lipson (1983) evaluated the comprehension performance of Jewish and Catholic children after reading passages describing the Bar Mitzvah and the First Communion and found that their performance on measures of free recall and on open-ended questions was better for the passage that was most directly related to their religious background. There is also evidence that when children are asked to recognize true statements about passages they have read, they are more successful when they possess either accurate prior knowledge or have no prior knowledge about a topic prior to reading. Further, they are least successful when they have incorrect prior knowledge (Lipson, 1982).

There are several other factors related to prior knowledge that have been found to influence children's performance on measures of comprehension. For example, we know that middle school students perform better on both recall measures and multiple-choice comprehension questions when the theme of a passage is familiar. Further, it has been demonstrated that children's ability to recall and answer questions is enhanced when reading materials contain words that occur with a high frequency in our language (Freebody & Anderson, 1983; Raphael et al., 1981; Wittrock, Marks, & Doctorow, 1975). As noted by Johnston (1984a), the results of research on the effects of prior knowledge indicate that two individuals who are equal in reading comprehension but who differ in prior knowledge are likely to demonstrate different levels of comprehension on the same text. This is important because these differences are likely to show up in assessments of reading comprehension ability.

In addition to passage familiarity, research has shown that other characteristics of the text such as its organization and structure have an effect on students' performance on measures of comprehension. Specifically, we know that middle school readers are better able to answer multiple-choice questions for well-organized as opposed to poorly organized text (Raphael et al., 1981). Therefore, even when the topic of a text is familiar, students of the same ability will perform differently depending on the presentation of the information. Further, junior high students seem to produce better recalls after reading a text with a comparison structure than after reading a text with a description structure (Brandt, 1978). There is also evidence that both good and poor readers perform better on recall tasks after they have read narative material as opposed to expository text (Berkowitz & Taylor, 1981). Once again the results of current research suggest variablity, not stability, in a reader's performance under different reading conditions.

Factors associated with the measurement tasks themselves have also been found to influence students' performance on measures of comprehension. For example, we have evidence that intermediate grade level students are better able to identify the main idea of simple expository paragraphs when they are asked to choose the best title than when they are asked to write a summary sentence (Williams, Taylor, & Ganger, 1981). This appears to be true for learning disabled students as well (Taylor & Williams, 1983). We also know that direct information about the tasks that are to follow reading can have a powerful influence on children's performance. Children who are given information about the postreading tasks answer more comprehension questions correctly and recall more than children who are not given this information. This is true of both learning disabled and normally achieving students (Wong, Wong, & LeMare, 1982).

Questioning tasks are probably the most frequent means of evaluating reading comprehension. The literatue on questioning suggests that there are a number of factors related to question construction that influence children's performance. Drum, Calfee, and Cook (1981) analyzed several standardized, multiple-choice tests of reading comprehension to determine the factors that contribute to individual differences in children's performance. Among other things, the results of this study indicate that performance decreases as the plausibility of the incorrect choice increases. There is also evidence that children's performance on question measures is influenced by both the type and the content of the questions they are asked. Evidence presented by Pearson et al. (1979) and Raphael, Winograd, and Pearson (1980) indicates that implicit or inferential questions are more difficult to answer than explicit or literal questions. Further, Wixson (1983, 1984) demonstrated that both the type of question asked and the information that is being questioned influence what is recalled and the types of inferences children make. Specifically, text-explicit questions result in fewer inferences, whereas text-implicit questions result in more text-based inferences and knowledge-based questions result in more knowledge-based inferences. In addition, students tend to recall the information that they have been questioned about to the exclusion of other information. Thus, it appears that the task itself can influence students' performance on various measures of comprehension ability.

The influence of contextual factors on reading performance obviously extends beyond the specific text or task condition to the setting in which the reading takes place. For example, Mosenthal and Na (1980) found differences in students' performance on a recall task admistered in two different settings—a formal testing situation and an informal reading lesson situation. These results suggest that students' performance in formal testing situations may not be representative of their performance on similar tasks in the classroom.

A final noteworthy factor that plays a major role in determining children's performance on measures of reading is motivation (see Johnston & Winograd, 1983; Paris, Olson, & Stevenson, 1983; Wigfield & Asher, 1984). As Paris, Lipson, and Wixson (1983) suggest, the possession of skills is not sufficient to ensure skilled performance. Children can choose to use their skills or not. Factors such as interest, the amount of time and effort required, willingness to take risks, achievement, self-concept, and fear of failure can influence a child's performance.

Whether people perform and learn in a particular situation depends on whether they *can do* what must be done and whether they *want to do* it (Adelman & Taylor, 1977). *Can do* is a matter of knowledge and skill, while *want to do* is matter of motivation. Learning and performance require both skill and will

(Paris, Lipson, & Wixson, 1983). However, it is important to realize that motivation is not simply a matter of reinforcement incentives, but that expectations, aspirations, values, and beliefs *combine* with skill to direct behavior. Within this context, motivation can be viewed in terms of : (1) how learners perceive the value of the learning situation, and (2) their ability to function appropriately within the situation (Adelman, 1978).

Recently researchers have begun to explore these affective factors as they relate to learning. For example, Butkowsky and Willows (1980) demonstrated that poor readers had significantly lower initial expectations for success than did average and good readers. When these same readers were confronted with repeated exposure to failure, the good and average readers demonstrated greater persistence than did the poor readers. In addition, 68 percent of the poor readers attributed their failures to low ability while only 12 to 13 percent of the good and average readers did so. The behavior demonstrated by the poor readers in this experiment has been characterized as one of "learned helplessness" (Dweck, 1975). They believed that no matter how hard they tried the outcome would be failure; therefore, they stopped trying. Fowler and Perterson (1981) have demonstrated that the persistence at reading tasks demonstrated by learned helpless readers ages 9 to 13 can be increased by attribution retraining. The results of these studies suggest that readers do make choices about how much time and effort to devote to a task. These are the motivational realities that influence children's performance on measures of reading, yet typically are neglected in cognitive accounts of reading ability.

In summary, reading disability, like ability, is interactive and therefore subject to variation. When reading disability is viewed from the same perspective as reading ability, it becomes clear how difficult, and probably fruitless, it is to search for a single cause. We are suggesting that an interactive view of reading be adopted for both reading ability and disability. An interactionist perspective is well suited to the understanding of both able and disabled readers, because it predicts variability in an individual's performance across texts, tasks, and settings. From this perspective, children's performance on various reading measures is considered an indication of what they can and will do under a specific set of conditions, rather than a set of fixed abilities or disabilities. When reading ability and disability are both viewed within the context of an interactive model, the necessity for identyfying the disability is eliminated and our attention is refocused on how each child performs under different conditions and which set of conditions is most likely to facilitate learning.

INTERACTIVE ASSESSMENT

Current approaches to the assessment of reading (dis)ability are concerned with explaining the variability between individual's performance in terms of relatively fixed traits inside the learner, rather than explaining within-individual variability in terms of specific interactions among reader, text, and context (Johnston, 1984b). Generally, standardized tests are designed to *control* "nuisance" factors such as prior knowledge, text organization, topic interest, and so forth. Therefore, they tend to be insensitive indicators of individual performance and are designed inadequately to provide diagnostic information about specific reading areas, much less about interactions that might be manipulated for instructional purposes (Thorndike, 1973–1974). In addition, such instruments are particularly vulnerable to the criticism that assessment bears little relationship to the reading tasks presented in other instructional settings where reading is required. Given what we know about the dynamic nature of the reading process, it is both unrealistic and undesirable to attempt to design assessment procedures that do not account for the factors that are known to influence the reading process. A more productive approach is to measure such nuisance factors and take them into account as valuable sources of information (Johnston, 1984a).

An interactionist perspective on reading ability and disability suggests that assessment must move away from the search for pathology and toward the specification of the conditions under which a child can and will learn. Hunt (1961) describes the problem of learning as the problem of the match between the child and the circumstances he or she encounters. He goes on to say that the notion of the proper match between child and circumstance is what teachers must grasp if they are to be effective. Within this context, (dis)ability is no longer seen as an absolute property of the reader, nor is difficulty considered to be an absolute property of a particular reading skill or task. Both a reader's ability and the difficulty of the reading activity are seen as relative properties of the interaction among specific reader, text, and instructional factors. Therefore, assessment needs to be focused on an evaluation of the existing match and the identification of the optimal match between a reader and the conditions of instruction.

The purpose of assessment, then, is to find patterns of *interactions* that allow us to make relatively good decisions about instruction. Few standardized tests provide this kind of information. Therefore, we often find it necessary to devise our own diagnostic strategies, with heavy reliance on trial remediation in assessing a child's ability (Vellutino et al., 1977). As Hunt (1961) suggests, the matching process is essentially a matter of empirical trial and error until those situations that call forth learning are discovered. This approach to assessment is consistent with the view that testing and teaching must become integral events (Glaser, 1981; Vygotsky, 1979).

We are not suggesting that current testing instruments be abandoned entirely, but that assessment move forward from a different perspective. We must look to the individual in interaction with specified texts, tasks, and methods. In the past, such specification has been incidental to the goal of identifying the reader's problem. Interactive assessment assumes that any assessment will remain incomplete if we look only to the ways in which the individual's knowledge and skill contribrute to or interfere with reading achievement. Although recent suggestions that assessment be focused on the instruction in contrast to the learner (e.g., Engelmann, Granzin, & Severson, 1979; Messick, 1984) are a step in the right direction, this approach to assessment also results in an incomplete evaluation. What is needed are approaches to assessment that permit an evaluation of the interaction between the learner and the conditions of the learning situation. We turn now to some representative practices that appear to have potential as rich sources of information about the conditions under which a reader can and will perform and learn.

Interviews

Recent evidence provided by Paris and his colleagues (Paris, Cross, & Lipson, in press; Paris & Jacobs, in press; Paris & Myers, 1981) shows that interview measures of reading knowledge are strongly realted to reading comprehension skill. This suggests that interviews offer considerable promise as a method of assessment. Questions related to readers' perceptions of their interactions with different classroom reading materials and tasks can provide useful information about the match between a reader and instruction that is unavailable otherwise.

Wixson et al. (1984) have developed an interview specifically designed to evaluate readers' awareness of the goals and purposes of reading activities, the demands imposed on them by specific reading activities, and the strategies they have available to carry out specific reading activities. Because the interview is designed to be used with actual classroom materials (a basal reader, a content-area text, workbook pages), the children's descriptions of their own abilities and the strategies they might employ is specific to the reading contexts they encounter daily. Such systematic probing can lead to a fairly detailed and differentiated profile of the child's knowledge and beliefs. For example, responses to the question, "If your teacher told you to remember the information in this story (chapter), what would be the best way to do this?" asked in the context of both a basal reader and a content-area text can provide information about a reader's level of strategy development and sensitivity to the varying demands that the same task can impose in different reading contexts. Some students provide responses such as "try hard" or "think about it" in both contexts, which may indicate a generalized lack of awareness regarding task demands and strategy usage. Other students' responses suggest that they have developed context-specific strategies for dealing with this particular task. Within the context of the basal reader, responses such as "Memorize the names of the characters," or "Think about the exciting action parts" suggest an awareness of the properties of narrative text that may serve as cues for remembering. Similarly, responses in the context of a content text such as "Take notes and study," "Write out the questions," "Have someone quiz you," and "Break it up into small parts and memorize it" suggest an awareness that remembering in this context requires a conscious effort on the part of the reader.

Both Paris and Jacobs (in press) and Wixson et al. (1984) report responses from children who possess mistaken notions about the goals of skilled reading. It appears, for example, that many children believe that the goal of reading is flawless word calling or that effective reading is equivalent to verbatim memory of text. Such inappropriate assessments by the reader may lead to a corresponding application of inappropriate strategies (e.g., pay attention only to the graphic cues or read it over and over again).

Interview data can also provide insights into learners' motivations and attributions for success and failure. For example, one of the first things we ask new clients in our reading clinics is how *they feel* about their reading and whether they believe they have a problem. To that question, Jonathon, age 10, responded, "I have to tell you something. I'm in the fourth grade, but I'm only using a third-grade reader. That's not very good." When pressed to discuss how he felt about his reading he responded, "Needs improvement—yeah, that's what it says, needs improvement." He also volunteered that his performance varied from day to day. "Like yesterday it was terrible, but today my teacher said 'Excellent'." Jonathon appears to rely heavily on external assessments of his ability and he believes that he is a poor reader. During more formal testing, he consistently minimized his successes with remarks like, "Sometimes the questions you ask are just too easy!"

Additional information is gleaned from questions asking children if they can identify any good readers among their peers. We then ask what makes them good readers. To this question Jonathon responded, "They try harder and say all the words right." Jonathon not only believes the goal of reading to be flawless decoding, but he believes that effort, not additional skill, stands between him and reading success. It is little wonder that he feels he does not have control of his reading performance.

Responses to interview questions like these can best be interpreted in combination with other sources of information. The value of interviews lies in their ability to suggest hypotheses for further evaluation that otherwise might never have been uncovered.

Verbal Reports

Verbal report procedures involve simply asking readers to stop at various points during their reading and "think aloud" about the processes and strategies they are using as they read (i.e., *how* they are reading as opposed to *what* they are reading). These procedures have been used with increasing frequency by researchers investigating reading performance and cognitive processing strategies (e.g., Garner, 1982; Olshavsky, 1976–1977). As a research methodology, verbal self-reports have been criticized for a variety of reasons (e.g., Nisbett & Wilson, 1977). However, as a clinical tool, we have found these procedures to be quite useful. Like interview data, verbal reports are attractive because they allow access to cognitive behaviors that are otherwise unobservable.

In combination with other assessment instruments, verbal reports can illuminate the ways in which readers attempt to process written text. The following excerpt from Stacy, an 11-year-old client, demonstrates that she is clearly using a meaning-focused strategy:

STACY: (*Reads title*) Space Ship Earth.
TUTOR: What were you thinking about when you read that title?

STACY: A space trip to earth. (*Reads first portion of text—haltingly and with many repetitions*) Boy! I had a lot of trouble with that one.

TUTOR: What makes you think you had trouble with it?

STACY: I kept messing up.

TUTOR: What do you mean by "messing up"?

STACY: I kept reading sentences twice.

TUTOR: What do you think caused you to read sentences twice like that.

STACY: Not understanding it.

TUTOR: Okay, did any of the words give you trouble?

STACY: No.

Stacy clearly belives that the reading process is driven by the search for meaning and her verbal reports reveal that her repetitions were attempts to understand what she was reading. Although miscues were obvious during this segment, Stacy's "fix-up" strategy was driven by a desire not to sound good but to construct a sensible text representation. Another verbal report protocol from this same child suggests that she also tries to bring her prior knowledge to bear on the text to make predictions.

STACY: (*Reads title*) "When Dinosaurs Lived on the Earth."

TUTOR: All right. Tell me something about what you were trying to think about as you were reading that line.

STACY: I was trying to figure out what the story is (going to be) about and was thinking that lately we've been—in social studies—we've been talking about paleontologists and stuff that dug up dinosaur bones.

Interactive assessment is continous, lasting as long as the working relationship with the child. Whereas specific aspects of the assessment will be specified and manipulated in the formal, early stages, the observation of interactions to glean information is a vital component of all work with the child. The excerpts from Stacy demonstrate the rich data that can be gathered as part of the diagnostic and instructional flow.

Like all aspects of reading and reading assessment, the verbal report data should not be construed as having fully described some static ability or set of strategies. Verbal reports are most likely to reflect what the reader is doing with a *specific text* under *specific conditions*. Farr and Mitchell (1981) have evidence that readers report using a variety of strategies within and across text types. For example, the tenth-grade good readers in their study reported using rereading as a strategy with expository text significantly more often than with narrative text. On the other hand, they more frequently reported using imagery (visualizing) with narrative text than with exposition. Qualitative differences in verbal reports have also been reported as a function of text difficulty (Olshavsky, 1978). Specifying the factors related to text and varying them systematically will greatly enhance the contributions of verbal report data to the total assessment.

READING (DIS)ABILITY / 141

Informal Reading Inventories

Informal reading inventories typically consist of graded word lists and a series of short, graded passages that are accompanied by 5 to 10 open-ended comprehension questions. Both teacher-made and commercially constructed informal reading inventories have been used extensively in reading assessment. They are used most often to obtain a reading ability level that is then used to place the child in appropriate reading materials. Measures of oral-reading accuracy, oral and silent-reading comprehension, and sight vocabulary are all obtained.

The use of informal reading inventories, as prescribed in the past, assumes that the reading process is static—that reading ability can be measured at some point in time using one set of materials to predict performance on other materials. As we have noted, such a view of reading is contradicted by the most recent theoretical and empirical reports. However, informal reading inventories are among the few instruments we have that allow us to observe the reader in situations that approximate actual classroom contexts. Consequently, we have continued to employ them in our work with children, but have introduced variations and controls that make them more useful in terms of interactive assessment.

We have found it especially useful to administer several informal reading inventories to each child during assessment (see Lipson et al., in press). When these tests are administered as directed, this practice often yields disparate placement estimates of reading ability. Thus, the examiner is forced to search for interactions that may be contributing to the variability in an individual's performance. Prior knowledge, text type and length, format, and prereading preparation have all been sources of variation in our work with children. In addition, the quantity and quality of postreading questions affects readers' performance. As children's performance is explored in detail to search for interactions, it is possible to find the strategies they are using and direct instruction accordingly.

The children's behaviors and comments as they perform under a variety of conditions are also useful. For example, a young boy who had been a willing examinee throughtout oral-reading testing, balked when he was asked to read silently. He was adamant, "I don't do so good when I read inside my head." Not surprisingly, his silent-reading comprehension was inferior to his oral-reading comprehension.

Oral Reading Children's productions during oral reading have long been used by both researchers and practitioners as a source of information about children's reading abilities. Early classifications of oral-reading errors lacked a theoretical or empirical base, although the implicit assumption was that children's errors were based entirely on the visual-perceptual aspects of the task. As a result of the work of the Goodmans and their colleagues (Goodman, 1969; Goodman & Burke, 1972), oral-reading errors have come to be perceived by many as resulting from the cue systems (e.g., context cues) used by the reader to process the text, hence the term *miscue*.

There has been a tendency, however, to charactize individual's miscues as static as well (see Wixson, 1979). Interactive assessment requires that miscues be evaluated not only for evidence of the cue system favored by the reader but also in terms of how cue usage changes as the text and task parameters change. Hutson and Niles (1981), for example, demonstrated that children made fewer semantically acceptable miscues as the material increased in difficulty. In addition, the frequency of totally wrong miscues increased. This suggests that we may get both a quantatively and qualitatively different picture of a reader depending on the material used. Often, in classroom, clinic, and laboratory settings, children who are not reading on grade level are evaluated with materials at or above their frustration level. In fact, the Goodmans suggest that the reader be evaluated with materials that will provoke a relatively large number of miscues. These practices can lead to judgements that the child has a deficit in using contextual cues whereas, in truth, it appears that all readers experience this difficulty when text difficulty is high.

Comprehension Children's comprehension is generally evaluated on informal reading inventories in terms of responses to open-ended postreading questions. Computing the percentage of correct answers for a given passage is only minimally helpful since it provides no information about *why* the child answered correctly or incorrectly. However, rich diagnostic information can be obtained by examining the answers to questions in terms of the source of the answer. Pearson and Johnson (1978) have developed a taxonomy of question-answer relationships that accounts not only for question type but for question type in relation to the source of the information required to answer the question. Raphael and her colleagues (Raphael & Pearson, 1982; Raphael et al., 1980) have found that when this taxonomy is used to examine question responses in terms of the likely source of the answer, it is possible to infer how the child is processing the text. For example, one young child performed poorly and consistently across all informal reading inventories, although there were peaks in her performance. An examination of her responses indicated that the child relied almost exclusively on preexisting knowledge rather than text information to answer questions. Thus, when asked, "What two things do birds like to eat?" she answered "Seeds and worms," a plausible but incorrect answer (the text explicitly says "stones and gravel"). When this pattern is observed consistently, it becomes clear that a child may be using a "perseverative reading strategy" (Kimmel & MacGinitie, 1984) that entails using prior knowledge to answer all questions regardless of the expected question-answer relationship.

Explorations of question-answer relationships can also suggest when comprehension problems are the result of inadequate word calling. If children miscue on a critical word in an informal reading inventory, it is entirely possible for them to have difficulty answering the comprehension questions. For example, a young child recently substituted *window* for *wide meadow* while reading. Two of the six comprehension questions that followed required references to that portion of the text. Clearly we cannot make judgments about a child's comprehension skills based only on a failure to respond to questions. We must look to what is required to answer the question and then determine if the information is available, has been misunderstood, or if the appropriate source is being tapped.

Diagnostic Teaching

We have briefly discussed several modifications in the initial assessment process. Although these provide rich data upon which to make initial guesses about instructional programs, diagnostic teaching is perhaps the most useful technique for identifying an optimal instruction match.

One of the most critical aspects of interactive assessment is the provision for systematic modification of the reading instructional situation in order to observe what the child does under specified conditions. We have chosen to call this *diagnostic teaching* because it captures the dual purposes of the endeavor. First, it allows for alterations in assessment conditions that clarify the diagnosis that has gone before. The level of teacher support, for example, can be systematically varied to observe the reader's performance under somewhat different conditions. Second, diagnostic teaching provides opportunities to try out methods of instruction that may be successful alternatives for working with a child. This last is a critical feature of interactive assessment precisely because it allows us to explore a child's performance under circumstances more like those encountered in the classroom on a regular basis.

During diagnostic teaching, the teacher can manipulate in a planned way any of the factors that are suspected to be contributing to or inhibiting reading achievement. Feuerstein, Rand, and Hoffman (1979) have suggested ways in which modifications in testing contexts may be introduced so that we may arrive at indexes of *learning*, rather than static measures of *capacity*. Cioffi and Carney (1983) have adapted several of Feuerstein's suggestions for use in reading assessment. They note that information appropriate for instructional use can be gleaned from traditional tests by altering the administration of the test. Accordingly, they suggest modifying the task in a variety of ways; for example, eliminating time constraints, providing appropriate prereading instruction, observing miscues under prepared versus unprepared conditions, and introducing instructional aids as needed. Ryan (1981) has also suggested several aspects of the task that might be manipulated to reveal an individual's repertoire of cognitive strategies including: instructions, degree of tutorial assistance, difficulty of the material, required response (recognition versus recall), time constraints, and task setting. In practice, diagnostic teaching often follows some initial estimates gained from other sources, such as those described previously. Thus, the factors to be manipulated are frequently identified prior to the initiation of the diagnostic teaching.

Specific adjustments in instruction are the most obvious candidates for manipulation. For example, Tom, age 7, demonstrated dramatic shifts in attitude and ability during the initial diagnostic session. He read correctly only 58 of the first 100 words on a list of common words and had difficulty recognizing the words in the first preprimer of the basal series in which he had been placed. In addition, he performed in a listless, bored manner. However, during the inteview, he indicated that he enjoyed being read to and demonstrated a wide knowledge of the books that had been read to him. Further, during a test of listening comprehension, he listened attentively and became very animated as he retold the story in elaborate detail. An observation in his classroom revealed his instruction was focused on readiness skills—specifically sound-symbol correspondence—and that he had not yet been give a book to read. Diagnostic teaching revealed that teaching him words taken from his own dictated stories provided a more appropriate instructional match for Tom. After only 20 sessions, he read the second-grade passage of an informal reading inventory with 96 percent accuracy and answered four of the five comprehension questions correctly.

Another instructional manipulation that has proven effective on a number of occasions is the use of direct instruction in task appraisal and control strategies (e.g., Paris, Cross, & Lipson, in press; Duffy & Roehler, 1982). Paris, Lipson, and Wixson (1983) suggest that the need to incorporate information about the *when* and *why* aspects of skill and strategy usage may be at least as important as providing information about the *what* and *how*. For example, when Ray, age 9, was asked during an initial interview if he thought he had trouble in reading, he replied, "Only with the hard words." Subsequent observation revealed that when he failed to recognize a word as he read, he quickly became frustrated and discouraged saying, "I can't" or "I don't know," whereupon he lost all interest in continuing to read. Through diagnostic teaching we discovered that when Ray was provided with explicit instruction about alternative strategies for identifying unknown words while reading and about *when* and *why* it was most appropriate to use these strategies, he was able to read in an uninterrupted manner. It is also important to note that diagnostic teaching enabled us to identify an instructional procedure that Ray could and would use independently, because it made sense to him.

In summary, we have described several assessment procedures that can be used to obtain information about the interaction between a reader and the conditions of the instructional context. The focus in interactive assessment is not on the reader or on instruction but on the interaction between them. Within this context it is important to remember that each encounter with a child must be viewed not as a success or a failure, but as a source of information that can be used for instructional planning.

CONCLUSION

Research suggests that reading ability and disability are both interactive processes. When reading ability and disability are both viewed from an interactionist perspective, there is no longer any need to continue the debate about who is disabled or what is disability. Variability in performance is expected for *all* readers as a result of the interaction between the reader and the reading situation. Therefore, the goal in assessment is not the identification of a disability but rather the specification of the conditions under which a particular child can and will perform and learn.

It is clear that this goal will not be accomplished easily unless our approach to assessment changes. Within an interactionist framework, it is no longer meaningful to evaluate a reader outside the context of the reading situation, nor is it useful to evaluate an instructional context in isolation from the reader. What is needed is an approach that focuses on the *interaction* between the reader and the conditions of the reading situation as a means of identifying an optimal *match* between reader and instruction.

The dynamic nature of reading and learning requires that interactive assessment be viewed as an ongoing process. Each encounter with a child must be seen as an opportunity for interactive assessment. In this manner, teaching and testing become integral events. By adopting an interactionist perspective of reading (dis)ability, we have taken a positive step toward providing instructional programs that are responsive to the needs of all children.

REFERENCES

Adelman, H. S. (1978). The concept of intrinsic motivation: Implications for practice and research with the learning disabled. *Learning Disability Quarterly, 1,* 43–54.

Adelman, H., & Taylor, L. (1977). Two steps toward improving learning for students with (and without) "learning problems." *Journal of Learning Disabilities, 10,* 455–461.

Anderson, R. C. et al. (1977). Frameworks for comprehending discourse. *American Educational Research Journal, 14,* 367–381.

Asher, S. (1980). Topic interest and children's reading comprehension. In R. J. Spiro, B. C. Bruce, & W. F. Brewer (Eds.), *Theoretical issues in reading comprehension.* Hillsdale N.J.: Erlbaum.

Barr, R. (1974–1975). The effect of instruction on pupil reading strategies. *Reading Research Quarterly, 10,* 555–582.

Berkowitz, S., & Taylor, B. (1981). The effects of text type and familiarity on the nature of information recalled by readers. In M. L. Kamil (Ed.), *Directions in reading: Research and instruction, 30th yearbook of the National Reading Conference.* Washington, D.C.: National Reading Conference.

Brandt, D. M. (1978). Prior knowledge of the author's schema and the comprehension of prose. Ph.D. diss., Arizona State University.

Brazee, P. E. (1976). A qualitative and quantitative description of eighth grade students' oral reading in both narrative and expository materials. Ph.D. diss., University of Northern Colorado.

Butkowsky, I. S., & Willows, D. M. (1980). Cognitive-motivational characteristics of children varying in reading ability: Evidence for learned helplessness in poor readers. *Journal of Educational Psychology, 72,* 408–422.

Christie, J. F. (1977). The effect of later appearing syntactic structures on seven- and eight-year-old children's oral reading errors. Ph.D. diss., Claremont Graduate School.

Cioffi, G., & Carney, J. J. (1983). Dynamic assessment of reading disabilities. *The Reading Teacher, 36,* 764–768.

DeLawter, J. A. (1975). The relationship of beginning reading instruction and miscue patterns. In W. D. Page (Ed.), *Help for the reading teacher: New directions in research.* Urbana, Ill.: National Conference on Research in English. ERIC Clearinghouse on Reading and Communication Skills, National Institute of Education.

Drum, P. A., Calfee, R. C. & Cook, L. K. (1981). The effects of surface structure variables on performance in reading comprehension tests. *Reading Research Quarterly, 16,* 486–514.

Duffy, G. G., & Roehler, L. R. (1982). The illusion of instruction. *Reading Research Quarterly, 17,* 438–445.

Dweck, C. S. (1975). The role of expectancies and attributions in the alleviation of learned helplessness. *Journal of Personality and Social Psychology, 31,* 674–685.

Engelmann, S., Granzin, A., & Severson, H. (1979). Diagnosing instruction. *Journal of Special Education, 13,* 355–364.

Farr, P. A., & Mitchell, J. (1981). *Towards an understanding of reader's comprehension of expository and narrative text.* Paper presented at the National Reading Conference, San Diego, Calif.

Feuerstein, R., Rand, Y., & Hoffman, M. B. (1979). *The dynamic assessment of retarded performers.* Baltimore, Md.: University Park Press.

Fowler, J. W., & Peterson, P. L. (1981). Increasing reading persistence and altering attributional style of learned helpless children. *Journal of Educational Psychology, 73,* 251–260.

Freebody, P., & Anderson, R. C. (1983). Effects of vocabulary difficulty, text cohesion, and schema availability on reading comprehension. *Reading Research Quarterly, 18,* 277–294.

Garner, R. (1982). Verbal report data on reading strategies. *Journal of Reading Behavior, 14,* 159–167.

Glaser, R. (1981). The future of testing. *American Psychologist, 36,* 923–936.

Goodman, K. S. (1969). Analysis of oral reading miscues: Applied psycholinguistics. *Reading Research Quarterly, 5,* 9–30.

Goodman, Y. M., & Burke, C. L. (1972). *Reading miscue inventory.* New York: Macmillan.

Hunt, J. Mc V. (1961). *Intelligence and experience.* New York: Ronald.

Hutson, B. A., & Niles, J. A. (1981). How similar are patterns of miscue in oral reading and cloze tasks? *Reading Improvement, 18,* 144–149.

Jenkins, J. R., & Pany, D. (1978). Standardized achievement tests: How useful for special education. *Exceptional Children, 44,* 448–453.

Johnston, P. H. (1984a). Prior knowledge and reading comprehension test bias. *Reading Research Quarterly, 19,* 219–239.

Johnston, P. H. (1984b). Assessment in reading. In P. D. Pearson (Ed.), *Handbook of reading research.* N.Y.: Longman.

Johnston, P. H., & Winograd, P. N. (December 1983). *Passive failure in reading.* Paper presented at the National Reading Conference, Austin, Tex.

Juel, C. (1980). Comparison of word identification strategies with varying context, word type, and reader skill. *Reading Research Quarterly, 15,* 358–376.

Kibby, M. W. (1979). Passage readability affects the oral reading strategies of disabled readers. *The Reading Teacher, 32,* 390–396.

Kimmel, S., & MacGinitie, W. H. (1984). Identifying children who use a perseverative text processing strategy. *Reading Research Quarterly, 19,* 162–172.

Lipson, M. Y. (1982). Learning new information from text: The role of prior knowledge and reading ability. *Journal of Reading Behavior, 14,* 243–262.

Lipson, M. Y. (1983). The influence of religious affiliation on children's memory for text information. *Reading Research Quarterly, 18,* 448–457.

Lipson, M. Y. et al. (in press). Explorations of the interactive nature of reading: Using comercial IRIs to gain insights. *Reading Psychology.*

McDermott, R. (1977). Social realtions as contexts for learning in school. *Harvard Educational Review, 47,* 198–213.

Menosky, D. M. (1971). A psycholinguistic description of oral reading miscues generated during the reading of varying portions of text by selected readers from grades two, four, six, and eight. Ph.D. diss. Wayne State University.

Messick, S. (1984). Assessment in context: Appraising student performance in relation to instructional quality. *Educational Researcher, 13,* 3–8.

Meyer, B. J. F. (1975). *The organization of prose and its effects on memory.* Amsterdam: North-Holland.

Mosenthal, P., & Na, T. J. (1980). Quality of children's recall under two classroom testing tasks: Towards a socio-psycholinguistic model of reading comprehension. *Reading Research Quarterly, 15,* 504–528.

Nisbett, R. E., & Wilson, T. D. (1977). Telling more than we know: Verbal reports on mental processes. *Psycholgical Review, 84,* 231–279.

Olshavsky, J. E. (1976–77). Reading as problem solving. *Reading Research Quarterly, 14,* 654–674.

Olshavsky, J. E. (1978). Comparison profiles of good and poor readers across materials of increasing difficulty. In P. D. Pearson & J. Hansen (Eds.), *Reading: Disciplined inquiry in process and practice, 27th yearbook of the National Reading Conference.* Washington, D.C.: National Reading Conference.

Paris, S. G., Cross, D. R., & Lipson, M. Y. (in press). Informed strategies for learning: A program to improve children's reading awareness and comprehension. *Journal of Educational Pschology.*

Paris, S. G., Lipson, M. Y., & Wixson, K. K. (1983). Becoming a strategic reader. *Contemporary Educational Psychology, 8,* 293–316.

Paris, S. G., & Jacobs, J. (in press). The benefits of informed instruction for children's reading awareness and comprehension skills. *Child Development.*

Paris, S. G., & Myers, M. (1981). Comprehension monitoring in good and poor readers. *Journal of Reading Behavior, 13,* 5–22.

Paris, S. G., Olson, G. M., & Stevenson, H. W. (Eds.). (1983). *Learning and motivation in the classroom.* Hillsdale, N.J.: Erlbaum.

Pearson, P. D., Hansen, J., & Gordon, C. (1979). The effect of background knowledge on young children's comprehension of explicit and implicit information. *Journal of Reading Behavior, 11,* 201–209.

Pearson, P. D., & Johnson, D. D. (1978). *Teaching reading comprehension.* N.Y.: Holt, Rinehart & Winston.

Raphael, T. E. et al. (1981). The effects of some known sources of reading difficulty on metacomprehension and comprehension. *Journal of Reading Behavior, 13,* 325–334.

Raphael, T. E., & Pearson, P. D. (in press). Increasing students' awareness of sources of information for answering questions. *American Educational Research Journal.*

Raphael, T. E., Winograd, P., & Pearson, P. D. (1980). Strategies children use in answering questions. In M. L. Kamil & A. J. Moe (Eds.), *Perspective in reading research and instruction, 29th yearbook of the National Reading Conference,* Washington, D.C.: National Reading Conference.

Rousch, P. D. (1972). A psycholinguistic investigation into the relationship between prior conceptual knowledge, oral reading miscues, silent reading, and post-reading performance. Ph.D. diss., Wayne State University.

Ryan, E. B. (1981). Identifying and remediating failures in reading comprehension. In T. G. Waller, & G. E. MacKinnon (Eds.), *Advances in reading research.* N.Y.: Academic.

Sarason, S. B., & Doris, J. (1979). *Educational handicap, public policy, and social history.* N.Y.: Free Press

Stein, N. L., & Glenn, C. G. (1979). An analysis of story comprehension in elementary school children. In R. O. Freedle (Ed.), *Advances in discourse processes (Vol. 2): New directions in discourse processing.* Norwood, N.J.: Ablex.

Taylor, M. B., & Williams, J. P. (1983). Comprehension of learning-disabled readers: Task and text variations. *Journal of Educational Psychology, 75,* 743–751.

Thorndike, R. L. (1973–1974). Reading as reasoning. *Reading Research Quarterly, 9,* 135–147.

Thornton, M. F. (1973). A psycholinguistic description of purposive oral reading and its effect on comprehension for subjects with different reading backgrounds. Ph.D. diss., Wayne State Univerisity.

Vellutine, F. R. et al., (1977). Has the perceptual deficit hypothesis led us astray? *Journal of Learning Disabilities, 10,* 375–388.

Vygotsky, L. (1979). *Mind in society.* Cambridge, Mass.: Harvard University Press.

Wigfield, A., & Asher, S. R. (1984). Social and motivational influences on reading. In P. D. Pearson (Ed.), *Handbook of reading research.* N.Y.: Longman.

Williams, J. P., Taylor, M. B., & Ganger, S. (1981). Text variations at the level of the individual sentence and the comprehension of simple expository paragraphs. *Journal of Educational Psychology, 67,* 484–489.

Wittrock, M. C., Marks, C., & Doctorow, M. (1975). Reading as a generative process. *Journal of Educational Psychology, 67,* 484– 489.

Wixson, K. K. (1979). Miscue analysis: A critical review. *Journal of Reading Behavior, 11,* 163–175.

Wixson, K. K. (1983). Postreading question-answer interactions and children's learning from text. *Journal of Educational Psychology, 30,* 413–423.

Wixson, K. K. (1984). Level of importance of postquestions and children's learning from text. *American Educational Research Journal, 21,* 419–434.

Wixson, K. K. et al. (1984). An interview for assessing students' perceptions of classroom reading tasks. *The Reading Teacher, 37,* 354–359.

Wong, B. Y. L., Wong, R., & LeMare, L. (1982). The effects of knowledge of criterion tasks on comprehension and recall in normally achieving and learning disabled children. *Journal of Educational Research, 76,* 119–126.

9

A New Focus on Free Reading: The Role of Trade Books in Reading Instruction

Linda G. Fielding • Paul T. Wilson • Richard C. Anderson

INTRODUCTION

Electronic technology is a dominant force in modern life. Watching television, listening to the radio, playing the stereo, and increasingly, using a computer take up significant portions of the average adult's time every day. Perhaps partly as a result few adults do very much reading, especially leisure reading. Today's students are subject to the same electronic influences. Schools do very little to understand or channel these influences, preoccupied instead with the traditional tasks of teaching the basics of reading and writing.

Literacy skills acquired in school directly relate to how literate students can be when they get out of school. Recently, though, we have begun to consider the influence that flows in the other direction; that is, the influence of students' out-of-school activities, particularly book reading, on the development of reading proficiency. Our purpose in this chapter is to translate what we have learned about literacy development outside school into suggestions for better ways to foster literacy in school.

FREE READING AND READING ACHIEVEMENT

Over the last two-and-a-half years, we have done two comprehensive investigations of how fifth-grade students spend their time out of school. In the first study, 53 students filled out a log sheet every day for a total of 8 weeks indicating the

Table 9.1 **Mean (S.D.) Minutes Per Day on Various Activities**

Activity	Study I		Study II	
Reading books	11.7	(15.9)	9.2	(17.2)
Reading comics	3.9	(5.9)	1.3	(3.3)
Reading newspapers and magazines	4.7	(7.1)	4.8	(6.7)
Reading mail	1.2	(1.8)	1.5	(3.0)
Listening to music	26.6	(28.3)	34.0	(53.8)
Watching TV	122.0	(73.7)	136.4	(94.9)
Eating dinner	25.7	(7.9)	27.8	(11.2)
Talking on phone	8.0	(9.2)	8.4	(10.4)
Going out	93.4	(45.1)	100.8	(50.0)
Practicing	14.5	(13.9)	13.5	(15.8)
Doing homework	16.7	(19.2)	21.0	(18.6)
Playing games	18.4	(18.5)	16.9	(23.5)
Working on hobby	10.7	(18.1)	11.2	(20.8)
Doing chores	16.3	(16.9)	14.6	(13.2)
Other	—		37.0	
Total minutes	374.3	(111.4)	439.6	(169.2)

numbers of minutes they spent on a range of free-time activities. In the second, more extensive study, 105 children filled out a similar log sheet for 26 weeks. Table 9.1 lists the average amounts of time that these children spent on a selection of free-time activities.

Of particular interest is the amount of time the children spent reading books. In both investigations, the children averaged about 10 minutes per day reading books. This represents a little more than 2 percent of their free time.

Ten minutes a day is an average amount that is inflated because of a few very long times; there were some avid readers who were reading upward of 80 minutes every day. In fact, a child who reads books as much as 10 minutes a day is a comparativily avid reader, who actually falls at the seventieth percentile among the children we studied.

Fifty percent of the children in the two samples were reading from books 4 minutes a day or less. Thirty percent read 2 minutes a day or less. Almost 10 percent never reported reading any book on any day. For the majority of the children, reading books occupied 1 percent of their free time or less.

The problem is not that students cannot read, but that on most days they do not. The average child in our studies read from a book only about one day in every five, although the average amount of time spent reading on that particular day was a respectable 46 minutes. Almost one-third of the children we studied claimed half or more of their total time reading during the entire two- to six-month period in a single day. Data from the log sheets indicated that although these children hardly ever read from books they were quite capable of reading 120 to 150 minutes in one day when, for instance, they had a book report due.

When children are capable of doing this much reading it is a pity that they do not do it more often. The reason we say this is that amount of book reading is fairly strongly related to growth in reading proficiency. We found that among all the ways children can spend their leisure time, average minutes per day reading books was the best and most consistent predictor of standized comprehension test performance, size of vocabulary, and gains in reading achievement between second and fifth grade.

Other researchers have verified the impact of leisure reading on school achievement. Heyns (1978) found that the amount of reading students did was the only summertime activity that made a unique contribution to achievement, and the effect was independent of family socioeconomic status. Similarly, in a study of Irish schoolchildren, Greaney (1980) found positive relationships between amount of reading of books and comic books and reading achievement, again independent of family background factors.

Our research and that of others (Greaney, 1980; Walberg & Tsai, 1984) indicates that there is particular form to the relationship between amount of book reading and reading achievement. Specifically, the first few minutes a day of reading are associated with sharp increases in achievement. After that, for each additional minute of reading there are smaller and smaller increments in achievement. The data suggest that if children could be induced to spend as few as 10 minutes a day, on average, reading books their reading proficiency might improve considerably.

WHY READING TRADE BOOKS IS VALUABLE

The traditionally accepted reason for reading books is that the collected wisdom of the ages is stored in them. So through reading books it is possible to gain access to the cultural heritage of all mankind. Recent research gives a fresh perspective to this time-honored justification: Not only is understanding the cultural heritage an end in its own right, but one of the major influences on reading comprehension is the knowledge that the reader already possesses about the topic and the form of the text being read. (See Anderson & Pearson, 1984, Pearson & Gallagher, 1983, or Wilson & Anderson, 1983, for reviews of this research.)

Wide reading of books can make a significant contribution to the development of students' knowledge. For instance, fiction can provide insights into different kinds of people, interpersonal relationships, and moral dilemmas that can be difficult to learn from real life.

Knowledge building is cumulative, and the relation between knowledge and comprehension is reciprocal. Already-possessed knowledge enables the comprehension of today's text, and the knowledge acquired from today's text enables the comprehension of tomorrow's. The student who does not read much does not know much. Furthermore, the student who does not know much cannot comprehend much.

In addition to serving as a source of new topical knowledge, book reading helps students deepen their knowledge of the forms of written language. This is one of the unique contributions from reading books, especially trade books. Basal readers and textbooks do not offer the same richness of vocabulary, sentence structure, or literary form as do trade books.

Analyses comparing the stories in basal readers with trade books show that the ones in primary-grade basals have fewer plot complications, involve less conflict among and within characters, and offer less insights into character's goals, motives, and feelings (Bruce, 1984). This is regrettable, because it probably makes the stories less interesting and harder to comprehend. A diet consisting only of basal stories probably will not prepare children well to deal with real literature. A practical solution for the classroom teacher is to supplement the basal reader with trade books.

Content-area textbooks in use in American classrooms are also deficient in several respects (Anderson & Armbruster, 1984; Armbruster & Gudbrandsen, 1984). Too many social studies and science texts are simply "baskets of facts," little more than loosely connected lists of propositions about a topic. The structure of textbook chapters is likely to be murky. There are simple structures that are well accepted among the canons of exposition, such as cause-effect, temporal sequence, or comparison-contrast. Yet it is seldom that one finds a content-area textbook selection that is clearly organized according to one of these structures. Students are more likely to encounter these structures and to learn to understand and appreciate them when they read good nonfiction trade books.

Besides its contribution to knowledge of text content and knowledge of text structure, independent reading of books is probably a major source of vocabulary growth. A synthesis of available evidence suggests that children in Grades 3 through 12 learn about 3,000 new words a year (Nagy, Herman, & Anderson, 1985). Some of these are acquired as the result of direct instruction, but a moment's reflection will show that this source can account for only a modest proportion of the total. To learn 3,000 words a year would require learning about 15 words every school day. Even the most determined advocates of direct vocabulary instruction do not introduce this many new words a day, let alone teach them to the level of mastery.

Another source of vocabulary growth is oral language experience. This is obviously the principal source for young children, and no doubt continues to be important throughout the life span. However, there is reason to believe that beginning in about the third grade, reading becomes a more important source of vocabulary growth than oral language for most people.

Oral and written language have different *type-token ratios*. Each different word in the language is a type. Each time that word occurs in actual usage, the occurrence is counted as a token. In oral language every individual word is used relatively often, so that there is a high ratio of tokens to types. In simple terms, in oral language, each word gets repeated frequently. In written language there is less repetition of words, so there is a lower ratio of tokens to types. Because there is less repetition of words and, it turns out, greater use of synonyms, there is a greater chance of encountering new words in print. Children who read more will encounter more new words in meaningful contexts, and thus will have a greater opportunity to expand their vocabularies. Nagy, Herman, and Anderson (1985) concluded on the basis of their research that book reading accounts for at least a third, and quite possibly most of the yearly vocabulary growth of the typical child in the middle grades.

Because of the heavy controls on the vocabulary of made-for-school reading material, trade books are a richer source of new words than textbooks. Also, the syntax, or sentence structure, of school reading materials is less varied than that of trade books (Davison, 1984). Thus, the child who spends time reading trade books has more opportunity to unravel the intricacies of written language than the child whose reading is restricted to textbooks.

A further advantage is that independent reading can be thought of as *self-initiated practice*. As with almost any skill, practice makes perfect. Our data indicates that some children do 10 to 20 times as much independent book reading as others. This means that they are getting vastly more practice and helps to explain why children who read a lot make more progress in reading.

Practice improves the automaticity of the basic skills of word indentification (LaBerge & Samuels, 1974; Perfetti & Lesgold, 1977). A reading skill at the *accuracy* level can be performed only if considerable attention is invested in it; reading skills at the *automatic* level, though, can be performed without exhausting the reader's attention. Since attention is limited, it is crucial for young readers to attain automaticity in lower-level word identification skills so their attention can be directed toward higher-level comprehension processes.

In comparison, for instance, to workbook pages or computer drills, the reading of books provides practice in a form that is likely to be particularly effective in increasing the automaticity of word identification skills. Reading books allows practice on chunks of information larger than isolated words, and the ability to automatically process larger chunks of information will increase overall reading fluency. Reading books also provides enjoyable practice for the child's developing skills of automaticity in decoding. This reinforces the instructional goal of having more of the children's attention available for understanding what they read.

In summary, reading books, especially trade books, in addition to being just plain fun is probably a major source of topical knowledge; knowledge of syntax, text structures, and literary forms; and vocabulary growth. Independent reading of books can be regarded as self-initiated practice that exercises all aspects of reading including, notably, word indentification skills.

THE WELL-SPRINGS OF AVID READING

Just as some children learn to read before any formal school instruction (Durkin, 1966; Taylor, 1983), some also become avid readers without direct intervention on the part of teachers. Studying the conditions under which children naturally become avid readers may shed light on what teachers might do to promote avid reading among more children. To this end, we interviewed eight average readers and the eight most avid readers from our first study as well as their parents (in all but one case, mothers). Our findings generally corroborate those of others who have interviewed early readers, avid readers, or their parents (Durkin, 1966; Ingham, 1981; Taylor, 1983).

The parents we interviewed gave us information about the home literacy environment, the expectations they as parents established, and the support they offered. None of the parents were surprised to find that their children were among the most avid readers in their classes. These parents viewed reading as essential to success in life and had always maintained a home atmosphere in which books were important and plentiful.

In the few cases in which neither parent was an avid reader, a grandparent or older sibling, or in one case a baby sitter, provided an early model of avid reading. All children were read to from the time they were very young; a few parents reported still reading to their sixth-grade children or noticing the older children listening when stories were read to younger siblings. Reading was viewed as a source of pleasure and relaxation as well as a source of new information and was a part of the home lives of the avid readers from their earliest memories.

The parents of avid readers believed in the importance of a stable family structure in which there were rules, guidance, and expectations. They sometimes set limits on the amount of time their children could spend watching television or talking on the telephone, usually expected their children to be at home at certain times, and frequently set a time by which children were expected to be in bed.

Although the parents of avid readers encouraged reading they rarely required it, preferring instead to surround their children with reading materials, model the uses of reading, suggest reading when the children wanted something to do, and set limits on some other activities such that reading became a more attractive option. A number of children, for example, read in bed at night when the only other option was sleeping!

Interestingly, a number of the parents credited required school reading for some of their children's at-home reading. They were generally in favor of this though they did not approve of requiring specific books or requiring book reports. They sometimes disapproved of their children's personal book selections, but they generally gave the children freedom of choice.

Few of the parents of avid readers could remember whether or to what degree their children could read before entering school six or seven years earlier. They did, however, remember their children's early interest in books and print. To us, this underscores the tendency we noticed for parents of avid readers to set up optimal conditions for literacy without pushing it, or even seeming to worry too much about it. The few who remembered working on some specific reading drill at home reported poor results. This does not mean that the parents did not take part in their children's learning. They reported answering children's questions; getting involved in children's projects, report writing, and book reading; and helping their children study for tests.

Interviews with the avid readers themselves revealed information about additional influences of which the parents were not aware. Beyond being read to, encouraged to read, shown the importance of reading, and surrounded by books at home the children mentioned several other influences that contributed to their being avid readers. Most interesting was that avid readers seemed to belong to *communities of readers*. They reported talking to peers, siblings, parents, or teachers about books they had read and getting recommendations for future reading from these same people. The avid readers never seemed to be at a loss for something to read. Although only a few of them read more than one book at a time they all had plans for what they would read next.

The avid readers were more aware than their parents of past or present teachers' influence on their reading habits. They mentioned teachers having books available in the classroom, reading out loud to the class, recommending books to them, talking to them about books they had read, requiring them to read a certain number of books in a grading period, or just being such good teachers that children came to love reading by being in their classes. According to the children themselves, teachers can have a significant influence on the development of avid reading.

A noteworthy observation from the children's interviews is their admission that except for one or two of them, reading is not always their number one favorite way to spend free time. Watching television, playing video or computer games, and participating in sports were often favored over reading. But for these children reading remains a frequent activity, perhaps because it is something they can do any time, without involving anyone else. As one child put it, "It's always been there and it always will be."

Other researchers (e.g., Greaney, 1980; Ingham, 1981) have noted that avid readers are generally more involved in many activities than less avid readers, spending less time, as Greaney put it, "lying about." But for less avid readers perhaps reading does have to compete for time with other activities. In fact, when we asked these avid readers why they thought some children liked to read and others did not they suggested two distinguishing features: They said that children who do not like to read probably have not had help in finding books that would be interesting to them and that children who read infrequently are so involved in other activities that they do not realize that reading can be fun, too.

WHAT TEACHERS CAN DO TO PROMOTE BOOK READING

The amount of out-of-school time that most children devote to reading is alarmingly small. An implication of this fact is that schools ought to be doing more to promote independent reading. There are several reasons for believing that this would pay dividends in reading achievement. In this section we will address the characteristics of an independent reading program that would actually foster increased reading.

A key feature of any program to promote independent reading is ready access to many books—preferably, a virtual *book flood*. If we were going to place a bet on one approach, we would favor a thoughtfully constructed in-class library of paperback trade books that the children are encourged to use in a number of different ways by an interested and motivated teacher. The in-class library program should be supplemented in collaboration with the school and public librarians.

We know of two evaluations of book floods. One, done in the Fiji Islands with children who were not native speakers of English, produced striking improvements in reading achievement that were still evident when the children were retested a few years later (Elley & Mangubhai, 1983). The other, done in Bradford, England, produced positive though less dramatic results. Children from schools that participated read more books, had better attitudes toward reading, and made larger gains in reading comprehension than children from comparison schools (Ingham, 1981).

In our opinion, good school and community libraries, although a valuable resource, cannot match the ready availability of books in classroom collections. Research has demonstrated that children who become avid readers typically have books immediately accessible to them in their homes (Durkin, 1966; Taylor, 1983). Providing a school enviroment that approximates the home conditions giving rise to avid reading could be especially helpful to children whose parents are not able to supply a steady flow of new books. As Heyns concluded, "the public provision of books is far more critical to families that do not or perhaps cannot purchase children's books or provide home libraries than for families that do" (1978, p. 181).

It stands to reason that a classroom library that is continuously available to children would make deciding to read easier and more likely. If children are absent on the day the class goes to the school library, leave their books at home, or do not like their selections, others can be selected with a minimum of fuss if there is a collection of books right in the classroom.

Classroom libraries will not be economically feasible in every school, or at least will not be given a high priority by those who hold the purse strings. If a classroom library is not affordable, an individual teacher might arrange to borrow 50 or so carefully selected books from the school library every month or two so there are at least some books immediately accessible.

A good starting point for building a classroom library is the annual Children's Choices list, published in the October edition of *The Reading Teacher* since 1974, consisting of favorite books of children at varying stages of reading maturity. Other obvious candidates are Caldecott and Newbery award winners. One caution, however. The children likely to be helped the most by having a library in the classroom are the ones who are neither frequent nor very good readers. So care must be taken to select some books that will appeal to less able readers, to include books that are not necessarily award winners *if these are the books that children want to read.*

Further evidence from the Bradford, England, project makes it clear that the easy access to books afforded by a classroom library is not alone sufficient to increase reading (Ingham, 1981). A number of the teachers did nothing to encourage use of the class library, knew little about the books it contained and so were unable to suggest titles to children, and even limited their students' use of the library. Some of the teachers stopped taking their children to the school library once they had a classroom library. Thus, in some classrooms having a library actually restricted the children's reading choices. The moral is that a teacher should build on the children's experience with the classroom library by actively encouraging them to seek books from school and public libraries, too. A classroom library should become a springboard into wider reading.

Our own findings and our analysis of other research suggests that in addition to easy access to books there are three other important features of a successful independent reading program: motivational activities designed to interest children in books, guidance in choosing books by someone who knows both the children and the books, and time set aside during the school day for independent silent reading.

Early readers and avid readers learn at home that reading is a source of pleasure. Teachers should try in a similar fashion to provide enjoyable experiences with books in the classroom. One approach is Holdaway's (1979) Shared Book Experience, a classroom method modeled on the home experience at its best. The foundation of the method is a teacher's skillful oral reading of children's books, often with pictures and print enlarged so that they are visible to the whole class. Repeated reading of a book in this manner, Holdaway argues, helps children learn enough of the story that they can soon "read" the book independently. Notice how similar this method is to the experience many children have at home when their parents read to them.

For older readers and longer books a teacher's oral reading of a few chapters, perhaps with some encouragement to predict what will happen next, may be all it takes to encourage children to finish the book on their own. In fact, in the book-flood experiment in the Fiji Islands (Elley & Mangubhai, 1983), a common activity in the successful classrooms was the teacher's reading aloud to the class from English (second language) storybooks.

Children enjoy the freedom to make their own decisions about what to read, but at the same time our results and the results of others (e.g., Ingham, 1981) indicate that children do appreciate suggestions and benefit from encouragement and discussion. Although some ideas about what to read can be inspired by a teacher's oral reading of books, guidance often needs to be more personalized, reflecting awareness of and interest in what individual children have just read and what topics they are interested in. Here a teacher's familiarity with the classroom collection becomes crucial.

Teachers who have read a lot of children's books, and who continue to read them on a regular basis, can lead more children to frequent reading than teachers who are not familiar with children's books. A male teacher in the Bradford experiment (Ingham, 1981) illustrates this point. Familiar with many books of interest to boys, he put this knowledge to work by personally recommending books to the individual boys in the class. However, by his own admission he knew little about girl-oriented books. At the end of the study, many of the boys in his class had noticeably increased the amount of reading they did; few of the girls had, however.

In an ideal classroom teachers would have read all of the books in the classroom library and would continually update their repertoire of children's literature. In *real* classrooms, where teachers are pressed for time as it is, firsthand knowledge of all books will not be possible. To supplement what we hope will be a constantly broadening firsthand knowledge of children's books, teachers can read synopses and sometimes short critiques of children's books in annotated bibliographies (See Appendix 1 for a list of bibliographies we have found useful). They can and should seek the help of school librarians. Usually lovers of children's literature themselves, school librarians are generally very happy to share some of what they know about children's books with teachers. We see continually expanding knowledge of children's books as essential to being a first-rate reading teacher.

We suggest that teachers encourage informal sharing among children of opinions about books, which will help build a community of readers within the class. During these discussions, avid readers will be a bountiful source of information about children's books. Ingham (1981) noted a twofold advantage to book discussions in the classrooms she visited. First, children learn from their peers about new books that they might read. Just as important, teachers who listen in and participate learn more about books that they have not yet found time to read themselves, and they learn more about the reading interests of their students—information that they can then use in their own discussions with children.

A final condition that we think is essential for a successful classroom reading program is *time for everyone to read*. The fairly common practice of letting children read when they finish their work is inadequate for several reasons. First, it caters to those who finish their work early—the very children who are probably already good readers. Second, it promotes the misconception that skill work has priority over real reading. Finally, it does not provide the quiet, relaxed atmosphere or the teacher modeling of silent reading that are possible when the whole class reads silently at a designated time.

For these reasons we advocate uninterrupted sustained silent reading (McCracken, 1971). Based on our finding that an average of 10 minutes of reading a day produces positive results, we recommend a total classroom silent reading time of about 70 minutes per week, divided among three weekly sessions. Since it is clear that some children, given choices, do not read in their spare time, the provision of in-class time for practicing reading coupled with guidance in book selection is important. We see a well-run sustained silent reading period as a functional way to increase engaged learning time (Fisher et al., 1980).

If teachers could reallocate their instructional time to allow 20 or 30 additional minutes of large-group time per day, their independent reading program would have a good foundation. At least three days a week, 20 minutes or so could be used for everyone, including the teacher, to read silently. The rest of the time could be used for the teacher to read to the class and for the children to discuss books and recommend them to each other.

To recapitulate, favorable school conditions will increase the amount of reading children do, their enjoyment of reading, and their reading achievement scores. Notice, too, that favorable school conditions can be expected to have a kind of multiplier effect: Children who get started on good books in school will continue to read these books ouside of school, further extending the amount of reading they do.

What can independent silent reading replace in an already crowded school day? Our answer is workbook pages! Many workbook pages and skill sheets are of poor quality and the activities they incorporate have little basis in research. Teachers may not be aware that research suggests that *amount of time spent on workbook pages and skill sheets is unrelated to gains in reading,* whereas, of course, amount of classroom time spent in silent reading is postively related (Leinhardt, Zigmond, & Cooley, 1981). We suggest judicious paring of workbook activities down to that core that actually helps children improve important reading skills. To do this, see Osborn's (1984) practical guide for evaluating workbook exercises. Reinforced by reading motivation activities and whole-class sustained silent reading, children could learn to use some of the time they formerly spent on seatwork for independent reading while the teacher works with other groups.

In summary, our most important message to teachers and teacher educators is that teachers and schools can be important influences in helping their students to develop a lifelong reading habit through a new focus on free reading. An in-class library, coupled with the motivation and time for all students to use it and personalized suggestions about what they can read, is a relatively inexpensive, easy, rewarding way for teachers to improve children's literacy development.

APPENDIX 1: ANNOTATED BIBLIOGRAPHIES OF CHILDREN'S BOOKS

American Library Association. (1981). *Let's read together—Books for family enjoyment* (4th ed.). Chicago: Author.

American Library Association. (1977). *Notable children's books 1940–1970.* Chicago: Author.

American Library Association. (1981). *Notable children's books 1971–1975.* Chicago: Author.

Council on Interracial Books for Children. (1976). *Human—and anti-human—values in children's books.* New York: Author.

Kimmel, M. M., & Segel, E. (1983). *For reading out loud!* New York: Delacourte.

Sutherland, Z. (Ed.). (1973). *The best in children's books—1966– 1972.* Chicago: University of Chicago Press.

Sutherland, Z. (Ed.). (1980). *The best in children's book—1973– 1978.* Chicago: University of Chicago Press.

Tway, E. (Ed.). (1981). *Reading ladders for human relations* (6th ed.). Washington, D.C.: American Council on Education.

White, M. (Ed.). (1979). *High interest easy reading, for junior and senior high school students* (3rd. ed.). Urbana, Ill.: National Council of Teachers of English.

White, M. L. (Ed.). (1981). *Adventuring with books* (new ed.). Urbana, Ill.: National Council of Teachers of English.

Williams, H. E. (1980). *The high/low consensus.* Williamsport, Pa.: Bro-Dart.

Williams, H. E. (1980). *Independent reading, K-3.* Williamsport, Pa.: Bro-Dart.

REFERENCES

Anderson, R. C., & Pearson, P. D. (1984). A schema-theoretic view of basic processes in reading comprehension. In P. D. Pearson (Ed.), *Handbook of reading research* (pp. 255–291). New York: Longman.

Anderson, T. H., & Armbruster, B. B. (1984). Content area textbooks. In R. C. Anderson, J. Osborn, & R. J. Tierney (Eds.), *Learning to read in American schools* (pp. 193–226). Hillsdale, N.J.: Erlbaum.

Armbruster, B. B., & Gudbrandsen, B. H. (1984). *Reading comprehension instruction in social studies programs or, on making mobiles out of soapsuds.* Tech. Rep. No. 309. Urbana, Ill.: University of Illinois, Center for the Study of Reading.

Bruce, B. (1984). A new point of view on children's stories. In R. C. Anderson, J. Osborn, & R. J. Tierney (Eds.), *Learning to read in American schools* (pp. 153–174). Hillsdale, N.J.: Erlbaum.

Davison, A. (1984). Readability—appraising text difficulty. In R. C. Anderson, J. Osborn, & R. J. Tierney (Eds.), *Learning to read in American schools* (pp. 121–139). Hillsdale, N.J.: Erlbaum.

Durkin, D. (1966). *Children who read early.* New York: Teachers College Press.

Elley, W. B., & Mangubhai, F. (1983). The impact of reading on second language learning. *Reading Research Quarterly, 19,* 53–67.

Fisher, C. W., et al. (1980). Teaching behaviors, academic learning time, and student achievement: An overview. In C. Denham & A. Lieberman (Eds.), *Time to learn* (pp. 7–32). Washington, D.C.: U. S. Government Printing Office.

Greaney, V. (1980). Factors related to amount and type of leisure time reading. *Reading Research Quarterly, 15,* 337–357.

Heyns, B. (1978). *Summer learning and the effects of schooling.* New York: Academic.

Holdaway, D. (1979). *The foundations of literacy.* Sydney: Ashton Scholastic.

Ingham, J. (1981). *Books and reading development.* London: Heinemann.

LaBerge, D., & Samuels, S. J. (1974). Toward a theory of automatic information processing in reading. *Cognitive Psychology, 6,* 293–323.

Leinhardt, G., Zigmond, N., & Cooley, W. W. (1981). Reading instruction and its effects. *American Educational Research Journal, 18,* 343–361.

McCracken, R. A. (1971). Initiating "sustained silent reading." *Journal of Reading, 14,* 521–529.

Nagy, W. E., Herman, P. A., & Anderson, R. C. (1985). Learning words in context. *Reading Research Quarterly, 20,* 233–253.

Osborn, J. (1984). The purpose, uses and contents of workbooks and some guidelines for publishers. In R. C. Anderson, J. Osborn, & R. J. Tierney (Eds.), *Learning to read in American schools* (pp. 45–111). Hillsdale, N.J.: Erlbaum.

Pearson, P. D., & Gallagher, M. C. (1983). The instruction of reading comprehension. *Contemporary Educational Psychology, 8,* 317–345.

Perfetti, C. A., & Lesgold, A. M. (1977). Discourse comprehension and sources of individual differences. In M. A. Just & P. A. Carpenter (Eds.), *Cognitive processes in comprehension* (pp. 141–183). Hillsdale, N.J.: Erlbaum.

Taylor, D. (1983). *Family literacy,* Exeter, N.H.: Heinemann.

Walberg, H. J., & Tsai, S. (1984). Reading achievement and diminshing returns to time. *Journal of Educational Psychology, 76,* 442–451.

Wilson, P. T., & Anderson, R. C. (1983). What they don't know will hurt them; The role of prior knowledge in comprehension. In J. Orasnu (Ed.), *Reading comprehension: From research to practice.* Hillsdale, N.J.: Erlbaum.

PART 3

THE CONTEXTS OF WRITING INSTRUCTION

The third question addressed in this volume focuses on contexts of writing, asking, *How can contexts for developing children's understanding and use of the writing process be characterized?* As is true of reading, writing occurs within and is influenced by the social context. This is particulary emphasized within a focus on the process of writing, in contrast to examining only final written products. Specifically, when focusing on process, the context in which written work proceeds becomes a crucial area of study. Thus, the third section is concerned with the variety of contexts in which writing occurs. DeFord's chapter provides a basis for examining how the writing environment influences what young writers produce. In effect, she examines the outcomes of different models of guidance used by teachers. She details three different environments: traditional, literature based, and mastery learning. She demonstrates, through samples of children's writing, that differences in their writing can be attributed to the social context of the classroom. When both students and teachers construct a writing environment and determine what can be written, more meaningful text is produced. A similar theme, and supporting evidence, is presented in the chapter by Tierney, Leys, and Rogers. They analyze lessons from two classrooms—a traditional approach to reading and writing instruction and a conference approach—in terms of the focus of teachers' and students' statements. They use the differences and similarities between the two classrooms to discuss the nature of writer-reader collaborations. They, too, underscore the point made by Rogoff that both teachers and learners construct their contexts for learning, showing how the students through their journals help to form the direction for their instruction.

The importance of creating a challenging and meaningful environment is clearly outlined in the DeFord and the Tierney, Leys, and Rogers chapters. Complementing these chapters are discussions of what must be considered in developing such atmospheres in schools. Hansen and Rubin and Bruce, take similar approaches to considering the development of a writing-communicative evnvironment, emphasizing that we are *all* learners, albeit with different goals. Hansen discusses the lessons her students, teachers, and administrators learned in moving to a conference approach teaching writing; Rubin and Bruce discuss the lessons learned by students, teachers, and software developers in creating a communicative environment using the microcomputer. In both chapters it is clear that learning must occur at many levels, from learning the skills of writing to learning how to encourage communication through writing, and that learning is a social process.

Together these chapters provide a basis for understanding the relationships between environments and written products within the school classroom. Since communication is at the root of successful guided participation, they also detail clearly the exciting learning that can occur on many levels once a course is begun toward creating a meaningful communicative environment.

10

Classroom Contexts for Literacy Learning

Diane E. Deford

Child language researchers have understood the importance of context in making sense of children's language learning for over three decades. In studying the development of verbal abilities, they have always had to rely on social and contextual information to fill in the limited surface forms of child language (Cook-Gumperz & Gumperz, 1976). Context is thought of as the physical setting, the people within the setting, what the people are doing and saying, and where and when they are doing it (Erickson & Shultz, 1981). A study of context, then, requires a linguistic and paralinguistic analysis of conversations and actions within the environment they take place along with a description of the participants' intentions (Cook-Gumperz & Gumperz, 1976).

From these analyses of language and contexts, researchers learned very early on that children understand "language is doing things with words to achieve practical ends" (Halliday, 1976), having the need to make sense, to fit words into appropriate social and/or contextual settings. Children bring this same language-learning process into school settings. But once children are in school, their ideas about language are often superseded by the folk linguistics of the classroom, with its categories and classes, its rules and regulations, its dos and don'ts (Halliday, 1976). Halliday suggests that prior to school children use language as a *resource* for reflection and action; for thinking about the world and self; for structuring experience and expressing personality; and for acting on the world organizing the behavior of others, and getting them to provide goods and services the child wants. Once in school, language is used as a set of *rules* as well as a set of resources.

Within the home, a child seeks to make sense of new information in light of previous experiences with various contextual settings. Rogoff (this volume) suggests that the most influential feature of mother-child interactions in instructional settings may be the guided participation of the child in the activity, with the adult and child coordinating responsibility for structuring and pacing the interaction. She found that mothers simultaneously attempted to maintain the child's attention, evaluate the pace of instruction, maintain social status relative to the child, and work on a specific component of the task. In the 32 mother-child dyads Rogoff and Gardner (1984) observed, 47 percent of the mothers tied the new task to the child's everyday context in introducing the task, and 84 percent did so at some point in the instructional session. In this way the adult managed to construct an instructional context that established references to what the child already knew. This allowed the child to build new information or skills into their already existing knowledge. The children put themselves in a position to observe what was going on, involved themselves with the ongoing activity, influenced the activities they particpated in, and demanded some involvement with the adults who were their guides in the learning task.

Prior to entry into school, then, children learn the linguistic, intellectual, and social aspects of their society. Social interaction, active participation, and meaningful demonstrations within familiar contexts have been key characteristics of their learning environment. As a means of understanding the transition into the world of formal schooling and children's literacy learning, a study of three classroom contexts was undertaken. This chapter describes children's interactions with teachers and peers in three very different first-grade contexts as they learned about and explored written language. Each of the teachers dealt with children's previous language knowledge in different ways and acted upon a variety of *language rules* that were used in explicit and tacit ways to extend children's language learning (i.e., "Everything you write must be spelled correctly"). Social interactions, the nature of children's participation, and the types of demonstrations varied as well. This study points up the importance of conversational communication and the environment devised for literacy learning in children's understanding of written language.

CONVERSATIONAL COMMUNICATION

From studies of language used in classrooms, it is evident that conversation is more than a set of utterances with a single thematic connection (Cook-Gumperz & Gumperz, 1976). Acts, or language alone, do not make conversational communication unique; but the examination of acts and language in relation to the apparent goals of the interaction makes conversational communication distinct from connected utterances. Context influences our sense of appropriateness of rules and the interpretation of speech acts. In a classroom setting, a statement such as "We don't sit on tables" is understood as, "Don't sit on this table, or else" (Sinclair & Coulthard, 1975). In another context the same statement might be interpreted as an explanation or an apology. Successful interaction in a given situation depends on a language user's ability to read and respond to these situational cues in what is deemed an appropriate manner.

What this suggests is that language users (e.g., teachers and students) bring expectations based upon past experiences about how and when people talk, what constitutes an appropriate topic, and what constitutes appropriate participation (Green & Smith, 1983). Green and Smith indicate that some of the rules that govern these interactions have been identified as gaining access to conversations (Gumperz, 1977; Stoffan-Roth, 1981); taking turns at talk (Cahir & Kovacs, 1981; Sacks, Jefferson & Schegloff, 1974); constructing narratives (Michaels & Cook-Gumperz, 1979; Tannen 1979); interacting appropriately (Goffman, 1980; Hymes, 1974; Wilkinson, 1982); demonstrating group membership (Erickson & Shultz, 1981, 1982); and interactional synchrony or how all of these rules are orchestrated (Erickson & Shultz, 1982).

Given that language is not always explicit, participants within conversational communications make inferences based upon their understanding of the rules that have been signaled, and negotiate meanings as necessary within face-to-face interactions (Green & Smith, 1983). Within classroom interactions about writing instruction, for example, a teacher may caution children to make sure they spell everything correctly, or may mark spelling errors with a red mark after a paper is completed. In either instance, the writer understands that spelling is important in the teacher's evaluation of good writing. Future writing will be influenced by this critieria in such a way that writers may be more concerned with the mechanics of their writing than in what they want to communicate through writing. In this way, writers seek to negotiate with the rules for language use specified within the classroom setting.

ENVIRONMENT DEVISED FOR LITERACY LEARNING

Each teacher also has a set of expectations about how print should be used within the classroom environment. These notions are a result, certainly, of negotiations among beliefs about how learning best takes place; what constitutes worthy instructional materials; what indicates growth in reading and writing; what is evaluated as *good* in the use of the reading and writing processes; and what *givens* there are within the social environment of the school (materials, services, administrative criteria, etc.). Students come to the instructional environment with a set of expectations about how they function in the world. If story reading (Heath, 1983) has been a valued experience in their home, then they have developed an understanding of stories, how they operate, and how story-reading time is carried out. The sum total of these beliefs serve to define the context for literacy learning and the interactions that take place within that environment.

Language is fundamental for conveying the resulting context as teachers use language to make demonstrations *about* language and evaluate the language children are using (see Figure 10.1). Children, on the other hand, learn language, learn through the use of language, and learn *about* language [knowledge about

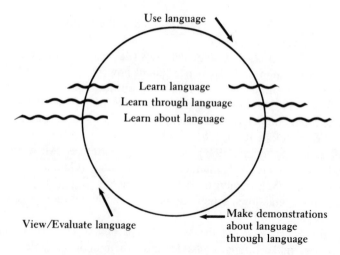

Figure 10.1 **Language Model of Teaching and Learning**

the abstract characteristics of langage and how to talk about this (Halliday, 1975)] within the variety of contexts in which they find themselves.

If, for example, a teacher believes that children learn oral or written language by practicing specified forms until mastery occurs, then the environment will facilitate practice and use an operational definition for mastery as the criterion. The materials will be sequentially organized, and practice periods built into the day. Tests will be give to assess mastery levels, and instruction and further practice will be provided in areas of need. Control of the materials and pacing of instruction is in the hands of the teacher and the curriculum guide, ostensibly in response to student performance. These beliefs will serve as a frame of reference for a teacher in selecting materials for instruction and for presenting and guiding the use of these instructional materials. These values will be communicated to the students, both verbally and nonverbally. Students will adhere to and improvise upon the contextual demands, or will find ways to change the nature of those demands through active, or passive, negotiation.

EXPLORATION OF THE CLASSROOM CONTEXT

The remainder of this chapter explores how specific values and beliefs about written language are constructed and communicated by teachers and children within classroom environments. The three classrooms studied were part of a research project funded by the Spencer Foundation. These classrooms were selected because (1) the teachers were identified as exemplary, yet (2) the teachers constructed contexts for literacy learning that differed dramatically from each other. All teachers were approximately the same age and were either working on advanced degrees or had recently completed their master's degrees.

The purpose of this research was to document the different ways these teachers dealt with language through ethnographic techniques of interviews, field notes, audio- and videotaping and triangulation procedures through which teachers and children confirmed the interpretation of data. We visited each classroom on three separate two-week intervals. Writing samples produced during the weeks of our classroom visits were collected, photocopied, and returned to the teachers. Videotapes of four children of high- and low-writing ability as defined by the teacher were used for case study analysis of the writing process in each room. Two researchers were present at all times of data collection, each taking independent field notes.

Each teacher believed strongly in the goals they held for their literacy program. In terms of basic organization, these classrooms will be characterized as traditional, literature based, and mastery learning. Curriculum models derived out of our observations were confirmed by the teachers participating in the study. The major features of the classroom organizations are set forth in Table 10.1 for an overall comparison. Each classroom environment will be described in detail in the following sections with attention given to the character of the rooms, the organization and management of the curriculum, the schedules, typical days, reading and writing instruction, and interpersonal communication.

The Traditional Classroom

The traditional classroom teacher described her classroom as a colorful, enticing room for learning. She incorporated a variety of teaching resources into the day with television, music, educational computer programs, learning centers, language experience stories, art, children's literature, basal and content materials, and games to carry out the curriculum. Parent volunteers helped with individualized practice or work sessions. The context was formed in this classroom by the teacher

Table 10.1 **Classroom Organization**

	Traditional	Literature	Mastery Learning
Reading	Basal Literature supplement	Literature	Programmed basal Mastery overlay

Class grouping	Heterogeneous
	  ability
		Heterogeneous
		Flexible
			Tracked—
			  homogeneous
			  ability

Content	Segmented	Integrated	Segmented

Physical features	Desks & learning
	  centers
		Work areas &
		  tables
			Desks

Writing feedback	Mechanics & message	Message	Mechanics
Writing	Teacher assigned	Student initiated	Teacher assigned

Display	Commercial &
	  student writing
		Student writing	Commercial &
			  student writing

(see Figure 10.2), who interpreted and presented the curriculum in light of her own personal goals, the resources she marshalled in support of those goals, and her evaluations of students' needs. Although there was a district-adopted curriculum guide, the teacher was free to determine emphasis, timing, and means of expressing the stated objectives. The students were warmly invited to participate in this context through a series of teacher-guided experiences.

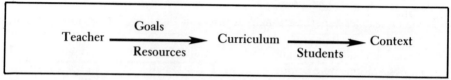

Figure 10.2 **Traditional Curriculum Model**

Within this greater curriculum model, the traditional teacher set up a series of general rules for classroom participation, some explicitly stated, others inferred from teacher-student interactions. The overriding teacher needs were for: (1) a productive, smoothly flowing, moderately quiet day and (2) providing for student capabilities within assignments so as little confusion as possible resulted. The four rules for students within this classroom were:

1. *Work time*   Complete work with thoroughness and neatness; do one center as part of your seatwork; be quiet enough that others will be able to work.
2. *Sharing time*   Respect others, listen, and understand what others have to say.
3. *Line-up time*   Maintain order and quiet through the halls.
4. *Transition time*   Follow directions, move smoothly from one activity to another.

There was usually a low hum of activity throughout the work period that occurred during reading-group time, but if talk became too loud the teacher would quietly deal with the problem and continue with her group. The teacher had attended a workshop on assertive discipline control and used a modification of this program for allowing students ownership and control of their behavior. There was a lot of cooperation and mutal respect exhibited among teacher and students. The teacher exhibited a concern for individual needs and encouraged children's use of their own backgrounds of experience in discussions held throughout the day.

A typical day began with opening exercises (i.e., Pledge of Allegiance) and quiet informal conversations between the teacher and individual children. They started the work day with a schedule review and sharing time followed by phonics, math, and reading groups. The transitions between each activity were marked by group songs or movement games like Simon Says. After lunch a book was usually shared or group- or individual-language experience stories produced, with the remainder of the day reserved for science, health, social studies, art, and music on rotating cycles. The teacher often ate lunch with her children and then returned to the classroom before them to prepare for the afternoon.

Reading group was generally based upon the basal program, with seatwork made up of workbook pages and phonics worksheets. Occasionally, a children's literature book was a focal point in the reading lesson, and other times the basal story was used in a buddy-reading experience. Seatwork activities included a math sheet and some writing or reading activity. If the seatwork was a writing activity, the topic was teacher assigned. At the beginning of the year these assigned writings consisted of fill-in-the-blank exercises, word categorization activities for practice of phonics generalizations, and copying or handwriting practice experiences. Toward the end of the year, assigned writing consisted of pen-pal letters, stories written about pictures, or extensions to literature books (see Figure 10.3). Usually there was a group discussion before the children wrote to bring out personal experiences and ideas, with the teacher writing words they might encounter on the board for them. There was an initial emphasis on mechanics and careful writing, with more stress on the message as the year progressed. Very little writing was student initiated.

The 21 children in this classroom were cooperative and responsible workers. They participated actively in teacher-lead discussions and tried diligently to complete their work. Once assigned work was completed they could choose an activity from available learning centers or select a game to play so long as they did not disturb others who needed quiet time. Children talked quietly to their neighbors while they did their seatwork. Conversations centered mostly around work ("How far have you gotten?" "How do you spell *where*?"), events happening at home with their families, and activities that were part of the school agenda (recess, lunch, and so on). Child-child conversations occurred openly during this period of time with most other conversations characterized as teacher-child or teacher-group throughout the rest of the day.

The teacher sought to anticipate student needs prior to initiating a lesson as a means of limiting the children's confusion. The lessons were thoroughly planned, allowing few child-initiated decisions and usually structured so that they could be completed in one work period. Most conversational exchanges prior to the onset of work periods were to clarify directions the teacher had established for doing activities. Once the work period began, the children worked within the confines of the lesson frame so the teacher could be free to conduct reading groups.

The Literature-Based Classroom

The classroom teacher using literature as a reading and writing focus stated that her room was a place for children to learn through talk, play, reading, and writing. She immersed the children in print, from story books and infomational books to student-produced print that was displayed around play-work areas (i.e., housekeeping, blocks, sand box, art, library, and math-science). Parents were invited to par-

Figure 10.3 **Range of Traditional Classroom Writing**

Figure 10.4 **Literature-Based Curriculum Model**

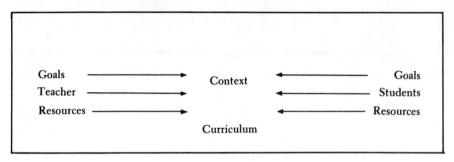

ticipate in small-group projects or field trips, or just to come observe. Additionally, other children from the school visited the classroom to read with her students as well. Children brought in materials from home to share, such as birds' nests, pictures, books, dolls, and so forth, which then became part of the environment for varying periods of time. The context for literacy was formed by the teacher and children as they wrote, read, and explored the environment inside and outside their room (see Figure 10.4). Teacher goals and student goals were negotiated to produce the curriculum and context.

The rules the teacher and children set together revolved around issues of productive work and social/child development. The teacher extended children's language and work through individual conferences and personal conversations centered around negotiated writing-reading interests. The rules apparent within this setting were:

1. *Work time* Complete work initiated (with teacher and peer guidance), even though it may take a week to complete a project.
2. *Sharing time* Respect others and value what they've contributed to the classroom environment.
3. *Play areas* Set personal goals (with teacher guidance) that balance play with work and do not allow play to interrupt other students at work.
4. *Clean-up time* Clean up the areas you have been working in. If something is left to be done, be responsible for doing it. When finished with your jobs, move to the library area and select a book to read or share.
5. *Reading time* Read either alone or in small groups, but read.

There was moderate talking throughout the two work periods in the day. If noise became too loud, the teacher would turn off the lights or quietly say, "Freeze." The students resumed working with a moderate noise level. The students helped each other or asked for help from adults within the room if they had problems. The teacher built sharing into both reading and writing by asking the children to share their books (trade or self-authored) with classmates during the day.

A typical day began with the children at the library area sharing a book with a friend or reading by themselves. After attendance and lunch count were taken, the teacher read a book and discussed it with the group. Then children with unfinished projects were quickly set to work and students who were starting new projects talked with the teacher before they began. Once everyone was working the teacher moved from student to student conferencing about their work in progress, answering questions, guiding them through problems, and working with specific students individually or in small groups. The projects varied from bookmaking (i.e., poetry, stories, informational prose, songbooks, letters) to math, science, or art experiences (i.e., charts comparing the illustrations used by Tomie De Paola, weighing and measuring, surveys about how many pets each student had at home). Once the work period ended and the room was cleaned up there was usually time for student sharing or for reading another book. This schedule was repeated in the afternoon, with students grouped and regrouped for special activities or time with other teachers.

Reading, writing, and instruction were not necessarily separate activities; they were handled individually or in small-group situations, with the teacher assessing and teaching on a daily basis from information gathered during the work period. Instruction occurred through a variety of topics and materials. Field trips were numerous, even if only to another room to watch a chicken hatching. These experiences became topics for the reading and writing that occurred within the classroom where the children and the teacher worked together to make decisions about writing and reading themes. The children also used literature books as the basis for their writing. However, the teacher consistently encouraged them to make the story their own (see Figure 10.5). For example, she stressed independence in writing and spelling, but guided them individually over problem spots. Reading in content areas was facilitated through surveys, and measuring-and-weighing activities that emerged from student's questions and problems. In addition, the teacher assigned math practice sheets to be completed within the work period. Science, social studies, and health were woven into the group discussions, field trips, writing, and reading. The writing that grew out of the total context was literature based, personal, and informational; other forms, such as poetry and letters, occurred less often.

The children in this room were active, independent, and generally responsible for the social climate within the room. They helped each other and collaborated on projects out of friendship or common interests. They talked to each other and adults in the room freely, with home and school activity providing significant topics in their conversations and their writing ("These are pictures of my cat. I'm writing a book about my pet."). Child-child conversations and teacher-child conversations were most common and teacher-group interactions occurred less often. Children were consistently involved in the decisions about work and play. It was not unusual for the class to run smoothly with the teacher out of the room (the hallway was used to extend classroom space).

The teacher supplied a variety of materials, then structured open-ended activities and helped students make decisions about personal directions and out-

Billy (5 yrs.)   Old Befana, how old are you   I am 5.
I will be 6 in Mar. I like my cookie
and book mark!

Jim and the Beanstalk by Jenny and Kristina

Page 1. Early one morning Jim woke up
and saw a great plant growing
outside

Page 2. I'll see how high it goes And
he began to climb up the plant.

Page 3. When he got to the top he
went inside.

Page 4. When he reached the top of the
plant Jim saw a castle.
"I'm Hungry he said. Ill ask
at the castle
for breakfast. I Hope. They
Have. some. Cornflakes

Page 5. Jim ran to the castle and knocked
on the. Door. He waited. and.

waited. until. the door was slowly
opened by a very old giant AHa said
the Giant a boy a nice juicy boy
Three fried boys. on a slice
of toast That's What I used to
enjoy

Page 6. The Giant shared his break of beef
and beer with Jim is your name Jack
he asked   no   he said   Jim

Page 7. Don't you have any glasses asked
Jim only beer Glasses said the
Giant. I mean reading said Jim.
they Go on your nose

Page 8. Jim came down The Tree and There
was his mother   The End

Figure 10.5   **Range of Literature-Based Writing**

comes. Whereas all students might work within the thematic study of Tomie De Paola books, some might write a book, some might complete a school wide survey, and some might make posters, dioramas, and puppets. Teacher planning for student projects ususally extended from several days to several weeks during which time the teacher evaluated progress continuously until the projects reached completion.

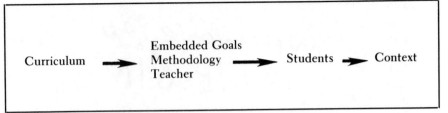

Figure 10.6 **Mastery Learning Curriculum Model**

The Mastery Learning Classroom

In the mastery learning room, the teacher's stated goal was to create a comfortable but productive environment for work. The sound of the teacher and students within the reading group dominated. Students outside the reading group worked quietly, or moved about the room getting supplies related to their work. Time throughout the morning was spent in direct instruction or individual practice and work. After reading groups were completed, the teacher or an aide was available to direct unit tests on an individual basis for students who had finished their practice. Parents were not used within the instructional program. The literacy context was directed by the curriculum, the teacher serving as mediator and manager of the reading and writing program (see Figure 10.6). Students worked efficiently and comfortably within this environment knowing clearly both the goals and evaluation process.

The explicit and implicit rules generated were most often the direct result of the management system used to deliver content of the curriculum. The programmed reading material vocabulary was worked into this system of program management. It provided for introduction, practice, review, and testing sequences within the reading and writing program. There was direct teaching, oral and written practice, proofing, correction, and testing that was an overlay to the programmed, individualized basal. The rules in operation were:

1. *Work time*   Complete work neatly and accurately; work quietly at desk; progress consistently through the programmed reader; complete all work before lunch recess.
2. *Line-up time*   Maintain order and quiet in the halls and within the room.
3. *Group-Response time*   Whenever a new word or skill is introduced, whether during reading group or writing time, everyone must participate in the choral responses to teacher questions unless otherwise requested.
4. *Written work*   Spell words taught in class correctly and spell other words you may need the best you can.

Students cooperated in following work-time rules, and there was seldom an interruption in the flow of reading-group lessons. The weekly library visits were carried out without teacher direction, and movement within the room for supplies was in keeping with the class policies. If students were unable to work within a work group, their desks were moved to the perimeter of the work space to insure better concentration. If the teacher had corrective feedback for students it was carried out in private conversations.

Each day began with students completing a math worksheet at their desks until the bell rang. Once attendance and lunch count were taken, the children moved to the front of the room to listen to the teacher explain their work assignments. While they returned to their desks and began working the teacher conducted reading-group lessons at the back of the room. The reading groups worked through their word lists and the introduction and practice of vocabulary in oral and written forms. Once the groups had met there was often time to complete work and read from books in the class library until it was time for lunch. The afternoon was used to practice writing and deal with content-area instruction or any special classes such as art, physical education, or music.

The classes were tracked by ability, and students were further ability grouped for reading. The children moved independently through their workbook pages reading each word, statement, or paragraph three times and writing any required response on a practice sheet of paper. If there were pages to read in their basal readers they read them as directed by their teacher. After doing their assigned pages within a given unit, they took a practice test individually, then worked with a partner to practice taking the test. They went to the teacher or the teacher's aide for their final test.

Assigned writing was also part of their seatwork for the day. This was usually a sentence or story-writing exercise using the characters from their programmed readers, or a writing experience using a picture stimulus, or a story starter (see Figure 10.7). Students were held accountable for accurately spelling words that had been taught during the year, but were encouraged to spell others on their own. Mastery levels set for reading-word lists, writing, and comprehension were 96 percent, 90 percent, and 83 percent respectively. All words were to be read and spelled in a timed task with 100 percent accuracy in order to move on to the next unit.

Most conversational exchanges were teacher-group directed. Child talk was generally limited to teacher-lead interactions, and work-period conversation seldom rose above a whisper. If conversations did occur they were related to the assigned task—such as comparing work progress. Student-initiated conversations were usually for the purposes of clarifying work assignments or indicating individual readiness for testing. Once reading groups were completed, the teacher moved about the room to check on work, provide guidance, or chat informally with individual children.

Routines were established for instruction and practice through the adopted curriculum. The teacher carried out the plans and goals within the curriculum as the group needs demanded. The activities of the day were planned so they could be complete within the morning work period, and they usually required little in the way of explanation. If a new activity was introduced, several examples were

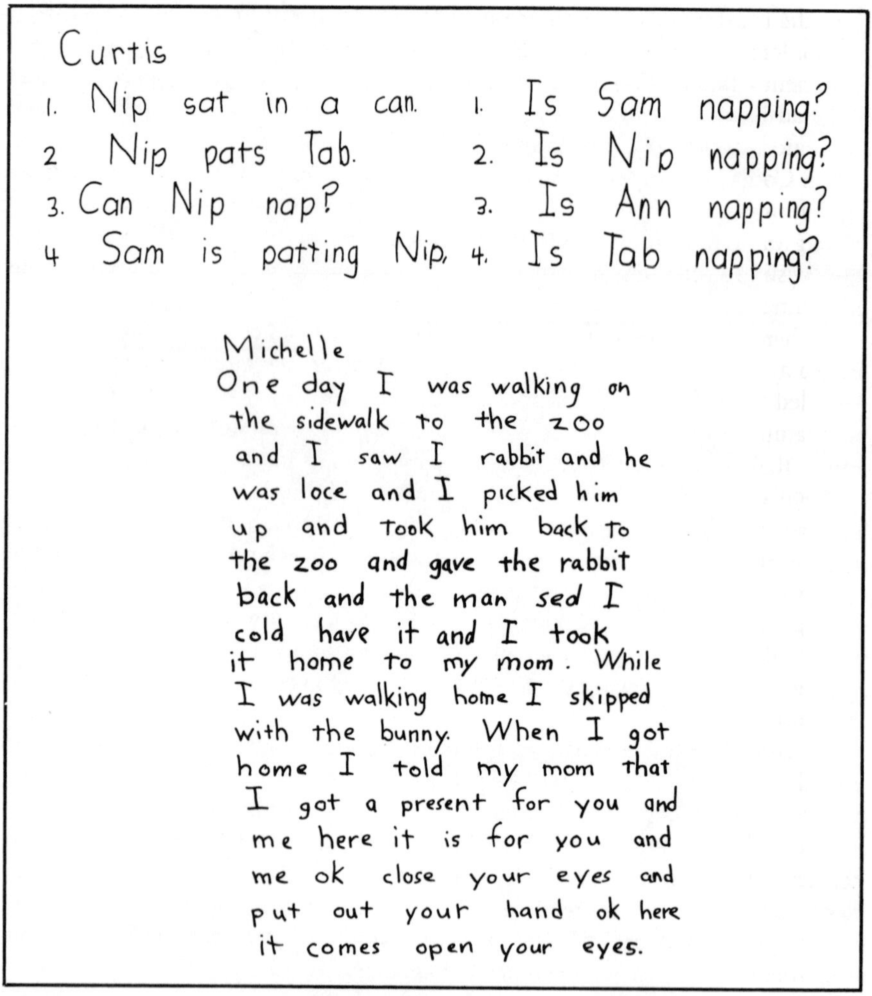

Curtis

1.	Nip sat in a can.	1. Is Sam napping?
2	Nip pats Tab.	2. Is Nip napping?
3.	Can Nip nap?	3. Is Ann napping?
4	Sam is patting Nip,	4. Is Tab napping?

Michelle
One day I was walking on
the sidewalk to the zoo
and I saw I rabbit and he
was loce and I picked him
up and took him back to
the zoo and gave the rabbit
back and the man sed I
cold have it and I took
it home to my mom . While
I was walking home I skipped
with the bunny. When I got
home I told my mom that
I got a present for you and
me here it is for you and
me ok close your eyes and
put out your hand ok here
it comes open your eyes.

Figure 10.7 Range of Mastery Learning Writing

provided before the children were asked to work on their own. Very little in the way of child-initiated writing occurred.

IMPACT OF CONTEXT ON WRITING

The videotape transcriptions and the information gathered from teacher interviews and field notes indicated there was a unique culture that evolved in each of these classrooms—complete with values, norms, beliefs, and organizational structures. The context in which literacy was presented surrounded and influenced the community of writers and readers. This environment either facilitated or constrained the reading and writing processes and the choices children made as they read and wrote.

The analysis of children's in-process writing and the samples they produced form the basis of subsequent comments. The writing samples were analyzed as to the content and characteristics of form, such as number of words. As a means of documenting specific instructional and contextual cues, percentages of words used that had been cued within the instructional setting (i.e., word lists, books) were calculated. Words that the children brought to the writing setting were also computed. Components of cohesion analysis (Halliday & Hasan, 1976) were used for an examination of text unity. These data suggest that the form and the content of writing varied as a function of the classroom context. The amount of borrowing, improvising, revision, and rehearsal found in students' writing were key points of differentiation.

There were specific links between the classroom context and children's writing. In all classrooms, writers *borrowed* from the contextual and instructional cues provided (linguistic, pragmatic, literary, or basal program) in learning to write. If, for example, the teacher suggested or assigned the topic, most students, if not all, found it difficult to go beyond that topic. If only controlled vocabulary was represented in the print environment, children tended to use only that vocabulary. In these instances, the children felt compelled to stay within specified guidelines. If literature was emphasized, then it was more likely that the literature would find its way into student texts. In other words, what children read they tended to use in writing. The reading material emphasized in the reading program was the most influencial factor in determining the form as well as the content of children's writing.

In all classrooms, the children *improvised* upon the contextual and instructional cues provided. However, the quality and quantity of language information provided within the environment, as well as the teachers' directions, influenced how much borrowing or improvising occurred. The amount of improvising was related to the number of options the writers felt they had within the writing process. The students from the literature program were able to choose their own topics. They wrote on a greater variety of topics representing a larger body of literary forms, and they tended to borrow elements from a number of books and improvised upon them rather than parroting whole texts.

The narrower the guidelines provided by the teacher, the less range there was in students' vocabulary or topic selection. The traditional and mastery-learning teachers both set strict guidelines. In the traditional room, the children began to invent more toward the end of the year. Their writing became longer and more creative and cohesive as the teacher placed fewer restrictions on writing topics. The mastery-learning class tended to write a lot but say very little—they used more "and then's" and repeated vocabulary in a stilted manner. They were much more limited to vocabulary they knew how to spell. The pictures they were often given (picturing the beginning, middle, and ending of a story) used characters from their reading books. This could account, in part, for the fact that these children used the same vocabulary over and over again (e.g., *Nip, Ann, Sam, hill, sat, came, went, ran*), with little plot or theme development exhibited in their writing. There was much more borrowing than improvising apparent from writing samples collected in these situations.

Revision and *rehearsal* only occurred in the literature-based classroom. In this room, there were many opportunities to share written materials over a period of time, so revisions were considered with each rereading. There was peer sharing during writing and sharing during reading and writing done with the teacher. The teacher then suggested that the children share their work with others throughout the school or classroom once it was completed. The writing usually remained in the classroom so it could be reread in the future. This celebration of writing may have contributed to the conversations often noted about "my next book" and the fact that there was a stronger sense of what Graves (1983) refers to as *voice* in their writing. Another aspect of rehearsal in this room was found in their art work. These students usually created all of their pictures first, then shared what they were going to write even before putting pencil to paper. In this way, conversation and rehearsal served as a tool in their writing, much as did their pencil.

In both of the other rooms, there was a tendency to produce a written text within one day. The students then turned it in to the teacher to be graded—never to be read again within the confines of class time. Consequently, rehearsal and revision was limited to the time frame allocated to one product. Many of the revisions noted from the videotapes involved corrections of spelling or spacing. There was much erasing, some rereading, and little rehearsing observed during writing except where children might draw pictures before they wrote. There were no instances of children knowing in advance what they were to write about in either of these two rooms. Within the traditional room, some of the students' writing was bound together in class books. It was not until the end of the year that the teacher indicated these were being taken home at night to be read.

And finally, the focus that the teacher set within the classroom was carried out in students' use of the process. If the teacher was concerned with spelling, punctuation, and form, the students exhibited more concern with these issues. If the focus was on the message, they took greater care in communicating their message and less time asking about spelling. If the teacher always assigned the writing topic, children depended on this. Any attempts to open the options by the teacher created pandemonium.

CONCLUSION

From these analyses of first-graders' writing, three major recommendations are offered that follow from factors influencing writing production in the contexts studied. These recommendations concern: (1) the organization of writing programs; (2) the assignment of topics for writing; and (3) what materials are appropriate for learning about reading and writing.

Too often children were expected to generate an idea and produce a completed written product within 30 to 40 minutes. This practice did not encourage revision or rereading and did not allow children the opportunity to rehearse or clarify their own intentions. If time is necessary for writers to personalize their writing, then *time* within the classroom day needs to be reconceptualized. The first recommendation, then, is that writing, as a part of the curriculum, needs to be allocated in time blocks and organizational frames that provide multiple opportunities for revision and rehearsal, with appropriate teacher guidance *during* the process. When children were given opportunities to write and share during repeated instances, they exhibited a greater sense of voice and ownership in their writing, and quality improved.

The second recommendation concerns the traditional practice of assigning topics for writing. In the literature-based classroom, writing of any one product could occur during more than one day, and students collaborated with each other and the teacher during the writing process. These students also tended to generate new ideas for future writing within this conversational writing time. The teacher guided students over problems with topic selection, but did not assign classwide topics. The fact that students needed very little teacher guidance could also have been a function of the amount of options they had for writing within this classroom. Children may need to initiate their own topics to explore their own potentials in style, voice, and form in writing.

And finally, the language cues provided within the instructional setting (verbal, nonverbal, and written) had an impact on children's growing concepts of written language. These cues set the frame for how writing must occur and what the writing could look like as well as influenced the children's use of language. Within the rationale for this chapter, the research indicated that in the process of learning, learners borrow from and improvise upon that which already exists. The data from this study offered further support of this notion. The last recommendation is that we need to provide texts and language information within our classrooms that are worthy models for developing readers and writers. Stories, letters, informational prose, and poetry find their way into children's writing if they are valued in the instructional environment. By simplfying and contriving literacy events we make reading and writing more difficult. If we provide materials that reflect the quality and forms for language found in print within the world around us, children, in turn, may come to value reading and writing because they have been approached as readers and writers rather than children who have much to learn.

REFERENCES

Cahir, S. R., & Kovacs, C. (1981), *Exploring functional language*. Washington, D. C.: Center for Applied Linguistics.

Cook-Gumperz, J. (1981). Persuasive talk—The social organization of children's talk. In J. Green & C. Wallet (Eds.), *Ethnography and language in educational settings* (pp. 25–50). Norwood, N.J.: Ablex.

Cook-Gumperz, J., & Gumperz, J. (1976). *Context in children's speech*. Papers on language and context, working paper no. 46. Language Behavior Research Lab, University of California, Berkeley, Calif.

Erickson, F., & Shultz, J. (1981). When is a context? Some issues and methods in the analysis of social competence. In J. Green & C. Wallet (Eds.), *Ethnography and language in educational settings* (pp. 147–160). Norwood, N.J.: Ablex.

Erickson, F., & Shultz, J. (1982). *The counselor as gatekeeper*. New York: Academic.

Goffman, E. (1980). *Forms of talk*. Philadelphia: University of Pennsylvania.

Graves, D. H. (1983). *Writing: Teachers and children at work*. Exeter, N.H.: Heinemann.

Green, J. L., & Smith D. (1983). Teaching and learning: A linguistic perspective. *The Elementary School Journal*, 83(4), 353-391.

Gumperz, J. (1977). Sociocultural knowing in conversational inference. In M. Saville-Troike (Ed.), *Twenty-eighth annual round table monograph series on language and linguistics* (pp. 191-211). Washington, D. C.: Georgetown University Press.

Halliday, M. A. K. (1975). *Learning how to mean: Explorations in the development of language*. London: Edward Arnold.

Halliday, M. A. K. (1976). *Ideas about language*. Inaugural lecture at the University of Sydney, Australia.

Halliday, M. A. K., & Hasan, R. (1976). *Cohesion in English*. London: Longman.

Heath, S. (1983). *Ways with words: Language, life, and work in communities and class-rooms*. Cambridge, Mass.: Cambridge University Press.

Hymes, D. (1974). *Foundations in sociolinguistics*. Philadelphia: University of Pennsylvania Press.

Michaels, S., & Cook-Gumperz, J. (1979). A study of sharing time in first grade students: discourse narratives in the classroom. In *Proceedings of the Berkeley Linguistics Society* (Vol. 5, pp. 647-660). Berkeley, Calif.: Berkeley Linguistics Society.

Rogoff, B., & Gardner, W. P. (1984). Adult guidance of cognitive development. In B. Rogoff & J. Lave (Eds.), *Everyday cognition: Its development in social context* (pp. 95-116). Cambridge, Mass.: Harvard University Press.

Sacks, H., Jefferson, G., & Schegloff, E. (1974). A simplest systematic for the organization of turn-taking for conversation. *Language*, 50(4), 696-738.

Sinclair, J. & Coulthard (1975). *Towards an analysis of discourse*. London: Oxford University Press.

Stoffan-Roth, M. (1981). Conversational access gaining strategies in instructional contexts. Ph.D. diss., Kent State University.

Tannen, D. (1979). What's in a frame? Surface evidence for underlying expectations. In R. Freedle (Ed.), *Advances in discourse processing* (Vol. 2, pp. 137-181). Norwood, N.J.: Ablex.

Wilkinson, L. C. (1982). *Communicating in the classroom*. New York: Academic.

11

Learners Work Together

Jane Hansen

The principal walks into a second-grade classroom during writing and counts only 10 of the 25 students writing. Four other students are at a table with the teacher. That's 14. Eleven others! Mr. Lowy approaches two buddies as they shuffle through a plastic tub of books. They notice him: "Mr. Lowy, can you help us find Andy's book? I want him to read it to me." Mr. Lowy helps and then wonders about the nine students he has not accounted for yet. Mark walks toward Christopher with a piece of paper in his hand and says, "Christopher, how does this sound: 'This just goes to show you'd better do what your parents say.' Is that a good ending?"

"Well, it's pretty hard to tell. Maybe you'd better read your whole piece to me." Mr. Lowy looks around. Three students are looking at the new chickens instead of writing! He marches over just as Seth exclaims, "Hey, guys, look! That one is starting to get a feather on his wing!" They all scrawl the date and data in their notebooks. Mr. Lowy turns and Matt appears, "Mr. Lowy, can I read this to you?" Later, Mr. Lowy waves to the teacher and leaves the writing workshop.

Mr. Lowy took a writing course the previous summer and he and his fellow students spent their time on two activities: writing and responding. He found the writing hard, but loved it. When he and the other students responded they listened and talked. During the response sessions it was mainly the writer who talked, and sometimes there was quite a lot of talking in their workshops.

The professor rarely lectured. Rather, she wrote and responded, too, as she modeled a way to teach with an emphasis on the process rather than the product of learning. The students perceived their teacher as a learner also, rather than as a person who has finished learning.

In the fall of 1983, Ann Marie Stebbins, Ruth Hubbard, Donald Graves, and I started a two-year research project to study the learners in the Mast Way kindergarten through fifth grade elementary school in Lee, New Hampshire. The project has now reached the half-way point. We have traced some of the problems educators solve as they learn to teach writing with an emphasis on the process, and as they begin to use the same learning principles when they teach reading. The project is based on the notion that children are informants (Vygotsky, 1978; Harste, Burke, & Woodward, 1984). (For an expanded discussion see Rogoff, this volume.) The teachers have no teachers' manuals to lead them when they teach writing and reading. Instead, they use their students as their guides when they make decisions about what to teach next.

While we collect some data on all the children and teachers in the school, we concentrate our data collection on five case studies: the librarian; a first-, a third-, and a fourth-grade teacher; and the principal. Each of us goes to the school at least twice a week to spend time in the classrooms, and we meet with each teacher after each visit.

Also, we write with 16 members of the staff weekly. The school has two sections at each grade level plus various specialists. Eleven of these staff members, in addition to the core of five, chose to participate in these writing workshops. Thus, the weekly writing group consists of the principal, librarian, physical education teacher, learning disabilities teacher, Chapter 1 tutor, a parent volunteer, 4 researchers, and 10 classroom teachers. The staff members find themselves in an environment such as they establish in their classrooms.

The teachers analyze the factors that help them with their own writing and not only include these elements within their writing programs but try to keep these learning principles constant when they design similar reading programs. The teachers learn the power of the group. They want the group to meet again the second year of the research project because when the group continues to meet they continue to write; when they find themselves on their own it's hard to keep their momentum alive. They want their students, also, to be interested in writing. Of the various features of the writing environment the students' desire to write relates most directly to the writing workshop and the community of writers.

THE STUDENTS AS LEARNERS

Workshop

The workshop represents a shift within writing instruction from a product to a process emphasis. When teachers emphasized the product, the students wrote alone at their desks and placed their papers on the teacher's perennial "stack of papers to correct" (with a red pen at the dining room table every other Sunday evening). However, with a process emphasis the teachers help their students and the students help each other while they are in the process of writing.

For example, in Phyllis Kinzie's fourth-grade classroom the following interchange is typical. Mrs. Kinzie stops at a cluster of writers and asks, "Margo, what are you working on today?"

"My trip to Boston, but I'm not sure which part they [the other students in the class] will be most interested in."

"What was the most fun to you?"

"I think the flat tire we had on the way down. The highway patrolman was so funny. Guess what he did. . . ."

Mrs. Kinzie listens. So do two of the students who are working in the same cluster of desks. When Margo finishes her story Carmen responds, "Really? What happened next?" Mrs. Kinzie leaves, knowing they will continue without her. She stops as Andrew looks up at her, "Guess what I just found out. A mouse gnawed at Mozart's violin once! How can I fit that into my report about him? I thought I was done, but I want it in. I could put it at the end so everyone will laugh, but I just don't know."

"If you read it to me I'll listen for some possibilities." Andrew reads, and Mrs. Kinzie and the three other students at his cluster listen. When he finishes, Liz, immediately comments, "I didn't know anything about Mozart. He sure lived a long time ago."

Andrew elaborates on life hundreds of years ago and pauses.

Katrin offers, "Well, I have two ideas about your problem with the mouse. . . ."

Andrew, Liz, and Katrin talk. Katrin's ideas spark an idea from Andrew, and he puts an asterisk in his draft where he wants to insert his mouse anecdote.

These students are in the process of writing and they want help. They know their teacher and friends will help them generate options so they can decide what to do. Not only is help readily available from either the teacher or peers but they aren't afraid to ask for it. The teacher has created an enviroment in which she expects the students to take risks (see Au & Kawakami, this volume). They know writing is a decision-making process, and the decisions are not easy to make.

Papert (1980) says students should realize it is acceptable to not always do their tasks right on the first try. Their teachers, in turn, should know the students are learning how to do new things, and learning takes time. An unsuccessful effort is the test of a hypothesis, and students respond by generating another hypothesis or by asking others to help them generate options. They then run another test. The learning process is a succession of trials and errors, and Papert complains about educators who give students the impression that the only acceptable behavior is polished performance. He suggests we change our focus in education.

No one can ensure writers their pieces will be accepted by their audience, so writing workshops can be tense. Writing is a nebulous task, and uncertainty reigns because the quality of the product can not be objectively assessed. Eudora Welty won a Pulitzer prize for *The Optimist's Daughter,* but not all readers like it. However when a student shares a draft, the others respond to the content by telling the writer what they learned, what they heard, and/or what they liked. The initial response is acceptance. This places the amorphous task in a predictable environment.

Often the writers read drafts to others without specific concerns in mind. They want to know if a draft is clear and are receptive to questions about parts the listeners do not understand. The questions do not make the writers uncomfortable. Rather, the writers seek questions so they can organize their thoughts better and ensure that others will understand them. For example, a student named Tom went to two friends to find out if his piece about his swim meet was clear. After he read it they congratulated him on his PR (personal record) and asked, "How many laps did you swim?"

"It's always three laps."

"Always?"

"Well, what I mean is. . . ." Tom explained and decided to insert a sentence into his text.

The questions asked of Tom exemplify an environment in which students learn from each other. The writers choose their own writing topics, and they choose topics they know more about than other students in the class. Thus, their peers ask questions, because they are interested in what the writer knows, and they want to learn more.

Writing workshops extend the prevalent scene within which young children try to figure out how to make oral language clear. When children try to tell their mothers something, mothers seldom respond by correcting their mechanics or criticizing their efforts. They want to know what their children say and respond to the content of a message as best they can. Children want their mothers to understand them so they repeat themselves, and gradually their speech improves (Lindfors, 1980; DeVilliers & DeVilliers, 1982; Dale, 1976; Menyuk, 1980). A meaning emphasis fosters children's language growth for their five preschool years, and language teachers carry this focus on meaning—rather than correction—into writing workshops.

Donaldson (1979) laments the unrealistic model of language acquisition she finds in many classrooms. She points to the inconsistency of language teachers trying to establish quiet, nontalking enviroments. Communicators, both speakers and writers, interact.

Community

The concept of community is another feature that affects the writing environment. It enriches the workshop scene so that it is not a place where students help each other only out of a sense of duty. The students interact regularly and not only know what each other knows but know each other well. They learn to respond to each other with positive feedback, and this response pattern produces an internal atmosphere of respect. Students help each other by opening options to the writer so the writer can make better decisions about writing.

Everyone in the writing community has the same activities. There is not a system of groups in which some children do one kind of work while others do another kind. They all write and respond. They decide what they want to write about, what genre they want to use, when to share, and with whom to share. When we did our research project in Ms. Blackburn's classroom (Graves & Hansen, 1983; Hansen, 1983; Blackburn, 1984), we collected data on who the children chose to work with when Ms. Blackburn let them choose their workmates rather than placing them in groups according to achievement level. Students who would normally be placed in a low group with other low students chose to work with better students who were able to help them. They wanted to learn. Goodlad (1983) says teachers should eliminate ability grouping. Teachers increase their students' opportunities to learn when the students identify each other by what they know rather than by the differential among them.

In education we often say we want to produce independent learners, but then we group our students so they must depend on us. Students can become independent learners if they find something they want to learn about, if they know what kind of help they need, if they know where to go for help, and if supportive help is available to them. Learners need many sources from which to glean information.

We have a videotape of Johanna, a second-grade girl who takes the viewers on a tour of her classroom at Mast Way while her class is in the midst of their reading workshop and, later, during their writing workshop. She explains what each child or cluster of children is doing. She also explains what many of the children have done in the past and knows many of their future plans. She knows what her classmates can do in the areas of both reading and writing, and she "shows them off" to her video audience. Johanna, an average student, revealed the children's confidence in each other one day in April when Ms. Funkhouser stopped by a cluster Johanna was in during reading. Ms. Funkhouser asked, "Can I help? Do any of you need me?"

"No, Ms. Funkhouser. At the beginning of the year we did, but now we don't."

Everyone knows their first task in any interaction is to support the learner who wants help. Students crave reinforcement when they share one of their own pieces of writing, and they know how the other writers feel. The students want each other to do well.

THE TEACHERS AS LEARNERS

Workshop

The teacher sets the tone for the workshop. She works. Emig (1982) says the only way teachers can help their students learn to write is to become learners and writers. She goes on to say students' writing can be enhanced by working with other writers, perhaps especially the teacher. "Teachers . . . who don't themselves write cannot sensitively, even sensibly, help others learn to write. Teachers of writing, then, must themselves write" (pp. 144). The students see their teachers write, and the teachers ask them to respond to their writing. The teachers tell their students about their writing problem.

In contrast, in a product-oriented classroom the focus is on material learned, so teachers are the model of material learned. They know a lot and pour their knowledge into the waiting students (Lapp et al., 1975). But they do not portray themselves as learners. In this situation, learning is a mysterious task left unrevealed to those students who become learners by finding the process of learning on their own.

Teachers of writing are learners. Professional writers say they are always learning to write (Murray, 1982), so a writing teacher is a learner, and her students appreciate seeing her as a learner. Ms. Rief's (1984) students work with her in a writing workshop for their eighth-grade English class. Recently, some of these students told the teachers in a university writing class that the most important thing Ms. Rief does when she teaches writing is "she writes."

Besides sharing her own writing in the workshops, a teacher learns from the students. A teacher listens. This is a new task for most teachers. When researchers observe in classrooms around the country, in most of the classrooms they hear the teachers talking two-thirds of the time (Rosenshine & Berliner, 1978). That leaves little talking time for each student to say, "Guess what!" and share with a friend. Yet, before the students began school, most of them frequently shared their discoveries. Their families encouraged their excitement about learning. However, each year in school they lose some enthusiasm. The difference between the interest of kindergarten students and sixth-grade students is great. For years we have cherished quiet classrooms and teachers who talk, but in a writing-process classroom the majority of the talk is student talk (Sowers, 1983). The teacher listens to the students so she can learn what they know, and this interest in their knowledge reinforces their enthusiasm.

Community

Teachers want the community feeling to grow, because it leads to a decrease in discipline problems. In a "quiet rows" classroom students who cause trouble usually do it for one of two reasons. Either they do not understand their work and, therefore, they do not know what to do so they cause trouble; or they have finished their work and do not know what to do. In a writing workshop children usually write about topics of their choice, so their interest is high. When they have a problem they go to someone for help so they do not have "frustration time" to fill. Furthermore, they do not "finish" their work because whenever they complete one piece of writing, they start another. The students help each other keep their writing going.

Teachers realize the impact of peers from their own writing community experiences. Patricia McLure, a first-grade teacher at Mast Way, wrote and shared her writing with her own peers for the first time this year. She was afraid, but when the date arrived for her to read her writing at the teachers' writing workshop she did, even though she had not volunteered for five months. Her colleagues' responses gave her the courage she needed to write again (McLure, 1984).

At midyear we interviewed the Mast Way teachers about their weekly writing workshops, and one of them said:

> The best thing is we've learned to support each other. On the first night you told us how to respond. You didn't say *support*, but that's what it was. You told us we had to support each other. So, we did. And, we do each week. By now, it's spread to situations other than the weekly writing seesions. We know each other better than we ever have and we support each other more. It's great.

The importance of support has become a cornerstone on which the project rests. Teachers, in general, seldom discuss their teaching. Yet, when people talk about what they do (i.e., the process they use) they gain control (Roehler & Duffy, 1984; Eisner, 1979). Teachers need support in order to have the convidence to explore new and different ideas in their classrooms. Elementary teachers typically work in isolation, but they need to interact in order to generate options about their teaching (Stuetzel & Allington, 1983). The Mast Way teachers' writing workshops provide the format for them to get to know each other so, as a consequence, they do interact more about their teaching than most staffs. When they sit around a table their discussions are not the complaint sessions we associate with teachers' lounges. They try to think of ways to urge each other onward.

THE PRINCIPAL AS LEARNER

Workshop

Principals trust teachers' ability to make decisions as teachers trust their students' ability to make decisions. A principal can not organize a school on a top-down policy if teachers do not manage their classrooms on a top-down policy. A school needs a consistent philosophy in the classrooms and in the office (Lieberman & Miller, 1979; Pratzner, 1984). Our research project is based on the decision-making model of a classroom where the writers make many decisions. Therefore, when this model is superimposed on the school, the teachers know they must make decisions.

It takes confidence, knowledge, and skill for teachers to set up classrooms with an emphasis on the process of learning. They do this best when their superiors listen to them, provide occasions for them to share their teaching, and support their decisions. When educators emphasize the process of learning, they give more attention to the process of trying than to the act of succeeding.

Principals should be the kind of people who try new things, take risks, fail, talk about personal failures with others to get feedback, try another hypothesis, and pursue. Such principals expect teachers to do likewise. They assume their teachers will have some failures when they try new ideas, but the teachers know they are on safe ground, because their principals are the first to tell them they, also, are learning.

These principals know a lot about teaching writing, so they can help their teachers. They may have visited other schools, sat in the midst of writing workshops, asked students and teachers how things work, and talked to other principals. And, these principals write. They respond to their teachers concerns about teaching similarly to the way the teachers respond to their students' concerns about writing. First, they confirm for teachers what they know about teaching, and then they ask teachers questions that explore the cutting edge of their teaching skills.

The school is the workshop in which teachers and principal learn from their explorations. A principal sets the tone for a workshop when the principal is the number one learner in a school.

Community

Mr. Lowy, and principals like him, worries about what parents will say when their children write drafts, because first drafts contain errors. But parents come to conferences with excitement about their children's writing. The teachers keep all rough drafts in school in a complete writing portfolio for each student and use these records to show progress. The children take home final copies and read them to anyone who will listen. That is what they are used to doing with their writing. They share it. The children's enthusiasm spreads to their parents.

Mr. Lowy also worried about what the parents would think about a change in the reading program when some teachers taught their students to choose their books in reading as a parallel to teaching them how to choose their own topics in writing. The students chose books they wanted to read, and if the book they chose did not turn out to be a good one, they returned it to the shelf (Hubbard, 1984; Atwell, 1983). Thus, the books they read they liked. They took their books home as often as they wanted to, and because they liked them they took them home often. The parents came to conferences and said, "I see my child read more than he ever did before. More than his two older sisters ever did when they went to school."

The parents of Pam Bradley's fourth-grade students like the way their children talk about books. The children have learned to share books of professional authors in reading workshops similarly to the way they share their own writing during writing workshops. When the children take books home, the parents and children can talk critically about them. The reading community extends beyond the walls of the building.

This large reading community begins with the writing communities in the classrooms. One day in February, Christopher shared his story about Holly, his parrot, with his class (McLure, 1984). Everyone in Chris' first-grade class had read their own writing to the class long before this, but Chris held back. Finally, the combination of trust within his class and excitement about his book brought him to the author's chair. When he finished reading his short book his friends asked him many questions about Holly, and he talked about her for 20 minutes. The children clapped for him.

The next morning he burst into school, wrote a second book about Holly, and read it to the class that day.

REFERENCES

Atwell, N. (1983). Writing and reading literature from the inside out. *Language Arts, 61*(3), 240–252.

Blackburn, E. (1984). Common ground: Developing relationships between reading and writing. *Language Arts, 61*(4), 367–375.

Dale, P. S. (1976). *Language Development.* N.Y.: Holt, Rinehart and Winston.

DeVilliers, P. A., & DeVilliers, J. G. (1982). *Early language.* Cambridge, Mass.: Harvard University Press.

Donaldson, M. (1979). *Children's Minds.* N.Y.: Norton.

Eisner, E. W. (1979). *The educational imagination.* N.Y.: Macmillan.

Emig, J. (1982). Non-magical thinking: Presenting writing developmentally in school. *The web of meaning.* Montclair, N.J.: Boynton/Cook

Goodlad, J. (1983). *A place called school.* N.Y.: McGraw-Hill.

Graves, D., & Hansen, J. (1983). The author's chair. *Language Arts, 60*(2), 176–183.

Hansen, J. (1983). Authors respond to authors. *Language Arts, 60*(8), 970–977.

Harste, J. C., Burke, C., & Woodward, V. A. (1984). *Language stories and literacy lessons.* Portsmouth, N.H.: Heinemann.

Hubbard, R. (1984). Drawing parallels: Real writing, real reading. In J. Hansen, T. Newkirk, & D. Graves (Eds.), *Breaking ground.* Portsmouth, N.H.: Heinemann.

Lapp, D. et al. (1975). *Teaching and learning.* N.Y.: Macmillan.

Lieberman, A., & Miller, L. (1979). The social realities of teaching. In A. Lieberman & L. Miller (Eds.), *Staff development: New demands, new realities, new perspectives.* N.Y.: Teachers College Press.

Lindfors, J. W. (1980). *Chilren's language and learning.* Englwood Cliffs, N.J.: Prentice-Hall.

McLure, P. (1984). Chris shared with the class today. In *Children who write when they read.* Durham, N.J.: Writing Process Lab, University of New Hampshire.

Menyuk, P. (1980). What young children know about language. In G. Pinnell (Ed.), *Discovering language with children.* Urbana, Ill.: National Council of Teachers of English.

Murray, D. (1982). *Learning by teaching.* Montclair, N.J.: Boynton/Cook.

Papert, S. (1980). *Mindstorms: Children, computers, and powerful ideas,* New York: Basic Books.

Pratzner, F. C. (1984). Quality of school life: Foundations for improvement. *Educational Researcher, 13*(3), 20–25.

Rief, L. (1984). Writing and rappelling: A matter of fear and trust. *Learning,* September, 72–76.

Roehler, L. R., & Duffy, G. G. (1984). Direct explanation of comprehension processes. In G. Duffy, L. Roehler, & J. Mason (Eds.), *Comprehension instruction.* N.Y.: Longman.

Rosenshine, B., & Berliner, D. C. (1978). Academic engaged time. *British Journal of Teacher Education, 4,* 3–16.

Sowers, S. (November, 1983). *Authorship in first-grade: Children write when they read.* Paper presented at the National Council of Teachers of English, Denver, Col.

Stuetzel, H. C., & Allington, R. L. (1983). Teacher effectiveness on decisions made during reading instruction. In J. Niles & L. Harris (Eds.), *Searches for meaning in reading language processing and instruction*. Rochester, N.Y.: National Reading Conference.

Vygotsky, L. S. (1978). *Mind in society: The development of higher psychological processes*. M. Cole et al. (Eds.). Cambridge: Harvard University Press.

12

Comprehension, Composition, and Collaboration: Analyses of Communication Influences in Two Classrooms

Robert J. Tierney • Margie Leys • Theresa Rogers

In this chapter we explore the collaborative nature of the reading and writing experiences of elementary school-aged children. First we describe the different types of collaborations involved in the acts of reading and writing, presenting past research and theory that relate to this topic. Then we describe analyses of the dynamics of various teacher and student interactions within two classrooms and discuss how these dynamics shape the collaborative nature of the experiences of selected readers and writers

Our goal will be to support a thesis that emerged from these data. Namely, we need an expanded theory of reading and writing processes—a theory that welds thought processes and reading-writing outcomes to the transactions that occur as readers and writers collaborate with peers, their teachers, and themselves, as well as published authors and readers. Our claim is that the opportunities readers or writers have to engage in collaborations contribute to how they learn to evaluate their own comprehension and compositions, and to how they develop an awareness of the strategies they enlist to make meaning.

The material in this chapter was originally a paper presented at the conference on "Contexts or Literacy," Snowbird, Utah, June 29, 1984. It stems from a larger research study conducted by R. J. Tierney and M. E. Giaccobe, "Reading and Writing Relationships: Processes, Products, and Communicative Contexts." We would like to acknowledge Avon Crismore who has assisted with various aspects of the project planning and data collection.

Table 12.1 Examples of **Reading–Writing** Collaboration

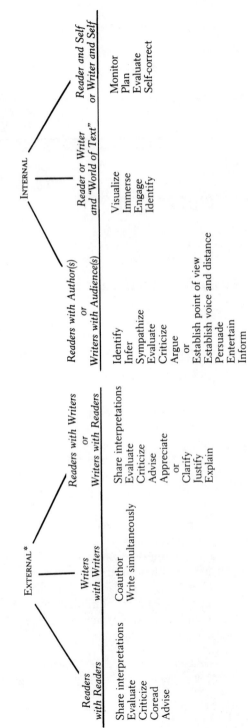

EXTERNAL*		INTERNAL	
Readers with Readers	Writers with Writers	Readers with Writers or Writers with Readers	Readers with Author(s) or Writers with Audience(s)	Reader or Writer and "World of Text"	Reader and Self or Writer and Self
Share interpretations Evaluate Criticize Coread Advise	Coauthor Write simultaneously	Share interpretations Evaluate Criticize Advise Appreciate or Clarify Justify Explain	Identify Infer Sympathize Evaluate Criticize Argue or Establish point of view Establish voice and distance Persuade Entertain Inform	Visualize Immerse Engage Identify	Monitor Plan Evaluate Self-correct

* External collaborations can take place in the following contexts—whole class, small group, or one-on-one conferences (student to student, student to teacher, student to family, student to others).

THE COLLABORATIVE NATURE OF READING AND WRITING

Elementary-aged readers and writers may be involved in various types of collaborations (see Table 12.1). At one level, children may be involved *externally* in, for example, coauthoring, conferencing with peers, or discussing ideas or problems with their teacher or family. Each of these collaborations may make a unique contribution to both the process and the eventual product of the reading or writing experience. For example, as several educators have hypothesized, peers can play a key role in contributing to a child's developing a sense of audience and certain revision and self-appraisal strategies (Graves, 1983; Kirby & Liner, 1981; Newkirk, 1984). At a second or *internal* level of communication, writers and readers are involved in myriad social interactions with the page and with themselves. As writers, they may become involved in the stories they are writing as characters or narrators while, at the same time, they may be thinking about what they are trying to say and what the effects of their writing upon their readers might be. This audience—their readers—may include known peers or a larger public; it may also include themselves as their own readers, judging what they have written on the basis of criteria they have gleaned from past reactions and their own internalized criteria. As readers, they may find themselves absorbed in the stories they are reading while they simultaneously monitor their own progress as readers and consider who wrote the piece and why.

Witness, if you will, some of the dimensions of the following third-grader's experience as a reader and writer. This is one of 24 children with whom we spent a year talking about reading-writing relationships while examining their reading and writing and watching their classes. What we share is restricted to just 2 of over 300 pages of transcribed interviews, journal entries, and stories we gathered from this one child alone (see Figure 12.1). They include a page from her reading journal and a page from her writing journal, together with comments from her teacher. We learned a great deal about this child's reading and writing experience from these pages.

In her reading journal entry, she discusses aspects of the visual experience she enjoys as she reads as well as her sense of the author's craft. Her comments reflect different levels of involvement: with herself ("it really was neat"), with the authors ("they did an excellent job"), and the world suggested by the text ("in my head I could really see ghosts and stuff"). By examining the teacher's entry, we became aware of some aspects of the student's "external" collaborative experiences: the student's relationship with her teacher and future interaction with peer authors. A similar analysis was performed on her writing journal; her comments about her own writing reflect levels and types of involvement similar to those in her reading journal. In terms of external collaboration, she discusses coauthoring with a peer and seeks advice from her teacher. In terms of internal collaboration, she is obviously monitoring her own progress ("we have a lot but we are fixing up some"), and is aware of her reader ("so if you see it you'll know").

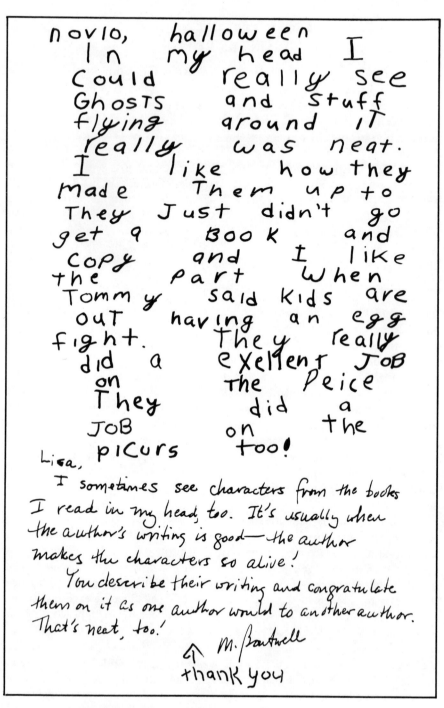

nov10, halloween
In my head I
could really see
Ghosts and stuff
flying around it
really was neat.
I like how they
made Them up to
They Just didn't go
get a Book and
copy and I like
the part when
Tommy said kids are
out having an egg
fight. They really
did a exellent Job
on the Peice
They did a
Job on the
picurs too!

Lisa,
I sometimes see characters from the books
I read in my head, too. It's usually when
the author's writing is good—the author
makes the characters so alive!
You describe their writing and congratulate
them on it as one author would to another author.
That's neat, too!
M. Bantwell
thank you

Figure 12.1 Reading and Writing Journal Entries

Jan. 11
=83=

Today I am writing
musical inster ments with
ROBIN we have
a lot so far
but we are fixing
up Some so if
you see it yu'll
know we are sort
of having a little
trouble because
we have to
interview mRS. PaTTacK
and she wasn't
there when we
went But we will
keep triing

Lisa

Lisa,
Congratulations on your Plane trip
story! So much detail and feelings!!
As far as interviewing, perhaps you
could put a note asking for an
appointment in her box in the teachers' room.
Have you and Robin written down what
questions you plan to ask her? Also, would
you like to borrow my tape recorder?

M/Boutwell

Figure 12.1 **Reading and Writing Journal Entries** (continued)

As stated earlier, readers and writers are involved in both external and internal collaborations. Externally, they are engaged in collaborations with a variety of people. Internally, they are engaged in interacting with the text and their reading of that text. They are involved in a variety of ways with the characters, events, or subject matter—the world of the text. They interact with their perceptions of readers as they are writing and the writer as they are reading. They also interact with an *innerself* who monitors, plans, and also acts as an audience of what is written or interpreted. What compounds the complexity of these interactions is that as a reader or a writer one can respond to or be influenced by peers. At the same time, one can react to the content, identify or empathize with the characters, and even be aware or such responses.

Unfortunately, there are very few theories that describe these various levels of collaborative involvement as they occur simultaneously and in conjunction with comprehension and composition. Most theories tend to describe only selected facets of a reader's experience and discuss them as though they occur separately (Bruce, 1981; Collins, Brown & Larkin, 1980; Rumelhart, 1980). Further, of those theorists who do consider these levels of involvement (Applebee, 1978; Britton, 1970; Galda, 1982; Rosenblatt, 1976) many underestimate the ability of readers and writers to be engaged simultaneously as objective observers and subjective respondents. It is not surprising, then, that some theorists misjudge the contribution of these involvements to comprehension and composition. Likewise, most of the research bearing on these issues appears in disparate fields or, in an effort to control variables, deals only with selected aspects at any one time. For example, there is a body of research that has examined the issue of character identification and perspective taking and its influence on story comprehension (Hay & Brewer, 1982; Jose & Brewer, 1984; Pichert, 1979; Spiro, 1977). Other studies have examined the nature of author-reader relationships and their influence upon reading and writing behavior (Tierney et al., in press). Research in social psychology has examined the influence of group experiences and peer relationships upon self-image, social awareness, and social negotiations (Asher, Renshaw, & Hymel, 1982). Some reading studies have examined the similarities and differences between peer and teacher-student interactions in school and out of school (Heath, 1982; Au & Mason, 1981; Phillips, 1982). Selected writing studies have examined the nature and role of collegial support within the context of business writing, as well as peer and teacher support in the context of school writing (Odell, 1984; Gere & Stevens, in press; Freedman, 1984, Freedman & Sperling, in press).

Even among educators, there has been a tendency to consider these issues separately rather than together. For example, writing and reading educators have discussed in some detail the importance of a sense of audience and developing the *other* or *inner* self as reader, planner, and judge (Brown, 1982; Murray, 1982). Some of these educators have discussed the role of a writer's peers, family, teachers, and others in developing these abilities and acting as the writier's readers (Ferreiro & Teberosky, 1982; Freedman, 1984, Freedman & Sperling, in press; Griffin, 1982; Newkirk, 1984). Other educators have discussed the importance of having readers appreciate the writer's craft (Graves & Hansen, 1983; Smith, 1983; Bruce, 1981; Tierney & LaZansky, 1980).

As we have indicated, what appears to be lacking is a coordinated examination of collaborations—a sociocognitive examination of the various communicative contexts within which reader and writers reside. With this in mind, we decided to initiate such a pursuit in the context of a larger study in which we were examining various aspects of the nature of reading-writing relationships. While working with the larger study, we came to believe that at the heart of the reading and writing processes are the various collaborations and negotiations between readers and writers and the role these collaborations play in helping children to develop awareness of the strategies involved in comprehension and composition.

The intent of this chapter, then, is to describe the nature of those collaborations in which elementary-aged readers and writers engage. We chose to explore the collaborations in two classrooms in order to provide some contrasting perspectives on how such collaborations might relate to and support each other. One class (Prairie School) was a third grade in which a basal reader approach was supplemented by a rich variety of trade books. The students also had creative writing lessons twice a week. The other class (Atkinson Academy) was a third grade that used a conference approach to reading and writing and provided students with extended reading and writing opportunities.

We took several different approaches toward capturing and analyzing the collaborations that occurred in the classrooms. We analyzed teacher interviews, videotapes of classroom lessons, and student-generated remarks from parallel reading and writing interviews. Our transcripts represented over 200 hours in each classroom and about 4,000 pages across all classrooms and children. To capture the collaborations, we specifically focused on an examination of: (1) the nature of the classroom rules that defined the range of the interactions among peers and between the student and teacher; (2) the two teachers' perceptions of the nature of the collaborations established in their classrooms; and (3) the children's perceptions of the nature of their collaborations.

NATURE OF THE CLASSROOM RULES THAT DEFINE THE RANGE OF INTERACTIONS

As we stated earlier we were interested in two levels of collaboration (internal and external) and their interrelationship. Each of these levels includes three types of collaborations. At the external level readers or writers interact with peers, colleagues, teachers, and parents in these contexts: (1) readers with readers, (2) writers with writers, and (3) readers and writers interacting with authors and audiences. At the internal level readers or writers interact with (1) an author or audience, whether known or imagined, (2) the characters, events, or objects that are part of the world of the text, and (3) themselves as planner, monitor, or evaluator.

Our first step in objectively describing some facets of these collaborations was a microethnographic analysis of a reading and writing lesson (event) in each class. This analysis provided us with a picture of the interactions that were in operation between teachers and students and among peers. Also, it served as a backdrop for understanding the nature of some of the internal collaborations in which students engaged.

Before describing the results, we will explain what this analysis entailed. As ethnographers define it, an event is a unit of analysis that is homogenous with respect to participants, topic, purpose, and rules of interaction (Savill-Troike, 1982). The way the rules are understood by the participants are the "norms of interpretation" for those particular rules. For instance, a typical classroom rule is that children must raise their hands if they want to speak. The interpretation of that rule by participants is that children must bid for a turn to speak. An event is made up of a sequence of acts each having an interactional function. An act can be a statement, a request, or a meaningful gesture. For example, a typical class-room event has an act sequence with a triad structure: a teacher asks a question, children raise their hands and, when chosen, answer, and the teacher evaluates the response. So, a microethnographic analysis of an event includes a description of the following elements: setting, participants, function, purpose and goals, act sequence, rules of interaction, and norms of interpretation.

Table 12.2 represents a summary of the microethnographic analysis of read-ing events in Praire School and Atkinson Academy. The act sequence of the reading event in the Prairie School followed a fairly typical pattern. The teacher initiated with a question, children raised their hands to gain permission to speak, and the response from the child called upon was evaluated by the teacher. If the response was not deemed appropriate the teacher either asked for more informa-tion, asked another child for more information, added information, or asked for another response. Almost all of the interactions (97 percent) were between the teacher and the students. One way to interpret these rules is that the teacher is the participant who knows the appropriate questions and is the judge of the "right-ness" or "wrongness" of the answers.

In contrast, the act sequence described in the Atkinson school event was guided by a different set of rules and norms. Here, although there were still more interactions (57 percent) between students and the teacher than between students, students initiated the discussion and called on others to respond. As a result, more of the substantive questions (about the text) came from students than from the teacher. Also, the students were allowed to evaluate the questions that were asked and could choose not to answer what they deemed to be irrelevant or redundant questions. The teacher still managed the structure of the event and many typical classroom rules were in effect, but the substance of the interactions—the interpre-tations, evaluations, and sharings—were largely supplied by the students.

What appeared to differentiate the act sequences between the two schools was the nature of the collaborations. Both teachers controlled the flow of ideas. What was different about the collaborations was the extent to which the Atkinson teacher afforded students the opportunity to interact with each other as evaluators and advisors on the substance or content of texts. The Prairie teacher, in contrast, tended to mediate not only *who* shared, but *what* was shared.

During writing, similar constraints were in effect. A writing assignment given in the Prairie School classroom followed a discussion of the basal story by Sharon

Table 12.2 Summary of Microethnographic Analyses of Reading Event Sequences in Two Schools

PRAIRIE SCHOOL	ATKINSON ACADEMY
The lesson analyzed below took place in a classroom at The Prairie School. Prairie is a university-affiliated laboratory school that admits students with abilities representative of the whole nation by matching test scores to norms from nationally standardized tests.	The lesson analyzed below took place in Atkinson Academy. Atkinson is a public school in a small rural community in New England.
Setting	*Setting*
Only a section of the classroom is visible on the screen. There is a rectangular table with nine chairs situated parallel to a blackboard. Beyond the head of the table is a bulletin board with samples of the students' writing hanging diagonally in neat rows. The lesson takes place on a Tuesday morning in February.	Atkinson is a small school in New Hampshire, housed in a traditional, white clapboard building. The classroom has a workshop atmosphere with low trapezoid tables, makeshift cinderblock bookshelves filled with books, an old sink, and coats hanging from hooks in the wall. In one corner is a $9' \times 12'$ rug, where the students and teacher gather for share meetings.
Participants	*Participants*
Four third-grade students are seated in chairs along one side of the table and one is sitting at the foot, so none of the children have their backs facing the blackboard. The teacher, a woman about forty years old, is seated at the head of the table. She is dressed in a suit with a scarf tied in a bow—the students are dressed in jeans and tee shirts. This, the second reading group to meet that morning, is the middle group (in terms of ability).	Twenty third-grade students in jeans and tee shirts are sitting in a circle around the rug; some are leaning against a wall, some against a bookcase, and one or two are in easy chairs. The teacher, a woman in her thirties dressed in corduroy jeans and a sweater with long hair pulled back in a clip, is also sitting in the circle on the floor.
Function, Purpose, Goals	*Function, Purpose, Goals*
The purpose of this lesson is to discuss a basal story that the students have recently finished reading. The teacher is assessing their understanding of this particular story and teaching them	The event is a share meeting in which a few students tell other students and the teacher about a book they are reading. The purpose of the share meetings is to give students an opportunity to share

Table 12.2 **Summary of Microethnographic Analyses of Reading Event Sequences in Two Schools** *(continued)*

PRAIRIE SCHOOL	ATKINSON ACADEMY
general principles of interpretation. (For example, she stops periodically to explain generic terms and to make comments such as, "We don't all interpret stories the same way.) She is specifically focussing her lesson on characters.	their appreciation for or problems they are having with a book.
	"The children come together as a group a couple times a week and share what they have been reading, problems they come across, and kids respond to them. When they [the children who are sharing] are having trouble, others will sort of support them and they are real patient with that person [who is] explaining what they are doing." [Excerpt from teacher interview.]

Act Sequence

As the tape begins, the children are already seated and still. The act sequence goes as follows:

Teacher asks a question.
Children raise their hands.
Teacher scans group to see who has their hand raised.
Teacher repeats all or part of the question.
More children may raise their hands.
Teacher turns her body toward a child and calls on him or her.
Child gives an answer.
Teacher either:
Nods in agreement.
Asks for additional information.
Turns toward another child for additional information.
Adds information herself or asks another child for a different response.

Occasionally the teacher goes to the board to record students' responses and, following that, will praise the whole group.

4 interactions with other students:

2 are disagreements (e.g., "I don't think she was nice!)

Act Sequence

The tape begins when all the participants are seated. The act sequence goes as follows:

The teacher gives students permission to begin.
The chosen children [the actor(s)] stand up and give some background and discuss "good parts" or problems.
Other children or the teacher may raise their hands.
The actor calls on the teacher or on a child.
The teacher or the child either asks a question or makes a statement.
The actor answers the question or responds to the statement.
(The last four acts are repeated.)
The teacher requests that only one more question be asked.
(The same four acts are repeated once or twice.)
The teacher asks if the actors are finished.
Actors respond.
The teacher says, "Thank you."
The actors sit down.

The whole cycle is repeated (in this case, once)

Table 12.2 **Summary of Microethnographic Analyses of Reading Event Sequences in Two Schools** *(continued)*

PRAIRIE SCHOOL	ATKINSON ACADEMY
2 are corrections (e.g., "No, it was 7 [not 12]")	*10 interactions with other students:*
	1 is a comment for the actors (You can't read that in one day!)
149 interactions are between the teacher and a student:	9 are questions (e.g., Did you think you would be interested when you started reading the book. What's the best part?) or requests (Can I read it after you?)
148 are teacher questions or a student response to the teacher's question	
1 is a directive from the teacher	
TOTAL: 153 interactions	*13 interactions are with the teacher:*
	4 are comments or questions about the actors' reading
	9 are teacher directives addressed to the actors
	TOTAL: 23 interactions

Rules for Interaction

PRAIRIE SCHOOL

1. The teacher leads the discussion and the participants follow a fairly strict turn-taking sequence. (Some are called on frequently and others not at all.)
2. Children must raise their hands to bid for a turn from the teacher.
3. Only one person may speak at a time.
4. Turn taking is interrupted only when one participant substantively disagrees with another participant's response.
 (*Example:* When the first child was finished, another immediately gave a very different answer. The teacher explained that both responses were acceptable and did not reprimand.)
5. Children must attend to whoever is speaking within the group; they may not turn to look at or communicate with the rest of the class. (If this rule is broken the teacher gazes at the guilty child until he or she is still.)

Rules for Interaction

ATKINSON ACADEMY

1. The teacher chooses the actors who will share.
2. The students are not supposed to ask questions until the actor is done with the initial presentation (when this happened, the teacher told the actor to continue with his presentation).
3. The teacher has first priority in speaking when she raises her hand, and she can tell the actor(s) who to call on.
4. If the teacher's hand is not raised, the actor(s) can call on any child he or she chooses, and may choose not to answer a particular question if a good reason is supplied (e.g., That is like Tom's question [which was already answered]).
5. The teacher decides when enough questions have been asked.
6. When the teacher says, "One more question" and then asks if the actor is done, she expects him or her to say, "Yes."
7. When the teacher says, "Thank you" the actor is supposed to sit down.

Table 12.2 Summary of Microethnographic Analyses of Reading Event Sequences in Two Schools *(continued)*

PRAIRIE SCHOOL	ATKINSON ACADEMY
Norms of Interpretation	*Norms of Interpretation*
The teacher is the judge of "rightness" or "wrongness" of answers. Hand raising is a signal that a participant knows the answer and is evaluated by the teacher as an act in itself whether or not a response is given. Children are expected to remain attentive throughout a lesson. If the teacher turns bodily toward a student who does not have his or her hand raised, the student is being reprimanded. A child may never be called upon even though he or she raises a hand. Perhaps the student has not read the story or, in the past, has not given appropriate responses.	The students seem to understand that "normal" classroom rules are still in operation during these meetings—the teacher still guides and sometimes controls the interactions. The teacher has conferenced individually with students and knows who is ready to present and so calls on those students. It is considered impolite and counterproductive to interrupt the actor's presentation. The teacher contributes to and controls the question asking so that those who have something substantial to say will get a chance. Actors may not answer a question that is not considered substantial or at least different. The teacher decides when enough time has been given to actors, because they have a certain amount of time to hear what seems to be a predesignated number of presentations. The actors are expected to conform to this by listening and paying attention to signals such as "One more question" and "Thank you."

Bell Mathis called "A Sidewalk Story." Parts of the lessons are transcribed in Table 12.3 to give you a sense of the whole lesson. The discussion centered around the main characters, and the children were asked to describe each character as the teacher wrote their answers on the board. The actual writing assignment begins on line 57. The students were asked to write a biography of one of the characters, presumably using lists already on the board to describe these characters.

The assignment in the Atkinson classroom followed a discussion of a book called *Soup* by Robert Peck. During the discussion, the students were asked to talk about how Robert Peck let his readers know about the characters—particularly Soup, an autobiographical character. The teacher then moved into a discussion of a piece written by one of the students in the class (line 24) and asked how Lisa let them know about the character named Natasha. After some discussion, the assignment (given on line 37) was to analyze how it is they as authors have let their readers come to know their characters. They are then asked to write about this in their journals.

These lessons with very similar objectives represent a rich display of how the two teachers support various types of collaborations in their classrooms. In both classrooms students were encouraged to consider their perceptions of the characters in stories. Both teachers highlighted the author—Mathis and Peck—and both encouraged the students to consider their peers' ideas. But there are some key differences in the two teachers' approaches. The Atkinson teacher urged the students to think about themselves as writers and readers; the Prairie teacher did not encourage such an immediate sense of authorship and readership in the students. What is interesting to note about the Atkinson School is that the students were encouraged to move in and out of various collaborations. They progressed from thinking about how a relatively unknown author developed his characters (readers with readers and readers with writers), to how a classmate developed her characters (readers with writers), to how they, as writers, develop their own characters (writers and world of text), to writing about that (writer and self). There was an obvious and deliberate attempt by the Atkinson teacher to interface the students' experience with published authors, their peers' work, and their own reading and writing.

Table 12.3 **Prairie School and Atkinson Academy Writing Assignments**

PRAIRIE SCHOOL WRITING ASSIGNMENT

1. T: There were lots of different characters in your story, this one was the com-
2. plete story. Yours was what we would say is the abbreviated form or the con-
3. densed version of the story. I'm going to write on the board the names of
4. the different people, the important characters in the story. All right—Chris,
5. can you think of one of the names.

6. c: Lily.

7. T: Good, we'll write her name up here. Another name—Cathy?

8. c: How about . . . *(inaudible)*

9. T: Oh, yeah, she was another important person in the story, wasn't she? Good.
10. Pete?

11. c: Mrs. Brown.

12. T: All right. Let's put Mrs. Brown up here also. And somebody that was in
13. here.

14. T: Who else was in the story? Chris?

15. T: We would call them, these would be called the key or major characters and
16. then we would have some minor characters. Well, let's just go along with
17. these people first. I want you to think of words that would tell about each
18. one of these. Something that you could say about each one of them.
19. Cathy.
20. c: Nice.

Table 12.3 **Prairie School and Atkinson Academy Writing Assignment** *(continued)*

21. T: Nice.

22. C: Fresh; friendly.

23. T: Friendly. Those are good words to use. Chris.

24. T: Okay. How could you describe Mrs. Brown?

25. C: *(Inaudible)*

26. T: All right, well, Chris might have a little different idea—we always don't
27.   interpret stories the same way. And what did you think—you thought
28.   she was . . . She was a little bit, wasn't she, so what word do want to
29.   use?

30. C: Have we said *grumpy*?

31. T: Grumpy, okay. Another one that you can think of. Marcie?

32. C: This one's for Frazier.

33. T: For Frazier—good.

34. C: Kind to others.

35. T: Kind to others—good, Marcie.

36. C: Because he bought Lilly the earrings.

37. T: That's right. All right. Kind to others.

38. T: She was a very caring person. She did—good, Marcie. All right now, if you're
39.   really thinking about her feelings so what would you say—

40. C: *Caring.*

41. T: Excellent. You gave a very good example, Marcie, why she was caring.
42.   Steve?

43. C: She thought that she could do the same as Mrs. Ruth did because she was
44.   poor and had to get her house back . . . .

45. T: We have things under each person. Some, I think you can see, are more
46.   important than others. Who was the most important person in the story?

47. C: Lilly and Tanya.

48. T: You feel they both were very important?

49. C: Lilly, because she did most of the stuff.

50. T: Okay. Chris?

51. C: Lilly.

52. T: You feel that also? What about you, Cathy?

53. T: I love the way you're really picking up the feelings and what—sometimes

Table 12.3 **Prairie School and Atkinson Academy Writing Assignment** (*continued*)

54.   they say—what's written between the lines of the story. It might not be
55.   there just exactly sentence by sentence by sentence but you're also discover-
56.   ing things that we say sometimes are written *between the lines*, they're not
57.   just written there, you have to think about them, you're doing a good
58.   job.

59. T: All right, go back to your desks. I want you to select one of these people—one
60.   of the major characters in the story and write about that person and just
61.   almost as though you were writing a biography. We've read lots of bio-
62.   graphies about famous people and written about them. You don't have to
63.   make it very long, but tell as much about the one of those people as you can
64.   and you select which ever one you would like to. Do you have any questions
65.   about what you're supposed to do? Any questions, Marcie? Steve? Okay, go
66.   back to your desks, you've been a good group . . . .

ATKINSON ACADEMY WRITING ASSIGNMENT

1. T: —Yesterday we talked about how he used Rob and what his relationship
2.   was. I would like to talk to you about how he did that—How Robert Peck
3.   described himself as a child, how did he develop his own character and how
4.   did he do it with Soup?

5. C: He picked out all the bad things—where he got in trouble.

6. T: Okay. A lot of his adventures and a lot of them went wrong, right? And
7.   what did he tell us about Soup as a person—

8. C: Well, first he had . . . . *(Inaudible)*

9. T: Okay, so first he was using Rob and then they became friends. Was Soup
10.   always using people?

11. C: No.

12. T: Okay, what else do we know about Soup?

13. C: He always wanted Rob to do certain things.
14. T: Okay, he was using Rob to do the kinds of things he liked to do but he was
15.   playing it safe. What about the time with the junkman? *(Explains episode)*
16.   How did Soup feel then?

17. C: Funny.

18. T: Well, why did he feel funny?

19. C: Bad . . . . *(Inaudible)*

20. T: Okay, so both he and Rob felt bad. So, Robert Peck, in doing that, let us
21.   know what Soup was like, as a person. Both sides of him, and he let us know
22.   about Rob and their friendship. He developed those characters the way he
23.   wrote them. Okay, what about the character that you're developing. Well,
24.   what about Natasha, Lisa's [a student] Natasha. In *Natasha and her Run*
25.   *Away Imagination*. How did we get to know her?

Table 12.3 **Prairie School and Atkinson Academy Writing Assignment** *(continued)*

26. c: She showed us how she had a big imagination—she—so she left—

27. t: Okay, so she left. And then what happened?

28. c: And then she ran away—and she kept seeing things—

29. t: Okay, and Lisa put us into her imagination, so we aren't sure what was true
30. and what wasn't true. Right?

31. c: Most of the time.

32. t: Okay, most of the time until Natasha was discovered. That time when
33. her mother was calling her to come home and then all of a sudden her
34. mother disappears. I thought her mother was really there at first, did
35. you?

36. c: Yeah!

37. t: Yeah, right. So the way Lisa wrote that we got to know that character and
38. what was going on in her mind. What I would like you to do today is to go
39. to whatever you're writing and look at it—the characters—and see how
40. you've developed them. How you let us know about personality of that
41. character and what's going on with that character. Now say you're not
42. working on something that has a character—go back to something you've
43. written before. And check it out. And I'd like you to write about that in your
44. journals so we can discuss it tomorrow, okay?

45. c: About what?

46. t: About how you developed your characters—you're not working on a char-
47. acter right now, Ken. But remember when you did the Snoopy one? Go
48. back and look at how you let people know about him.

49. t: Okay? If you have any questions, I'll come around anyway.

50. c: I'm just starting my book and—

51. t: Then you can plan out . . . . How are you going to show us what the char-
52. acters in that haunted mansion are going to be like. Okay? . . . let's get going.

TEACHERS' PERCEPTIONS OF THE NATURE OF COLLABORATIONS IN THE CLASSROOMS

The teachers' comments were difficult to categorize since many of the same comments could serve as evidence of the awareness of more than one type of collaboration. Indeed, the comments highlight the ways in which the collaborations are inextricably interwined. However, for purposes of presentation, we categorized those comments made by the teachers regarding their perceptions of collaborations in terms of their primary focus.

External Collaborations

In terms of external collaborations, the teachers' comments reflected marked differences in who controls the flow of interactions. The Atkinson teacher stated that in literature group there is "cross-dialogue between them [the students] and what the author might mean, and how this ties into what we have already found out, and what it would mean for what is going to happen next. . . ." In contrast, the Prairie teacher described a fairly typical basal-directed reading lesson with teacher as sole questioner.

> In reading groups we usually introduce the story, there would be some kind of motivation to read the story, we might discuss words. . . . The children would read at their desks. Then it would be more or less interpreting the story—I would ask questions that were literal or factual, and then some questions that were more or less evaluating what they thought of the story.

In writing the Atkinson teacher allows the children to choose their own topics and to confer with other students to "help them along with the process" as they compose.

> Before they start writing, they have a choice—and they should choose something they care about and are really interested. . . . Sometimes they will talk to friends to get some ideas. Once they start writing their story or report, they conference with other kids on what really sounds best. I go around conferencing all the time—I might ask questions, they might read it to me, they might just tell me about it. . . . They are sharing their process of writing with people as they go along.

During her writing lessons the Prairie teacher generally initiated the topics.

> As far as the chronological order for a typical week's writing lesson, we would do some motivational activity, we would follow it up maybe with some suggestions from the students, too. Then we would do the writing and I would walk around the room giving encouragement and suggestions. I might say, as they are writing, "What about this word?" For example, they might have a word that should be capitalized—or they will discover they have left out a word.

In terms of reader-writer collaborations, the Atkinson students were given imput from the teacher who helped them wrestle with a problem by brainstorming. Also, while they were writing, they conferenced with other students or brought the piece to share meeting. "They share their processes as they go along and celebrate. They bring it to share meeting because they have more children, more variety of answers and responses." In the Prairie classroom the writing was finished, corrected by the teacher, and sent home. Sometimes their work was displayed on a bulletin board; but as the teacher commented, "they don't all make a mad dash over there."

Internal Collaborations

In terms of the internal collaborations of readers and authors, both the Atkinson and Prairie teachers emphasized the importance of thinking about the authors and their intentions. The Atkinson teacher said:

> I emphasize inferential comprehension—where the author is taking us—also to think about what they are reading, to kind of critically analyze it, and to figure out "well, this might be what the author says but maybe that isn't really the way I see it."

Questions the Prairie teacher asked her students included: Why do you think the author wrote the book? What was his purpose? and Do you think the author liked children?

Comments that reflected the Atkinson teacher's perceptions of the writer-audience collaborations of her students included, "All the time they are doing their writing, they will be conferencing and talking to other kids about it. This helps them get it the way they want it." The Prairie teacher said, "If they can pretend they are talking as they are writing, just saying something to me only putting it on paper, because most of them can talk a lot."

Both teachers encouraged character identification, or collaboration, between the reader and the world of the text. The Prairie teacher asks the students what-do-you-think and evaluating questions—"Would you have done this?" or "Would you let [the character] have another turn?" The Atkinson teacher said, "The students really become part of the characters, acting out parts to figure out how a character felt."

In term of writer and world-of-text collaborations, the Atkinson teacher said, "They are writing things that are meaningful to them, things they care about, things that are important to them." She compared writing to thinking out loud—how things fit in, how are they meaningful to you and where do you see them going? The Prairie teacher talked about familiarity of content ("I think they have to have something they are familiar with"); clarity ("Look over your work and reread it and see if there is something that doesn't make sense"); and neatness ("Often when they are writing they are scratching out and they want [their writing] to look nice").

Finally, in terms of reader-self and writer-self collaborations, the Atkinson teacher stressed the development of strategies and encouraged self-reflection on their reading and writing processes in conferences and in journals.

> When I am conferencing with each child, especially the ones that don't have many strategies, I can help them and introduce some. . . . When the student finishes reading, I ask, "What did you do differently in reading this book?" Before they start writing, they brainstorm what they are going to do. . . . Some will write different leads, some will think about it over and over in their heads. . . . They decide through conferences or share meetings how they want it. They are constantly rereading it. Eventually they have gone through the process of really evaluating it themselves, getting it the way they want it.

The Prairie teacher gave her students "suggestions for different kinds of questions you might ask yourself when you are reading a book. They are going to look at these questions and be more critical." She also felt that for some students it was important to "gather their thoughts" before they started to write: "Sometimes we need to do a little thinking before we start writing."

It is interesting that whereas there are marked differences in the two classrooms both teachers were concerned with each of the collaborations discussed in this chapter. What differentiates the two classrooms are some of the dimensions related to these collaborations. There appear to be at least four dimensions upon which the classrooms vary: support for self-initiation, peer interaction, emphasis on process, and sense of students as writers and readers. In the Atkinson School students are encouraged to make choices, seek support from, and offer support to their peers while they read and write; appreciate the process of writing as much as the product; and consider themselves authors and interpreters of texts. In the Prairie classroom children had less opportunity to choose their own topics and books, less interaction with peers, and more emphasis on the product of writing (neatness, grammar, punctuation) than the process. Also, most of their compositions or interpretations were mediated and evaluated only by the teacher. The next section will enable us to observe rather than infer what this might entail in terms of student reading and writing behavior.

CHILDREN'S PERCEPTIONS OF THE NATURE OF THEIR COLLABORATIONS

In the first two sections of this chapter, we have discussed the collaborative nature of reading and writing in two third-grade classrooms from our perspective as researchers and from the perspective of the classroom teachers. In this section we present a third perspective, that of the students.

To determine how the children perceived these collaborations, we examined the transcripts of the parallel reading and writing interviews we had conducted with individual students. Each interview, one for reading and one for writing, had two sections: (1) an unstructured conversation with the students where they shared with us their writing, their peers' writing, their favorite books, their content-area texts, and their basal and, (2) specific questions on a range of topics including each of the aforementioned collaborations.

For the Atkinson children we had two additional sources of information: (1) their reading and writing journals and (2) their reading and writing folders. Most children wrote in their journals on a daily basis; sometimes it was in response to a question posed by the teacher, such as, "How are you doing on the report?" or "How are reading and writing the same to you?" or "How do you get to be a good author?" Sometimes they talked about who they had worked with, problems they were having with a piece of writing or understanding a book, or they described their reaction to a book or piece that they were writing. The teacher read these and from time to time made comments in the form of a dialogue with the child. Figure 12.2 provides an example of such entries. In their folders, the children listed all the books they had read or pieces they had written, when a piece was started and finished, and whether or not they had abandoned it. They also listed problems they had had, new things they had learned, who they had collaborated with (such as coreading and coauthoring), and who they had conferenced with about their reading or their writing.

In analyzing the children's perception, we first determined what constituted reliable evidence for the existence of a collaboration. To determine if a child was involved in an internal collaboration (e.g, projection into the world of the text) we considered their responses during the unstructured conversation in conjunction with their answers to specific questions. For the Atkinson children we also searched through their journals and folders for corroborating comments. For example, one child answered "yes, always," to the question, "As I read, I feel as if I am one of the characters or people in the story," but this behavior was not supported by her answers to other pertinent questions or by her general comments. Therefore, we did not consider her answer as evidence that she was involved in this internal collaboration. We felt that if children had truly acquired a strategy their use of it would be selective and evidence for the existence of it would appear in several areas of the interviews. Another child responded "sometimes" to this same question. But in one journal entry he wrote, "The book I'm reading, *The Lions, the Witch, and the Wardrobe*, has a lot of feelings in it. I could see things. It's like I was in it." Also, in the interview he discussed books where he did project and ones where he did not. For this particular child we decided that there was quite strong evidence that he was involved in an internal collaboration with the world of the text as he read.

It should also be noted that we have only included the comments from one of the four groups of students interviewed in each school—those students identified as good readers and good writers. We have studied these children first to establish what the most developed level of children's collaborations are in these classes. It should also be noted that there were no differences among schools in the performance of these students on the same standardized reading achievement tests.

Our discussion of the students' perceptions are presented in terms of the previously discussed external internal collaborations. We included comments from four children: Shelley and Mike, who are students at Prairie School and Lisa and Chris, who are students at Atkinson.

External Collaborations

At Prairie School, while there were fewer formalized opportunities for readers and writers to share their work than there were at Atkinson, the children did share. Furthermore, they said that they enjoyed doing it and that it was helpful to them. As Shelley, one of the students at Prairie School, stated, "I like to ask people to read my writing; I ask them if they like it—I want to get their opinion. I usually give it to Jennifer, because she sits next to me." Or, as Mike, who liked to share but was quite selective, stated, "[Sometimes I give it to] my family or someone, [sometimes] I keep it a secret—some friends might not like it."

While writing is the subject of most of the Prairie students' comments about sharing, some remarks were offered about their interactions with others about reading. As Shelly suggested, she liked to talk to other people about books that she reads, but she did not do it very often. She also talked to peers when she was selecting a book: "I like to read what my best friend reads—especially Judy Blume." Using peers to advise on topic or book selection was more prevalent in reading than writing. The teacher usually gave the writing assignments and also most of the feedback students received. Shelley and Mike both mentioned the teacher as the primary person who provided feedback on their writing. This was usually in the form of an overall reaction, evaluative comment (such as "very good work") or comments about spelling and punctuation.

At Atkinson the class day was organized so that the children had time set aside for both large- and small-group meetings. The children also had more freedom of choice of assignments in both reading and writing. This structuring of class time had a direct effect on the external communicative context for these children. For example, Chris thoroughly enjoyed these share and conference times, for both reading and writing. He liked the sense of satisfaction—the entertainment value—as well as the feedback his peers give him. In the interview he said , "You know how we were talking about changing this part down here about the minisub? Well, I wouldn't have noticed that if they hadn't told me at share. I would have just went on with the book. They ask a lot of questions." He also said, "When I have a problem—it's that I mostly get stuck I don't know what to put next—so I go conference with somebody to see what they think; we try it out." Similarly, Lisa said that "sharing always helps me improve my writing. There are lots of people there asking questions and telling me if it's good or not . . . if they don't understand a part I can change it."

As at Prairie, the children at Atkinson acted as advisors for each other when they were selecting books to read and also topics to write about. They publish a book four times a year called *Room 5 Celebrates Reading,* which contains book reviews they have written. During the interviews several children talked about reading their friends' reviews and using this information when choosing a book to read. Sometimes the children asked the teacher for advice about a book or topic, and the teacher sometimes gave them suggestions in her comments to them in their journals.

The children at Atkinson saw themselves as authors—not quite as skilled as published authors—their term for commercial authors—but authors nonetheless. Readers in this classroom talked to the author of a book and asked questions or gave comments. Chris mentioned that he had read a friend's book at home "and it [said] 'both my grandmothers came for Christmas Eve'. . . . I asked her [Jill, the author] on the phone." Lisa also commented that she will go talk to class authors, "[sometimes] I think about why he or she wanted to write the book . . . sometimes, if the author is in the room, I ask why."

The Prairie school children did not talk about being authors talking to authors. Shelley mentioned once in her reading interview that she really liked reading her best friend's story about friends and she told her so. She also said,

"Mostly the teacher reads my things. When they're on the bulletin board I hope other people do, too."

At Atkinson another way that the children collaborate is that they coauthor and coread. Chris says, "Me and Stephen are a team at working on science books. So far we've written *The Planet* and *the Universe*. That's our speciality. Arik and Tommy write animal stories." Lisa wrote in her journal about reading a book with her friend Jill during reading time at school and then again on the weekend.

Internal Collaborations

In terms of thinking about the projected author of a text, Shelley (a Prairie student) said in her reading interview that "sometimes I think about what that person [the author] looks like and what he or she would be doing at that time when he or she was writing that book."

When the interviewer asked Mike, also at Prairie, "As you read, do you act or imagine that you are the author?" He replied, "Sometimes—if this is not a good story, I could feel [for him] if someone told him that he wasn't a very good writer or something."

When Shelley was asked if she thinks about what the reader is like as she writes, she said, "I'm not sure, I don't know." But Mike answered that question by saying, "Like if it's a very good reader, then I can write some hard things for him—good readers know a lot of things, so I would write some hard topics."

Overall, the Prairie School children indicated that they think about authors quite a lot when they read, but that they have a limited sense of their audience when they are authors.

The comments from the Atkinson children, on the other hand, showed that they had a well-developed sense of authorship and readership. For instance, in his writing interview Chris discussed the reason for a revision in one of his books: "Well, some people don't know what elliptical means so I just decided to put that there so they wouldn't get mixed up." His revised text read, "Edmund Halley was the first to state that comets are members of our solar system traveling in elliptical (which means a long oval) orbits." Later on that page he had done the same thing with the word *immemorial*.

Lisa stated that "writers have to know if the reader is going to understand. . . . Sometimes it only matters if I like what I write; sometimes it only matters if the readers like it." She also said, [sometimes after reading a book] I think about the author, why he or she wanted to write the book . . . [with my tongue twister book] maybe he [the author] liked tongue twisters and had a lot of them he wanted to write down and he wanted to remember them so he wrote it."

When Chris was asked if he ever pretends that he is the author of what he reads, he answered, "Yes, well I do most of the time. Especially with C. S. Lewis [his favorite author at the time of this interview], because it says C. S. and it's me, Chris Straw!"

Another type of internal collaboration is that of involvement with characters, events, and content—the world of the text—while reading or writing. The children at both schools talked about being able to "make pictures in their heads" while reading or writing and often feeling like one of the characters. Also, they said at times they felt like observers as if they were there in the story, able to see what was happening, but not actually part of it.

Shelley, from Prairie, commented:

Sometimes when I read a page I can picture, get a picture in my mind and figure out what they are doing, and what is going to happen. I can't do it when I am reading my science or reading book [her basal], only in library books.

Mike, from Prairie, said, "When I am writing a story I feel that I am the main character and I am doing a lot of the things—especially in mysteries."

Chris made a very similar comment and then discussed how he tried to make it easier for his readers to be able to picture:

Well, on the second page it says, "Brad Wilson was walking down a dirt road," and they have a dirt road in their mind, but when I say "which is really a mud road because of a good day's rain," they have a clue and they keep it in their heads. [This is from his mystery, *Brad Wilson, Undercover Detective.*]

Lisa said that it is important in "both reading and writing . . . to make pictures in my mind." With her writing she used this to monitor her work to see if it was good or not. If she can't picture it, then she feels it was not well written.

It is interesting that all of the children mentioned that sometimes the pictures in a book got in their way—they preferred to create their own. Lisa said, "Sometimes I think about why they did a picture that doesn't match with the words."

A third type of internal collaboration is when readers or writers interact with themselves, to monitor or plan or evaluate; that is, to serve as their own audience. Shelley talked about being her own audience: "Sometimes I imagine that I am the one who is going to read it, and I think about what other people would think." When it came to monitoring her writing she said that she can find some problems, but she also said that she expects her teacher to "pick up" on her problems and then, point them out to her. "If I don't catch it Mrs. Black will, and then she'll tell me to figure out how to fix it."

Mike discussed being able to monitor his reading without any problems, "Most of the time [I can tell when something I've read doesn't make sense]. Sometimes when I read a book, I [find] a sentence I think doesn't make sense and then if I read it a couple of times more I can figure out how it makes sense." Nevertheless, he often had either his mother or his teacher, and occasionally both, go over his written work to look for mistakes.

The Atkinson children also discussed monitoring and evaluating their reading and writing. But it is very interesting to see how they also used their peers and teachers during conferences and share meetings as monitors and evaluators (e.g., Chris's and Lisa's earlier comments about share meetings in the external section illustrate how peers ask questions, tell them where more information is needed, etc). In reading, Chris commented that "if you are in a confusing part of a book and rereading doesn't help, I would go talk to someone who already read it and liked it."

These children also talked about serving as their own audience for their writing; for example, Lisa says, "I read my work as another person, I like to have a hint of what the other people may say about it."

Taken together the comments from the four students show that they are involved in a variety of reader-writer collaborations. Their statements serve as validation that the collaborations we have defined are not just figments of researchers' or teachers' imaginations, but that they do exist in varying degrees in the two third-grades that we studied. If you recall, these children were all considered good readers and good writers; it will be interesting to see, as we continue examining our data, the levels of involvement for children with less well-developed abilities. The children's comments also suggest that although our categories are useful labels, they must not be thought of as discrete. The collaborations within which readers and writers engage are highly interrelated.

We are also tempted to posit support for the suggestion that differences in the two classrooms influence the nature of the collaborations within which these young readers and writers reside. For example, at Atkinson the large- and small-group situations provide opportunities for interactions between actual authors and readers that are not present at Prairie School. What appears to emerge in conjunction with these collaborations are opportunities for children to share their ideas, strategies, and understandings; and to develop, fine-tune, and expand selected monitoring abilities, including a fuller sense of audience.

FINAL DISCUSSION

Our argument throughout this chapter has been that we need an expanded theory of reading-writing relationships—a theory which welds thought processes and reading-writing outcomes to the transactions that occur as readers and writers collaborate. Our data clearly establish this collaborative phenomena and take us a step closer to appreciating how social negotiations pervade reading-writing strategies. We have suggested, for example, that young readers' or writers' external collaborations (e.g., with peers) may contribute to how they evaluate their own comprehension and compositions, including their involvement with the text, strategic behavior, and sense of relationship to a counterpart—the author or reader. We believe our data supports this argument.

We have also tried to illustrate the ways in which different classroom structures and rules constrain or allow for various collaborative experiences of the participants.

From a broader perspective, we would like our data to be interpreted as contributing to the rudiments of a sociocognitive theory of reading and writing—a theory that would have at its core the premise that reading and writing are acts of both cognition and social negotiation. Such a theory, borrowing from such disparate fields as literary theory, social psychology, cognitive development, and instructional theory would have as its goal ways of assessing the relationships between social interaction, learning, and performance.

REFERENCES

Applebee, A. N. (1978). *The child's concept of story.* Chicago: University of Chicago Press.

Asher, S., Renshaw, P. D. & Hymel, S. (1982). Peer relations and the developement of social skills. In S. G. Moore & C. R. Cooper (Eds.), *The young child: Reviews of research* (Vol. 3). Washington, D.C.: National Association for the Education of Young Children.

Au, K. H., & Mason, J. M. (1981). Social organizational factors in learning to read: The balance of rights hypothesis. *Reading Research Quarterly, 17,* 115-152.

Britton, J. N. (1970). *Language and learning.* Baltimore: Penguin.

Brown, A. L. (1982). Learning how to learn from reading. In J. A. Langer & M. T. Smith-Burke (Eds.), *Reading meets author/Bridging the gap.* Newark, Del.: International Reading Association.

Bruce, B. (1981). A social interaction model of reading. *Discourse Processes, 4,* 273-311.

Collins, A., Brown, J. S., & Larkin, K. M. (1980). Inference in text understanding. In R. J. Spiro, B. C. Bruce, & W. F. Brewer (Eds.), *Issues in reading comprehension.* Hillsdale, N.J.: Erlbaum.

Ferreiro, E., & Teberosky, A. (1982). *Literacy before schooling.* Trans. from Spanish, 1979. Exeter, N.H.: Heinemann.

Freedman, S. (April, 1984). *Evaluation of, and response to student writing: A review.* Paper presented at the American Education Research Associaltion, New Orleans.

Freedman, S., & Sperling, M. (in press). Teacher student interaction in the writing conference: Response and teaching. In S. W. Freedman (Ed.), *The acquisition of written language: Revision and response.* Norwood, N.J.: Ablex.

Galda, L. (1982). Assuming the spectator stance: An examination of the responses of three young readers. *Research in the Teaching of English, 16*(1), 1-20.

Gere, A., & Stevens, R. (in press). The language of writing groups: how oral response shapes revision. In S. W. Freedman (Ed.), *The acquisition of written language: Revision and response.* Norwood, N.J.: Ablex.

Graves, D. H. (1983). *Writing: Teachers and children at work.* Exeter, N.H.: Heinemann.

Graves, D., & Hanson, J. (1983). The author's chair. *Language Arts, 60*(2), 176-183.

Griffin, C. W. (1982). Theory of responding to student writing: The state of the art. *College Composition and Communication, 33*(3), 296-307.

Hay, A., & Brewer, W. F. (1982). *Children's understanding of the narrator's point of view in prose.* Tech. Rep. No. 294. Urbana: University of Illinois, Center for the Study of Reading.

Heath, S. B. (1982). Questioning at home and at school: A comparative study. In G. Spindler (Ed.), *The ethnography of schooling.* New York: Holt, Rinehart & Winston.

Jose, P. E., & Brewer, W. F. (1984). The development of story liking: Character identification, suspense and outcome resolution. *Developmental Psychology, 20*(5), 911-924.

Kirby, D., & Liner, T. (1981). *Inside out: Developmental stragegies for teaching writing.* Montclair, N.J.: Boynton/Cook.

Murray, D. (1982). Teaching the other self: The writer's first reader. *College Composition and Communication 33,* 140-147.

Newkirk, T. (1984). *"Be Like Us:" The writing teacher as representative of an interpretative community.* Diss., University of New Hampshire.

Odell, L. (1984). *Writing in the workplace.* Paper presented at the Conference for College Composition and Communication, New York.

Phillips, S. (1982). *The invisible culture: Communication in classroom and community on the Warm Springs Indian Reservations.* New York: Longman.

Pichert, J. W. (1979). *Sensitivity to what is important in prose.* Tech. Rep. No. 149. Urbana: University of Illinois, Center for the Study of Reading.

Rosenblatt, L. M. (1976). *Literature as exploration* (3rd ed.). New York: Noble & Noble.

Rumelhart, D. (1980). Schemata: The building blocks of cognition. In R. J. Spiro, B. C. Bruce, & W. F. Brewer (Eds.), *Theoretical issues in reading comprehension.* Hillsdale, N.J.: Erlbaum.

Spiro, R. J. (1977). Remembering information from text: The "state of schema" approach. In R. C. Anderson, R. J. Spiro, & W. E. Montague (Eds.), *Schooling and the acquisition of knowledge.* Hillsdale, N.J.: Erlbaum.

Tierney, R. J., & LaZansky, J. (1980). The rights and responsibilities of readers and writers: A contractual aggreement. *Language Arts, 57,* 606–613.

Tierney, R. J. et al. (in press). Author's intention and reader's interpretation. In R. J. Tierney, P. Anders, & J. Mitchell (Eds.), *Understanding readers' understanding.* Hillsdale, N.J.: Erlbaum.

Saville-Troike, M. (1982). *The ethnography of communication.* Oxford: Basil Blackwell.

Smith, F. (1983). Reading like a writer. *Language Arts, 60*(4), 558–567.

13

Learning with QUILL:
Lessons for
Students, Teachers, and
Software Designers

Andee Rubin • Bertram C. Bruce

She sat silently in the back of the room. Every line in her scowling face demanded, "Show me! Show me how this computer stuff is going to teach my kids how to write!" At the end of the three-day training session on QUILL, a set of microcomputer-based writing activities, we were sure that this was one fourth-grade teacher who would never beome a successful user. Soon, however, reports started to filter back about a teacher everyone was calling "Mrs. QUILL." It was our scowling resister. By the end of the school year, her class had written letters to their local congressman and to President Reagan, organized a "Face the Students" session with their congressman, and traveled to Washington, where they met with Maureen Reagan. The initial letters, lists of questions for the "Face the Students" session, and thank you letters to the Reagans were all written using QUILL. The project was aided by a local parent who knew the congressman and was impressed by his child's school activities. Several local newspapers carried accounts of the class's letter-writing activities and journey to Washington.

Many people learned important lessons from this teacher's experience. She, herself, learned that computers could enhance her classroom, even in the unlikely area of writing. The students in her class learned that writing could be used to accomplish goals they cared about, even in the unlikely place called school. We as software designers learned that even unlikely teachers could use QUILL in educationally exciting and valuable ways, if QUILL was consistent with their educational goals and techniques. In this case the teacher had always valued letter writing as a language arts activity. She ran a well-organized yet flexible classroom into which it was possible to integrate the use of a computer. Using QUILL and the microcomputer she was able to establish a new and meaningful context for developing literacy in her classroom.

This chapter describes the effects QUILL has had on classroom contexts for communication and literacy. More generally it investigates the changes an open-ended innovation can bring about for teachers and students. Educational tools that allow significant flexibility require teachers to participate actively in their implementation. Thus, individual classrooms may choose different activities, teachers may focus on their own special interests, and students may use the tools in significantly different ways. Given this freedom teachers often create educational activities that the innovation developers never considered.

The computer is a particularly interesting medium for investigating these concepts because it is often thought of as an instrument for controlling students and classrooms. We hear about "teacher-proof" software and "individualized instruction." In contrast, open-ended software such as QUILL is teacher dependent and provides a context in which students can work at their own rate only if teachers provide that opportunity (Bruce, 1985; Levin, 1982; Rubin, 1982; Collins, in press).

Our contention is that open-ended software—like other flexible educational contexts—provides opportunities for learning that go beyond transferring knowledge from the machine to the student. In this chapter we discuss lessons teachers, students, and software designers learned during the past two years of working with QUILL. They span traditional lessons in language arts, lessons about the writing process, lessons about classroom organization, and philosophical lessons about the interaction of purpose and tools in writing. These lessons provide powerful evidence for the educational value of software and other innovations that can provide multiple opportunities for learning.

WHAT IS QUILL?

QUILL (Collins, Bruce, & Rubin, 1982; Rubin, Bruce, & The QUILL Project, in press; Bruce & Rubin, 1984) is a set of microcomputer-based writing activities for students in Grades 2 through 12. The software is based on recent research in composition and encompasses the prewriting, composing, revising, and publishing aspects of the writing process (Bruce et al. 1982; Flower & Hayes, 1981; Graves, 1982; Newkirk & Atwell, 1982). To aid students in becoming more experienced writers, QUILL includes two tools for writing: PLANNER, which helps students plan and organize their pieces, and WRITER'S ASSISTANT (Levin, Bortua, & Vasconcellos, 1982), a text editor that facilitates the revision process by making the addition, deletion, and rearrangement of text easier. QUILL also provides students with two contexts for writing designed to foster communication by providing audiences for student composition. The first, MAILBAG, is an electronic mail system with which students can send messages to individuals, groups, or an electronic bulletin board. The second, LIBRARY, is an information management system in which writing is accessed by title, author, or keywords.

QUILL was used in over 150 classrooms across the country from Massachusetts to Alaska (Barnhardt, 1984) from 1982 to 1984. These sites provide the basis for the examples used throughout this chapter.

LESSONS FOR STUDENTS

Student Lesson 1

There are many legitimate reasons for writing and reading, even in school. Students typically find the purpose of writing in school to be mystifying. The assignment often involves half an hour of sitting alone, writing about a topic that they may find either boring (e.g., compare *Hamlet* and *Huckleberry Finn*) or silly (e.g., describe how it would feel to be an ice cream cone). In most cases everyone in the class must write on the same topic, and teachers who assigned the topic are then expected to read and evaluate themes on a subject that is not meaningful to them either. The final indignity is that most of the teachers' responses to the writing tend to focus on grammatical or mechanical errors rather than on content.

Students in several QUILL classrooms realized—some for the first time—that writing could be different from this dreary picture. In most cases this came about through teachers consciously setting up a communicative environment where the audience and purpose for writing were both specific and real. QUILL contributed both by providing examples of such contexts and by being an easily adaptable tool around which to build communicative events. The examples below illustrate these contexts.

On a trip through Alaska to visit QUILL classrooms we carried a disk called "Supermail." Students in each classroom wrote messages to children in classrooms they knew we would later visit. Students in some of the later classrooms read these messages, gaining ideas for messages of their own. Some even set for themselves the task of outdoing their peers. Thus, writing became meaningful as a form of communication, sometimes even as competition for readers from an audience of their peers. One example of this "competition from afar" began with the following piece, written by two eighth graders in McGrath, Alaska (population: 500, reachable only by air).

CALLING ALL MEN

Sheila Forsythe   Althea Jones

Hi,

This note is to all you good looking guys out there in the world. There are two of us writing so we'll tell you a little bit about ourselves. Our names are Sheila Forsythe and Althea Jones. We're both 14 and stuck in a small town in Alaska called

McGrath. We have a pretty big problem and we hope that you guys will help us out. We have a very short supply of foxy dudes here. So if you are a total fine babe PLEASE I repeat PLEASE write us!!!!

Write:

Sheila Forsythe and Althea Jones
General Delivery
McGrath, Alaska 99627

and hurry!

Keywords: /Mcgrath/Male Order Men/

The two authors acknowledged that it was important to call attention to their letter by their choice of keywords. The first keyword—McGrath—was an obligatory identification of the source of the message. But the second (including the misspelling) was their own invention. Since the Supermail disk was actually a LIBRARY disk, students chose which entries to read by scanning the list of keywords. These girls were correct in their assessment of their audience: groups of boys in later classrooms did choose their message. Not to be outdone, two girls in the next town, Holy Cross, wrote the following message on the Supermail disk:

GOOD LOOKING JUNEAU BOYS

Two Holy Cross Girls   Josie and Evelyn

Our names are Josie Adams and Evelyn Fields. We like skiing, basketball, hockey, writing letters to cute boys, and we would be more than pleased if any of you cute boys would write to us. We don't have any boyfriends. So you don't have to worry about that! We also would like you to send a picture when you write. (You are going to write aren't you?) We will send you a picture too. Josie is 14 and Evelyn is 13. Well, please write soon! We are waiting for your letter!!!!!

WE SEND YOU OUR HEARTS!

SINCERELY, JOSIE AND EVELYN.

Keywords: /Juneau Boys/H.C.R. Girls/

These two girls used a slightly different strategy for attracting readers; they knew the disk would be traveling to Juneau next, so they specifically aimed their "personal ad" toward Juneau boys, including them in both the title and keywords. They also spent considerable time and effort drawing the heart (an idea they appropriated from the younger students in the school who had spent the morning making word pictures with QUILL) so their message would compete effectively with the one from McGrath. Incidently, boys in both Juneau and Oregon, where the disk later traveled, took all four girls' addresses with the intention of writing to them during the summer.

Some students discover that writing can be meaningful for self-expression as well as for communication. This was evident in a poignant episode concerning Peter, a sixth grader in an inner-city school. Peter's home situation was troubled and he did not do very well in school. In January he ran away from both home and school and spent several nights sleeping in an abandoned car. After a few days he reappeared in his classroom and asked if he could use the computer. When the teacher told him he would have to wait his turn, he offered to use the computer in the morning before classes began. One of the first pieces he wrote after returning to school was the following:

PETER'S ISLAND

PETER

HI SWEET POLLY LOVERS . . . HERE IS A REVIEW OF THE LATEST NEW T. V. SHOW . . ."PETER'S ISLAND."
ONE DAY THERE WAS A BOY NAMED PETER. HE WANTED TO RUN AWAY BECAUSE EVERY BODY DID NOT LIKE HIM SO HE RAN AWAY HE HEARD OF A BOAT GOING OUT TO SEA SO HE WENT TO GET ON THE BOAT AND ON THE SECOUND DAY AT SEA THERE WAS A BAD STORM AND HE WOKEUP HE WAS IN THE SEA LAYING ON A BOARD AND HE WAS GETTING TIRED AND HUNGRY SO WENT TO SLEEP AND ALL MOST DIED BUT WHEN HE WOKEUP AND HE WAS ON A ILAND AND HE LOOK AROUND AND SEEN A DOLPHIN BUT MICHAEL KEEP SAYING WHO SAVED HIM THEN HE KNOW WHO SAVED HIM THE DOLPHIN AND HE LIVED THE REST OF HIS LIFE ON THE ISLAND WITH THE DOLPHIN

THE END.

Keywords: /peter/boat/boy/

In this piece Peter adopted a TV-announcer's role, a strategy that he had used in the past. There seem to be two plausible purposes for Peter's piece. One is his way to come to terms with running away. He may also have seen it as a message to his teacher asking for help or understanding. Peter eventually became one of the most prolific writers in the class. In his classroom girls dominated the keyboard; yet Peter always made sure he had writing time. Later in the year he became the food editor of the class newspaper and wrote a book five typed pages in length.

Student Lesson 2

Revision is both possible and desirable.

According to some, the computer's most important contribution is that it "takes the sting out of revision" (Romick, 1984). Professional writers recognize the importance of revision; some analyses of the writing process suggest that 14 percent of the time is used in prewriting, only 1 percent in actually composing, and 85 percent in rewriting. The distribution of time allotted to the writing process in schools does not reflect this in any way. Few teachers give their students the opportunity to revise, and those who do usually face a chorus of moans from their students who hate copying over. The students rarely understand all that revision can entail, perhaps because of their long exposure to a focus on mechanics and neatness (Scardamalia, 1981). While the presence of a text editor does not guarantee informed revision, it does make it possible without the undue hardship that results from rewriting entire texts.

Some students, in fact, carry revision to extremes. One sixth-grade girl in Hartford was fascinated by the fact that she could potentially produce a perfect paper. While she had been one of the most prolific writers in the class, she was slowed down considerably by her habit of correcting every typo as she noticed it, rather than waiting until she had completed a chunk of text. However, her meticulousness illustrated her real concern with the appearance of her writing.

Most teachers who used QUILL were not accustomed to commenting on the content of students' writing; their training and the demands of achievement tests had encouraged them to focus on mechanics. The training they received during workshops on QUILL, combined with the possibility of their students making substantial changes easily using QUILL, led some of them to respond more substantively to their students' writing. The result of such feedback can be seen in the changes on two drafts of a "New Jersey resolution" written by two fourth-grade boys; the assignment was to develop a resolution that the legislature could pass to help improve New Jersey.

Drugs Are Dumb

Benjamin M.   Darren S.

    What is bothering us the most in New Jersey is underaged kids are taking drugs. Their not getting enough education. Some kids even get killed!

    Adults should educate their children not to take drugs. To get help you should go to a psychiatrist. Try not to take drugs.

    It would take a few months or weeks to get over this problem. It is important to solve this problem because sometimes people get killed.

Keywords: /psychiatrist/drugs/children/killed/education/

Their conversation with their teacher about this piece focussed on the need for snappy conclusions and on how long it would really take to kick a drug habit. Benjamin and Darren then produced the following final draft.

Dangerous Damaging Drugs

Benjamin M.   Darren S.

What is bothering us the most in New Jersey is underaged kids are taking drugs. They're not getting enough education. Some kids even get killed! Adults should educate their children not to take drugs or not to get involved with drugs. To get help you should go to a psychiatrist. Try not to take drugs. If you take drugs, go for help! It would take an unlimited amount of time to get over this problem. It is important to solve this problem because sometimes people get killed. So be smart, make sure you don't take drugs!

Keywords: /psychiatrist/drugs/children/killed/education/

In addition to correcting mechanical errors and responding to their teacher's comments, the two boys revised their previous title, extending the alliterative theme, and increasing the chances for it to attract a reader's attention. This use of the text editor for both revision and editing within a number of drafts is an important step beyond the way writing instruction is handled in many classrooms.

LESSONS FOR TEACHERS

Teacher Lesson 1

Truly communicative writing in school is possible, legitimate, and necessary.

Teachers are sometimes suspicious of the notion of "communicative writing" in school, associating it with surreptitious note passing, giggling, and other disruptive activities. Part of the goal of the QUILL training workshop and teacher's guide was to convince teachers that communicative writing was a legitimate part of writing in school, and that assessing the communicative value of any written piece should be a primary concern. The Cookbook, a handbook of suggestions for teachers on how to use QUILL, suggested sending messages on MAILBAG as a beginning activity to acquaint both students and teacher with QUILL. A sixth-grade teacher in Oregon discovered that his students took advantage of this opportunity to write him serious notes about their opinions of school. Some typical examples are: "I think it's a good idea to write our schedule for the day on the board," and "I'd like to do more art in school."

A teacher in a combined sixth-, seventh- and eighth-grade class in Holy Cross, Alaska, took advantage of a real-world situation to create a truly communicative task for her class. Villages in Alaska like Holy Cross (population: 275) receive an inordinate number of requests for information about their village. In Holy Cross, the city council gives all such requests to the school. After answering several of the letters individually, this teacher decided to have her class construct a tourism brochure about Holy Cross. They decided what the brochure should include, took responsibility for varous sections, did the required research, and wrote the text. The finished product includes several hand-done drawings as well as sections on schools, clothes, trapping and hunting, fishing, businesses, government, communication, recreation, and population.

A third way teachers discovered to include functional writing in a school was through class newspapers. Since the computer is a useful aid for the most onerous parts of putting together a newspaper—text preparation, editing, and formatting—many classes published regular editions, as often as monthly. Without the advantages of the computer, the typical pattern one finds is that one or two issues are published with the bulk of the preparation done by the teacher. The issues end when the teacher gets tired of staying up all night typing dittos. Newspapers in QUILL classrooms were produced for both in-school and out-of-school audiences; the assumed readership included the members of the class, friends, and their families. A newspaper produced by a sixth-grade class in Massachusetts included the following column, editorial in nature and clearly directed to other class members.

Kids' Behavior Toward Substitute Teachers

When we have a substitute teacher you are supposed to treat them like your own teacher. Some of the kids in the classroom don't treat the substitute teacher with any respect. They treat them like another kid. They call the substitute names, or yell out disturbing the teacher. Some of the girls act like it is their regular teacher, but some of them act fresh. You hardly ever see a boy act nice to the substitute teacher. They always for some reason act nice to our regular teacher, but not to substitute teachers.

These writing activities demonstrate not only the possibility and legitimacy of communicative writing in the classroom, but its necessity. Students contributed enthusiastically to the newspaper and brochure projects in part because they knew there was a real audience for the information they possessed. This crucial element had been missing in many other less successful classroom writing activities.

Teacher Lesson 2

Changes in the classroom social structure that allow more student interaction can lead to better writing.

One of the unsuspected advantages of having only one computer in each classroom is that teachers immediately acknowledge the need for students to work at the computer in pairs or small groups. In most classes, individual work during writing is the rule; with QUILL it has become the exception. The need to have students work on the computer together has led several teachers to realize the potential benefit of collaborative work. A sixth-grade teacher from Oregon commented that papers produced by pairs of students have fewer grammatical errors;

he hypothesized that both students' independent writing would improve as a result of working with another student. The following conversation, observed in another sixth-grade class, illustrates one benefit of student collaboration. The first student had written a message to students in other cities using the Supermail disk: "We are in Mr. Kinder's class." His partner immediately reminded him that "the kids who read that won't know who Mr. Kinder is!"

One of the most dramatic examples of the influence of social structure on writing occurred in a sixth-grade classroom in Hartford. Students had seen a Black History show given by the younger classes in the school. Upon returning to their room several students opted to write reviews of the show. Once they had completed a draft at their desks, students were assigned consecutive numbers that designated their turn to enter their draft on the computer. A backlog soon developed, and several students ended up standing around the computer reading each other's first drafts. One girl, named Margaret, had written a lukewarm review of the show. Part of her piece read:

> The scenery was pretty good, and the light was bright enough, but the sound was not that good. Mr. Hodges was speaking very loudly and was good on the stage. I think the show deserves three stars because it was very good.

While she was waiting to use the computer, Margaret read a first draft by her friend Marines. Marines' review claimed that "the light was a little dull." She also complained about the glee club: "They were almost all weak. The audience couldn't hear them. They sounded soft then they went loud. It was a disaster!"

Margaret was aware that her review and Marines' expressed different opinions—and that hers might be ignored in the face of Marines' strong views. She also had an explanation for Marines' criticism of the glee club. This explanation was included in her final draft:

> The scenery wasn't very much, and the light was kind of dull, and the sound wasn't very good. Mr. Hodges was speaking loud and clearly, and he was great on the stage. When the Glee Club was singing so nice, Marines got very jealous and asked Mrs. Evens to be in the Glee Club. But when Mrs. Evens said no she wrote bad things about the Glee Club on the computer up-stairs.

Notice that while she had underminded Marines' opinion of the glee club, she has also changed her own description of the lighting to agree with the other girl's (see Bruce, Michaels, & Watson-Gegeo, 1984, for a more detailed analysis).

None of these incidents would have occurred in the traditional model of writing instruction—students sitting alone, writing, turning in a paper, and receiving a grade. The presence of QUILL in the classroom contributed to creating a positive context for writing by shaking up the teaching of writing, making it necessary for students to write together in order to have sufficient computer time. The challenge for teachers is to channel these social interactions to improve students' writing.

LESSONS FOR SOFTWARE DESIGNERS

Software Designer Lesson 1

A teacher's instructional philosophy is a more powerful determinant of software use than the software itself; that is, the teacher's contribution overwhelms that of the software.

Many software designers overestimate the effect their software will have on education. On a global scale, predictions are made of revolutions in education and a technologically literate citizenry due largely to the use of new software (Papert, 1980). Our experience has shown that, especially in the case of open-ended software like QUILL, the software makes an important but not an enormous contribution to what happens in the classroom. A much more potent effect comes from the teacher.

One example can be found in teachers' use of MAILBAG in their classrooms. One of our most successful classrooms, particularly in their use of electronic mail, was a fourth-grade class who used the QUILL software in its very early stages. Even using a relatively primitive system, messages flew among the students and between students and their teacher. The teacher made it clear to her students that she believed this written exchange among the students served an important educational purpose.

In contrast, a teacher in another class later in the project viewed students' use of MAILBAG as illegitimate writing once they started using it to write love notes and immediately made it unavailable. By this time, the MAILBAG had been polished and was easier to use, but the teacher clearly indicated she felt it lacked any educational value.

The process of educational change involving QUILL seemed to proceed in two stages. First, the software made possible a new writing genre (written conversations, in the case of MAILBAG). Second, the teacher responded to this new genre in her own way. In the most positive cases teachers transferred the children's new-found sense of communicative writing to other genres and modalities. In the most negative cases teachers rejected the new genre as illegitimate.

Teachers demonstrated interesting differences in communicating with students using MAILBAG. A sixth-grade teacher in Hartford adopted two separate personae in writing to his students. The first was a perfectly serious one used when he carried on straightforward—and sometimes quite personal—written conversations with his students. The following exchange is typical:

Bathroom

Marlowe B.

There is a lot of trouble in the bathrooms. There's been writing on the new paint job, and there's been someone who's been peeling the paint off the radiator.

If people keep messing up the bathroom, Ducky said that she was going to close the bathroom until we learn not to write in it. And there's been plenty of noise in there. If we don't have to go to the bathroom, don't go in.

Keywords: /bathroom/clean/

Girls' Bathroom

Dr. A.
Dear Pee Wee,

Thank you for being concerned about the girls' bathroom. I feel sorry for the girls who are messing it up. They must be a little "messed up" themselves.
When I see Ducky, I'll try to remember to tell her what you did.

Dr. A.

When he was not being serious, this teacher adopted a frivolous personality called Dunedeen, a mischievous monster who sent anonymous messages to several students each week. These messages, predictably, provoked similar unserious replies. Both sets of messages were filled with "hahahaha" and epithets such as "Squarehead." The point to emphasize is that students responded in kind to whatever personality the teacher adopted. The teacher was careful to separate the two because they required such different responses from his students.

A fourth-grade teacher in New Jersey used MAILBAG quite differently. One of the suggestions in the teacher's guide for using MAILBAG is Classroom Chat, an adaptation of the popular newspaper column, Confidential Chat. By sending anonymous messages students can discuss personal problems with other chatters in the class without revealing their identity. In the newspaper prototype writers usually adopt a pseudonym that refers to their problem (e.g., Hassled Mom or Concerned Commuter). This teacher decided to use this idea to give her class an assignment. She sent the following message, complete with pseudonym:

The Shower Problem

I. Needabath
Dear Classy Computer Kids,

There are five members in my family and only one shower. Because I'm the youngest member of our family, I'm the last one in line to take a shower. By then, there's usually no more hot water and not too much time for me to wash behind my ears! It's a horrible way to start a day. What can I do to solve this problem?

Cold, late, and dirty,
I. Needabath

The assignment produced the following predictably tongue-in-cheek responses, which hover between reality and fantasy much as the original letter did.

Buying A Shower

Jill Y.   Suzanne H.

Dear Ichabod Needabath,

The next time your parents have a garage sale, go to your room and pick out things you don't use anymore. Put them with the rest of the items that are going to be sold. (Make sure you ask your parents first.) Take the money that you make from the sale and dig deep into your piggy bank for more. Go to your parents and give them your money. Ask them (nicely) if they will buy a shower with the money you have. (Some other family members can use it after you.) If at first they say no, tell them it will be better for the whole family. Good luck, Icky!!

Showers

Dear I. Needabath,

I think you should tell the first person that takes a shower you have to go the bathroom. Then they should let you go before they take a shower. Quickly lock the door and take your shower. You will have enough of time to wash behind your ears.

Sneaky and Desparate,
Kerry N. and Jenny B.

An interesting problem emerged in this activity: The form of the teacher's message mimicked that of the standard Confidential Chat letter, but the students in the class all knew who had sent the letter and, even more important, that it posed a fake problem. Thus, their assignment was to pretend they were answering a real letter from a needy person yet they knew it was an imaginary letter from their teacher. While students produced imaginative pieces, observers in the classroom reported they were confused about their audience (their teacher or I. Needabath) and their purpose (real or fantasy) while they were writing. This lack of clarity was most obvious when they were signing their names; many were not sure whether to use their own names or to make up pseudonyms.

While the software was identical in our two examples, the outcome was notably different. These differences can be attributed to the teacher's style and values. QUILL contributed the concept of MAILBAG and a medium through which students could send messages, but the content of the writing belonged to the teacher and the students.

Software Designer Lesson 2

There is an important difference between using a computer for editing and for communication.

When we began designing QUILL we underestimated the importance of this distinction. We knew there were text editors available for schools but thought they were insufficient. We wanted to create software informed by recent work on the writing process. In fact, one of our early designs required children to access the text editor by declaring the part of the writing process (drafting, revising, editing, etc.) on which they were working. It seemed clear to us that an effective writing curriculum should be embedded in the writing process. A corollary was that a piece of writing software had to embody writing process concepts.

We were surprised later to find that the usefulness of QUILL in many classrooms derived not from our (perhaps insufficient) attempts to reflect the writing process, but from its ability to support the establishment of environments for communication, for example, the exchange of personal mail, sharing writing with others, and publishing newspapers. In contrast, we found some classrooms where QUILL's communication environments were not used. For example, in one junior high classroom the teacher did not want to allow direct communication among students since, she feared, it might encourage obscene language. In that case a simple text editor, such as WRITER'S ASSISTANT, would have been more appropriate.

While QUILL includes a text editor as a tool, it is only part of a larger environment that provides purposes and audiences for writing. For private writing (e.g., diaries) or public writing that is only to be shared in printed form (e.g., professional papers), a text editor might be sufficient. In fact, in those cases the environments of QUILL could be cumbersome and interfere with writing. Students in many situations, however, would benefit from more attention to the social aspects of writing. Social environments and interactions with peers and teachers provide a sense of purpose and audience for young writers, especially if they have access to software that can provide support for the processes of drafting, editing, and publishing their work.

SUMMARY

These six lessons arose during two years of field testing QUILL in second-through eighth-grade classrooms. During that time we also learned much about the importance of administrative support to the success of educational innovations. Teachers taught us a great many lessons about creative and effective uses of QUILL that we had never imagined. Had we designed a program that required multiple-choice answers or merely asked students to edit a flawed piece, we would have missed important aspects of the learning process. The final lesson for software designers is just this: We will all learn more if the software is flexible and adaptable. Put in less computer-oriented terms, it applies to other educational contexts as well. QUILL's open-ended nature and attention to process provided a context in which both students and teachers increased their awareness of literacy. Similarly, other flexible contexts for language instruction can lead to significant and truly individualized learning for all the participants.

REFERENCES

Barnhardt, C. (April 1984). The Quill Microcomputer Writing Program in Alaska. In R. V. Dusseldorp (Ed.), *Proceedings of the third annual statewide conference of Alaska Association for Computers in Education* (pp. 1–10). Anchorage, Alaska: Alaska Association for Computers in Education.

Bruce, B. (1985). Taking control of educational technology. *Science for the People, 17,* 37–40.

Bruce, B., Michaels, S., & Watson-Gegeo, K. (1985). How computers can change the writing process. *Language Arts, 62,* 143–149.

Bruce, B. C. et al. (1982). Three perspectives on writing. *Educational Psychologist, 17,* 131–145.

Bruce, B., & Rubin, A. (September 1984). *Final report on the utilization of technology in the development of basic skills instruction: Written communications.* Washington, D.C.: U.S. Department of Education.

Collins, A. (in press). Teaching reading and writing with personal computers. In J. Orasanu (Ed.), *A decade of reading research: Implication for practice.* Hillsdale, N.J.: Erlbaum.

Collins, A., Bruce, B. C., & Rubin, A. D. (1982). Microcomputer-based writing activities for the upper elementary grades. In *Proceedings of the Fourth International Learning Technology Congress and Exposition* (pp. 134–140). Warrenton, Va.: Society for Applied Learning Technology.

Flower, L. S., & Hayes, J. R. (1981). Problem solving and the cognitive process of writing. In C. H. Frederiksen, & J. F. Dominic (Eds.), *Writing: The nature, development and teaching of written communication* (pp. 39–58). Hillsdale, N.J.: Erlbaum.

Graves, D. H. (1982). *Writing: Teachers and children at work.* Exeter, N.H.: Heinemann.

Levin, J. A. (1982). Microcomputers as interactive communication media: An interactive text interpreter. *The Quarterly Newsletter of the Laboratory of Comparative Human Cognition, 4,* 34–36.

Levin, J. A., Boruta, M. J., & Vasconcellos, M. T. (1982). Microcomputer-based environments for writing: A writer's assistant. In A. C. Wilkinson (Ed.), *Classroom computers and cognitive science* (pp. 219–232). New York: Academic.

Newkirk, T., & Atwell, N. (1982). *Understanding writing.* Chelmsford, Mass. The Northeast Regional Exchange.

Papert, S. (1980). *Mindstorms.* Brighton: Harvester.

Romick, M. (April 1984). The computer chronicles. In R. V. Dusseldorp (Ed.), *Proceedings of the third annual statewide conference of Alaska Association for Computers in Education.* Anchorage, Alaska: Alaska Association for Computers in Education.

Rubin, A. D. (1982). The computer confronts language arts: Cans and shoulds for education. In A. C. Wilkinson (Ed.), *Classroom computers and cognitive science* (pp. 201–217). New York: Academic.

Rubin, A. D., & Bruce, B. C., & The QUILL Project. (in press). QUILL: Reading and writing with a microcomputer. In B. A. Hutson (Ed.), *Advances in reading and language research.* Greenwich, Conn.: JAI Press. (Also published in 1981: Reading Education Rep. No. 48. Urbana, Ill.: Center for the Study of Reading.)

Scardamalia, M. (1981). How children cope with the cognitive demands of writing. In C. H. Frederiksen, & J. F. Dominic (Eds.), *Writing: The nature, development and teaching of written communication* (pp. 81–104). Hillsdale, N.J.: Erlbaum.

PART 4

INFLUENCES ON CONTEXTS OF LITERACY INSTRUCTION

The fourth question we address considers, *What influences appropriate contexts for learning to read and write?* There are many areas beyond the immediate social organization of the reading and writing contexts that greatly influence the development of literacy. If both adult and child contribute to the context for learning, the child's perceptions of the learning environment are critical for successful learning. Weinstein considers the important issue of relationships between students and teachers. She focuses on the students' perceptions of how their teachers view them in terms of academic ability. She provides impressive evidence that children are sensitive to their teachers' perceptions about their skills regardless of age, ethnic group, or ability level. Both negative and positive perceptions can have a direct impact on children's successful development of reading and writing abilities and their ability to influence and modify their teacher's instruction.

While many suggestions have been proposed for developing children's literacy levels, an important point is noted by Schwartz. He outlines the need to develop the teachers' knowledge base if we are to expect to effect widespread change in children's learning in school settings. Schwartz differentiates between expert and novice teachers' types of knowledge and how this knowledge influences their construction of the learning environment for a given child. A parallel point is made by Winograd as he details the need for knowledge to be developed and synthesis reached between researchers suggesting avenues for change and policy makers who actually implement the programs being proposed. Finally, Clark argues for the need to develop shared knowledge and mutual respect between researchers and teachers; the researchers to be aware of the needs and goals of the teachers who are the acknowledged experts of their own classrooms, and the teachers to be aware of the amount of "answers" that researchers can and cannot be expected to provide.

The last chapter in the volume provides a synthesis of the chapters in terms of the four questions proposed in the preface, discussing the implications of the wealth of ideas presented throughout the volume. A look toward the future of instruction in the skills of literacy is taken, focusing on how contexts of school-based literacy may be characterized in the near future and on directions for future research to encourage the development of these contexts.

14

The Teaching of Reading and Children's Awareness of Teacher Expectations

Rhona S. Weinstein

Success in schooling rests upon learning to read and upon the continued development of this capacity, fine-tuned for the purposes of gaining and critically analyzing new and increasingly complex information. Despite our commitment toward universal literacy, progress toward this goal has met with somewhat mixed results.

Educators express concern over declining reading attainment scores (as compared to an earlier decade), a decline most consistently seen in the upper grades (Chall, 1983). Yet the mean level of reading attainment of a population represents only a part of the picture. Underlying these average gains and losses is a continued, still-apparent trend for groups of children to increasingly fall behind others in reading attainment over the course of schooling.

This chapter underscores the role of self-fulfilling prophecy effects as one causal element in explaining our slow progress toward universal literacy. Certain beliefs and practices of reading instruction as it occurs in the context of classrooms and schools carry messages concerning expected student performance. Recent research on the student mediation of self-fulfilling prophecies highlights that *children are aware of these messages* and internalize the view communicated. This awareness has clear psychological, social, and academic consequences that

Work on this chapter was supported by a grant from the Spencer Foundation, which is gratefully acknowledged. The studies described in this chapter were funded by grants from the National Institute of Education (NIE-G-79-0078 and NIE-G-80-0071) and the National Institute of Mental Health (IROI MH 34379). The opinions expressed here do not necessarily reflect the position or policy of these agencies, and no offical endorsement should be inferred.

may play a role in failures to learn to read and in the slower development of reading skills.

The purpose of this chapter is to introduce findings drawn from student mediational work in terms of what this knowledge base can teach us about the instruction of reading in the classroom. Before examining this literature, it is important to outline in brief the extent of the problems we face in reaching universal literacy.

STATEMENT OF THE PROBLEM

The problem is two-fold. First, educators have become increasingly concerned with the large numbers of children who experience severe problems in *learning* to read. Second, the gap between those who are learning and those who are having problems widens over the course of schooling. The number of children who are experiencing problems in learning to read had been estimated by governmental committees to be 10 to 15 percent (Carroll & Chall, 1975), although only 2 percent have been earmarked for special services by Public Law 94–142. Perhaps because of the growing industry in the identification of learning handicaps, the number of childern identified as learning disabled has grown phenomenally from 120,000 in 1968 to 1,281,395 in 1979 (Leinhardt, Zigmond, & Cooley, 1981). Yet, recent research suggests that beyond their *relatively* poor performance in reading, the characteristics of children identified as learning disabled are quite diverse and do not largely conform to the descriptions set down by federal law and the professional literature.

In a recent study of a representative sample of a learning disabled population, Shephard, Smith, and Vojir (1983) found that 57.4 percent of the children identified could not be characterized as hyperactive, brain injured, having statistical discrepancies between ability and achievement, or showing signs of perceptual processing disorder. Instead, the low achievement of these misidentified children stemmed from other sources such as language interference, emotional and behavior problems, or largely unknown sources, in that these children were described only as "slow learners" and "below grade-level achievers." Further, when Ysseldyke and colleagues (1979) compared a sample of identified learning disabled children with nonidentified children who had comparable levels of underachievement on a battery of psychological tests, the results documented considerable similarity between the two groups.

Other researchers have demonstrated that characteristics of children, teachers, and schools play a role in who and how many are identified as belonging to different categories. Boys have been found to be overrepresented in those children identified as learning disabled, as have low-socioeconomic status (SES) children (Balow, 1971). Teachers in open classrooms have been found to rate fewer children as moderately maladjusted than teachers in traditional classrooms (Hochschild, 1976). Smith (1982) has also shown that bureaucratic pressures to serve handicapped youngsters and to adjust demand to supply result in differing patterns in the identification of the learning disabled. The distribution of ability (narrow or wide) in a school alone would result in different types of children being identified.

Evidence also suggests that the gap in reading attainment between groups of children widens over the course of schooling. Chall and Snow (1982) found that low-SES children were about equal in reading, writing, and word meaning to the norms for a middle-class population at Grade 2. However, by Grade 6, attainment was considerably lower as compared to middle-class norms. Similarly, in a recent study of the achievement pattern of minority groups in a large urban school district, McLean (1984) reports that although both black and white students achieved above national norms in the first grade (on the California Achievement Tests), each year black children fell steadily until they were far below the norms by eleventh grade, whereas white students remained at the same level in the distribution of students nationwide.

These recent results continue to mirror patterns described earlier by Coleman et al. (1966) and Jencks (1972). These patterns of differential achievement between groups of children that systemically *widen* over the course of schooling clearly suggest that the educational process itself plays a role in determining such differential outcomes. Despite many attempts to equalize educational opportunities for groups of children who differ in socioeconomic status and race, this widening gap in attainment persists.

Thus, what these studies suggest is that certain groups of children have more difficulty learning to read in the earliest stages of schooling (and it is not clear that they deserve the term *learning disabled*), and the differences in reading attainment widen over the school years. We have had a long history of believing that the problem lies in the child. We have tests and labels that support this child deficit characterization, yet the variability that underlies the learning disabled population is a clear indication that something more is taking place.

LOOKING TO THE INSTRUCTIONAL CONTEXT

Many have argued that a child's failure to learn to read might be evidence that the instruction itself was lacking (Bateman, 1979; Calfee, 1982; Roehler, Duffy, & Meloth, this volume). Others suggest that the match between the child's cognitive stage or style and instructional strategy was amiss. Still others point to the instructional context in which reading takes place. In the Resnick and Weaver (1979) volumes on reading, both Simons and Cazden cite the classroom interactions with the teacher as a potential cause of reading difficulties of some children. More of this perspective is represented in the first *Handbook of Reading Research* edited by Pearson (1984) and in attention to sociolinguistic research on reading (Bloom & Green, 1984), social and motivational influences on reading (Wigfield & Asher, 1984), and multiple aspects of instructional practices in reading.

Yet clearly, in the history of research on reading, a focus on the context in which reading instruction occurs has been severely underrepresented. Instead, research has been largely concerned with understanding the reading process occurring between learner and text (Venezsky, 1984). Yet stripped of its instructional and social context, this knowledge base cannot, in and of itself, help explain why some children are and some children are not learning to read. As Gordon has stated, "reading instruction, learning to read, and reading behavior all occur in situations that support, interfere with or are neutral to the phenomenon" (1979, p. 373).

What are these variables or contexts that we must address? The sociolinguists argue that for children reading is an activity conducted in groups in interaction with teachers and peers (Cazden, 1979; Guthrie & Hall, 1984). These ethnographic studies of classroom events implicate *social interactions* in the classroom as possible causes of the reading difficulties experienced by children. Bloom and Green suggest that:

> From this perspective, reading is viewed not only as a cognitive process, but also as a social and linguistic process. As a social process, reading is used to establish, structure, and maintain social relationships between and among people. As a linguistic process, reading is used to communicate intentions and meanings, not only between an author and a reader but also between people involved in a reading event. (1984, p. 395)

Sociological perspectives on the teaching of reading highlight the *organization and management of instruction*, what Otto, Wolf, and Eldridge (1984) call "the setting up and maintaining of a total environment which includes curricular, organizational, and instructional aspects" (p. 799). The allocation and organization of learners and resources occurs at multiple levels of a school district, and the prevailing conditions of a classroom reflect in part decisions made at higher levels of the educational organization (Barr & Dreeben, 1983; Winograd, this volume). Variations in classroom structures in the organization of reading instruction are hypothesized to explain differences in students' perceptions of their ability (Rosenholtz & Simpson, 1984) as well as differences in reading outcomes.

Psychological process-product approaches to the study of teaching have identified *teacher behaviors* that predict student achievement in subject areas such as reading (Anderson, Evertson, & Brophy, 1979) and math (Good, Grouws, & Ebmeier, 1983). The majority of these variables concern teacher-student interactions during instruction, with documented differential patterns of teacher treatment toward different types of students (e.g., Allington, 1980).

Cognitive psychological approaches have highlighted the conceptions and decision making that teachers bring to instruction (Shulman, 1975), which in turn influence their instructional practices and their consequences for students. How teachers group their students for reading instruction (Shavelson, 1982) and how teachers' conceptions of reading influence their choice of methods (Buike & Duffy, 1979) are some of the questions addressed.

Each of these traditions has research findings which point to the existence of different environments for different groups of children within the same classroom for the teaching of reading. Research on self-fulfilling prophecy effects in schooling underscores how differential treatment can communicate teachers' expectations to students in ways that bring about the expected performances. Expectancy processes are clearly at work in the teaching of reading.

SELF-FULFILLING PROPHECY EFFECTS IN THE TEACHING OF READING

A large body of literature now exists on teachers' expectations for their students' performance and the potential for self-fulfilling prophecy effects to occur in classrooms (recently reviewed by Brophy, 1983). While the majority of the research has been conducted without systematic attention to the teaching of specific subject matters, the implications of this work for the teaching of reading can be usefully drawn. In addition, the teaching of reading provides a particularly interesting case in point for expectancy theory because of several salient features of its instructional context.

Context has been largely absent from expectancy research because the evolving model of how expectancy effects occur in the classroom has been largely *dyadic*. It is viewed as an influence process expressed in a *social interaction sequence* between a teacher and a student.

Despite more attention given in the model to the information processing in which teachers and students engage in interpreting each other's behavior (Cooper, 1979; Braun, 1976; Darley & Fazio, 1980; Weinstein, in press), this model is still limited in its conceptualization of how expectations can function as self-fulfilling prophecies in the classroom. Growing from our work with students' perceptions of differential teacher treatment in the classroom, I have become more aware of the limitations of a strictly dyadic interactional model of expectancy influence. Talking with children about how they learn about their "smartness" in classrooms has broadened our perspective of the types of cues to which children are attentive, key participants who provide cues, and levels of instruction at which they come into play.

THE COMMUNICATION OF TEACHERS' EXPECTATIONS AS REFLECTED IN CHILDREN'S PERCEPTIONS

It should not be surprising that children not only become aware of teachers' expectations for them but are also influenced by them. Yet we have rarely asked students (particularly elementary school students) what they see, how they understand it, and how they feel. We assume that because they are children they are probably not aware of the implicit layer of expectations held by teachers and schools for their learning. Recent research has clearly demonstrated otherwise.

In research on teacher expectations, the student mediation question has been directed at how differential teacher treatment (as a communication of differential teacher expectations) leads to the enhancement or deterioration of student performance. Existing theory has distinguished between direct and indirect effects of teacher expectations on student performance (Brophy & Good, 1974; Good, 1980). Differential teacher behavior, such as the provision of opportunity to learn material, can *directly* affect student achievement gains without involving student interpretive processes. Differential teacher treatment can also provide information to students about expected ability, thus influencing self-image and motivation, and through these processes *indirectly* impact on achievement.

Recently, studies of classroom expectancy effects have begun to examine these processes within the student that may mediate between hypothesized differential teacher treatment and student performance. This growing body of literature is reviewed elsewhere (Weinstein, in press). The intent in this chapter is to highlight selected findings that have implications for how we understand the instruction of reading in classrooms and its potential for communicating self-fulfilling prophecies.

Differential Teacher Treatment of Peers

In a series of studies, using the teacher treatment inventory (Weinstein & Middlestadt, 1979) to assess student's perceptions of the frequency of their teachers' interactions with a hypothetical high and low achiever in their classroom, my colleagues and I have found that children are clearly aware of differential teacher treatment in the classroom. Looking across subject matter, children report that some classroom teachers treat high and low achievers very differently. In these classrooms students described low achievers as the recipients of more negative feedback and teacher direction as well as more work and rule-oriented teacher behavior than high achievers. High achievers were reported to receive higher expectations from the teacher, more opportunity, and more choice than low achievers. These findings have now been replicated with older elementary school students (Weinstein et al. 1981) and with students as young as first grade (Weinstein & Marshall, 1984). Further, neither high or low achievers were found to be more sensitive in detecting differential treatment by the teacher. Thus, differential treatment was likely to be perceived by all when it occurred.

Our classrooms were also found to vary in the extent of differential treatment perceived by students, mirroring the results from classroom observational studies of teacher treatment (Good, 1980; Brophy, 1983). That is, large differences in teacher-child dyadic interaction patterns were perceived in some classrooms and little difference in treatment was reported in other classrooms. Further, teachers were perceived to differ from each other in their treatment of low achievers more than in their treatment of high achievers.

Differential Patterns in Self-Perceptions of Treatment

Not only are students aware of differences in their teachers' interactions with their peers as described above, but students also report that their own interactions with the teacher differ in systematic ways from those the teacher has with peers. In a study of fourth and sixth graders by Cooper and Good (1983) students described their own treatment from the teacher by rating nine teacher-student interactions for whether these interactions occurred more often, about the same amount, or less often with them than with classmates. Students for whom teachers held higher expectations saw themselves as having more frequent teacher-initiated public interactions, less frequent teacher-initiated private interactions, more praise, and less criticism then their classmates. These results mirrored teachers' perceptions except for the perception of frequency of praise where teachers perceived low-expectation students as the more frequent recipients.

In another study, expectation-related differences in students' reports of their own treatment appeared in classrooms where students described their teachers as highly differentiated in the treatment of high and low achievers, but not in classrooms where few differences were perceived (Brattesani, Weinstein, & Marshall, 1984). Low-teacher-expectation students (as identified by the teacher) perceived more frequent negative feedback and direction from the teacher than did high-teacher-expectation students. High-teacher-expectation students perceived higher expectations, greater opportunities, and greater choice from their teachers than did low-teacher-expectation students. These results suggest that students perceive teacher treatment toward themselves that is congruent with their status as high- or low-teacher-expectation students, but *only* in those classrooms where student reports indicate greater availability of differential achievement cues from the teacher as reflected in differential treatment patterns.

These findings suggest that students are attentive to differences in the ways in which their teachers work with other students and that such differences can provide clues to students about the implicit ability expectations underlying *their own interactions* with a teacher. Knowledge of teacher interactions with peers appears to be an important piece of the puzzle in interpreting one's own interactions with a teacher.

Awareness of Differential Treatment and Student Outcomes

Students awareness of differential teacher treatment has been found to be predictive of the expectations children hold for future reading performance, their actual performance, and their views of their peers.

In their observations of differential teacher practices toward peers and toward themselves, children infer where they stand as an achiever within the classroom achievement hierarchy. For example, we have found that in classrooms where students reported a great deal of differential teacher treatment (that is, cues about ability were more readily apparent) fourth through sixth graders' own expectations for their future performance in reading were more closely aligned with their teachers' expectations for them relative to the others in the classroom than in classrooms where little differential treatment was perceived (Brattesani, Weinstein, & Marshall, 1984). Thus, expectation differences between children were *accentuated* in classrooms where students reported more differential ability cues. Other research has already underscored the positive relationships between expectations of success on a task or confidence level and academic performance, task persistence, and task choice (as reviewed by Meece et al., 1982).

Further, in classrooms where children reported greater differential treatment by the teacher (presumably, communicating differential expectations), the effects of teachers' expectations on student year-end achievement were more pronounced, over and above the effects of prior achievement.

Finally, in classrooms where teachers were perceived to greatly differentiate their treatment of high and low achievers, students perceived high and low achievers to differ more from each other on academic task behaviors in the classroom (Marshall et al., 1982). Thus, high- and low-achieving students appear more different to their peers in their work habits in classrooms where teachers are perceived to treat them very differently than in classrooms where the treatment is perceived to be more similar.

In a related set of studies (although student awareness of ability cues was not directly assessed), variations in classroom organization structure that maximized ability comparisons were found to be related to student, teacher, and peer consensus about relative ability. Rosenholtz and Simpson (1984) present a strong case for the social construction of ability conceptions in classrooms. In classrooms with "unidimensional organization" where curricular tasks are uniform, children have little autonomy, evaluation is salient, and grouping patterns highlight comparisons, students' self-reported ability levels have been found to be more widely dispersed, and students' perceptions of their own ability more congruent with peers and teachers' ratings. They suggest that:

> consensus between teachers and peers (in their evaluations of individuals) acts to tighten the system of feedback and press individuals toward ability formation. When teachers and peers agree, not only do fewer optional sources of self-definition exist, but also the "official" evaluations of the teacher are systematically supported by peers' conversation concerning ability. (Rosenholtz & Simpson, 1984, p. 41)

Supportive evidence is also found by Filby and Barnett (1982) who report greater agreement among students about who are the best classroom readers in whole-class reading instruction than in staggered reading instruction where the available information was more restricted. The major basis for the discrimination was an analysis of oral reading performance. Similarly, in classrooms with competitive reward structures versus cooperative reward structures (Ames, 1981), self-perceptions of performance differences were also accentuated.

These related studies highlight how differential treatment patterns and certain classroom organization practices accentuate student ability differences that are internalized by students in their views of themselves and each other.

Complexity of Ability Cues Children Distill from Teacher Practices

Subtle Cues An interview study with first- through sixth-grade students illustrates the subtle distinctions that children make in interpreting teacher behavior (Weinstein & Middlestadt, 1979). As one example, classroom observations systems

record the frequency with which teachers call on individual students as one indication of opportunities to perform. Children tell us that they can distinguish
between subtypes of call-ons that differ in the implicit message about expected
performance conveyed to students. For example, the teacher "calls on the smart
kids for the right answer . . . she expects you to know more and won't tell
answers." With regard to low achievers, the teacher calls on them sometimes "to
give them a chance," or because they "goof off," or the teacher often "doesn't call
on them because she knows they don't know the answer." Students appear to
differentiate between instances of call-on behavior in complex ways, relying on
both verbal and nonverbal cues. They are sophisticated interpreters of the classroom culture.

Multiple Levels of Cues   In an interesting case study of a single first-grade classroom, Eder (1983) describes students' awareness of differential peer performance
both across the various reading groups as well as within each reading group. The
primacy of within-group comparisons (mediated, she suggests, by reading aloud
practices) is reflected in differential academic self-concept scores of students, tend-
ing to favor the high-standing members over the low-standing members within
each group.

Wide-ranging Cues   The majority of cues that children report concern some
aspects of what teachers say and do. In an interview study of 133 students from 16
fourth-grade classrooms (Weinstein, 1981) 66 percent of the cues that the children
reported as informing them about their smartness concerned teacher practices
("my teacher doesn't need to help me"), 2 percent involved peer behaviors ("cause
the other kids ask me to help them"), 4 percent referred to parental practices ("my
mom checks over my papers and tells me"), and 25 percent concerned self-
evaluations and task-mastery information ("I am good at figuring things out").

However, the range of teacher beliefs and practices that children cite is quite
far-reaching. Just looking across the series of studies concerned with student perceptions of differential teacher treatment, we have learned that children can distinguish between the following.

1. *Teacher beliefs about ability.* Some classrooms are places where students
reported feeling they can become smart. In these classes "people who used to not
be smart, they're smart now." In other classes, student achievement is viewed as
low, across the board. One child reports the teacher as saying "statistics (on report
cards) don't lie . . . 'cause people . . . can't read too good in my class." In another
class students can report with precision exactly where they stand on the hierarchy
of relative ability. For example, one child explained his achievement level in the
following way: "Because I know there are ten All-stars and there are two people in
my group that read and do math better than me. . . . All-stars are the highest
group, and I'm in the Blazers, the second highest group."

2. *Grouping arrangements for instruction.* Children can dicipher the relative
order of grouping arrangements. One child described it that "our teacher wouldn't
say, you know—like the lowest group in our class is the Blue Bee and that's a

math-group book and they're the lowest in our class. But she would say Blue Bee and we all know that's the lowest in the class." The ordering is also clearly an ability ranking as evidenced in this child's wish: "I wanted Miss——to put me in a smarter group."

3. *Text and curriculum materials.* Children know which is the higher-level material; for example, "He is the only one in the highest book in our class," and "One person will be doing the harder work."

4. *Allocation and monitoring of classroom tasks.* Children are aware of differences in the treatment of high and low achievers with regard to (1) the degree of *choice* given over involvement at all or over which materials are to be used (high achievers could "read any book they want" whereas for low achievers, "the teacher makes them read and they can't choose what they read because they need it"); (2) *pacing* (high achievers are allowed to go at faster rates in learning materials than low achievers because "the teacher thinks we can do things"); (3) *time allocated for task completion*; and (4) *teacher monitoring of work* (the high achievers don't have "to get things done by an exact time," and they are "let on their own more . . . [the teacher] doesn't look at us to see if we are cheating" whereas with low achievers "the teacher helps them more . . . helps them a lot means they are not so smart"). From the children's perspective, high achievers are expected to do well, their learning is not as structured and monitored, and they are given more freedom to choose books and activities of interest to them—their classroom experience is perceived as more *intrinsically motivating.* Low achievers, in contrast, are made to work in teacher-determined and monitored ways, because *they need it* and ironically are given less time to finish things than are high achievers despite perhaps a need for more time and for a more motivating context.

5. *Motivating, evaluating, and enabling responsibility in students.* Children's comments underscore how evaluative an environment the classroom is. For example, sometimes the teacher says, "Well, the best reader in this group is so-and-so." The public nature of the evaluation is particularly striking, "like she [the teacher] likes to call out the grades and see how poorly some people did." In classrooms where students reported greater differential teacher treatment, students also reported more public teacher communication about poor performance (Weinstein, 1981). Special opportunities and responsibilities are reserved for the smart ones, "The way you know a person is smart, Miss—— always picks them to go to different places," or "But she's not so smart because she is missing so much [music]," or the teacher "gives smarter kids a special assignment . . . it's like they feel more responsible, I guess." In children's descriptions, evaluation is continuous; rewards, motivating opportunities, and responsibilities are scarce and distributed to a select few.

6. *Teacher-child interaction pattern.* Our work with the teacher treatment inventory demonstrated that children were aware of differences in the frequencies with which teachers interacted with different students on a variety of behavioral dimensions. Interviews with children also highlight the qualitative distinctions children make within each type of behavior, for example, praise. One child de-

scribed that "sometimes she says, 'Oh, that's very poor reading' to someone else and she says pretty good to me and sometimes. . . . I kind of marked myself in the middle on reading because . . . to other people she says excellent reading."

Thus, these studies illustrate the kind of observers children are: they are aware of subtle and implicit feelings on the part of teachers, they make within-group and between-group comparisons in teacher treatment and in peer behavior, and they attend to multiple aspects of the organization and implementations of instruction.

In these studies conducted to date, individual differences in student perceptions of teacher treatment have not been found to be large. All children (whether they are high or low achievers) seem to be aware of differential treatment patterns when they occur. This awareness has also been found in children as young as first graders. Future research must explore the extent to which individual differences and developmental differences play a role in students' interpretation of the classroom reality and in their susceptibility to expectation effects. At this point, however, all children show some awareness and some effects.

IMPLICATIONS: READING INSTRUCTION AS A SOURCE FOR SELF-FULFILLING PROPHECIES

Learning about the social context of instruction from students' perceptions underscores the complexity of expectancy processes as they unfold in classrooms. Dyadic social influence processes between a teacher and a student cannot adequately capture the levels at which expectations operate nor the critical elements that interactively impact on students during the course of instruction.

We must look to the social context in which reading is taught in classrooms and school—its elements interact in ways to create self-fulfilling prophecies for student performance that directly shape student achievement through lack of opportunities to learn certain reading skills (for example, less exposure to comprehension); directly shape certain ways of working independently and with choice; and indirectly impact on achievement through a gradual erosion of self-image, expectancies for performance, and motivation. The study of these indirect routes of influence as mediated by children informs us about the conditions under which children work in the classroom in learning to read.

What can we learn from children's view of these differentiated treatments in classrooms? If we are to understand how the instruction of reading takes place, we have to delve deeper into a reexamination of beliefs about ability that underlie many of the teaching practices now in place. We have to recognize that all children are part of the teaching context and that gathering children together for instruction occurs at multiple levels. We have to take up the question of "appropriate treatments"—whether they are or not and what to do given that their implemention (in selective and systemic ways) conveys information to students about their relative ability. Finally, we have to realize that the effects that follow are cumulative.

Beliefs about Ability

We need to examine in depth the nature of teachers' and schools' beliefs about ability that underlie fitting curriculum to children. What are the prevailing beliefs and implicit assumptions about ability that hinder teaching reading in classrooms? In *The Mismeasure of Man*, Gould (1981) poignantly traces how throughout history we have reduced a multifaceted notion of intelligence to a single entity. He argues that we have engaged in:

> the abstraction of intelligence as a single entity, its location within the brain, its quantification as *one* number of each individual, and, the use of these numbers to rank people in a *single* series of worthiness, invariably to find that oppressed and disadvantaged groups, races, classes, or sexes . . . are innately inferior and deserve their status. (Gould, 1981, p. 25)

Rosenholtz and Simpson (1984) show how this institutionalized conception of ability in schools generates ability conceptions in students that match those of the society. This unidimensional conception of intelligence assumes strong relationships between performance among diverse cognitive tasks. Reading ability is seen as a unitary skill, as a proxy for intelligence. And in classrooms reading ability becomes predictive of performance on other subjects such as math. As Rosenholtz and Cohen argue, reading ability comes to function as "a status characteristic—that is, an index of how smart one is expected to be on a wide variety of tasks" (1983, p. 516). Thus, value is placed on only one ability rather than many, largely limiting opportunities for recognizing achievement, diagnosing learning styles, and acknowledging what cross-cultural research evidence has taught us—that different environments encourage the development and use of different cognitive skills (Ogbu, 1978).

Our measurement of ability also assumes that ability is distributed among a population along a normal curve; thus, reading ability is also so dispersed. When we gather children together for instructional purposes within a classroom, school, or district it follows in this view that some children will be excellent readers, some will be good readers, and some will be poor readers. Regardless of the particular mix of children, this assumption leads to realtive distinctions, with a press to determine the clues for identifying and selecting among alternative students. Opportunities for stereotypic perceptions are many. Witness the unintended consequences for reading instruction—the need to find learning-disabled children within a defined population group regardless of the spread of student abilities (Smith, 1982) and the tendency to assign below-grade-level reading material to the bottom reading group regardless of the achievement level of the students (Anastasiow, 1964).

Beliefs that ability is largely inherited, stable, and unchangeable over time, or that the rate and pattern of learning to read is indicative of intelligence all constrain our commitment to the *teachability* of the student. This belief ignores evidence of wide differences in the rate at which children pass developmental milestones including the readiness to read that may not be predictive of later capabilities (this has been particularly true of boys). The Palardy study (1969) is instructive in this regard. He compared the students' reading achievement scores of two groups of first-grade teachers—one group believed that boys and girls had an equal chance to learn to read and the other that girls would learn more quickly than boys. Although fall achievement scores did not differ, by spring (in classrooms where teachers believed girls would be more successful) girls outperformed boys, whereas no sex differences in reading achievement appeared in the other group. Wigfield and Asher (1984) contend that even accurate expecations could function as a more subtle form of bias. They underscore that "it is an educator's task to go beyond the data given, that is, to expect a child's behavior can be transformed with appropriate instruction and structuring of the educational environment" (1984, p. 435).

Finally, we have an instituationalized tendency to seek psychological or intrapsychic solutions to problems of learning. If problems in learning to read arise the cause is most likely presumed to reside in the child; we operate from a deficit-oriented focus. Years of special education expeditures have not largely eradicated the learning problems we set out to remediate. Is it remediation we are after, or adequate trials of well-matched instruction in social settings that are conducive to learning for all children despite vast individual differencies. The responsibility for problems in learning should lie with teachers, and the solution should lie in an assessment of the match between instructional methods and learners' needs. The press for mainstreaming children back into regular classrooms is in response to the negative social and psychological consequences of segregated treatments. Yet resegregation can still occur at multiple levels unless underlying beliefs about ability are addressed.

This simplification of children's ability becomes compounded in the primary instructional practice underlying the teaching of reading in classrooms, that of ability-based grouping. While expectancy effects result from "false beliefs" that teachers hold about student ability, ability-based reading groups over-simplify the differences between students within a group and between groups of students and thereby institutionalize false beliefs. The lock-step characteristics of basal reading series keeps students in place, making changes between groups very difficult. In fact, empirical research concerning the movement between reading groups (once membership is assigned) documents relatively little change. Reading-group membership has been found to be largely fixed (Weinstein, 1976). Brophy (1983) also suggests that expectancy effects may be magnified in the context of grouping for reading instruction.

That children come to see their ability in ways congruent with teacher views of their ability is one lesson clearly learned from talking to students. Further, that variations exist between classrooms in the extent to which student conceptions match a rank-ordered teacher conception of ability is encouraging news. Classrooms in which students report less differential teacher treatment, or in which teachers use practices that minimize public single-ability comparisons appear to have different self-perception outcomes—differences that may be critical in fostering motivation in the learning-to-read process. The poignancy of the precision with which children know their place in the relative achievement hierarchy in certain classrooms is underscored by the fact that given another classroom and another mix of student abilities their relative place may in fact be quite different. Clinical practice with children with learning problems provides numerous examples of the negative effects of such beliefs. Further, there is scant evidence that such rankings have anything to offer us in our task of teaching all children to learn to read.

The Gathering of Children for Instruction

Learning to read or learning in general is not just an activity among teacher, student, and text, but a group activity. Children learn about themselves not only from the interactions they have with their teacher but also from how the teacher relates to peers. Because of teacher dominance in elementary school classrooms, teachers define relationships that children have with one another. Concepts of peer abilities and peer traits emerge from these patterns of interaction. That high and low achievers are viewed by peers as being more different in behavior in classrooms where students report large differences in teacher's interactions with high and low achievers has enormous implications for potential friendship choices between achievement groups and the potential for growth by low achievers who are seen by others and by themselves as so different. Patterns of teacher interactions with peers provide the criteria for evaluating one's own interactions with teachers. Thus, models of the instructional context have to include what peers are doing, how the teacher interacts with them, and how they perform as part of the context in which reading is taught.

Thus, the unit of analysis for the transmission of expectancies is not only a dyadic relationship between teacher and individual student. The multiple levels at which we gather children together for instructional purposes are all potential sites for the communication of expectations—within reading group, between reading groups, within the class, in versus out of class (pull-outs), between schools, and between countries (as one example, grade-level expectations). We need to examine expectations at each level exploring how the relative mix of student abilities interacts (or does not interact) with what unfolds.

Appropriate Treatments

We need to reexamine our notions of appropriate treatments for children in high and low reading groups. Hiebert (1983) reviews the research on within-classroom ability-based reading groups that documents that instruction differs widely for the various groups as do the interactions between teachers and students in pacing through materials, focussing on decoding versus comprehension skills, and interrupting for errors. Low reading-group members have been found to spend more time on decoding tasks and less time on meaning-related activities (Allington, 1981; Alpert, 1975; Gambrell, Wilson, & Gantt, 1981); to spend more time on reading orally than silently, thus covering less material (Allington, 1977, 1980; Grant & Rothenberg, 1981); to move through materials more slowly (Allington, 1981); have fewer opportunities to answer analytic questions (Seltzer, 1976); and to be interrupted more for the same errors (Allington, 1980) than high reading-group members.

These studies suggest that children in low-reading groups receive fewer opportunities for differentiated reading instruction 'and, in fact, cover far less ground in the curriculum. These differences in pacing, for example, become even more compelling in light of Barr's (1975) finding that teachers from year to year keep the same pace within high and low reading groups regardless of the abilities of the children within these groups.

Thus, it is not surprising that outcomes of appropriate treatment among achievement levels are very different. Poor readers demonstrate little use of context in deciphering words they do not know and they show poor comprehension skills. Is this a result of their systematically not being taught? Comprehension is often not dealt with until basic decoding skills are mastered. Such coverage or lack thereof is, of course, related to achievement (Borg, 1979): where one is not taught, one cannot perform on achievement tests. Studies show that reading-group membership itself contributes 25 percent of the variance in predicting year-end achievement scores over and above entering achievement differences (Weinstein, 1976). Further, in a recent study Gamoran (1984) demonstrated the significant *social effects* of grouping practices in predicting year-end achievement *after controlling for instructional differences between the groups.* These effects appeared in classrooms where the stratification between reading groups was accentuated (elitist classes), but not in classrooms where groups were less stratified (egalitarian classes). These social outcomes may be due in part to the fact that the repetitive remedial process that can characterize the teaching of low reading groups can delay further progress through the erosion of student and teacher interest. Students report that certain of the exciting events of instruction are given out after the basal reading curriculum is finished as extras to high achievers. Yet these very opportunities (choice of books, focus on comprehension and understanding, classroom responsibilities) are perhaps more motivating to students than the regular materials and tasks. Additionally, the high achievers are more often just left alone; as Rohwer (1980) argues, the smart learn because we have not tampered with them. For the high achievers, we have created a motivational environment that is task-mastery oriented (Nicholls, 1979)—self-chosen tasks focus attention on the mastery of the task. Whereas for the low achievers where we structure, monitor, and interrupt, we have created conditions for ego involvement in which engagement becomes a means of gaining approval from the teacher. Interest in reading itself is less and less stimulated.

Even if educators could agree that these differences in treatment documented between high and low groups were appropriate differences matching the needs of the learners, we must consider the unintended side effects that children come to infer from these differential practices, their own and their peers' ability relative to each other. Although Brophy (1983) in his review suggests that children exaggerate these differences, the point remains that their perceptions are important in and of themselves. Children's perceptions of differential treatment by the teacher predict the degree to which these teachers' expectations for students influence students' own expectations and their own achievement. Thus, despite the fact that treatments may be appropriate in the abstract, their noticeable and systematic application to the same groups of children labels the children and conteracts the potential positive effects of differentiated teaching. The true goal we seek is a combination of truly differentiated teaching (so *individualized* that rigid and systematic differences between types of students are not identifiable) with generalized teaching to all of certain skills and areas that we expect all students to master. As Slavin argues, we must "accept nothing less than universal reading and math literacy in elementary schools" (1983, p. 137).

Cumulative Effects

Finally, we must realize that the effects we are looking at are cumulative. What begins as small differences in student skills grows due to coverage differences and to accompanying changes in children's behavior, self-esteem, and motivation. Children complete each school year more different from each other than when they began. Each new school year brings easier grouping decisions based on history: where students are in the basal reading series, what they have covered in reading skills, and how independently they can work (all of which may follow from their reading-group membership). To the extent that expectations for other subject matters follow from reading performance, the cumulative effects become even more rapid. A case example of such overgeneralization concerns a second grader in our clinic who was having difficulty in learning to read and was assigned to remedial math despite a math achievement score in the ninety-sixth percentile.

Expectation effects are compounded over years of schooling. Sadly, we have too few longitudinal studies of individual students' careers in schooling (Rist's 1970 case study is one example) that demonstrate how differences persist and widen over the years. Thus, what may be a small effect in a given year may during the course of schooling make a sizeable difference.

Certain aspects of our current reading practices also ensure this cumulative effect. The teaching of reading typically shares the following characteristics:

1. Reading is the first subject area taught for children, the learning-to-read process is the first time evaluations of performance are made on the basis of normative and relativistic standards.
2. Reading is viewed as the most important subject, literally a key to other areas of learning.
3. Reading is largely taught in ability-based reading groups.
4. The reading curriculum relies heavily on ability-sequenced basal readers.
5. The teaching of reading is heavily teacher dependent.
6. Oral-reading performance is the primary teaching and evaluation tool.

These aspects of reading instruction are interactive and all heighten the public nature of the conditions under which students engage in learning to read and the potential consequences of failure in future reading learning as well as in other areas of the curriculum. The large individual differences between students placed within a reading group are masked (Shavelson, 1982) and the differences between groups are magnified in the implementation of instruction. The structures (grouping and basal texts) promote an artificial stability in progress, reinforced by narrow options for evaluation—that of oral-reading performance. These practices accentuate the cumulative effects of failure.

The early instruction of reading in our schools is a particularly ripe site for expectancy processes to flourish and to become compounded. These social processes could explain why groups of children experience failure in learning to read and fall farther and farther behind during the course of schooling. Our current teaching practices heighten relative differences between students and provide children with clear images of their potential for success in reading. Children are aware of these messages and internalize them. Such shaping of ability messages has motivational and achievement consequences for children who turn away from further learning. Sadly, these expectations that guide group placement and the allocation of instruction are likely to be false despite teachers' accuracy in their judging of students' general ability—false because of their globality (ill-matched to the multidimensionality of reading ability), because grouping simplifies as well as exaggerates differences between students, because attention is paid to relative differences regardless of absolute levels of accomplishment, and because the structure of teaching reading institutionalizes stability of perceptions.

That variations between classrooms exist *in the extent to which* children report systematic differential teacher treatment toward high and low achievers and *in the extent to which* students' own self-perceptions and achievement are so shaped gives hope that these negative self-fulfilling prophecies can be changed. To do so, however, we have to explore more fully the social context in which reading is taught in classrooms.

REFERENCES

Allington, R. L. (1977). If they don't read much, how they ever gonna get good? *Journal of Reading, 21,* 57-61.

Allington, R. L. (1980). Teacher interruption behaviors during primary-grade oral reading. *Journal of Educational Psychology, 72,* 371-374.

Allington, R. L. (November 1981). *Amount and mode of contextual reading as a function of reading group membership.* Paper presented at the annual meeting of the National Council of Teachers of English, Washington, D.C.

Alpert, J. L. (1975). Do teachers adapt methods and materials to ability groups in reading? *California Journal of Educational Research, 26,* 120-123.

Ames, C. (1981). Competitive versus cooperative reward structures: The influence of individual and group performance factors on achievement attributions. *American Educational Research Journal, 18,* 273-287.

Anastasiow, N. J. (1964). Frame of reference of teachers' judgements: The psychophysical model applied to education. *Psychology in the Schools, 1*, 392–395.

Anderson, L. M., Evertson, C. M., & Brophy, J. E. (1979). An experimental study of effective teaching in first grade reading groups. *The Elementary School Journal, 79*, 193–223.

Balow, B. (1971). Perceptual-motor activities in the treatment of severe reading disability. *Reading Teacher, 24*, 513–525.

Barr, R. (1975). How children are taught to read: Grouping and pacing. *School Review, 75*, 479–498.

Barr, R., & Dreeben, R. (1983). *How schools work*. Chicago, Ill.: University of Chicago Press.

Bateman, B. (1979). Teaching reading to learning disabled and other hard-to-teach children. In L. B. Resnick & P. A. Weaver (Eds.), *Theory and practice of early reading* (pp. 227–259). Hillsdale, N.J.: Erlbaum.

Bloom, D., & Green, J. (1984). Directions in the sociolinguistic study of reading. In P. D. Pearson (Ed.), *Handbook of reading research* (pp.395–422). New York: Longman.

Borg, W. R. (1979). Teacher coverage of academic content and pupil achievement. *Journal Educational Psychology, 71*, 635–645.

Brattesani, K. A., Weinstein, R. S., & Marshall, H. H. (1984). Student perceptions of differential teacher treatment as moderators of teacher expectation effects. *Journal of Educational Psychology, 76*, 236–247.

Braun, C. (1976). Teacher expectations: Socio-psychological dynamics. *Review of Educational Research, 46*, 185–213.

Brophy, J. E. (1983). Research on the self-fulfilling prophecy and teacher expectations. *Journal of Educational Psychology, 75*, 631–661.

Brophy J. E., & Good, T. L. (1974). *Teacher-student relationships*, New York: Holt, Rinehart & Winston.

Buike, S., & Duffy, G. G. (April 1979). *Do teacher conceptions of reading influence instructional practice?* Paper presented at the American Educational Research Association, San Francisco.

Calfee, R. (1982). A model for school change. *The Standford Educator, 8*.

Carroll, J. B., & Chall, J. S. (1975). *Toward a literate society*. New York: McGraw-Hill.

Cazden, C. B. (1979). Learning to read in classroom interaction. In L. B. Resnick & P. A. Weaver (Eds.), *Theory and practice of early reading* (pp. 295–306). Hillsdale, N.J.: Erlbaum.

Chall, J. S. (1983). Literacy: Trends and explanations. *Educational Researcher, 12*, 3–8.

Chall, J. S., & Snow, C. (1982). *Families and literacy: The contribution of out-of-school experiences to children's acquisition of literacy*. Washington, D.C.: National Institute of Education.

Coleman, J. S. et al. (1966). *Equality of educational opportunity*. Washington, D.C.: Department of Health, Education and Welfare.

Cooper, H. M. (1979). Pygmalion grows up: A model for teacher expectation communication and performance influence. *Review of Educational Research, 49*, 389–410.

Cooper, H. M., & Good, T. L. (1983). *Pgymalion grows up: Studies in the expectation communication process*. New York: Longman.

Darley, J. M., & Fazio, R. H. (1980). Expectancy confirmation processes arising in the social interaction sequence. *American Psychologist, 35*, 867–881.

Eder, D. (1983). Ability grouping and students' academic self-concepts: A case study. *The Elementary School Journal, 84*, 149– 161.

Filby, N. N., & Barnett, B. G. (1982). Student perceptions of "better readers" in elementary classrooms. *The Elementary School Journal, 5*, 435–449.

Gambrell, L. B., Wilson, R. M., & Gantt, W. N. (1981). Classroom observations of task-attending behaviors of good and poor readers. *Journal of Educational Research, 74*, 400–404.

Gamoran, A. (April 1984). *Egalitarian versus elitist use of ability grouping.* Paper presented at the meeting of the American Educational Research Association, New Orleans.

Good, T. L. (1980). Classroom expectations: Teacher-pupil interactions. In J. McMillan (Ed.), *The social psychology of school learning* (pp. 76–122). New York: Academic.

Good, T. L., Grouws, D. A., & Ebmeier, H. (1983). *Active mathematics teaching.* New York: Longman.

Gordon, E. W. (1979). Implications for compensatory education drawn from reflections on the teaching and learning of reading. In L. B. Resnick & P. A. Weaver (Eds.), *Theory and practice of early reading* (pp. 299–319). Hillsdale, N.J.: Erlbaum.

Gould S. J. (1981). *The mismeasure of man.* New York: Norton.

Grant, L., & Rothenberg, J. (April 1981). *Charting educational futures: Interaction patterns in first and second reading groups.* Paper presented at the annual meeting of the American Educational Research Association, Los Angeles.

Guthrie, L. F., & Hall, W. S. (1984). Ethnographic approaches to reading research. In P. D. Pearson (Ed.), *Handbook of reading research* (pp. 91–110). New York: Longman.

Hiebert, E. H. (1983). An examination of ability grouping for reading instruction. *Reading Research Quarterly, 18*, 231–255.

Hochschild, R. M. (1976). Teacher rated maladjustment in open, transitional and traditional classroom environments. *Dissertation Abstracts International, 37B*, 2508B. University Microfilms No. DAH 76-26531.

Jencks, C. (1972). *Inequality: A reassessment of the effects of family and schooling in America.* New York: Basic Books.

Leinhardt, G., Zigmond, N., & Cooley, W. W. (1981). Reading instruction and its effects. *American Educational Research Journal, 18*, 343–361.

Marshall, H. H. et al. (March 1982). *Students' description of the ecology of the school environment for high and low achievers.* Paper presented at the meeting of the American Educational Research Association, New York.

Meece, J. L. et al. (1982). Sex differences in math achievement: Toward a model of academic choice. *Psychological Bulletin, 91*, 324–348.

McLean, J. E. (April 1984). Racial and school differences in quality. In W. B. Brookover (Chair.), *Equality of educational programs within a school district.* Symposium conducted at the meeting of the American Educational Research Association, New Orleans.

Nicholls, J. G. (1979). Quality and equality in intellectual development: The role of motivation in education. *American Psychologist, 34*, 1071–1084.

Ogbu, J. U. (1978). *Minority education and caste: The American system in crosscultural perspective.* New York: Academic.

Otto, W., Wolf, A., & Eldridge, R. G. (1984). Managing instruction. In P. D. Pearson (Ed.), *Handbook of reading research* (pp. 799–828). New York: Longman.

Palardy, J. (1969). What teachers believe—What children achieve. *The Elementary School Journal, 69*, 370–374.

Pearson, P. D. (Ed.). (1984). *Handbook of reading research.* New York: Longman.

Resnick, L. B., & Weaver, P. A. (Eds.). (1979). *Theory and practice of early reading.* Hillsdale, N.J.: Erlbaum.

Rist, R. C. (1970). Student social class and teacher expectations: The self-fulfilling prophecy in ghetto education. *Harvard Educational Review, 40,* 411-450.

Rohwer, W. D. (1980). How the smart get smarter. *Educational Psychologist, 15,* 35-43.

Rosenholtz, S. J., & Cohen, E. G. (1983). Back to the basics and the desegregated school. *The Elementary School Journal, 83,* 515- 527.

Rosenholtz, S. J., & Simpson, C. (1984). The formation of ability conceptions: Developmental trend or social construction? *Review of Educational Research, 54,* 31-63.

Seltzer, D. A. (1976). A descriptive study of third grade reading groups. Dissertation Abstracts International, 36-09A, 5811. University Microfilms No. 76-6345.

Shavelson, R. J. (March 1982). *One psychologist's (not very representative) view of teachers' decisions about grouping students.* Paper presented at the meeting of the American Educational Research Association, New York.

Shephard, L. A., Smith, M. L., & Vojir, C. P. (1983). Characteristics of pupils identified as learning disabled. *American Educational Research Journal, 20,* 309-331.

Shulman, L. S. (1975). Teaching as clinical information processing. In N. L. Gage (Ed.), *National conference on studies in teaching.* Washington, D.C. National Institute of Education.

Slavin, R. E. (1983). Realities and remedies. *The Elementary School Journal, 84,* 131-138.

Smith, M. L. (1982). *How educators decide who is learning disabled.* Springfield, Ill.: Charles C. Thomas.

Venezky R. L. (1976). The history of reading research. In P. D. Pearson (Ed.), *Handbook of reading research* (pp. 3-38). New York: Longman.

Weinstein, R. S. (1976). Reading group membership of first grade: Teacher behaviors and pupil experience over time. *Journal of Educational Psychology, 68,* 103-116.

Weinstein, R. S. (April 1981). Student perspectives on achievement in varied classroom environments. In P. Blumenfeld (Chair.), *Student perspectives and the study of the classroom.* Symposium conducted at the meeting of the American Educational Research Association, Los Angeles.

Weinstein, R. S. (in press). Student mediation of classroom expectancy effects. In J. B. Dusek (Ed.), *Teacher expectancies.* Hillsdale, N.J.: Erlbaum.

Weinstein, R. S., & Marshall, H. H. (1984). *Ecology of students' achievement expectations.* Final Report to the National Institute of Education, Washington, D.C.

Weinstein, R. S. et al. (1982). Student perceptions of differential teacher treatment in open and traditional classrooms. *Journal of Educational Psychology, 74,* 678-692.

Weinstein, R. S., & Middlestadt, S. E. (April 1979). *Learning about the achievement hierarchy of the classroom: Through children's eyes.* Paper presented at the meeting of the American Educational Research Association, San Francisco.

Weinstein, R. S., & Middlestadt, S. E. (1979). Student perceptions of teacher interactions with male high and low achievers. *Journal of Educational Psychology, 71,* 421-431.

Wigfield, A., & Asher, S. R. (1984). Social and motivational influences on reading. In P. D. Pearson (Ed.), *Handbook of reading research* (pp. 423-452). New York: Longman.

Ysseldyke, J. E. et al. (1979). *Similarities and differences between underachievers and students labeled learning disabled: Identical twins with different mothers.* Research Rep. No. 13. Minneapolis: University of Minnesota, Institute for Research on Learning Disabilities.

15

Teachers' Classroom Learning: Toward the Development of Expertise in Reading Instruction

Robert M. Schwartz

During the last decade a considerable amount of research has focused on illuminating factors involved in learning (for reviews of this work see Brown et al. 1983; Siegler, 1983; Stevenson, 1983). The topics included in this volume demonstrate that research has begun to emphasize learning within the applied domains of classroom reading and writing instruction. The following discussion draws upon the emerging perspective of cognitive learning theory to consider a particularly complex school learning task, teaching. This represents a shift in the typical focus on students as learners, to focus on teachers as learners in the context of the classroom.

For teachers to be efficient in their instructional role they need to learn what knowledge and strategies their students possess and to modify their instruction based on the information provided by students' responses. The first of these learning tasks is generally labeled diagnosis, the second, diagnostic teaching. This view of teachers as engaged in a continuous learning process contrasts with more static views of the profession. An implicit assumption of the static view is that the content of the message (i.e., the specific curriculum or set of materials) presented to students is more important than the structure of the instructional interaction. The current perspective suggests that any specific curriculum is insufficient without skilled teachers who can transform the available material in ways that maximize students' learning opportunities.

In examining teachers' development of expertise in reading instruction, the emphasis in this chapter is on the classroom context in which this learning occurs.

The initial discussion will examine the type and structure of knowledge teachers need to support reading diagnosis and diagnostic teaching. The teachers' knowledge base guides their interpretation of student behavior and selection of instructional activities. Individual differences among teachers in terms of their knowledge about reading and reading instruction can result in their making quite different diagnostic decisions about the same content or students. These knowledge-base issues will provide the foundation for subsequent discussion of teachers' classroom learning, development of diagnostic skill, and environmental factors that may inhibit teachers' classroom learning and development.

STRUCTURE OF TEACHERS' KNOWLEDGE BASE

Differences in content-specific knowledge can affect memory, interpretation, and prediction within a given domain. In a procedural skill such as reading or teaching, knowledge can take a number of different forms. Bisanz and Voss (1981) use the domain of baseball to provide a description of the types of knowledge involved in understanding procedural domains. They suggest that high- versus low-knowledge individuals could differ in three ways:

> First, there is knowledge of the baseball concepts per se, which permits the individual to understand the nature of the game actions and states—for example "inning," "run," "out." Second, there is knowledge of how particular game actions may produce differences in the game states—for example, how an infield ground ball may lead to changes in the number of outs. Third, there is knowledge of the possible sequence of game action and state changes that permit the individual to understand the "flow" of the game. This type of knowledge especially involves relating information about what previously occurred in the game to information that is occurring (or even will occur). (p. 229)

Analogously, in order to interpret students' reading behavior and design instruction, teachers' knowledge must include (1) basic concepts about reading and instruction; (2) possible actions and procedures designed to bring about changes in students' reading; and (3) a sequence of goals and subgoals that allows teachers to understand the course of skill development. For example, teachers have to be familiar with the concept of phonics and know how it can affect reading behavior, it relates to other aspects of beginning reading, and to provide appropriate phonics instruction if needed.

Differences among teachers in these forms of knowledge will affect their interpretation of student reading behaviors and their subsequent instructional planning. The more elaborate and integrated the instructor's knowledge base, the more precisely a student's state of reading development can be specified.

Barron and Schwartz (1984) argue that lack of categorical and hierarchical relationships among concepts in the knowledge base of teachers can lead to a variety of difficulties.

> For example, relatively large numbers of teachers enter the [initial masters level] course with an incorrect understanding of the term "word recognition." They con-

sider it the equivalent of "phonics." Typically, when such an individual encounters a child who is experiencing reading difficulties due to overattention to phoneme-grapheme correspondence, the teacher provides the child with more phonics instruction, rather than recognizing the need to teach utilization of syntactic and semantic cues. (p. 286)

This type of inappropriate interpretation reflects the level of development of a teacher's knowledge base. Providing knowledge about instructional concepts has been the traditional focus of teacher education programs; however, additional attention should be devoted to establishing relationships among these concepts and organizing them within a goal structure that teachers can use to conceptualize the development of reading skill. Since the structure of the instructional situation may complicate decision making, a minimum requirement to meet the demands of successful instruction is for teachers to have well differentiated and interrelated sets of conceptual categories. Figures 15.1 and 15.2 present structured overviews illustrating relationships among concepts related to reading instruction. The major categorical division separates concepts related to understanding words (Figure 15.1) versus those related to understanding ideas (Figure 15.2). These overviews are not intended to represent a complete, or single, most appropriate set of relationships. They are, however, representative of graphic presentations that can help make relationships among basic concepts explicit for teachers (Barron & Schwartz, 1984).

The internatization of this type of conceptual network should be facilitated by preservice and in-service teacher education programs. However, in the acquisition of such a complex body of knowledge it is likely that many teachers only partially comprehend particular concepts, and that content from different portions of these methods courses do not become integrated into a unified network of relationships. Barron and Schwartz (1984) have demonstrated that even in a graduate course that elaborates the relationships among concepts, experienced teachers are not likely to internalize these relationships without some specific activities that require them to restructure their emerging knowledge base. In their research on problem solving in physics, Eylon and Reif (1984) have reached similar conclusions concerning the difficulty of acquiring a hierarchically organized knowledge base and its importance in scientific reasoning.

In addition to such categorical structure-relating concepts and procedures involved in reading and instruction, teachers need to internalize a goal structure that sequences possible activities. This is the kind of knowledge that Bisanz and Voss (1981) found particularly important for comprehension. High knowledge "individuals are not simply better at remembering a 'chain' of events, but they are better at constructing an integrated representation in terms of the meaning of the game" (p. 231).

In learning "games" like reading, the primary goal is students' development of flexible and efficient processes. High-knowledge teachers should be better at comprehending and interpreting sets of student behavior in terms of progress toward this goal. Progress requires that teachers' knowledge base include a sequence of conceptual stages and stage goals. This stage and goal structure

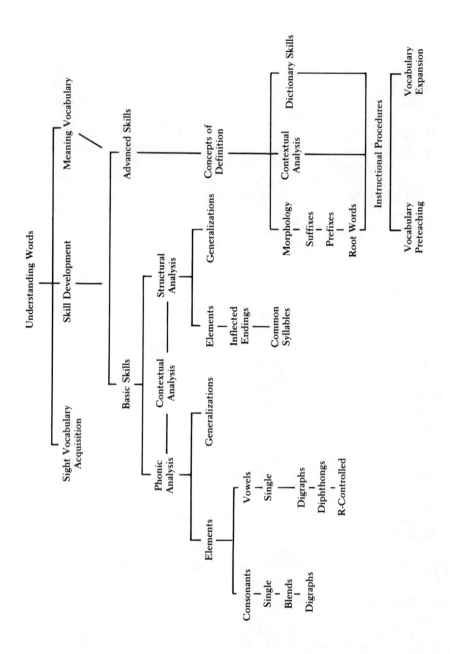

Figure 15.1 **A Graphic Presentation of Understanding Words**

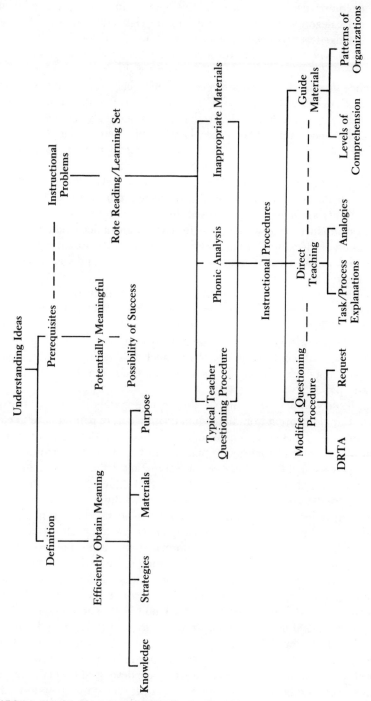

Figure 15.2 **A Graphic Presentation of Understanding Ideas**

should encompass the range of skill development in reading and other major conceptual categories. The following discussion elaborates the type of stage and goal knowledge teachers need to facilitate reading instruction.

For any type of ability or skill there exist different levels of proficiency. The development of a skill can be viewed in terms of the learner's progress through three conceptual levels or stages—preperformance, beginning, and advanced. The stages are characterized by the particular set of goals that constitute the primary focus for development. Stages will overlap and earlier goals may need to be reinforced and refined during later stages. Despite this overlap, determination of an individual's stage of development is of primary importance for diagnosis of performance in the skill and planning for future instruction.

To aid in the specification of these three stages of skill development in reading, consider the general progress in the acquisition of a motor skill where differences in ability are more easily observed. In tennis, for example, an individual in the preperformance stage would need to develop an understanding of the form and function of the game. Casual observations might increase interest in learning the skill and an awareness of basic concepts, such as forehand and backhand, that can facilitate later learning.

The beginning stage, whether structured by formal instruction or individual effort, will focus on performance of component skills—forehand, backhand, serve, and so forth. This is accompanied by increased knowledge that supports advanced performance (knowledge-relating procedures like lob and volley to game strategies.) A novice will continue to develop through this beginning stage if skill and knowledge components are combined with an attitude that the activity is meaningful and personally engaging.

For those who persevere through this beginning stage, the mark of advanced skill is a shift of attention from individual components of performance to efficient and flexible use of these components in game situations. Although an expert (such as John McEnroe) may continue to practice his backhand, his attention during a game is focused on the combination of factors that determine selection of shots and placement, rather than how to make the shot. Movement into the advanced stage is marked by increased flexibility in the coordination of processes, rather than absolute performance levels. Even those who are rated expert in a particular area seldom see this as the end of a developmental process. Instead, they are often particularly aware of aspects of their performance that could improve.

Stage analysis can provide the goal structure needed to interpret student reading behavior and to sequence instruction. The preperformance or prereading stage should foster an interest in reading and a desire to learn to read. This should be accompanied and enhanced by understanding the purpose and function of literacy and some of the basic concepts related to print and general language skill (Clay, 1972; Downing, 1979). A child does not need to master these initial goals before reading instruction can profitably begin; however, given a uniform approach to initial instruction, students who have developed further in these areas can be expected to benefit most. For children who see no purpose to reading or have not developed concepts of directionality, or print-to-speech match (Gillet &

Temple, 1982) these prereading goals can either become the focus of initial instruction or be developed in combination with beginning reading goals.

The division between prereading and beginning reading goals mirrors the shift in the learner from knowledge about the task to practice of the components of the task. Children who learn to read without instruction may not be conscious of the shift, while those who have difficulty in acquiring reading skill often become painfully aware of the components. For beginning reading the primary goals are:

1. *Development of a word recognition process.* Since students know many words and use them in their oral language, an initial goal of reading instruction is to enable students to recognized these familiar words in print. This requires the coordination of a set of component skills that include the use of relationships between letters and sounds (*phonics*), structural parts of words (-*s*, *ed*, -*ing*), and meaning clues from the sentence or setting in which an unfamiliar printed word occurs (*context*).

2. *Development of a sight vocabulary.* Since the word reconition process is difficult and requires close attention, it can interfere with comprehension processes. To avoid this difficulty a student must come to recognize words quickly, without the use of sound or meaning clues. As students progress in the beginning-reading stage they should come to recognize most of the words in their oral language as sight words. Sight vocabulary is an important set of knowledge needed to support advanced performance.

3. *View of reading as meaningful and personally engaging.* This is an extremely important goal of beginning reading. Unless students read for pleasure and to gain information it is very unlikely that they will do enough reading to accomplish the other beginning goals, or be motivated to move on to the advanced stage of skill development.

Portions of these goals seem to be part of most teachers' implicit theory of reading instruction. An overemphasis on one goal, or on a component of one goal, can lead to very different instructional decisions. Indeed, most of the historical trends and debates in reading instruction can be organized around the priority or importance attributed to one of these goals at the expense of the others. For example, language experience approaches stress Goals 2 and 3. By using group or individually generated materials, initial instruction attempts to maximize meaningfulness and student engagement, as well as to reinforce or develop prereading goals related to the function and form of literacy. Repeated reading of these student-generated materials is used to select words for additional practice to establish an initial sight vocabulary. Contextual aspects of word recognition are encouraged since words from a student's oral language are encountered in the context of meaningful experience stories. Phonic and structural components of the word recognition process are taught through the use of a child's developing sight vocabulary. Although the methodology includes all three goals, the lack of systematic materials and curriculum for instruction on the word recognition components (Goal 1) may result in students developing inefficient strategies. This in turn might prevent or frustrate attempts at reading other types of material (Goal 3), leading to a breakdown in the developing skill. Similarly, a program that over-emphasizes phonics in relation to the other aspects of word recognition or the other goals of beginning instruction may so distort the meaningfulness of the task that skill development would also be impaired.

Progress into the advanced-reading stage requires coordination of the above goals to the extent that students recognize most of the words in their oral language as sight words and find reading sufficiently engaging to continue skill development. As with other skills, advanced performance in reading is characterized by increasing flexibility and efficiency. Advanced-reading goals include the following:

1. *Development of explicit strategies to aid comprehension*. Attention must shift from decoding words to constructing meaning of larger passages. In selecting an appropriate strategy students must consider the type of material they are reading, their own knowledge base and characteristics as readers, and their purpose for reading.

2. *Development of study skills to support learning from content textbooks*. These skills include strategies to use before, during, and after reading to promote comprehension, learning, and memory for new information.

3. *Development of a large meaning vocabulary*. Although sight vocabulary must continue to grow, students at this level must also learn new word meanings from their reading. This word meaning process includes the use of various sources of information to determine components of meaning. The primary sources of meaning information are the context in which the word is found, meaningful aspects of word structure, and reference materials such as dictionaries.

This goal list is neither independent nor exhaustive. Each of the goals of advanced reading could be considered under the general concept of flexibility. Much of the current research on reading is designed to unpack the components of knowledge, strategies, task, and material variables that affect flexibility (see Wixson & Lipson, this volume; Johnston, 1983). Similarly, the beginning goals could be expanded to included knowledge aspects related to comprehension such as awareness of different text types and text structures. Although this information could support advanced preformance it is not the primary focus of beginning skill development.

Explicit comprehension strategies are assigned to the advanced stage primarily due to considerations related to capacity limitaions. During initial instruction it is important that the learning process be motivated by meaningful and engaging materials. This also requires that students comprehend what they read. But since word level processes requires considerable learner attention (Schwartz, 1980; Stanovich, 1980), teachers should structure the situation such that comprehension is insured. If materials place too high a demand on active attention toward comprehension of unfamiliar ideas, then overall meaningfulness will suffer. To insure comprehension while allowing students to focus on learning component skills, teachers can employ a variety of instructional strategies; for example teacher-directed previewing (Graves, Cooke, & Laberge, 1983) or prediction activities (Hansen, 1981; Stauffer, 1975) can increase meaningfulness. In the advanced stage instruction can focus on the transfer of process control to the students, engaging them in independent previewing and prediction as explicit strategies to increase comprehension. Thus, although the student should consistently see comprehension and meaning as the goal of reading, from an instructional perspective the initial focus is to support meaningfulness, with later emphasis on developing independent and explicit comprehension strategies.

TEACHERS' CLASSROOM LEARNING

Instructional activities partially define the context of learning for both students and teachers. The previous section provided some illustrations of how the teachers' knowledge base can influence instructional decisions. This section describes how instructional practice can lead to modification of instructional procedures and development of the teachers' knowledge base related to reading instruction.

Given the difficulty of learning relationships among concepts and procedures in a well-structured university course (Barron & Schwartz, 1984), it would be difficult for teachers to acquire such knowledge independently through instructional practice. However, given some partial knowledge of conceptual relationships and developmental goals, practice can provide the feedback necessary to support further refinement of the teachers' knowledge base. The rate of teachers' learning is likely to be directly related to the extent of their current knowledge and the value teachers place on this learning goal.

The type of teacher learning that occurs in the classroom may be difficult to identify. It will probably involve a gradual reorganization of known concepts rather than simply the acquisition of new ones. The structure of the knowledge base outlined here suggests that learning may result in (1) additional categories of information involved in reading and instruction, (2) new procedures for effecting changes in students' reading processes, and (3) more explicit relationships between the categories and procedures and the stages and goals that sequence skill development.

These forms of learning are interrelated. The following three learning scenarios demonstrate how teachers' conceptual knowledge drives instruction and how instructional practice can lead to modification of this knowledge base. The first example relates syllabication procedures to the word recognition process, the second involves the transformation of a comprehension strategy, while the third demonstrates the extension of a concept used in diagnosis.

Syllabication is a topic covered in most basal reader programs. Usually the students' reader and workbook present a number of syllabication rules and practice exercises. The complexity of these procedures often leads both students and teachers to treat this set of information as an independent and isolated skill. As teachers become more familiar with these procedures as well as the processes involved in word recognition, some coordination may be achieved. Instructional experience indicates that children often attempt to sound out words letter by letter. Syllabication procedures enable sound-symbol relationships to be applied to larger units of print. Since word recognition processes need only provide an approximate pronunciation to aid in identification of a known word, the syllabication procedure need not be exact. From this perspective it is more important that students be flexible in generating several possible patterns than that they apply a particular rule. As teachers learn these new relationships between syllabication and the word recognition process, the way that they teach syllabication may change. The purpose of instruction can now be made more explicit for students, with syllabication taught as one of a set of word recognition strategies instead of as an independent skill.

As a second example of teacher learning consider the use of the directed reading and thinking activity (DRTA) (Stauffer, 1975). This technique is usually presented in methods texts as a teacher-directed questioning procedure. The questioning process is designed to help students activate appropriate background knowledge and to establish a purpose for reading through prediction. With careful text analysis and question planning this technique can be very effective in promoting students' comprehension and their memory for the text. As teachers become more aware of goals for advanced reading, they may see the need to transform this technique from a teacher-directed activity to one that promotes independent comprehension. Instructional lessons can then be developed to support the independent generation of questions and predictions by students.

This transition in the use of the DRTA procedure indicates a new division in the teacher's knowledge base between teacher-directed and student-directed comprehension activities. The former may be linked to the meaningfulness goal of beginning reading and uses in content-area instruction, while the latter provides a strategy that can contribute to student flexibility in the advanced-reading stage. The establishment of these two branches of comprehension activities in a teacher's knowledge base may lead to further reorganization or establishment of new links between previously unrelated procedures (for example, relating study guide and teacher-directed DRTA procedures).

As a third example consider the relationship among concepts used in informal diagnosis. A reading problem is often defined by a gap of two grade levels between a student's instructional level and hearing capacity (see Gillet & Temple, 1982, for a discussion of these concepts). The hearing capacity reflects the highest level of text that a student can understand on a listening task. The capacity notion suggests that a student with a gap between listening comprehension and reading performance has the potential to improve, but is currently having difficulty constructing meaning from print. This concept of potential is similar to Vygotsky's (1978) discussion of zone of proximal development (see chapters by Gavelek and Rogoff, this volume). That is, the gap provides an indication of what the student might be able to achieve given teacher support and appropriate reading instruction.

For students in the beginning-reading stage, a listening task frees attention from the word recognition process and provides an indication of the extent of development to be expected as word processing demands are reduced. For students in the advanced-reading stage, however, interpreting listening comprehension scores in terms of capacity may be misleading. At this level attentional demands of word recognition have been reduced by the establishment of a large sight vocabulary. Thus, reading to students may no longer provide support for comprehension and could in fact attenuate performance, since silent-reading strategies cannot be applied (eg. previewing or reviewing). The capacity, or zone of proximal development, might better be extended into the advanced stage by comparing performance on unaided silent reading, with scores obtained in conjunction with a teacher-directed DRTA procedure. A difference in comprehension performance following these tasks could indicate a lack of active comprehension strategies and provide clues for further instruction. Similarity in scores may suggest that students already engage in this type of activity, or perhaps that vocabulary or general knowledge constrains current performance levels in both conditions.

This last example represents my own most recent development of knowledge about reading instruction. The concepts of listening comprehension, capacity, DRTA procedures, and zone of proximal development were each available, but originally isolated in my knowledge base. The new relationship among them developed out of considering these ideas in the context of the stage sequence for instruction. Thus, in my current view, I see capacity as requiring different operational definitions depending on the student's level of development in the reading process. This notion may prove to be immature or to need further modification, but at this time I can accept the relationship as providing an extension and elaboration of my original conception of capacity measures in diagnosis. My subsequent experience with students, both in instruction and research, will yield opportunities to confirm, reject, or modify this relationship.

DEVELOPMENT OF DIAGNOSTIC SKILL

The structure of the knowledge base and the learning examples described in the previous sections characterize teachers in the advanced stage of instructional skill development. They possess an elaborate set of conceptual and procedural knowledge that enables them to interpret student behaviors and transform curricular materials to maximize learning opportunities for their students. Transforming specific information in terms of a structured knowledge base related to reading instruction is a primary goal in the development of diagnostic expertise. Diagnostic skill follows a general developmental sequence similar to those described for procedural skills in tennis or reading. Rather than discussing the goals of this ideal developmental sequence (that can be generalized from the previous example), the next two sections will focus on contraints that may inhibit this development. The first constraint is partially successful instructional strategies; the second involves environmental factors that affect teachers' development.

Brown et al. (1983) summarize research on skill development in studying (see also Brown & Day, 1983; Brown, Day, & Jones, 1983), writing (Bereiter & Scardamalia, 1982; Flower & Hayes, 1981), and scientific reasoning (Kuhn & Phelps, 1982). In each of these complex learning tasks, Brown et al. (1983) characterized the process of development as:

> not just one of acquiring increasingly more refined and sophisticated strategies: development involves the systematic consolidation and growing conviction of the appropriateness of mature strategies combined with the rejection of plausible but less efficient habits. (p. 94)

Maintaining these less efficent but partially successful strategies inhibits further skill development. These strategies can be applied and used in a variety of situations, but tend to impede progress toward more efficient and flexible procedures.

Such partially successful strategies appear to constitute the dominant mode of school instruction and vary considerably from a flexible form of diagnostic teaching. Teachers attempt to present the curriculum rather than transform it in terms of developmental goals or individual student needs. To illustrate this point compare the following description of a partially successful writing strategy (Brown et al., 1983) with descriptions by Durkin (1978–1979; 1981) of classroom comprehension instruction and by Vinsonhaler et al. (1983) of diagnostic processes used by reading specialists:

> The knowledge-telling strategy [for writing] is distinguished by (1) a lack of goal-related planning; (2) a lack of internal constraints in the text, one sentence being as deletable as any other; (3) a lack of interconnectedness in the written output; (4) reliance on purely forward-acting serial production rather than recursive forward-backward revision process; and finally (5) a remarkable lack of anything other than merely cosmetic revision. (Brown et al. 1983, p. 93)

> Presumably, a classroom is a place where instruction is offered and received. However, in a classroom-observation study of the kind and amount of reading instruction that grades 3–6 provide, a different picture emerges (Durkin, 1978–1979). Instead of being instructors, the 39 observed teachers tended to be questioners and assignment givers. Since almost all their questions were attempts to learn whether the children had comprehended a given section or chapter, the teachers seemed more intent on testing comprehension than teaching it. They were also "mentioners," saying just enough about a topic (e.g., unstated conclusions) to allow for a written assignment related to it. (Durkin, 1981, p. 516)

> Individually . . . the diagnoses show significant deviations from the recommendations of experts. First, the diagnoses included a large number of one-time-only statements having questionable relevance to remediation. Second, the diagnoses systematically fail to mention the reading skills of greatest import to remediation. Third, even when important skills are mentioned in the diagnosis, these statements are not reliably linked with treatment. (Vinsonhaler et al., 1983, p. 160)

The assessment and assignment strategy described by Durkin (1978–1979; 1981) is partially successful in that some children in each of the observed classrooms were good readers. Whether student learning was actually facilitated by the instruction they reveived is debatable; nevertheless, student success allows teachers to feel comfortable with their instructional strategy. Of course some students experience difficulty in learning to read; for the more severe of these problems we have devised a labeling system that implies that the problem rests with the child rather than the instruction (learning disabled, dyslexic). As in the knowledge-telling strategy, assessment and assignment requires little goal-related planning, interconnectedness of instruction, or modification and revision of lessons.

The description of diagnostic reports by Vinsonhaler et al. (1983) bares even a greater resemblance to the knowledge-telling strategy since writing and diagnosis involve similar planning and production demands. In fact, the types of process and product analyses used to study writing might be useful in investigating the development of diagnostic expertise. Rather than using reliability as the primary criteria for judging the diagnostic process, these procedures might provide a description of qualitatively different forms of diagnosis. To illustrate what this shift from knowledge-telling to knowledge-transforming forms of diagnosis might involve, consider the case study data presented in Table 15.1.

The information presented in Table 15.1 is considerably simpler than the case studies used by Vinsonhaler et al. (1983). The first two columns show scores on an informal test of word recognition in isolation (WRI). This test consists of a series of graded word lists in which each higher-level word list is more difficult than the preceding list. Students are first given a short, flashed presentation (one-half second) of a word and asked to pronounce it. If the student is unable to initially identify a word, they are given an untimed exposure to the word and asked to try again. The percent correct under these criteria on each graded list is shown in the first two columns of the table. Scores in the next three columns are based on an informal reading inventory. This test consists of a series of graded reading selections ranging in difficulty from beginning elementary to secondary levels. Students are typically given a set of these passages to read orally. Following the oral reading of each passage the teacher asks a number of comprehension

Table 15.1 **Sample Case Study Data; Age 13, Grade 5**

| Level | Word Recognition | | | Comprehension | |
| | Isolation | | | | |
	Flash	Untimed	Context	Oral	Hearing
pp	100	100	—	—	—
p	90	100	100	90	—
1	80	100	98	75	—
2	50	90	96	40	—
3	—	90	—	—	85
4	—	85	—	—	75
5	—	80	—	—	70
6	—	60	—	—	50
7	—	—	—	—	—
8	—	—	—	—	—
9	—	—	—	—	—

questions based on the passage. When oral-reading performance falls below acceptable levels, the teacher will read some additional passages to the student, with each passage again followed by comprehension questions. Student performance on these tasks yields measures of word recognition in context, oral-reading comprehension, and listening comprehension, as shown in the next three columns of the Table 15.1. See Gillet and Temple (1982) for a discussion of these informal reading tests.

The following are three possible levels of diagnostic skill. Each level reflects an increase in teachers' knowledge base and ability to transform information about student performance in terms of this knowledge base.

Level 1 In this case the student would be viewed as having a problem in flashed word recognition and reading comprehension. The diagnostic interpretation is strongly tied to the form of test. Problem areas are determined from scores judged to be low in relation to grade level. Typical remedial suggestions would take the form of additional practice on tasks similar to the test, which in this case would involve the use of flash cards and additional comprehension assessment.

At this level of diagnostic skill, test results are not transformed in terms of general concepts involved in the reading process. Grade-level expectations are the main criteria used to evaluate performance, and students who perform at or above grade level are considered not to require diagnosis or diagnostic teaching.

Level 2 Particular test scores are transformed by teachers in terms of concepts related to the reading process. In the sample case, the flashed word-recognition score is interpreted as an indication of sight vocabulary. Scores from the informal reading inventory may be used to establish different performance levels for the student: independent, instructional, and frustration levels and hearing capacity (see Gillet & Temple, 1982). The diagnostic interpretation may take into account these levels, but decisions about the nature of reading process and instruction are still based primarily on grade level. Remedial recommendations may now take a more general form since instructional procedures and diagnostic information are both tied to general concepts. Thus, the teacher might decide to use a language experience approach to develop sight vocabulary, rather than flash cards. Because different categories of information are not interrelated or sequenced into stage goals, remediations will address specific problems; in the current case study, this includes sight vocabulary and comprehension.

Level 3 The student's performance is now transformed and interpreted in terms of hierarchically related concepts and instructional goals. The case study data is not interpreted as indicating a comprehension problem since listening comprehension remains strong through the fifth-grade level. Rather, the low comprehension score on the second-grade oral-reading passage is considered to result from attentional demands of word recognition. This hypothesis is supported by the low level of sight vocabulary. Phonic and structural aspects of the word recognition process seem relatively strong based on the score from the untimed portion of the

WRI test. Little information is available on the use of contextual clues to support word recognition. Detailed analysis of specific miscues on the oral reading passage may provide some information, but additional tasks may be needed to determine the extent to which available context clues are used to support the word recognition process. Though no information is available on the student's view of reading as meaningful and engaging, it might be predicted from the performance pattern that an interview would indicate that the student does little reading outside school. Thus, teachers apply their knowledge of the goals for beginning reading to organize and interpret available test data as well as to suggest additional information that might support or modify current hypotheses. Test results or observations are transformed in terms of a goal-directed process.

This integrated view of the student's current level of development may lead to a variety of instructional recommendations. These might focus on strengths (e.g., encourage outside reading in high-interest, high-knowledge areas), or weaknesses (e.g., direct attempts to build sight vocabulary). Whatever the focus of initial instruction, a program that interrelates stage goals will be necessary. Since instruction serves to foster development of expertise, diagnostic information can inform instruction for students at all levels of development, not just those who fall below the group average on current performance measures. Differences between estimates of capacity and performance are seen as providing more information about the student's skill development than comparisons of performance and grade level.

The assessment and assignment strategy described by Durkin (1978–1979) and the diagnostic performance characterized by Vinsonhaler et al. (1983) seem consistant with the decision processes used in Levels 1 and 2. Certainly, a well-developed conceptual knowledge base will not be sufficient to support classroom instruction without equally well-developed procedural knowledge. An interesting question for future research is the relationship among knowledge base variables, diagnostic decision processes, and classroom instruction.

ENVIRONMENTAL FACTORS

The previous discussion has focused on the relationship of the teachers' knowledge base to two types of classroom learning, one global and one specific. Global learning involves the continuous development and modification of the knowledge base related to reading and instruction. Specific learning requires the use of this knowledge base to interpret students' reading performance and to plan further instruction. If partially successful strategies are viewed as adequate, the teachers' need for further learning is removed. The classroom and school environment play an important role in determining the extent to which the goal of teacher learning is viewed by teachers and administrators as being central to the educational process and profession.

Excessive class size and limited planning time carry implicit messages about the importance of these learning goals. Little more than assessment and assignment can be expected with a half hour a day to plan instruction. Similarly, administrative and peer evaulation often stress goals other than learning. Universities and, to a somewhat lesser extent, high schools tend to evaluate their faculty in terms of specific content knowledge (and research), rather than their ability to transform that knowledge in ways that promote learning. At the elementary level more attention is given to instructional factors in evaluation, but this often centers on classroom management skill rather than diagnostic teaching ability. State and local assessment procedures attempt to hold teachers accountable for their students' learning, but since these assessments usually do not reflect a holistic view of reading, they tend to promote isolated skill instruction.

The belief that there is more to learn and that we are capable of further learning is the motivation that can drive students, teachers, and researchers toward the development of their particular forms of expertise. Social contexts that foster this learning goal will characterize effective classrooms, schools, and universities. As implied in this final quotation, if learning is not valued even an individual with an extensive knowledge base will not benefit from practice.

> Many have marked the speed with which Maud'Dib learned the necessities of Arrakis. The Bene Gesserit, of course, know the basis of this speed. For the others, we can say that Maud'Dib learned rapidly because his first training was in how to learn. And the first lesson of all was the basic trust that he could learn. It is shocking to find how many people do not believe they can learn, and how many more believe learning to be difficult. Maud'Dib knew that every experience carries its lesson. (Herbert, 1965)

REFERENCES

Barron, R. F., & Schwartz, R. M. (1984). Graphic postorganizers: A spatial learning strategy. In C. D. Holley & D. F. Dansereau (Eds.), *Spatial learning strategies: Techniques, applications and related issues* (pp. 275–289). Orlando: Academic.

Bereiter, C., & Scardamalia, M. (1982). From conversation to composition: The role of instruction in a developmental process. In R. Glaser (Ed.), *Advances in instructional psychology* (Vol. 2 pp. 1–64). Hillsdale, N.J.: Erlbaum.

Bisanz, G. L., & Voss, J. F. (1981). Sources of knowledge in reading comprehension: Cognitive development and expertise in a content domain. In A. M. Lesgold & C. A. Perfetti (Eds.), *Interactive processes in reading* (pp. 215–240). Hillsdale, N.J.: Erlbaum.

Brown, A. L. et al. (1983). Learning, remembering and understanding. In P. H. Mussen, J. H. Flavell, E. M. Markman (Eds.), *Handbook of child psychology: Vol. 3. Cognitive development* (pp. 77–166). New York: Wiley.

Brown, A. L. & Day, J. D. (1983) Macrorules for summarizing text: The development of expertise. *Journal of Verbal Learning and Verbal Behavior, 22,* 1–14.

Brown, A. L., Day, J. D., & Jones, R. S. (1983). The development of plans for summarizing texts. *Child Development, 54,* 968–989.

Clay M. M. (1972). *Reading: The patterning of complex behavior.* London: Heineman.

Downing, J. (1979). *Reading and reasoning.* New York: Springer-Verlag.

Durkin, D. (1978–1979). What classroom observations reveal about reading comprehension instruction. *Reading Research Quarterly, 14,* 481–533.

Durkin, D. (1981). Reading comprehension instruction in five basal series. *Reading Research Quarterly, 16,* 515–544.

Eylon, B., & Reif, F. (1984). Effects of knowledge organization on task performance. *Cognition and Instruction, 1,* 5–44.

Flower, L., & Hayes, J. (1981). Plans that guide the composing process. In C. Frederiksen & J. Dominic (Eds.), *Writing: The nature, development and teaching of written communication: Vol. 2. Writing: Process, development, and communication* (pp. 39–58). Hillsdale, N.J.: Erlbaum.

Gillet, J. W. & Temple, C. (1982). *Understanding reading problems: Assessment and instruction.* Boston: Little, Brown.

Graves, M. F., Cooke, C. L., & Laberge, M. J. (1983). Effects of previewing difficult short stories on low ability junior high school students' comprehension, recall and attitude. *Reading Research Quarterly, 18,* 262–276.

Hansen, J. (1981). The effects of inference training and practice on young children's reading comprehension. *Reading Research Quarterly, 16,* 391–417.

Herbert, F. (1965). *Dune.* New York: Ace.

Johnston, P. H. (1983). *Reading comprehension assessment: A cognitive basis.* Newark, Del. International Reading Association.

Kuhn, D., & Phelps, K. (1982). The development of problem-solving strategies. In H. W. Reese (Ed.), *Advances in child development and behavior* (Vol. 17, pp. 2–44). New York: Academic.

Schwartz, R. M. (1980). Levels of processing: The strategic demands of reading comprehension. *Reading Research Quarterly, 15,* 433–450.

Siegler, R. S. (1983). Information processing approaches to development. In P. H. Mussen & W. Kessen (Eds.), *Handbook of child psychology: Vol. 1. History, theory and methods* (pp. 129– 212). New York: Wiley.

Stanovich, K. E. (1980). Toward an interactive-compensatory model of individual differences in the development of reading fluency. *Reading Research Quarterly, 16,* 32–71.

Stauffer, R. (1975). *Directing the reading-thinking process.* New York: Harper & Row.

Stevenson, H. (1983). How children learn—The quest for a theory. In P. H. Mussen & W. Kessen (Eds.), *Handbook of child psychology: Vol. 1. History, theory, and methods* (pp. 213–236). New York: Wiley.

Vinsonhaler, J. S. et al. (1983) Diagnosing childen with educational problems: Characteristics of reading and learning disabilities specialists, and classroom teachers. *Reading Research Quarterly, 18,* 134–164.

Vygotsky, L. S. (1978). *Mind in society: The development of higher psychological processes* M. Cole et al. (Eds. and Trans.). Cambridge: Harvard University Press.

16

Contexts of Literacy:
Translating Research into Policy

Peter N. Winograd

The theme of this volume is the contexts of literacy. These contexts can range from a child reading a book alone, to a small reading group in a classroom, to funding decisions made at the national level. The context addressed in this chapter is found at the upper end of this continuum. Specifically, I want to examine state-level reading committees that decide how best to implement policy mandated by state legislatures. The work of these committees is important and difficult. It is important because the results from these committees determine, to a great degree, which aspects of reading teachers are supposed to teach, which commercial materials will be bought and used, which aspects of reading will be assessed, and presumably, which aspects of reading will or will not be learned by children. The work is difficult for a number of reasons, several of which provide the central focus of this chapter.

Before I discuss the problems faced by these policy committees, let me briefly describe their composition and their charges. Such committees are usually comprised of personnel from the state department of education, classroom teachers, curriculum coordinators, principals, and university professors. The committees are formed for a variety of reasons that include developing performance objectives in reading, local or statewide assessment instruments, or guidelines for evaluating commercial reading materials prior to adoption. In Kentucky, for example, the policy committee's task was to determine a list of essential skills in reading in order to meet the requirements of Kentucky Senate Bill 169 (1984) that states, in part:

271

By January 1, 1987, the state board of education shall assure that each pupil in the public schools of the Commonwealth is taught and is mastering the essential skills necessary to function in each basic skills area. . . .

Tasks such as these are extremely complex, and there are a number of perspectives on how best to accomplish them. Two perspectives, in particular, appear to be in direct conflict. For ease of discussion I will refer to these perspectives as that of a reading researcher and of a policy maker. While there are, obviously, other important perspectives represented on these committees (e.g., a teacher's), in this chapter I will focus on those of a researcher and a policy maker.

At issue is how to reconcile the conflicting perspectives and needs of the researcher and the policy maker so that these state-level committees and their directives do not become, in effect, a context against literacy. There seem to be two interrelated problems that contribute to the conflict. The first is a difference in objectives. The second is the changing definition of reading and the lack of a clear and common language to discuss that change. Each of these problems will be addressed in turn. Then I will focus on issues that need to be addressed if researchers and policy makers are to work together effectively.

READING RESEARCH AND ACCOUNTABILITY

Simply stated, researchers and policy makers have different objectives. The researcher's objective is to use his or her knowledge of how children learn to read to improve reading instruction in the classroom. The policy maker's objective is to set up an efficient system of accountability to ensure that children are taught to read. This fundamental difference in objectives is a major problem in translating research into policy. Understanding these differences is the first step to overcoming them.

The researcher's perspective results from their understanding of how children learn to read. In fact, researchers know a great deal about the process. Depending on the age of the child, and barring any sensory or physiological defects, copious amounts of book sharing, language experience, systematic instruction in aspects of word recognition, and modeling of comprehension strategies will result in a child learning to read. For some children book sharing and language experience is enough (Durkin, 1966). Although researchers may disagree about some of the specific details, most would agree that we know how to teach children to read. From a researcher's perspective, then, the question is how to incorporate as much as possible about what is known about teaching children to read into the committee's products (performance objectives, assessment instruments, etc.).

The policy maker's perspective has developed in response to the public's dissatisfaction with public education generally and reading performance specifically (Baratz, 1978). Such dissatisfaction runs in cycles, and recent reports like A Nation At Risk indicate that educational reform is again a topic of concern. A great deal of public attention has focused on the results of educational programs, especially results as measured by test scores. As far as the public is concerned, low scores on reading tests mean poor schools (Harper & Kilarr, 1978). Allow me an aside here. I am not denigrating the public's concern for educational improvement. The public has a valid interest in improving reading instruction; indeed, public involvement is essential to the improvement of reading instruction. What I am saying is that test scores are a focal point for the public; hence the issue from a policy maker's perspective is how to raise the test scores.

The way to raise test scores, according to policy makers, is by setting specific goals and then monitoring schools to see if the goals are achieved. In short, the way to raise test scores is through accountability. Accountability is not a new solution. The origins of accountability can be traced to the beginning of this century (Laffey, 1973). A more specific example of the kind of accountability that is currently facing researchers is the one described by Goodlad:

> The first step is to formulate some common, statewide goals. Second, these are to be translated into specific objectives for local schools. Third, there is to be a determination of needed change efforts on the basis of some kind of assessment of student performance in relation to objectives. Fourth, these needs are to be addressed through local innovative efforts directed at the improvement of weaknesses presumably revealed through assessment. Fifth, local evaluation capability is to be developed so that some kind of continuing self-appraisal will be built into local improvement efforts. Sixth, feedback to state authorities is then to be used to assist the state department of education in fulfilling its leadership roles, however it may perceive them. (1975, p. 108)

The steps outlined above seem like a rational approach to improvement of education in general and reading instruction in particular. There are certain conditions, however, that must be met if a system of accountability is to achieve its stated goals (Broudy, 1972; Cox, 1975). Two conditions are particularly relevant to the conflict between reading researchers and policy makers. First, there must be theoretical consensus and public acceptance on the aspects of reading that children should be expected to learn. Second, the standards for what constitutes success in reading need to be clear, and an efficient method of measuring success and failure needs to be established.

Both policy makers and researchers are aware of these conditions. Policy makers expect researchers, who are the experts in such matters, to be able to develop an exact list of specific objectives and an equally exact (and efficient) way of assessing whether these objectives have been met. In contrast, researchers expect policy makers to understand that reading is an "inexact process" (Harper & Kilarr, 1978), and that to reduce reading to a list of subskills that can be measured efficiently and exactly distorts and destroys the process (Page, 1978). These conflicting expectations lead to confusion, frustration, and resentment. Researchers view policy makers as "efficiency at any cost" bureaucrats and policy makers view researchers as irrelevant.

THE CHANGING DEFINITION OF READING

In addition to the difference in perspectives and objectives, researchers and policy makers face another problem, which was alluded to earlier. They lack a common definition of reading. The heart of the problem is that researchers' understanding of reading has evolved faster than that of the policy makers. This is as it should be. However, the lag in the way reading is conceptualized creates some real difficulties in communication. The work in progress by the Michigan Reading Association (MRA) in redefining reading provides an excellent example of the problem and an attempt to solve it.

In 1982 the MRA was asked by the Michigan Department of Education to review the state performance objectives in reading that were to be used in revising the state assessment test. The MRA agreed to undertake the task, and their first step was to consider how the state's current definition of reading would be changed to reflect recent research. The Michigan Department of Education's current definition and the MRA's concerns follow:

> "The department's definition of reading is based upon the assumption that the only legitimate, final outcome of reading instruction is comprehension. That is, although certain enabling word attack skills may be related to comprehension skills, mastery of these skills, in and of themselves and in the absence of comprehension is not a sufficient terminal objective for reading instruction."

> In many respects this statement still holds true today. However, in 1977 when the present definition was adopted, our understanding of reading in general and comprehension in particular was more limited than it is today. At that time reading was conceptualized as a series of skills that were viewed as sequential and hierarchical (e.g., literal, inferential, and applied comprehension). Consequently, the objectives and the reading tests were aimed at proficiency in component skill areas such as contextual analysis, dictionary usage, literal and inferential comprehension. While this view of reading was appropriate for that time, it no longer adequately reflects our knowledge of reading.

> In the six years since the present definition was adopted significant advances in fields such as anthropology, cognitive psychology, education, linguistics, and sociology have made it possible to broaden our view of reading. Recent research holds that reading is a dynamic process that involves the reader's ability to construct meaning through the interaction between information suggested by the written language and the reader's existing knowledge. In other words the reader is an active participant in the process. This interactive dimension focuses on how the reader derives meaning from print; what the reader brings to the reading situation in terms of experience, knowledge, skills and ability; how the information is presented in written text; and what effects context has on reading. As a result, difficulty is no longer viewed as an absolute property of a particular reading skill or task, but rather as a relative property of the interaction among specific reader, text, and instructional factors. (Wixson & Peters, 1984, p. 4)

The MRA went on to propose a revised definition commensurate with our current understanding of the reading process.

Reading is the process of constructing meaning through the dynamic interaction among the reader's existing knowledge, the information suggested by the written language, and the context of the reading situation. (Wixson & Peters, 1984, p. 5)

The MRA also identified some of the assumptions and implications inherent in their new definition of reading. The most pertinent to this discussion focused on the shift from the assumption that there is a specific set of skills, which if mastered, produces fluent readers to the assumption that the appropriate goal of instruction is to produce children who can process text flexibly and independently. Such a shift in assumptions has important implications for teacher training, reading assessment, classroom instruction, and policy making.

Developing a new definition of reading and identifying its assumptions and implications is an important first step. The next step is to inform policy makers so they can accept a new definition with its assumptions and implications. This can be difficult for several reasons. First, policy makers have a great deal invested in the current view of reading as a series of sequential and hierarchical skills. Such a view is particularly amenable to assessment for the purposes of accountability. Second, there is a great deal of ambiguity surrounding the terminology used to discuss reading. This is especially troublesome in the area of reading comprehension. At issue is how researchers can talk with policy makers about the interactive nature of reading comprehension without resorting to the language and connotations used to describe subskills.

Consider, for example, the ability to identify what is important in a text. This is an ability that most of the reading community considers worthwhile (Johnson & Barrett, 1981). For the moment, let importance be limited to what the author of the text considers important (textual importance) rather than what various readers might consider important for their own idiosyncratic purposes (contextual importance). Recent research has provided some insights into how fluent readers identify what is important in texts. In expository passages, fluent readers follow the organizational structure of the passage in order to determine which elements are important (Meyer, Brandt, & Bluth, 1980). In narrative passages, fluent readers try to understand what the main character's problem is and how he or she tries to solve it (Bower, 1978). How does one translate these insights about reading comprehension into the policy language used in, for example, performance objectives or curriculum guides?

Is it sufficient to simply state that the student will be able to identify the important information in a variety of passages and hope that sound procedures will be used to determine what information is important and what constitutes a variety of passages? Is it necessary to get more specific and state that the student will be able to recall the main idea and supporting details from expository passages and the basic plot from narratives? Is it necessary to get even more specific and distinguish between explicit main ideas and implicit main ideas? Consider, for a moment, the level of specificity commonly found on comprehension skills lists. The child will be able to:

1. Predict outcomes.
2. Draw conclusions.
3. Identify motives, behavior, and feelings of characters.
4. Identify explicitly stated main ideas.
5. Identify explicitly stated sequence.
6. Identify the unstated main idea.
7. Identify implied sequence.
8. Identify implied cause and effect.
9. Select an appropriate title for a story.
10. Identify the main idea of a story.
11. Recognize stated cause-and-effect relationships.

What is the effect of fractionating the comprehension process to this degree? One effect is that such specificity reinforces the view that reading is comprised of discrete and hierarchical skills that can be taught and tested in isolation. Another is that the habit of thinking about reading in this manner makes it very difficult to think about reading in any other fashion. Will researchers simply replace lists of comprehension skills like those above with new lists (e.g., different kinds of text structure, different reasons for reading, different amounts of background knowledge)?

The difficulty in translating a researcher's understanding of the process of text comprehension into a policy maker's language is a major problem that must be solved if current research is to inform reading policy. This is not likely to happen until researchers have a clearly articulated alternative to present to policy makers that will satisfy their needs. The most important stepping stone to helping policy makers accept a new conceptualization of reading is a clearly defined alternative to the old one.

ISSUES TO BE ADDRESSED

Recall that this chapter began by describing a very specific kind of context—a state-level committee meeting to implement policy related to reading. I have focused on how two of the many perspectives found on these committees are in conflict, and I have traced the source of this conflict to the tension between reading research and accountability and to the change in how reading is defined. In this section I want to raise some issues that need to be addressed if research is to be successfully translated into policy.

First, it is important to note that state-level committees and the legislators they serve operate in a larger context of literacy. Reading researchers are not the only ones with opinions to voice. Other people (e.g., legislators' constituents or citizens concerned about higher taxes) are likely to have suggestions based on their own perspectives and beliefs (Weir, 1983). Studies that have examined the relationship between social science and social policy (Caplan, 1979; Lindblom & Cohen, 1979) indicate that upper-level social policy decisions are more often based on soft knowledge than on hard knowledge. In this context soft knowledge refers to general forms of social science knowledge including opinions, assumptions, and beliefs, while hard knowledge refers to more specialized technical forms of social science knowledge (Caplan, 1979). The lesson to be learned from these policy studies is that it is important for researchers to disseminate their findings in understandable terms to the public in general and to decision makers in particular. If reading researchers wish to influence those outside the education community, then they must do it, in large measures, with soft knowledge. And it is important to educate the public because the more aware they are of the complexities inherent in improving reading instruction, the less likely they are to make simplistic demands for reform.

A second issue, closely related to the first, is that researchers and other educators need to deal with misinformation about reading. Consider, for example, the following excerpts from a book review that appeared in several Kentucky newspapers:

In 1955 Rudolf Flesch in his best seller, "Why Johnny Can't Read," told the American public specifically why public schools were failing: most students never learn to read. Why?

The reading textbooks teach by the look-and-say (sight-reading) method rather than by phonics. And now "Why Johnny Still Can't Read" tells us why again. The textbooks which are most widely used don't teach phonics or sounding out vowels and consonants.

Flesch makes good use of existing statistics to denounce the textbooks ". . . after 124 studies leaving look-and-say without a shred of scientific respectability, it is still used in 85 percent of our classrooms, poisoning the minds and crippling the educational growth of tens of millions of children. The educators have ignored this mountain of solid evidence and continued their programmed retardation in our schools."

This paperback edition of "Why Johnny Still Can't Read" is especially timely in Kentucky. The state textbook committee now is preparing a list of publishers and textbooks which will be available for adoption by Kentucky schools in 1985. The list comes out in May.

Of the current current reading books, adopted by Kentucky in 1979, only one, Economy Co., uses the phonics method. The other nine giants, Harper and Row, Rand McNally and Co, Scott Foresman and Co., for example, all teach the look-and-say (flash card) approach.

Flesch charges, "Clearly the U.S. literacy rate, now down to that of Burma and Albania, will drop even lower. The illiterates plus the slow readers are now a majority of the U. S. population."

With the present furor over money and education, suprisingly (sic), the classroom textbook hasn't received any attention.

This excellent book concludes by referring to Russia's use of phonics. Except for 2 or 3 percent, all Russian children can read at the end of first grade. "No words are taught by the sight method." (Drew, 1984)

The author of this review had mailed a copy to the Kentucky Department of Education and requested that it be distributed to the members of the textbook committee. Emotional, inaccurate articles like this are potentially very harmful, because they reach a much larger audience than do scientific reports based on factual data. The fact that serious members of the educational community dismiss and ignore such misinformation does not limit its effects on public opinion.

Third, researchers need to increase their efforts to translate current research into forms that are useful to teachers who must implement reading instruction in real schools. The current research into reading comprehension has resulted in a great deal of new information about how children comprehend what they read. This new information, however, still needs to be linked to an instructional framework that can be used by teachers with 20 to 30 students in their classes. The issue here is not reading instruction per se, but rather the management of reading instruction. The view of reading as a set of discrete and hierarchical skills will be very difficult to dislodge because it enables teachers to manage the teaching of reading to large groups of children and, at the same time, to focus instruction for individual children (Otto, 1977). Any new view of reading will have to address management needs or it will not find its way into widespread practice.

Fourth, researchers need to increase their efforts to develop more complete methods of assessing achievements in reading. At present, success in reading seems to be synonymous with performance on large scale, standardized test batteries. It is not unreasonable for states to conduct such large-scale assessment (Goodlad, 1975), and it is likely that the public will continue to use the results from these tests to monitor the effectiveness of the schools. However, performance on large-scale assessment batteries should not be the sole measure of reading achievement. Jackson (1968), for example, noted that experienced elementary teachers measured their success by observing student involvement or interest. Is there some way that measures of task involvement (Johnston & Winograd, 1983; Nicholls, 1983) or of amount of actual reading performed (Guthrie, 1981) can be used to augment the definition of success in reading? Broadening the definition of what constitutes success in reading may be one way to resolve some of the conflicts entailed in the current model of accountability.

Fifth, researchers need to examine the effects of various state-level committee decisions on teachers, classroom instruction, and classroom materials. When a state-level committee decides which essential skills must be taught and which performance objectives will be assessed, what effect does that have on the teacher as professional decision maker (Schwille, Porter, & Gant, 1979; Shannon, 1983)? Is there some way to use the influence of state-level committees to enhance the teacher's role rather than diminish it? How should state-level directives influence classroom instruction? It is reasonable to expect that teachers will address the objectives in some fashion, but how can this best be accomplished? If performance on a specific list of objectives is used to define success, how do we ensure that essential or minimal standards are not turned into maximum standards? Finally, what is the appropriate linkage between state-level objectives and teaching materials? Should schools adopt a basal series whose scope and sequence chart most closely matches the state's performance objectives? Again, how do we ensure that teaching materials do not simply become practice materials for the state tests?

The sixth issue became painfully evident as we attempted to address Kentucky Senate Bill 169. Recall that the purpose of this bill was to ensure that each pupil would master the essential skills in reading. What happens to students who do not meet the standards? Should, for example, third-grade teachers and third-grade children be expected to deal with an older child who should be in the eighth grade, but who has not passed the test? Remedial education is expensive and the public has shown little willingness to support it. If performance objectives are to be workable then they must be linked to some sort of remedial program. The kind of remedial program that is best for such children needs to be determined.

SUMMARY

One of the least examined contexts of literacy is that found when committees meet to formulate and implement state-level reading policy. This chapter focused on some of the difficulties that reading researchers have when using current research to inform that policy. Two problems, in particular, were identified. The first comes from a difference in agenda between researchers and policy makers. The second is related to the difference in how reading is conceptualized and to the ambiguities in the language used to discuss those differences. Finally, a number of issues were raised that need to be addressed if current research is to have a beneficial impact on state-level reading policy. I would like to conclude by pointing out that the policies formulated by state-level reading committees can be extremely useful in the effort to improve reading instruction. Let us hope that we are wise enough to use them constructively.

REFERENCES

Baratz, J. C. (1978). Policy issues in education: Reading and the law. In R. J. Harper & G. Kilarr (Eds.), *Reading and the Law* (pp. 11-15). Newark, Del.: International Reading Association.

Bower, G. H. (1978). Experiments on story comprehension and recall. *Discourse Processes, 1,* 211-231.

Broudy, H. S. (1972). *The real world of the public schools.* New York, N.Y.: Harcourt Brace Jovanovich.

Caplan, N. (1979). The two-communities theory and knowledge utilization. *American Behavior Scientist, 22,* 459-470.

Cox, C. B. (1975). Responsibility, culpability, and the cult of accountability in education. *Phi Delta Kappan, 58,* 761-765.

Drew, K. (February 12, 1984). "Look-and-say" reading method draws ire of author. *The Paducah Sun,* Paducah, Ky., E4.

Durkin, D. (1966). *Children who read early.* New York: Teachers College Press.

Goodlad, J. I. (1975). A perspective on accountability. *Phi Delta Kappan, 57,* 108-112.

Guthrie, J. T. (1981). Reading in New Zealand: Achievement and volume. *Reading Research Quarterly, 17,* 6-27.

Harper, R. J., & Kilarr, G. (1978). The changing theory of the reading process: Does society really know how it reads? In R. J. Harper & G. Kilarr (Eds.), *Reading and the law* (pp. 53-65). Newark, Del.: International Reading Association.

Jackson, P. W. (1968). *Life in classrooms.* New York: Holt, Rinehart & Winston.

Johnson, D. D., & Barrett, T. C. (1981). Prose comprehension: A descriptive analysis of instructional practices. In C. M. Santa & B. L. Hayes (Eds.), *Children's prose comprehension, research and practice* (pp. 72-102). Newark, Del.: International Reading Association.

Johnston, P., & Winograd, P. (December 1983). *Passive failure in reading.* Paper presented at the National Reading Conference, Austin, Tex.

Laffey, J. L. (1973). Accountability: A brief history and analysis. In R. B. Ruddell (Ed.), *Accountability and reading instruction: Critical issues* (pp. 1-11). Urbana, Ill.: National Council of Teachers of English.

Lindblom, C. E., & Cohen, D. K. (1979). *Usable knowledge: Social science and social problem solving.* New Haven, Conn.: Yale University Press.

Meyer, B. J., Brandt, D. M., & Bluth, G. J. (1980). Use of top-level structure in text: Key for reading comprehension of ninth-grade students. *Reading Research Quarterly, 16,* 72-103.

Nicholls, J. (1983). Conceptions of ability and achievement: A theory and its implications for education. In S. Paris, G. Olson, & H. Stevenson (Eds.), *Learning and motivation in the classroom* (pp. 211-237). Hillsdale, N.J.: Erlbaum.

Otto, W. (1977). Design for developing comprehension skills. In J. T. Guthrie (Ed.), *Cognition, curriculum, and comprehension* (pp. 193-232). Newark, Del.: International Reading Association.

Page, W. (1978). What kind of reading will the law prescribe? In R. J. Harper & G. Kilarr (Eds.) *Reading and the law,* (pp. 37-44). Newark, Del.: International Reading Association.

Schwille, J., Porter, A., & Gant, M. (1979). *Content decision-making and the politics of education.* Research Series No. 52. East Lansing, Michigan State Univerisity, The Institute for Research on Teaching.

Shannon, P. (1983). The use of commercial reading materials in American elementary schools. *Reading Research Quarterly, 19,* 68- 85.

Weir, M. W. (1983). Social science and social policy: A role for universities. In S. G. Paris, G. M. Olson, & H. W. Stevenson (Eds.), *Learning and motivation in the classroom* (pp. 307-320). Hillsdale, N.J.: Erlbaum.

Wixson, K. K., & Peters, C. W. (1984). Reading redefined: A Michigan Reading Association position paper. *The Michigan Reading Journal, 17,* 4-7.

17

Research into Practice:
Cautions and Qualifications

Christopher M. Clark

Earlier chapters in this volume have made a convincing case that the acquisition of literacy can be both enabled and constrained by the social context in which reading and writing are taught, learned, and used. Learning and teaching are social processes, and so is research on literacy and its dissemenation. The delicate process of establishing constructive links between research on literacy and the teaching of reading and writing depends on how teachers and researchers think about and act toward one another.

This chapter is addressed to both teachers and educational researchers. The message is an optimistic one, namely, that research on teaching and school learning can be even more useful to practicing teachers than it has been in the past. To realize this desirable state I believe that teachers and researchers must begin to think more flexibly and creatively about the nature and roles of educational research, the needs of the practical world of schools and classrooms, and new ways in which their two communities can communicate in mutually helpful ways. The chapter is divided into four sections, each headed by an exhortation: Let's get humble! Let's demand service! Let's get creative! and Let's get communicating! I hope that this chapter will serve as a constructive step in encouraging more use of educational research in the service of teaching.

Work on this chapter was sponsored by the Institute for Research on Teaching, College of Education, Michigan State University. The Institute for Research on Teaching is funded primarily by the Program for Teaching and Instruction of the National Institute of Education, United States Department of Education. The opinions expressed in this publication do not necessarily reflect the position, policy, or endorsement of the National Institute of Education. (Contract No. 400-81-0014)

LET'S GET HUMBLE!

Like many virtues, humility is a great deal easier to prescribe than to practice. As John Wesley said, "It is difficult to be humble. Even if you aim at humility, there is no guarantee that when you have attained the state you will not be proud of the feat." When I call for humility in connection with educational research and teaching what I am urging is a more modest sense of proportion about the size and scope of what social science has to offer practice. In research proposals and in the introductions to textbooks educational researchers often claim that the fundamental bedrock of effective teaching is, or should be, empirical research. "Research based" is a much sought-after prefix for texts, curricula, and teacher education programs, not unlike the Good Housekeeping Seal of Approval. The old saying, "To the carpenter, the world is made of wood," can also be applied to some educational researchers who tend to value teaching to the extent that it reflects their own research.

But, in my view, teaching is not primarily an applied science. Rather, teaching is a complex social, personal, political, and interactive human process. Empirical research on teaching and learning can be one element of what teachers take into account in their planning and teaching, but only one of many. Research can *inform* practice, but research—because of self-imposed constraints—can be much too narrow or highly constrained to literally serve as a *foundation* for practice.

One approach that I believe would help us to be more appropriately humble about the role of research in informing practice is to take some of the mystery out of the research process. People have a tendency to be somewhat awed by very complex research designs, analysis methods, and jargon-laden reports of results. Sometimes the complexity is necessary and the special technical terms crucial for precise expression of meaning. But meaning is obscured and potential usefulness to teachers reduced by unnecessarily complex designs and excessive use of technical terminology.

It helps me to reduce the mystery surrounding research in education when I remind myself that, when you boil them down, all research reports consist of descriptions of researcher's experiences and ideas. These experiences and ideas may be expressed in numbers or in words, more or less clearly, but there is always a person or group of persons behind the words and numbers. And these persons, the researchers, are not inaccessible beings set apart and somehow quite different from the other members of the community of educators. On the whole, they are quite willing to return telephone calls, respond to letters, and come to conferences to talk, to listen, to learn, and to teach. So perhaps one of the most valuable resources we have as a profession is access to dedicated and intelligent people who have spent years thinking about, observing, and writing about topics and situations that are of importance to educators.

At the same time it is important to remember that the world's foremost expert on a particular classroom or school setting is the teacher in that setting. The experience and expertise of a teacher may sometimes be enhanced or helpfully focussed by drawing on the experiences of others outside the classroom. But, in the final analysis, teachers are the planners, decision makers, and actors who have the most imtimate knowledge of and greatest influence in their classrooms. Teaching, like research, can be a constructively humbling experience.

LET'S DEMAND SERVICE!

The idea that the main role of research and researchers is to *serve* teachers is new and has not yet swept through the profession like wildfire. The concept of service is not well developed in our profession. But for teachers to be able to make more appropriate use of research and researchers' experience, a richer, more positive conception of service must emerge. Part of this new notion of service will have to be worked out in practice between individual researchers and teachers. What I have to offer to this process is a list of four ways in which research on teaching, and the researchers themselves, might serve teachers. The four modes of service are: information, inspiration, vision, and support.

Information

The most typical way in which research has served the practice of teaching is by providing information. The journals are full of descriptions of how teaching and learning worked under various conditions and in various settings. Most of this information is presented at a general level, having been derived from the averaging of many observations of many individuals or classes. And most of the information found in the research literature pertains to specific questions or hypotheses formed by the researchers. From a social science point of view this is good, reliable information. But precise answers to researchers' questions are unlikely to be of service to teachers. And general principles and average trends are as likely to misinform as to inform a particular classroom teacher dealing with a particular individual child.

So, in terms of information, the vast bulk of the research literature will be of little practical use to any particular teacher. This is not to say that such research should be stopped. Rather, we should treat the research literature on, say, literacy, as a kind of encyclopedia that we consult for information as we need it, with our own specific questions in mind and with a clear sense of the applicability of that information to our particular situation.

Inspiration

A second way in which research can serve practice is to provide inspiration. By inspiration I mean a picture of how schooling could be different, could be better, could become the world we imagined when we first signed on to become teachers. As the literary critic and historian Walter Pater wrote 100 years ago: "We need some imaginative stimulus, some not impossible ideal such as may shape vague hope, and transform it into effective desire, to carry us year after year, without disgust, through the routine-work which is so large a part of life" (*Marius the*

Epicurean, Chap. 25). I certainly need such a guiding pillar of cloud by day and pillar of fire by night to get me through the school year, and I think that research is one possible source of such inspiration.

My favorite example of an inspiring bit of research is the book *In the Early World* by Elwyn S. Richardson (1964). It was published in 1964 as Educational Research Series No. 42, by the New Zealand Council of Educational Research, so it certainly qualifies as research. (Sadly, I've heard that the book is now out of print.) The book is about learning to be literate in poetry, science, art, and community building in a two-room country school in New Zealand. The report spans a five-year period of life at Oruaiti School and is rich with the words and artifacts produced by the children and the stories behind the artifacts. *In the Early World* is the most vivid example of complete integration of learning with life, art with science, and people with people that I have ever read.

Now, the point of this example is not to urge you to recreate or to imitate the Oruaiti School of 20 years ago in the Utah or Michigan of today. No, the inspiration for me comes from knowing and being able to visualize a time and place in which, with simple materials, ordinary children, and a bit of imagination and risk-taking one teacher was able to foster the kinds of integrated learning experience that I value. Knowing that it is possible, knowing that it *did* happen, seeing the beautiful evidence in the haiku from which the book borrows its title, all of these help me to search for that extra spark, that constructive riskiness in my own teaching.

> The blue heron stands in the early world,
> Looking like a freezing blue cloud in the morning.
>
> —Irene

Vision

Research can serve to broaden and sharpen our vision of the world of schooling by offering us concepts, models, and theories through which we can see our familiar surroundings in new ways. I believe that professional boredom and burnout result, in part, from the feeling that one is trapped in a thoroughly predictable situation that is unlikely to change. But, even in such situations, it is possible to see the situation differently, with the help of an outsider's point of view. When anthropologists work in their own culture, as when ethnographers of education study American public school classrooms, one of their biggest challenges is to "make the familiar strange," to see with new eyes what they have learned to take for granted. When research provides tools for seeing the practical setting of the classroom in new ways, researchers are indeed serving practice.

An example of research in the service of vision comes from my own work with Susan Florio-Ruane on school writing. One analysis of a year-long descriptive study of the teaching of writing in elementary and middle school involved categorizing writing assignments on the basis of their forms and functions (Florio & Clark, 1982). Each of the major occasions for writing observed were sorted into one of four function categories: (1) writing to participate in community, (2) writing to know oneself and others, (3) writing to occupy free time, and (4) writing to demonstrate academic competence. And each function category was described in terms of its initiator, composer, writer, audience, format, fate, and evaluation. The importance of this example is not that the researchers' analysis is elegant, logical, and supported by data, or that the study was published in the journal *Research in the Teaching of English*. No, its importance lies in the fact that this descriptive framework helped at least one teacher to see his own classroom differently as an environment for writing. He used the form and function categories from our research to examine the opportunities that his own students had to write, to plan for changes in his curriculum, and to ask more penetrating questions about writing activity ideas that came his way. In short, this teacher used research to come to a new vision of what his teaching was and could be.

Support

Finally, research can serve practicing teachers by providing them with support for what they are already doing well. All too often, in my opinion, research in education is seen exclusively as a force for change. Usually, a call for change implies that what has gone before is faulty, inefficient, or inadequate to the task. Yet we know that American public schools are among the best in the world, and that truly terrible, damaging, and incompetent teaching is rare.

At the same time, teaching is an isolating and potentially lonely profession in which individual teachers rarely have the time or opportunity to learn about and discuss how their own teaching compares with others'. While research reports are certainly not a substitute for professional dialogue among teachers, research on teaching can provide both evidence for and explanation why good teaching works as it does.

In this connection, I think of an example from research on teacher planning. A number of studies of planning for the teaching of writing (reviewed in Clark, 1983) have confirmed that experienced teachers do not follow the so-called "rational model" of planning typically prescribed in teacher education programs (i.e., define learning objectives, generate alternatives, choose the optimum alternative, teach, and evaluate). Rather, teachers typically start with an idea for a writing activity, which they elaborate and adapt to their own classroom situations. Further, this research has documented the elaborate interconnections among different levels of teacher planning (e.g., yearly, term, unit, weekly, and daily planning). This line of research can be taken as supportive of teachers in at least two ways. First, it offers support to those teachers who do their planning in ways that are apparently adaptive to the complexity and constraints of the real classroom, but who might also feel guilty for not following the model that they were trained to use as undergraduates. Second, this research is a step toward acknowledging some of the invisible and unappreciated demands of the teaching profession and toward describing aspects of teaching that are truly professional in the sense that the work of designers, physicians, and lawyers is professional.

So, when I say, "Let's demand service!" what I am calling for is a combination of information, inspiration, vision, and support. Part of the responsibility for serving teachers rests with researchers; in the ways that they design their studies, share what they have learned, and call on practicing teachers to cooperate in the process. And part of the responsibility lies with teachers, who can begin to seek and also call for more relevant information, as well as inspiration, vision, and support from the research community.

LET'S GET CREATIVE!

When I call for more creativity in this context, I am calling for better ways to use the resources already available in the service of teaching. I am reminded of the brother of a neighbor of mine who worked for Libby Foods. For years he saw Libby discarding tons and tons of pumpkin seeds as a waste product of the processing of pie filling. After much stove-top experimentation he invented a snack food of processed pumpkin seeds that is now being marketed nationally. I'd like to apply that same kind of creativity to the research literature that we already have on the shelf to try to realize more of the potential that is there but is currently wasted.

Briefly, my proposition is that there are six different but related kinds of products of research on teaching that can be used to enrich the practice of teaching. The six classes of research outcomes are: (1) observed relationships among variables, (2) concepts, (3) theoretical models, (4) questions, (5) methods of inquiry, and (6) case studies. My hope is that by thinking more broadly and divergently about what research on teaching has to offer we might improve both the research on teaching enterprise and the practice of teaching itself. At the very least, both communities may come to believe that the grounds on which they could meet are larger in area and more varied and interesting in terrain than is typically thought. I will now discuss briefly each of the six classes of outcome of research on teaching, giving examples as I proceed.

Observed Relationships among Variables

Classically, the fruits of the research process are expressed as "findings and implications." The findings part of this dyad consist of brief summary descriptions of the observed relationships among variables studied, while the implications are inferences drawn by the researchers that typically go beyond the data. To oversimplify, findings are observed facts about the world and implications are what the investigator believes these facts suggest about how practitioners should behave in situations similar to the experimental one. The facts that many researchers on teaching pursue consist of causal statements about the relationship between particular teacher behaviors and measured student achievement. Still other kinds of facts about teaching have been pursued by researchers on teacher thinking who have sought to describe how teachers plan, process information, and make decisions (see Clark & Peterson, 1984). Both behaviorally and cognitively oriented research have played important roles in establishing research on teaching as a distinct and even thriving field, but the direct translation of findings and implications into prescriptions for teaching and teacher education has not worked well, for all of the reasons articulated by Cronbach (1975), Fenstermacher (1979), Phillips (1980), Floden and Feiman (1981), and Eisner (1984). In my judgement, the findings of research on teaching that describe observed realtionships among teacher and student visible or cognitive behaviors are the least likely to be directly useful in the classroom.

However, I do have a suggestion that might yield additional mileage from reexamination of this research. I have long believed that ineffective teaching—poor teaching, if you will—is due less to the absence of particular effective strategies and teacher behaviors than it is a consequence of the presence of things that teachers sometimes do that sabotage what could otherwise be good teaching. When, for example, students are faced with double binds and mixed messages about competition and cooperation, meritocracy and egalitarianism, equality of opportunity and self-fulfilling prophecies about the normal distribution of achievement, even technically excellent teaching may have mediocre effects. What I propose is to rephrase the big question of researchers on teaching effectiveness from "What kind of teaching (or teacher thinking) works best in almost all situations? (a discouraging question to pursue) to "What have some teachers done sometimes that have fouled things up?" Taking this perspective, could a reexamination of the literature of research on teaching yield ideas about what some of these avoidable impediments to good teaching and school learning are? And would it not make sense to include attention to these empirically observed impediments and pitfalls in our teacher preparation and professional development program? (Remember that the Ten Commandments have stood up for so long, in part, because they constitute a short list largely about what we should *not* do, rather than detailed prescription of what we should do. Perhaps proscriptions are more generalizable than prescriptions.)

The researchers who did the original work may have to be the ones who lead the search for evidence of impediments to good teaching, because explicit attention is seldom given to this side of teaching effectiveness when a study is first reported. Such evidence is more often present in the parts of the story that are left out of journal articles and technical reports or in sometimes speculative explanations of surprising or seemingly paradoxical findings. To illustrate from my own work, I was part of a team that did a laboratory study of teacher planning and teaching effectiveness in 1974 (Peterson, Marx, & Clark, 1978). One of our surprising findings was that among 12 teachers who thought aloud while planning there was a significant negative correlation between the number of planning statements they made and their students' postteaching achievement scores. Paradoxically, more planning was associated with lower achievement, and that is where we left matters in 1978. Now, with several years of hindsight, I believe that there is a more satisfying and logical explanation for this anomaly: the teachers with the largest number of planning statements were those who focussed their attention almost exclusively on reading and reviewing content to be taught, giving little or no planning time to the process of instruction. These teachers (legitimately) used their planning time as a study and curriculum review session and emerged with increased knowledge of their subject matter, but without a well-thought-out plan for instruction. This leads me to make a practical suggestion: that teachers and prospective teachers should pay attention to how they spend their planning time and what the balance is between attention to subject matter and attention to instructional process. Novices, especially, should be cautioned that planning for teaching is different from studying for a test (even though there is sometimes a testlike quality to observed sessions of practice teaching).

Concepts

A second category of outcomes of research on teaching is concepts. By concepts I mean verbal labels for phenomena that researchers have found useful in describing the dynamics of the classroom, aspects of teaching and school learning, and curriculum. From the researchers' point of view, concepts about teaching are seen as a means to the end of defining variables and subsequently measuring strength and direction of relationships among those variables. But my claim is that concepts themselves, when they are usefully descriptive of teaching, can be seen as valuable products of research on teaching. Examples of concepts of this kind include academic learning time (Fisher et al., 1980), academic work (Doyle, 1983), wait time (Rowe, 1974), the steering group (Lundgren 1972), withitness (Kounin, 1970), incremental planning (Clark & Yinger, 1979), and the occasion for writing (Clark & Florio, 1982). There are many more concepts of this kind that originated in research on teaching that are not obvious to the naive observer of the practice of teaching and that should be a part of the conceptual vocabulary of teachers. Concepts help us to organize, make sense of, communicate about, and reflect on our experiences. A teacher education or professional development program that equips its graduates with some of the means to make meaning, communicate, and reflect is on the right track.

Theoretical Models

A third kind of product of research on teaching that has potential application in teacher education is the theoretical model. By this I mean verbal or graphic representations of the relationships among concepts in teaching-learning situations. Theoretical models can serve all of the fuctions that I have attributed to concepts, and they also provide a more comprehensive framework for thinking about and perceiving classrooms in their complexity. Examples of theoretical models and constructs that could serve these purposes include the Carroll Model of School Learning (Carroll, 1963), Shavelson and Stern's (1981) and Peterson and Clark's (1978) models of teacher interactive decision making, Yinger's (1977) process model of teacher planning, and the participation structure model of the classroom (Phillips, 1972; Shultz, Florio, & Erickson, 1982). It is important, I believe, that abstractions of the kind that these models represent be taken as heuristic and suggestive rather than as prescriptions for "the correct way to think about teaching." Indeed, their principal value to educators may be that exposure to multiple theoretical models could encourage teachers to examine, make explicit, and refine their own implicit theories.

Questions

The fourth product of research on teaching on my list is questions. Here I commend to you both questions that are posed at the outset of a study and used to guide inquiry (typically called *research questions*) and also questions that are raised later when researchers are trying to make sense of the data and when calling for additional research. A teacher can learn a great deal about how to think about what is problematic in teaching by learning what the challenging and partially answered questions are that thoughtful researchers are asking. Even (or perhaps especially) when questions seem to have no definitive answer, they can serve to orient professional reflection. Similarly, researchers could learn a great deal from taking the concerns and dilemmas of practicing teachers into account as they frame the questions that guide their research. Examples of generative questions that are being addressed by researchers on teaching include: Why is writing so difficult to teach? What are the possibilities and limitations of small-group cooperative learning? What makes some schools more effective than others? What roles do textbooks play in school learning? How can individual differences in student aptitudes for learning be accomodated? What roles do teacher planning, judgement, and decision making play in classroom instruction? How do teachers' implicit theories affect their perceptions and behavior?

Methods of Inquiry

Fifth, research on teaching can be a source of methods of inquiry by inventing, demonstrating, and discovering the limitations of various techniques and tools for describing and understanding teaching. Teacher educators and teachers need ways of seeing, describing, and analyzing the complexities of teaching that go beyond what one can do with unstructured live observations. Researchers have developed many category systems for counting and rating the quality of teacher-student interaction (Simon & Boyer, 1970), including some that focus on dyadic interaction between the teacher and particular students (e.g., Brophy & Good, 1974). The technology of microteaching was originally developed to meet the needs of researchers on teaching and has been adopted as a useful part of many teacher preparations programs. More resently, researchers studying teachers' thought processes have employed stimulated recall, think aloud procedures, and structured journal writing to make visible the formerly hidden world of teaching. And practitioners of the ethnography of classrooms have provided us with clear examples of what their methodology can accomplish as well as improved guidelines for how to pursue this kind of inquiry and what some of its limitations are. All of these methods of inquiry offer interesting possibilities for adaptation in teacher preparation and professional development programs if an important goal of continuing education is to equip teachers to be reflective, analytic, and constructively critical of their own teaching.

Case Studies

Sixth, and finally, research on teaching has recently been producing case studies—rich and thick descriptions of classroom events ranging in duration from a few moments to an entire school year. Case studies can serve a number of valuable purposes for teachers, including illustration of concepts and theoretical models in context, providing opportunities to analyze and reflect on real classroom events from a variety of disciplinary points of view and illustrating how the perspective held by the researchers shapes and limits the form and content of the resulting case study. At Michigan State University my colleagues Robert Floden, Susan Florio-Ruane, and I have been using case studies from research on teaching to serve these purposes in our undergraduate and graduate education courses in educational psychology, the philosophy of education, and language arts methods.

In summary, I believe that research on teaching has a great deal to offer to the practice of teaching if we think more broadly than we are accustomed to about what research actually produces. Observed relationships among operationally defined variables in a particular study may be the primary product of research for the audience of other researchers. But teachers can and should be helped to become reflective and autonomous professionals by sharing with them the concepts, models, questions, methods of inquiry, and case studies that research on teaching also produces. Teachers, so prepared, must still face complex and demanding problem-solving situations in their own classrooms, and research on teaching probably will not make the process of teaching simpler. But creative use of the unexploited outcomes of research on teaching can be used to make teaching more appropriately complex.

LET'S GET COMMUNICATING!

My fourth and final exhortation, "Let's get communicating!", concerns the conditions for and methods of discourse between researchers and teachers and among teachers themselves. My claim is that neither teachers nor researchers are very adept at professional communication about professional matters. I suspect that none of us are fully satisfied by the traditional media of journal articles, textbooks, half-day in-service workshops, or evening and summer courses at the local university. Even when done well, these traditional approaches to professional communication fall short of genuine service to teachers.

For the past three years I have been working in a nontraditional format for professional communication called the Michigan State University Written Literacy Forum. The Forum is a collaborative effort by teachers and researchers aimed at developing effective means of bringing research on the teaching of writing into practice. Founded in September, 1981, the Forum has conducted inquiry into the relationship between written literacy research and practice through two kinds of activity: (1) Forum deliberations, in which the nine members (five teachers and four researchers) discussed and analyzed key issues in the teaching of writing, and (2) planning, delivery, and reflection on in-service workshops on writing instruction. In both of these major activities we drew from the substantial data base (Clark & Florio, et al., 1982) collected in the Michigan State University Written Literacy Project (in which all initial Forum members were participants), research literature on writing instruction, and extensive field experiences of the teachers and researchers themselves. By these means we sought to develop thoroughly grounded and practical ways of bringing the fruits of research on writing into action in the classroom.

The Written Literacy Forum was created as one possible answer to the challenge of bringing research and practice together. In creating it we attempted to modify the traditional culture of research that defines teachers as "subjects," researchers as "data analysts," and teacher educators as "change agents." Each participant in the Written Literacy Forum takes on all of these roles and more. New social, methodological, and theoretical forms developed as we collectively reflected on the teaching and learning of writing in schools. The Forum extends the conventional boundaries of teaching, research, and teacher education. In the affirmative social context of the Forum, trust and dialogue arose, yielding not only increased knowledge about the process of writing instruction but insight as well into the process of professional development as it is experienced by practitioners and researchers alike.

One example of the influence of Forum deliberations on our research agenda evolved from discussions by Forum teachers of the practical problem of when and how to provide constructive feedback to students during the composition process. This issue appeared to be a substantial problem for teachers from the primary grades through high school. Cases in which this problem was seen as serious were contrasted with situations in which providing constructive feedback was not problematic. These discussions, and the insights and questions that they stimulated, led to the drafting of a preliminary model of the process of school writing instruction that emphasizes social and contextual influences on the teaching of writing. This preliminary model is being elabaorated and tested in the current work of the Forum.

Forum deliberations have also influenced the practice of teaching. One example involves a primary-grade teacher and Forum member who reports that she has dramatically increased the number of opportunities for her students to do writing for audiences other than herself. This teacher attributes her decision to promote writing for audiences outside the classroom to her participation in Forum discussions of two issues: the fundamental function of writing as a medium that can bridge time and distance and the importance of writing activities feeling meaningful and consequential to authors. (Our earlier research on written literacy indicated that activities that seemed to students to have no purpose beyond pleasing the teacher were difficult to manage and rarely produced good writing.) The importance of this change in a teacher's practice lies not in the particulars of how she teaches differently. Rather, it is more significant that she has internalized a new question to pursue as she builds her own writing curriculum: How can I make this activity more meaningful and consequential for the young author?

My experience during the first three years of the Written Literacy Forum suggests that professional communication can be raised to new levels of usefulness when we invest the time and energy it takes to make it happen. Writing was a good choice of focus for our deliberations because it is a richly problematic part of the curriculum. But I see no reason why the Forum concept would not work equally well if the focus were other than writing. The general point holds: bringing the fruits of research into practice seems to require an intermediate step in which intelligent practitioners, through deliberation, make the important connections and adaptations themselves. As a researcher I may be able to facilitate this process a bit, but I certainly cannot expect to force my models on unwilling teachers. Face-to-face communication among teachers and between teachers and researchers is crucial to bringing research into practice.

CONCLUSION

In conclusion, teachers and researchers must cooperate if research on teaching is to be of real service to teaching. We need to get humble, to demand service, to get creative, and to communicate. Pursuing these four exhortations will look quite different in different professional settings. Unless we all take care to pursue each of them, research and practice will continue to go their separate ways.

REFERENCES

Baker, E. L. (1984). Can educational research inform educational practice? Yes! *Phi Delta Kappan*, 65 (March), 453–455.

Brophy, J. E., & Good, T. L. (1974). *Teacher-student relationships: Causes and consequenses*. New York: Holt, Rinehart and Winston.

Carroll, J. B. (1963). A model of school learning. *Teachers College Record*, 64, 723–733.

Clark, C. M. (1983). Research on teacher planning: An inventory of the knowledge base. In D. C. Smith (Ed.), *Essential knowledge for beginning educators*, 5–15. Washington, D. C.: American Association of Colleges for Teacher Education, 5–15.

Clark, C. M., & Florio (1982). *Understanding writing in school: A descriptive case study of writing and its instruction in two classrooms*. Research Series No. 104. East Lansing; Michigan State University, Institute for Research on Teaching.

Clark, C. M., & Peterson, P. L. (1984) *Teachers' thought processes*. Occasional Paper No. 72. East Lansing: Michigan State University, Institute for Research on Teaching.

Clark, C. M., & Yinger, R. J. (1979). *Three studies of teacher planning*. Research Series No. 55. East Lansing; Michigan State University, Institute for Research on Teaching.

Cronbach, L. J. (1975). Beyond the two disciplines of scientific psychology. *American Psychologist*, 30, 116–126.

Doyle, W. (1983). Academic work. *Review of Educational Research*, 53, 159–199.

Eisner, E. W. (1984). Can educational research inform educational practice? *Phi Delta Kappan*, 65, (March) 447–452.

Fenstermacher, G. D. (1979) A philosophical consideration of recent research on teacher effectiveness. In L. S. Shulman (Ed), *Review of research in education*, (157–185). Itasca, Ill.: Peacock.

Fisher, C. W. et al. (1980). Teaching behaviors, academic learning time, and student achievement: An overview. In C. Denham & A. Lieberman (Eds.), *Time to learn* (7–32). Washington, D.C.: National Institute of Education.

Floden, R. E., & Feiman, S. (1981). Should teachers be taught to be rational? *Journal of Education for Teachers*, 7, 274–283.

Florio, S., & Clark, C. M. (1982). The functions of writing in an elementary classroom. *Research in the Teaching of English*, 16, 115–130.

Kounin, J. (1970). *Discipline and group management in classrooms*. New York: Holt, Rinehart & Winston.

Lundgren, U. P. (1972). *Frame factors and the teaching process*. Stockholm: Almquist & Wiksell.

Peterson, P. L., & Clark, C. M. (1978). Teachers' reports of their cognitive processes during teaching. *American Educational Research Journal*, 15, 555–565.

Peterson, P. L., Marx, R. W., & Clark, C. M. (1978). Teacher planning, teacher behavior, and student achievement. *American Educational Research Journal*, 15, 417–432.

Phillips, D. C. (1980). What do the researchers and the practitioners have to offer each other? *Educational Researcher*, 9, 17–24.

Philips, S. U. (1972). Participation structures and communicative competence: Warm Springs children in community and classroom. In C. B. Cazden, V. John, & D. Hymes (Eds.), *Functions of language in the classroom*, 370–394. New York: Teachers College Press.

Richardson, E. S. (1964). *In the early world*. Wellington, New Zealand: New Zealand Council of Educational Research.

Rowe, M. B. (1974). Wait time and rewards as instructional variables, their influence on language, logic, and fate control: Part one—Wait time. *Journal of Research in Science Teaching*, 11, 81–94.

Shavelson, R. J., & Stern, P. (1981). Research on teachers' pedagogical thoughts, judgements, decisons, and behavior. *Review of Educational Research*, 51, 455–498.

Shultz, J., Florio, S., & Erickson, F. (1982). Where's the floor? Aspects of the cultural organization of social relationships in communication at home and at school. In P. Gilmore & A. Glatthorn (Eds.), *Children in and out of school: Ethnography and education* (pp. 88–123). Washington, D.C.: Center for Applied Linguistics.

Simon, A., & Boyer, E. G. (Eds.) (1970). Mirrors for behavior II: An anthology of observational instruments. *Classroom Interaction Newsletter*, special edition.

Yinger, R. J. (1977). *A study of teacher planning: Description and theory development using ethnographic and information processing methods*. Ph.D. diss., Michigan State University.

18

Contexts of School-Based Literacy: A Look toward the Future

Taffy E. Raphael

Each chapter in this volume has focused on the contexts in which students acquire written literacy through schooling. The guiding definition for the term *contexts* in this volume has been derived from several sources that emphasize the social and psychological, as well as physical, nature of educational settings (e.g., Bloome, 1985; Erickson & Schultz, 1981). Contexts take many forms from the observable physical environment in which instruction and participation in reading and writing exist, to the unobservable psychological context that individual readers, writers, and teachers bring to and create in the school setting. Essentially, we have assumed that contexts are constituted by what people are doing (e.g., academic tasks), as well as by when (e.g., historical period), where (e.g., school settings), and why (e.g., acquisition of written literacy) they are doing it. This definition provides the basis for examining the complexity of the environments in which literacy develops, including the multitude of encompassing and overlapping contexts: historical, social, psychological, cultural, academic, and so forth. The term *literacy* in this volume has been defined as the ability to read and construct meaning, and the ability to compose meaningful texts; that is, it has been defined in terms of written literacy. Thus, the authors throughout this volume have examined the development of children's reading and writing abilities within school settings and the factors that influence this development.

In this chapter a conceptual framework is presented to facilitate understanding and integration of information presented throughout this volume about the variety, multiple levels, and overlapping nature of contexts related to school-based

Special thanks for the useful comments on earlier drafts of this chapter go to Linda Anderson, Carol Sue Englert, and Becky Kirschner.

literacy. The first section of this chapter presents this conceptual framework for thinking about the findings and viewpoints presented in the previous chapters, mapping each one onto the framework for later discussion and integration. The second section applies the conceptual framework to the four questions posed in the preface of this volume. The third section provides suggestions for future directions, particularly research integrating reading and writing, studying both within the instructional contexts in which they occur.

TOWARD A CONCEPTUAL FRAMEWORK FOR THE CONTEXTS OF SCHOOL-BASED LITERACY

Like so many of the chapters in this volume, the proposed framework for conceptualizing contexts of school-based literacy is based in a Vygotskian perspective. Vygotsky (1978) proposed three related contexts—historical-cultural, social, and individual—in which the nature of development can be analyzed. In the first chapter of this volume Gavelek applied these three contexts, or levels of analysis, to the development of written literacy in school. The framework proposed in this chapter is an adaptation of Vygotsky's. Like Vygotsky's, all other contexts are embedded in the historical-cultural context. Within it are the individual (e.g., developmental level, knowledge base) and the social (e.g., home, school, instruction-group settings) contexts identified by Vygotsky, as well as the psychological (e.g., individual's perceptions, motivations), and the academic (e.g., subject area, academic tasks) contexts. While not necessarily exhaustive in scope, the proposed framework is a means for providing structure to a complex concept. Figure 18.1 indicates the considerable overlap among and between contexts, all contributing to a child's general development, or in this specific case, the development of written literacy.

Contexts that Influence Literacy Development

Historical-Cultural Context Since the historical-cultural context is the one in which all others are embedded, it is not surprising that many of the chapters in this volume (as well as scholarly works from numerous other sources) have sought to explain it. Examining historical-cultural contexts involves determining the impact of events over time that have resulted in and constrain today's practices. One area that has influenced the way we view literacy derives from the growth of cognitive psychology, described in Pearson's chapter. This growth has influenced perceptions about the reading process changing the view of reading from predominantly passive and static (i.e., readers perceive what is on the printed page and can thus determine the meaning) to constructive, dynamic, and active (i.e., readers bring relevant background knowledge to the comprehension process, actively construct meaning, draw inferences, connect new to already-known information). Pearson's chapter extends work (e.g., Mathews, 1966; Resnick & Resnick, 1977) that has examined the development of literacy in society and in school settings.

A second strong contextual influence on the way one thinks about practices

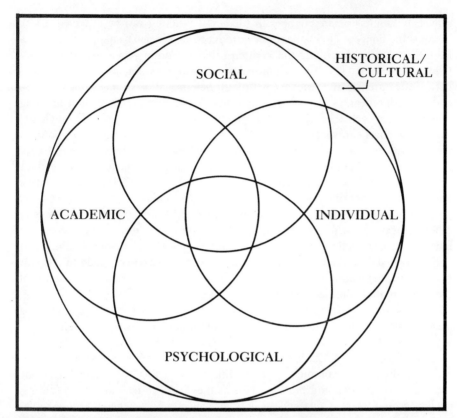

Figure 18.1 A Conceptual Framework for the Contexts of School-Based Literacy

for developing children's literacy is the culture in which literacy instruction is embedded. Culture, like context, is a term that embodies a number of different aspects. These include ethnicity of students and teachers and the individual cultures of schools, classrooms, and reading groups (Carew & Lightfoot, 1979; Cazden, 1981; McDermott, 1976). Considered still more broadly, other cultures related to literacy and schooling are those of the district and state agencies directing schooling, and colleges training pre- and in-service teachers and producing the research that guides this training. In other words, culture represents the sum of our development historically, whether development is considered broadly (e.g., society's culture) or more specifically (e.g., a given classroom or reading group).

One culture that has had a significant impact on instruction in literacy is the culture of colleges of education, discussed by both Schwartz and Clark. Cultures are built around shared belief systems and knowledge bases. Schwartz presents a convincing argument for the need to change the fundamental belief systems and knowledge bases of future and in-service teachers if major change in school literacy curricula can be expected to occur. For example, teachers cannot be expected to provide links between reading and writing, or to promote reading as a constructive, active process unless they themselves have such an understanding. Further, teachers, policy makers, and others must trust those who are change agents (e.g., university faculty) before changes in literacy instruction can be expected. Clark expands the concept of collaboration introduced in Pearson's chapter as a means for future change, describing the Written Literacy Forum as one example of collaborative efforts. The Forum provides opportunities for frequent meetings between researchers and teachers, with joint determination of the problems to be addressed. In effect, as Rogoff describes, they are cocontributors to their learning environments, each leading the other to the problem-solving goal. Through the Forum, teachers can suggest areas they are interested in learning more about; in concert with researchers, these new directions in developing school-based literacy can be explored. Winograd continues this theme, taking as his focus the need for collaboration between those scholars suggesting change, and the policy makers and teachers responsible for the delivery of new curricula.

Within the historical contexts of school-based literacy are embedded several other contexts. Most of the chapters in this volume have dealt with factors that fall into the intersection of two or more of these contexts. In the next section each context is first described and related to literacy with references made to relevant chapters in this volume. Then the intersection of contexts is explored in terms of the chapters that consider them jointly.

Social Context   One context that has received much attention in current literature is that of the social context in which reading and writing occur (Au, 1980; Cazden, 1981; Florio & Clark, 1982; Green & Bloome, 1984; Hansen, this volume, Rubin & Bruce, this volume). Work in this area desribes the interactions that occur among children and their teachers as they learn to read and write (during reading groups, in peer interactions, in conferences with teachers). For example, reading has been treated historically as a solitary activity, occuring within the cognitive activity of the individual reader. Recently, however, the social context in which reading occurs has been emphasized. Bloome describes three dimensions of reading as a social process:

> First, all reading events involve a social context. Social interaction surrounds and influences interaction with a written text. Second, reading is a cultural activity. That is, reading has social uses which are an extension of people's day-to-day cultural doings. And third, reading is a socio-cognitive process. Through learning to read and through reading itself, children learn culturally appropriate information activities, values, and ways of thinking and problem solving. (1985, p. 134)

This decription of the impact of considering literacy learning as a social process foreshadows the intersection of contexts to be discussed later.

Psychological Context   A second context related to the development of school-based literacy is the psychological one. This context of literacy development includes the perceptions students have about themselves as learners, perceptions about others' (e.g., their teachers') perceptions of themselves, motivational factors that drive them to apply the skills of strategic reading, attitudinal factors that lead them to understand the value of reading, and so forth. Paris, Lipson, & Wixson (1983) discuss the importance of psychological factors in terms of the different types of knowledge readers bring to the task of reading. Declarative knowledge, for example, is represented by students' understanding that reading is getting meaning from print and that writing involves communicating ideas. Procedural knowledge is involved when students learn strategies such as using surrounding text to identify an unknown word, using brainstorming to generate topics for writing, or making predictions from titles and headings. However, without conditional knowledge—knowing in what contexts to apply the strategies, having the motivation to act strategically, and believing they *can* act strategically (Weinstein, this volume)—students will become neither successful readers nor writers.

Individual Learner   Closely related to the psychological context is a third context of school-based literacy: that of the individual learner. This context includes such factors as children's ability levels, their developmental level, and their unique and shared experiences, all of which bear on their ability to read and write. They may be motivated (psychologically) to apply strategic knowledge such as making a prediction, but without experiences from which to make a prediction they are unlikely to be successful. They may understand that one important function of writing is to communicate, and they may want to communicate, but if the topic is unfamiliar or the task too difficult they will not be able to write successfuly. Individual differences as students respond to factors in their environment is at the center of Wixson and Lipson's discussion of a contextual view of reading ability.

Nature of the Academic Task   The nature of the academic task is a fourth context, one at the root of many children's ability to participate in reading and writing tasks. This context includes such factors as the difficulty of the text to be read, the type of text to which readers or writers must respond (i.e., narrative or expository), the type of writing assignment (e.g., impromptu or revision of previous writing), the subject matter under consideration (e.g., social studies or science), and the amount of support and time allotted to a given assignment. Chapters by Mason, Stewart, and Dunning; Au and Kawakami; DeFord; and others examine the role of the academic task in describing how tasks in reading and writing are conveyed to students.

The Intersection of Contexts

As Figure 18.1 depicts, contexts cannot function or exist in isolation. Children's performance in written literacy settings is a fuction of transactions among (1) the social interactions that occur, (2) their psychological (i.e., affective, motivational, attitudinal) framework, (3) the knowledge and abilities individuals learn and bring to the task, and (4) the academic task they face. The examination of performance in the intersection of contexts is an operational definition of the contextual view of learning.

Wixson and Lipson (this volume) discuss these interactions in their presentation of a contextual view of reading ability and (dis)ability. Taken most broadly, they argue that the contextual view helps to explain why students experience success under some conditions and failure under others. They suggest that current diagnostic practices are limited because they ignore contextual factors that influence reading ability and its measurement. They examine the importance of defining the context of academic tasks. For example, they note that the diagnosis of a student using standardized tests is not immediately useful for remedial instruction. The tests, even those with many subskill sections, provide only global information. Diagnostic settings with standard testing procedures ignore the very powerful influence of aspects of the psychological contexts including attitude and motivation. Further, standardized tests do not account for the contextual effects of academic tasks in that they may use only story narratives, randomly vary familiarity of the text topics, or ignore types of expository text structures. Thus, providing remediation becomes problematic without understanding the circumstances under which the student may be successful or unsuccessful. Compounding the problem, those who interpret diagnostic data often ignore the influence and variation in the social contexts in which the diagnostic instruments are administered—such as the adminstration of formal standardized tests in a group setting, individually administered informal reading inventories, or informal teacher observation during reading-group instruction. Wixson and Lipson cite case studies that suggest different evaluations will emerge under each circumstance, and thus such information as social context is critical for planning corrective opportunities. In sum, Wixson and Lipson imply that the learner is at the center of a complex and interrelated set of contexts; ignoring this complexity only undermines attempts to develop successful readers able to perform in a variety of settings.

Social Context and Academic Tasks   A number of other authors provide examples of studying intersections of contexts of the classroom and the academic tasks. For example, in their chapters, both DeFord and Tierney, Leys, and Rogers studied the relationship between the social context of the classroom and children's performance in academic writing contexts. Their findings are related to those of Mason, Stewart, and Dunning who examined the relationship between the social context of the kindergarten classroom, particularly regarding reading instruction, and kindergarten children's perception of reading. Together, their research provides a picture of how the social context of the classroom and the academic tasks presented jointly affect the nature of written literacy. In writing, peer interaction during composing provides a sense of purpose and audience, affecting students' development of goals of written literacy. In reading, young students, through teacher-student and student-student interactions during reading instruction, develop a foundation for perceiving the goals of the reading process. Further, what a teacher specifically communicates during these interactions is crucial. In a classroom in which literature was the basis of instruction in literacy, students tended to write longer and more complex stories. Those in a classroom in which mastery learning of discrete skills was stressed tended to focus on mechanics and the avoidance of errors, rather than to take risks by focusing on the content itself. Thus, the social setting in concert with the academic environment jointly influenced children's perceptions of goals and the means to achieve them.

Social Context, Psychological Context, and Academic Tasks   Several authors examined the specific intersection of the contexts of academic tasks and the psychological and social settings in which these tasks are introduced. For example, Roehler, Duffy, and Meloth and Paris consider students' development of metacognitive awareness through teacher modeling and through clarity of teachers' explanations. Roehler, Duffy, and Meloth describe the need for teachers' scaffolding of psychological constructs used in reading, using direct explanation of cognitive processes. Paris is concerned specifically with the development of conditional knowledge, teaching students when and how to apply cognitive strategies learned during reading instruction to the context of academic tasks.

Social Contexts, Psychological Contexts, and Individuals   Weinstein considers the intersection of the individual, social, and psychological contexts in her studies. She notes that disparties between lower- and higher-achieving students increase as students progress through school and then examines factors that contribute to this disparity. Students' attitudes and motivations are among the strongest predictors of success in academic contexts. Conversely, lack of motivation may be at the root of poor performance. Many factors affect motivation, among them students' perceptions of themselves. As Weinstein observes, these perceptions are often based on students' capability. The impact of the social context, defined in terms of the atmosphere created by the teachers, in which the students' are or are not able to discern their academic levels, and the expectations for their academic success is a strong determinant of students' evaluation of their own abilities, and thus potentially a major contributing factor to their development of literacy.

Social Contexts and Academic Tasks   Fielding, Wilson, and Anderson examined the intersection of the social contexts and academic tasks in their exploration of relationships between reading outside the academic environment and children's successes within academic contexts. They found a strong positive relationship, with the obvious implication that children should be encouraged to do more home reading. Since it is difficult for the schools to directly influence what children do in the context of their homes, Fielding, Wilson, and Anderson examine the intersection of the home and school contexts. They provide concrete suggestions for school-based literacy activities that have the potential to increase home-based literacy pursuits, demonstrating not only how contexts naturally intersect but how teachers can promote the integration of contexts.

Social Context, Cultural Context, and Academic Tasks   Two chapters focus on the intersection of cultural (e.g., ethnic background), academic tasks (i.e., categorization, reading comprehension), and social (i.e., home and school) contexts. These chapters provide insight into different ways to structure the learning environment with sensitivity to children's experiences, to help construct their learning environment. The cross-cultural research of Rogoff provides the basis for her five suggestions for creating appropriate learning tasks both for parent-child and for teacher-student academic interactions. She suggests that teachers and parents scaffold their children's learning by structuring situations in which the children may not be able to succeed independently, but in which the children will succeed in cooperation with an adult. The adult does not provide the actual steps or answers, but provides enough clues so that the children can induce the next step, or are led to determine an appropriate answer.

The notion of scaffolding within academic settings is demonstrated by Au and Kawakami's experiences with teaching disadvantaged Hawaiian students more effective reading comprehension strategies. These children had not experienced success in traditional turn-taking contexts in regular classes, apparently because of their fundamentally different view of cooperation and turn taking. The Hawaiian students, comfortable with cooperative learning, could not function in traditional reading groups (Au & Mason, 1981). Au and Kawakami describe how a Vygotskian-based reading program that incorporates many of the features described by Rogoff, (e.g., scaffolding by an adult mediator, coconstruction of learning based on the children's responses) greatly improved the Hawaiian students' reading comprehension skills.

In summary, considering the contexts of school-based literacy is a complex process. The terms themselves have different interpretations. The components that make up the general term, *context*, are themselves different types of contexts, each influencing the development of literacy both directly and in interaction among each other. The chapters in this volume provide a sense of the contexts that provide a perspective from which we can interpret the research of today. In the next section we apply this research to characterizing contexts of written literacy as we know them, and as we would like them to be.

DISCUSSING PREFACE QUESTIONS

Four questions were raised at the outset of this volume, asking: (1) What is the contextual view of the development of literacy? (2) How can contexts for learning to read and for developing strategic readers be characterized? (3) How can contexts for developing children's understanding and use of the writing process be characterized? (4) What influences the development of appropriate contexts for learning to read and write? In this section, the research described in the first section will be considered briefly in terms of each question.

What is the Contextual View of the Development of Literacy?

The first question raised in this volume concerned a definition or description of the contextual view of the development of literacy. The contextual view suggests that literacy develops in concert with a variety of influences—the home, the school, the individual, the culture—and that effective instruction to promote literacy must consider the interactions among and between these contexts. Gavelek provided the overview of this position, with particular emphasis on the influence of Vygotsky's theories of development. He suggests that the development of higher levels of cognitive processes can be greatly influenced by the opportunities for literacy found in schools. The school environment must be structured to allow peer-peer interactions, student-teacher interactions, and teacher-group interactions, all of which can be designed to provide opportunities to use literacy in the service of higher-level cognitive goals. Rogoff expanded on the Vygotskian perspective, providing cross-cultural examples of the contextual view. Her contrasts between formal and informal schooling provide a basis for conclusions that learning in academic and nonacademic settings is largely a function of the scaffolding provided by the instructor (i.e., mediator of learning) and the joint participation of both learner and instructor in determining the amount of assistance necessary.

Throughout the book are examples of applications of the contextual view. This view was applied most directly to a reconceptualization of reading disability in the chapter by Wixson and Lipson discussed in the first section, while chapters by Hansen, by DeFord, and others develop similar themes. Taken together, these chapters—and others throughout the volume—suggest that literacy development is neither automatic within the biological and genetic makeup of the child nor subject only to responses to environmental stimuli. Rather, as Gavelek (this volume) discussed, instruction is at the heart of literacy development, with both learner and teacher structuring the context in which literacy develops.

How Can Contexts for Learning to Read and for Developing Strategic Readers Be Characterized?

The second question concerned how we can characterize effective contexts for developing strategic readers. The chapters in the second section provide extensive information from which to construct our characterization. First, it is clear that the development of effective readers happens both within and outside the traditional reading group. As Fielding, Wilson, and Anderson suggest, there is a strong positive relationship between skilled readers and the amount of time spent in reading for pleasure. Thus, one characteristic of effective contexts for developing strategic readers is the opportunity to read with direct guidance from the teacher and to read individually or in concert with peers. Second, related to providing a rich literate environment is the need to integrate reading and writing instruction as one way to increase opportunities to read. As Rubin and Bruce and as Hansen suggest, when writers share their writing, the distinctions between reading and writing tend to blur; opportunities for reading increase when children read their own written work to peers. Third, developing strategic readers requires scaffolding in teaching both cognitive and metacognitive knowledge and skills. Au and Kawakami and Roehler, Duffy, and Meloth provide evidence that the teachers' role constructing a supportive environment in both is crucial. Through their questions and through direct explanation teachers lead children to develop the strategies necessary to read and to reflect upon the meaning of what they have read. This reflection is important if new strategies and new knowledge are to become part of a child's own repertoire. Paris describes how one program—Informed

Strategies for Learning—can be used to make the connections between instruction in metacognitive strategies and children's independent learning from text. Finally, Mason, Stewart, and Dunning suggest that the initial environments in which children are exposed to written literacy shapes students' perceptions of the reading process.

How can Contexts for Developing Children's Understanding and Use of the Writing Process Be Characterized?

The third question concerned how we can characterize effective contexts for developing writers. The four chapters in the writing section of this volume follow the central theme that children must learn that writing is a communicative process with a variety of fuctions. How such a concept develops is based heavily on the environment in which writing is taught. DeFord's chapter describes how powerful the environment can be in shaping children's view of writing, which in turn shapes the type of writing they produce. Children in classrooms that focus on descrete skills (e.g., on mechanics, writing on highly constrained topics) produces writers who apparently have little sense of the purpose of writing, and are subject to "writer's welfare" (Graves, 1983)—unable to generate text or topic independently. Their products are often stilted and lack the authors' "voice." In contrast, children in literature-oriented classrooms produce writing based on literature, with well-developed story lines and a strong sense of the voice of the author.

Tierney, Leys, and Rogers draw similar conclusions after examining transcripts of teacher-student and student-student interactions during writing instruction. The implications of this research are clear. The context in which students write exerts a powerful influence on their potential development as writers. Weinstein's research shows how clearly students perceive the implicit messages of their teachers—it is perhaps predictable that such perceptions would hold true in their perceptions of themselves as writers as well as readers.

These authors have made it clear that changing contexts for writing instruction involves the collaboration of researchers, teachers, administrators, curriculum developers, and students. This message, stated eloquently by Clark, is supported both in Hansen's and in Rubin and Bruce's chapters. These authors describe two examples of the efforts involved in moving toward a process approach to writing (Applebee, 1981; Graves, 1983; Murray, 1982; Hairston, 1982), drawing links between the composing process and that of comprehending texts. In both cases there was extensive involvement between the researchers and the school personnel at both the administrative and classroom levels. These programs were successful because the teachers made the decisions about implementation in their own classrooms and had support from researchers who did not have all the answers but rather were learning lessons of their own as they answered their initial questions and raised new ones. Thus, effective writing environments are process oriented, where writing is used to communicate, audiences exist beyond the teacher, and students self-select topics that have meaning to them as writers and as readers.

What Influences the Development of Appropriate Contexts for Learning to Read and Write?

The last question raises the issue of constraints. We have learned a great deal about what constitutes an effective environment for the development of school-based literacy. Yet current environments have been extensively criticized, both in terms of reading (e.g., Durkin, 1978-1979) and writing instruction (e.g., Harste, Burke, & Woodward, 1984). The knowledge base on instruction in written literacy has implications for major changes to improve curricula. Why have changes not occurred? The answers, as Winograd discusses, are not easy ones, First, there are tensions between those developing the improved methods and the policy makers in charge of change because, as groups, they must respond to different goals. The researcher tries to find the solution for improving an individual's performance considering the individual, psychological, social, and academic contexts in which the individual participates. The policy makers must look at the overall needs of large groups—for them, individual and psychological contexts must be kept in a subordinate position. Second, as Schwartz notes, teachers cannot be expected to teacher what they themselves do not know, and knowledge of appropriate teaching strategies is only part of the large picture. Teachers must also have the declarative knowledge about the processes involved in written literacy, how they interrelate, how ongoing diagnostic decisions must be made during instruction, how to adopt instruction during diagnostic teaching, and so forth. Finally, as Clark notes, communication between researchers and practitioners is often not satisfactory for either group. Practitioners may feel neglected during planning stages of studies or during the development of new curricula when their input would be valuable. They may not be consulted when initial questions are being raised, and thus the questions raised may not be pertinent to their classrooms. Researchers may feel inadequate when placed in a position in which they are expected to provide all the answers. Collaboration among the groups is clearly a continuing theme of this volume—among groups translating research into practice and among the research disciplines.

Where are we now? We can describe factors (e.g., social context, children's perceptions, policy implementation) that have a major influence on children's development of written literacy. Given these insights, we can identify characteristics of effective reading and writing programs, and we are aware of the constraints in widespread implementation of ideas. How should future efforts be characterized?

FUTURE DIRECTIONS

One goal of this volume has been to suggest relationships among the research areas of writing, reading, and teaching. The contexts in which instruction in written literacy occurs has been the "tie that binds." We have learned much in bringing together scholars from disparate areas, and future directions should underscore the integration of these lines of research. Thus, this section considers the question "Where should we go from here?"

Future research must begin applying what we have learned from descriptive studies, small-scale instructional studies, and research on pedagogy to long-term studies effecting change in teachers' thinking curricula, and students' performance levels. In considering written literacy, research exists in all of these areas. First, speculative papers have been written that convincingly argue the position that reading and writing are closely related processes (e.g., Squire, 1983; Tierney & Pearson, 1983). Second, research has demonstrated that instruction in story structures has had a positive influence on students' comprehension and composing processes (e.g., Gordon & Braun, 1982). Third, research has demonstrated the importance of instruction using a process approach and the positive influence of such instruction on children's generation of stories (e.g., Graves, 1983; Hansen, this volume; Calkins, 1983). Fourth, research has presented convincing evidence that to promote lasting changes in curricula teachers must be involved as collaborators in long-term projects that can lead to their own conceptual change (Barnes & Putnam, 1981; Clark, this volume; Hansen, this volume; Lanier, in press; Rubin & Bruce, this volume).

A number of efforts toward integration have begun. Duffy, Roehler, and Mason's (1984) book represents a first step in bringing together scholars who had previously interacted very little. Au and Kawakami's description of Kamehameha Early Education Program provides an example of research in reading instruction embedded within a study of cultural impacts on learning. One project (Raphael & Kirschner, 1985a, 1985b) currently in progress at Michigan State University seeks to combine several strands discussed throughout the volume.

The MSU project, partially funded by an Elva Knight Research Grant from the International Reading Association, is studying the instruction of expository reading and writing skills. This project, in its second year, has involved the partici- pation of eight fifth- and sixth-grade teachers and the students in their classrooms. It was designed to integrate research in the writing process (e.g., Applebee, 1981; Graves, 1983; Hansen, 1984; Murray, 1982), research in the structure of expository text structures (e.g., Anderson & Armbruster, 1981; Englert & Hiebert, 1984; Meyer, 1975), research in teaching students about sources of information (e.g., Raphael & Pearson, 1985; Raphael & Wonnacott, 1985), and research on teacher change (e.g., Barnes & Putnam, 1981; Clark, this volume; Lanier, in press). Researchers are ready to tie these strands together; to expect widespread change in classroom practice we must draw on sources from all related disciplines. Becky Kirschner, Carol Sue Englert, and I are attempting to integrate and apply these lines of research to a long-term instructional study involving active collaboration of teachers, and in some cases, their students. The study combines quantitative and qualitative research methods to examine the relative impact of providing (1) a social context that emphasizes the writing process, (2) instruction in expository text structures, or (3) a combination of both on students' ability to comprehend and to compose expository text.

The importances of communication, of lessons for students, teachers, and researchers stressed throughout the volume (see chapters by Clark, Hansen, Rubin & Bruce, and Winograd) has been an integral consideration in developing the research program. For example, throughout the year teachers have been partici-pating in weekly 60- to 90-minute meetings to share their observations of stu-dents' development of writing skills, discuss changes in their own conceptions of writing instruction, assess changes in their current practices, and provide input into the succeeding phases of the study. Researchers are participant observers in the fifth- and sixth-grade classrooms, which yields a wealth of observation informa-tion and informal interview data that provide the basis for modification as instruc-tion proceeds during the course of the academic year. This mutual participation has kept open communication channels vital for effecting change in instructional practice.

The importance of providing scaffolds, both for the students who participate in the reading and writing process and for the teachers providing instruction (initially using unfamiliar activities) has also been fundamental to the design of the project. Guidelines are provided at each stage of the process to scaffold stu-dents' thinking. They prompt students to consider appropriate strategies at differ-ent phases of their writing (e.g., to consider audience and purpose during rehearsal and other prewriting activities, to consider selection of form based on the questions they are answering during drafting) to scaffold the writing process not only for the students but for their teachers as well. Teachers' observations that students are eventually able to help edit each other's writing without the aid of guidelines suggests that they recognize the flexible and temporary nature of the scaffolding provided. Students' comments (after several weeks of intervention) that they wanted to have an editor help them and did not need the guidelines suggests that they were attempting to begin to assume control of aspects of the writing process.

Further scaffolding exists by gradually moving from the use of very familiar to unfamiliar texts during instruction. Specifically, students are introduced to the concept of text structures as these structures relate to authors writing to answer questions. The structures are demonstrated initially using one exemplar text for each structure. These exemplars were selected from a pool written by the students themselves. Second, students use their own generated texts to identify structures they have used. Third, students are shown well-structured social studies texts and discuss their characteristics. Fourth, they work with the less well-structured texts naturally occuring in their own social studies books. Finally, they write expository texts of their own, using information that they extract from their social studies books and other sources (e.g., guest speakers, library books). In this way, explicit connections are drawn between their writing and reading processes and those used by professionals who create their content-area texts.

The importance of creating a social context that promotes meaningful writ-ing has been considered in our project by having students prepare a favorite writ-ten piece for publication in a class magazine. The magazine provides a purpose for revision, considering audience, and recognizing the need for editing as well as revision, while providing a practical alternative to the publication of individual books. It also provides a basis for sharing information, which is fundamental to generating expository (i.e., informational) texts.

Thus, this project has focused on (1) promoting change in the teachers' knowledge base as a result of participating in and contributing to the instructional program; (2) developing appropriate social contexts for meaningful instruction in expository writing; and (3) enhancing students' understanding of relationships among writing in general, and expository writing in particular, and the strategies they use to read informational texts. Interviews with students have revealed growth in their understanding of what constitutes the writing process, the purposes for writing, and their sense of audience. Informal observations and interactions have also supported such growth. One day this winter afer three months of writing a student named Darryl informed us that our editing think-sheet had a problem because "it only asks for problems I think my author has, it doesn't ask for suggestions. The paper doesn't have problems, but I want to make some suggestions." It was clear he understood the role of an editor, in a very different way than he initially had when he looked only for spelling and punctuation mistakes. When a sixth-grade class voted to name their magazine "Our School's Sixth-Grade Authors," they emphasized during their prevote discussion that they were not just *writers*, they were *authors*. Teachers have indicated that they view writing instruction in a different light—stressing the value of the children's sharing of work, of a redefinition of their former role of evaluator to a "skilled and experienced editor," and of a belief that students need opportunity for rehearsal and revision, in addition to drafting.

Thus, it is clear that research efforts to improve current contexts of school-based literacy can incorporate the research from a number of related areas. While much has yet to be learned (e.g., how to adequately and appropriately assess growth in reading and writing skills, or how to diagnose deficiencies in children's performance), there is evidence to suggest that systematic applications of research to classroom practice should begin.

CONCLUDING COMMENTS

The intent of this chapter was both to synthesize the research presented in this volume and to consider how this information extends our current knowledge of school-related contexts in which literacy develops. In doing this a framework for conceptualizing contexts was proposed, the framework was applied to the research presented throughout this volume and other sources, and directions for future research discussed. The number of volumes (e.g., Goelman, Oberg, & Smith, 1984; Harste, Woodward, & Burke, 1984; Holdaway, 1984; Taylor, 1983) concerning literacy that have been published in the last three to five years is indicative of the importance attributed to it, and these volumes do not even begin to scratch the surface of the literature on literacy acquisition, development, and impact. While the chapters I discussed are extensive in their treatment of some aspects of the development of literacy in schools, more synthesis is needed. We did not address such issues as characteristics of literate home environments, literature in the workplace, or standards for literacy.

It is my hope that, regardless of perspective, readers finishing this book will have gained new insights and concerns for creating a literate nation. From reading the chapters in this volume I hope that researchers have begun to reconceptualize the questions to be addressed through continued development and refinement of our theories and through testing our theories using qualitative and quantitative research methods. I hope that teachers have gained concrete ideas for immediate implementation in class and, perhaps more important, a mind set for thinking about classroom literacy practices. I hope that adminstrators and policy makers have begun to consider the impact on individual teachers and students of global decisions conveyed through statewide assessment instruments, funding practices, and so forth. Finally, I hope that all of us have begun to think of the context of potential collaborators to which we all belong, for it is only through improving and increasing collaborative efforts that long-range critical changes in written literacy curricula are likely to occur.

REFERENCES

Anderson, T. H., & Armbruster, B. B. (1981). *Content area textbooks*. Reading Educator Rep. 23. Urbana, Ill.: Center for the Study of Reading.

Applebee, A. (1981). Looking at writing. *Educational Leadership*, March, 458–462.

Au, K. H. (1980). Participation structures in a reading lesson with Hawaiian children. *Anthropology and Education Quarterly, 11*, 91–115.

Au, K. H., & Mason, J. M. (1981). Social organizational factors in learning to read: The balance of rights hypothesis. *Reading Research Quarterly, 17*(1), 115–152.

Barnes, H., & Putman, J. (1981). Professional development through inservice that works. In K. Howey, R. Bents, & D. Corrigan (Eds.), *School-focuses inservice: Descriptions and discussions*. Reston, Va.: Association of Teacher Educators

Bloome, D. (1985). Reading as a social process. *Language Arts, 62*(2), 134–142.

Braun, C. & Gordon, C. (1984). Writing as metatextual aid to story schema applications. In J. A. Niles & L. A. Harris (Eds.), *Changing perspectives on research in reading/ language processing and instruction* (pp. 61–65). Rochester, N.Y.: National Reading Conference.

Calkins, L. M. (1983). *Lessons from a child: On the teaching and learning of writing*. Exeter, N.H.: Heinemann.

Carew, J.V., & Lightfoot, S. L. (1979). *Beyond bias: Perspectives on classrooms*. Cambridge, Mass: Harvard University Press.

Cazden, C. B. (1981). Social context of learning to read. In J. T. Guthrie (Ed.), *Comprehension and teaching: Research reviews* (pp. 118–139). Newark, Del.: International Reading Association.

Duffy, G. G., Roehler, L. R., & Mason, J. N. (1984). *Comprehension instruction: Perspectives and suggestions*. N.Y.: Longman.

Durkin, D., (1978–1979). What classroom observations reveal about reading comprehension instruction. *Reading Research Quarterly, 14*, 481–533.

Englert, C. S., & Heibert, E. H. (1984). Children's developing awareness of text structures in expository material. *Journal of Educational Psychology, 76*, 65–75.

Erickson, F., & Schultz, J. (1981). When is a context? Some issues and methods in the analysis of social competence. In J. Green & C. Wallat (Eds.), *Ethnography and language in educational settings*. Norwood, N.J.: Ablex.

Florio, S., & Clark, C. (1982). Functions of writing in the classroom. *Research in the Teaching of English, 16*, 115–130.

Goelman, H., Oberg, A., & Smith, F. (1984). *Awakening to literacy*. Exeter, N.H.: Heinemann.

Gordon, C., & Braun, C. (1982). Story structure: A metatextual aid to reading and writing. In J. A. Niles & L. A. Harris (Eds.), *New inquiries in reading research and instruction* (pp. 261–268). Rochester, N.Y.: National Reading Conference.

Graves, D. H. (1983). *Writing: Teachers and children at work*. Exeter, N.H.: Heinemann.

Green, J. & Bloom, D. (1984). Social processes in reading. In P. D. Pearson (Ed.), *Handbook of reading research*. N.Y.: Longman.

Hairston, M. (1982). The winds of change: Thomas Kuhn and the revolution in the teaching of writing. *College Composition and Communication, 33*, (February) 76–88.

Hansen, J. (1984). *Elementary teachers provide rehearsal time*. Paper presented at the National Council of Teachers of English, Detroit, Mich.

Harste, J. C., Woodward, V. A., & Burke, C. L. (1984). *Language stories and literacy lessons*. Exeter, N.H.: Heinemann.

Holdaway, D. (1984). *Stability and change in literacy learning*. Exeter, N.H.: Heinemann.

Lanier, J. (in press). Research on teacher education. In M. C. Wittrock (Ed.), *Third handbook of research on teaching*. N.Y.: Longman.

Mathews, M. M. (1966). *Teaching to read: Historically considered*. Chicago, Ill.: University of Chicago Press.

McDermott, R. P. (1976). *Kids make sense*. Ph. D. diss., Stanford University.

Meyer, B. J. (1975). *The organization of prose and its effects on memory*. Amsterdam: North Holland.

Murray, D. (1982). *Learning by teaching*. Montclair, N.J.: Boynton/Cook.

Paris, S. G., Lipson, M. Y., Wixson, K. K. (1983). Becoming a strategic reader. *Contemporary Educational Psychology, 8*(3), 293–316.

Pearson, P. D., & Tierney, R. J. (1984) *Learning to read as a writer*. Reading Educator Report. Urbana, Ill. Center for the Study of Reading.

Raphael, T. E., & Kirschner, B. M. (1985a). *Learning to write: Expository material*. Paper presented at the Institute for Research on Teaching Honors Colloquium Series, Michigan State University.

Raphael, T. E., & Kirschner, B. M. (1985b). *Improving expository writing ability: Integrating knowledge of information sources and text structures*. Paper presented at the American Educational Research Association, Chicago, Ill.

Raphael, T. E., & Pearson, P. D. (1985). Increasing students' awareness of sources of information for answering questions. *American Educational Research Journal, 22*(2), 217–236.

Raphael, T. E., & Wonnacott, C. A. (1985). Heightening students' awareness of sources of information for answering comprehension questions. *Reading Research Quarterly, 20*(2), 282–296.

Resnick, D. P., & Resnick, L. B. (1977). The nature of literacy: An historical exploration. *Harvard Educational Review, 47*(3), 370–385.

Squire, J. R. (1983). Composing and comprehending: Two sides of the same basic process. *Language Arts, 60*(5), 581–589.

Taylor, D. (1983). *Family literacy*. Exeter, N.H.: Heinmann.

Tierney, R. J., & Pearson, P. D. (1983). Reading as a composing process. *Language Arts, 60*(5), 568–580.

Vygotsky, L. S. (1978). *Mind in society*. M. Cole et al. (Eds. and Trans.). Cambridge, Mass.: Harvard University Press.

Author Index

NOTE: *Italic* denotes citation to a reference.

Subject Index

A

Accountability
  effects on students, 271
  policy, 272
  reading research, 274
Achievement differences, 234–235

B

Basal texts, 55
  and trade texts, 151

C

Classroom events
  definition of, 197
  rules governing, 197–198
Cognitive development
  higher psychological processes, 9
  memory development, 28
  sociohistorical factors, 3, 7
  theories of, 4–6
  transfer of, 13–14
Comprehension
  instruction, 45–46, 65, 80, 87, 260
  of text, 52–53, 72, 132
  use of questions, 81, 84–85
  strategic reading, 117–118
  vs. reading skills, 80, 258
Comprehension instruction, 52–53,
    80–83, 116
  direct instruction, 79
  individual differences, 84–85
  social mediation, 86, 120–121
  cultural factors, 64–65

Comprehension strategies, 45–46, 81,
    117–118, 263–264
Computers
  learning to write, 218
  role of teacher, 223
Context
  components of, 163–164
  conversational communication, 164
  definition, 163–164
  writing instruction, 176–177

D

Decoding, 46
Diagnosing readiness, 137
Diagnostic teaching, 143, 263
  instructional manipulation, 143
Dissemination, 185, 191

E

Expertise in teaching, 22
Explicit explanation, 56, 260

F

Free reading, 151
  group discussions, 157
  promotion of, 155–156
  vs. workbook exercises, 152

G

Guided instruction, 120–121

319